# Terrorism and Drug Trafficking in the 1990s

*Drug Trafficking After 1992: A Special Report* (Chapter 4 in this volume) is the first phase of a long term study of the Security and Response Implications of Drug Trafficking for the Single European Market. It deals with money laundering legislation as 'the spearhead of any successful attack on the business of drug trafficking' with particular reference to Britain and Italy. It has been made possible thanks to the support of the Commission of the European Communities.

# Terrorism and Drug Trafficking in the 1990s

*Edited by*

## Alison Jamieson

*Research Institute for the Study of Conflict and Terrorism*

**Dartmouth**
Aldershot · Brookfield USA · Singapore · Sydney

Published by
Dartmouth Publishing Company Limited
Gower House
Croft Road
Aldershot
Hants GU11 3HR
England

Dartmouth Publishing Company
Old Post Road
Brookfield
Vermont 05036
USA

**British Library Cataloguing in Publication Data**
Terrorism and Drug Trafficking in the
1990s. – (Research Institute for the
Study of Conflict & Terrorism Series)
I. Jamieson, Alison II. Series
303.62509049

**Library of Congress Cataloging-in-Publication Data**
Terrorism and drug trafficking in the 1990s / edited by Alison
Jamieson.
    p. cm.
Includes bibliographical references.
ISBN 1-85521-532-2 : $59.95
1. Terrorism—Case studies. 2. Drug traffic—Case studies.
I. Jamieson, Alison.
HV6431.T4614  1994                                              94–13470
363.3′2′09049—dc20                                              CIP

ISBN 1 85521 532 2

Printed in Great Britain by Ipswich Book Co. Ltd., Ipswich, Suffolk

# Contents

# Introduction

The studies presented in this volume were published between September 1989 and January 1993. In those 40 months we witnessed the collapse of communism and the disintegration of the Soviet Union, a full-scale war in the Gulf in which the use of weapons of mass destruction was threatened, and religious and ethnic struggles of such ferocity that the Holocaust – whose horrors were thought to be unrepeatable, at least within living memory – was re-evoked in the extermination and mass rape of minorities in former Yugoslavia.

Shrewd historians might have predicted the consequences of removing the lid from the cauldron of the Soviet empire, but few could have foreseen the rapidity and the violence of the changes that have occurred. By late 1993 the euphoria that greeted the fall of the Berlin Wall had evaporated. The harmony of a 'new world order' is proving elusive, if not impossible to achieve, and in the face of perceived governmental unwillingness or incapacity to react to the changes taking place, xenophobia and isolationism seem to be overruling the principles of liberal democracy.

All the political, economic and military institutions constructed for post-war Western society, including the European Economic Community, were created from a philosophy of bipolarism. We have not yet adapted our thinking to the changed circumstances, nor has there been time to devise new objectives and structures – for our intelligence services, for example – along post-communist lines, perhaps not least due to fears that the old world order may yet return.

## Trends and recent developments

Trends in terrorism and drug trafficking reflect global historical changes to a considerable degree. In this sense we can predict with some confidence that the phase of ideological terrorism of Marxist–Leninist inspiration, practised by groups such as the Red Army Faction (RAF) in Germany, the Red Brigades in Italy and Action Directe in France, is temporarily, if not definitively, over. Responsibility for sporadic actions continues to be claimed on behalf of the RAF and the RB but their continuity with the original members is tenuous and their potential following negligible.

In contrast, the collapse of communism and the supremacy of Western capitalism have given further stimulus to the spread of Islamic fundamentalism. Although the Islam revival that has swept the Middle East is primarily a peaceful movement seeking the return of religious purity, a minority, drawn largely from the most desperate and rootless members of society, has declared violent opposition to those Arab states – in particular Egypt, Algeria and Tunisia – in which the blend of Western with nationalist values is thought to have contaminated Muslim societies and led them astray.

The Islamic resistance movement, Hamas, is dedicated to the total destruction of Israel and the construction of a pan-Islamic union, and as such represents a major threat to the peace accord signed between the Palestine Liberation Organization and Israel on 13 September 1993. PLO Chairman Yasser Arafat won approval for the agreement from the Central Council of the PLO by 63 votes to eight, but the meeting was boycotted by the Popular Front for the Liberation of Palestine (PFLP) and by one wing of the Democratic Front for the Liberation of Palestine. In an interview given in October 1993 PFLP leader, Ahmed Jibril, pledged that the Palestinian armed struggle would continue, calling Arafat 'a traitor who will meet the same end as Anwar Sadat' and the peace accord 'a sell-out'. Attacks intended to sabotage the peace process carried out by both Israeli and Arab opponents led Arafat to declare a state of emergency in the Gaza strip in late October.

Countries which support Israel or the secular Arab states (France in particular) or which publicly encourage the peace initiative are vulnerable to terrorist attack, hence the murders and kidnappings of Western tourists and business travellers in Mahgreb countries. Muslim fundamentalists were indicted for the February 1993 bombing of the New York World Trade Center which killed six and injured 1000. Subsequent investigations revealed that other New York attacks were in preparation – all of them likely to cause major loss of life. Attacks against Western targets in Europe cannot therefore be excluded.

At the time of the Gulf war in 1991, a number of countries once accused of protecting, and even directing, terrorist actions began a gradual *rapprochement* with the West, resulting in a subsequent decline in incidents of state-sponsored terrorism. Colonel Muammar Qadhafi, once the unashamed provider of arms and explosives to the Provisional IRA, prevaricated for months in official deference to a UN require-ment that he hand over the two Libyans suspected of the Lockerbie bomb. Diplomatic relations were restored between Britain and Iran, even though the *fatwa* issued against the writer Salman Rushdie, far from being lifted, effectively continues to punish, as the shooting of Rushdie's Norwegian publisher in October 1993 confirmed.


## Immigration and social issues

Within Western Europe, the decline of ideological or doctrinal terrorism as practised by the far Left has been accompanied by a virtual cessation of the indiscriminate bombings associated with the far Right, such as the massacres at Bologna station and at the Munich Bierfest in 1980. The objectives of the far Right have shifted to more specific causes such as immigration and racial issues, where tension and growing intolerance have been promoted.

Conflict in Eastern Europe, particularly in former Yugoslavia, has intensified pressure upon the more affluent West to accept refugees and asylum seekers. This impression of an 'open-doors Europe' has aroused hostility in those sectors of the population who feel threatened by the influx of job and residence seekers: they have been manipulated by extremist agitators into a pliable instrument for publicity-seeking demonstrations of racial hatred.

The number of people seeking asylum in the EC almost doubled in the three years to 1992, when 557 000 knocked on the Community doors – 438 000 of them entered Germany alone. Germany, with 23 per cent of the EC's population, has a 43 per cent share of the non-Community immigrants within the EC. The German immigration law which came into force on 1 July 1993 overturned the guaranteed right of all foreigners to seek asylum (in operation since the end of the Second World War) and brought Germany into alignment with a general EC effort, led enthusiastically by French Interior Minister Charles Pasqua, to strengthen the EC's external barrier by means of 'zero immigration'. With 17 million unemployed and all 12 member states at different stages of economic recession, the EC has been forced to abandon altruism for a rearguard political defence of national interests. A meeting of immigration ministers in Copenhagen in June 1993 laid out the new Community guidelines for approval of visa, residence and asylum applications. Concessions granted to persecuted groups include the offer of 'temporary protection' but insist that refugees who enter the EC from a third country must be sent back there if it is considered safe.

## Policing and border control in the EC

Less than a year on from 1 January 1993, any attempt to analyse drug trafficking and terrorism trends purely in terms of the Single European Market would be premature and misleading. Many countries had all but dropped customs and passport controls well before that date but some, such as the UK, Ireland and Denmark, have continued to exercise controls on grounds of internal security. The other nine EC members, all signatories of the Schengen Accord, are committed to abolishing passport and customs controls by 1 February 1994 and intend to regulate illegal immigration and crime by means of the Schengen Information System (SIS), a computerized intelligence and information network based in Strasbourg which will permit instant access to each country's records. Italy and Greece, whose computer networks are not yet compatible with SIS, are likely to remain formally outside the free travel area until such time as they can comply. French fears that the ratification of Schengen would lead to increases in drug trafficking and illegal immigration were mollified by an assurance that each country could appoint liaison officers at each other's main ports and airports, while a compromise was found on arrangements for asylum seekers that has satisfied the original objection of the French Constitutional Court.

Britain's objections to abandoning passport controls have caused such tension with the signatories to the Schengen Accord that British police will not be permitted access to SIS unless passport controls are dropped. The Community runs a serious risk of a two-tier intelligence network and, unless this is resolved, it will certainly create difficulties for cross-border cooperation.


## Spain and Northern Ireland

There is no practical reason why the historic changes of the last four years should have had any effect on two of the longest surviving terrorist groups in Europe, ETA and the IRA, since their aims are theoretically independent of global political developments. Nonetheless there are signs of weariness in both organizations and, even more importantly, a real decrease in consensus with violent action from once tolerant, or even sympathetic, sectors of society. In September 1993, 70 000 people marched through the streets of San Sebastian calling for an end to ETA violence and urging the release of kidnapped businessman Julio Inglesias Zamora, punished for refusing to pay his 'revolutionary tax'. In the eyes of the majority of Basques, ETA violence has discouraged commercial and industrial investment without bringing any tangible benefits to the area. Zamora was released on 29 October on payment of an undisclosed ransom, after 117 days' imprisonment in a tiny cell.

Peace in Northern Ireland was still remote in the autumn of 1993, but for the first time in over 10 years, almost all the parties necessary for an agreement had begun to talk to one or more of the other parties. Parallel discussions were being pursued, firstly at a formal level between the British and Irish governments with the aim of jointly drafting a constitutional settlement for presentation to the parties in Northern Ireland by the end of 1993; secondly and informally, through a series of meetings between Provisional Sinn Fein President Gerry Adams and the leader of the Social Democratic and Labour Party, John Hume. At the conclusion of the talks, Mr Hume presented the Irish Taoiseach, Albert Reynolds, with a summary of their conclusions and specific proposals for a peace initiative. Mr Reynolds confirmed that the 'broad principles [of the document] could be a just and lasting peace process to be established and worked upon'.

Any solution will have to reconcile Article 1 of the 1985 Anglo-Irish agreement – whereby any change in the status of Northern Ireland may only come about with the consent of the majority of the people of Northern Ireland – with articles 2 and 3 of the Irish Constitution, which lays claim to jurisdiction over Northern Ireland. The Irish premier has indicated willingness for the wording of 'claim to jurisdiction' to be altered to 'aspiration', but such a change would require approval by popular referendum. On the loyalist side, the very fact of the Hume–Adams talks and the absence of official censure of them by the British government were interpreted as a betrayal, and inspired a new wave of loyalist-perpetrated atrocities.

The week that opened on 23 October 1993 with an IRA bomb that exploded in Belfast's Shankill Road killing 10 and injuring 50 culminated in a series of 'tit-for-tat' murders with a total of 23 lives lost. The immediate effect was to harden resolve on both sides not to yield. Nonetheless, peace prospects depend on the continuation, not the abandonment, of political discussions and on the hope that, sooner or later, the Northern Ireland community's tolerance of violence will give way to a resolve to end the self-perpetuating cycle of cruelty and suffering.


**The Mafia**

Although most peace agreements depend on compromise, compromise can be a fatal weakness in dealing with terrorism or organized crime. For decades successive Italian governments were hard on terrorists (especially from the far Left) but soft on the Mafia. The full implications of this choice were only beginning to emerge at the end of 1993, more than a year after the brutal murders in Palermo of Judge Giovanni Falcone, his wife and three bodyguards and of Judge Paolo Borsellino with his five bodyguards. Whilst a political consensus was found to track down, try and ultimately defeat the Red Brigades because they were an enemy external to, and in open confrontation with, the state, the Mafia, it now appears, prospered because it was able to penetrate the heart of Italy's state institutions: government, public admin- istration, judiciary, security services and police forces. With hindsight, it is scarcely surprising that diligent and honest representatives of those same institutions were brushed aside when they became too irritating – they could not be permitted to destabilize the 'business committees' and secret brotherhoods who for decades, together with the men of violence, systematically arranged the economic and political affairs of entire areas of Italy by means of a sordid horsetrading of impunity, votes, jobs, favours and protection.

The judges of the first Palermo 'maxi-trial' wrote, '... in order to obtain certain benefits the Mafia needs the keys of power. Unfortunately we did not have the means of identifying the keys or those who possessed them.' In October 1993, 17 national members of parliament, about half of them former government ministers, were suspected of crimes relating to Mafia association: 20 judges were alleged to have taken bribes in exchange for 'adjusting' criminal proceedings and court verdicts in favour of *mafiosi*, and two high-ranking intelligence officers had been arrested for Mafia collusion. In its annual report, published in October 1993, the Parliamentary Antimafia Commission concluded:

> Without these connections the Mafia would have been defeated within a brief passage of years and would not have survived the modernisation of the country. . . . If all those who have held or who hold positions of political responsibility at all levels had done their duty we would have had neither mourning nor Mafia massacres, and today this country of ours would be truly free.

The anti-Mafia drive in Italy is at last becoming effective, thanks to a combination of popular revolt at grass-roots level and sound legislation and, perhaps for the first time, genuine political commitment. Severe blows have been inflicted on all the major Italian organized crime groups: in the year from August 1992 284 important fugitives were arrested; 22 000 suspected *mafiosi* had been identified, of whom almost 3000 were in prison; assets seized and confiscated amounted to over £1 billion and £45 million respectively; while the number of collaborators, often referred to as *pentiti*, had risen to over 500.

The repercussions of the capture of many senior Mafia bosses and their imprisonment in top security prisons with little or no access to the outside world, the severity of new legislation and the stripping away of the political and judicial protection that ensured the annulment of trials and guilty verdicts had not fully been felt by the autumn of 1993. The spate of unattributed bombings in Rome, Florence and Milan in the spring and summer may have been an exploratory attempt to see whether the country could be intimidated into giving up its serious anti-Mafia intentions, or may have been linked to forces external to the Mafia but with a common interest in throwing Italy's painful democratic renaissance off course. It is believed, however, that if the ruthless strategies of the *Corleonesi* clans continue to predominate, then a precisely targeted retaliation campaign is in store for the future.

## Drug trafficking trends

Drug trafficking continues to be the most lucrative international activity for Italian organized crime, but the European market is more competitive than it was several years ago. Increased activity in Western Europe by Chinese trafficking groups in particular seems to have forced the various regional organized crime groups in Italy to form a loose cartel whereby importation, refining, distribution and sales are shared out. According to the Customs Cooperation Council, cocaine seizures in Europe rose by 42 per cent in the first half of 1993: 9800 kg were seized compared to 6914 for the first six months of 1992. Cannabis seizures were up to 91 metric tonnes compared with 80, whilst heroin seizures, down in Western Europe, rose sharply in the East.

*Change the strategies?*

The anti-narcotics strategies being pursued by Western governments are widely perceived as having failed, but there is an understandable reluctance on the part of governments to abandon prohibition, repression and interdiction efforts. Meanwhile in the background, tentative efforts to introduce partial legalization of consumption and/or possession of certain drugs are gaining ground even in traditionally conservative circles. Based on the hypothesis that addicts provided with regular supplies of drugs under medical supervision are less likely to turn to crime to sustain their habit and that the criminal underworld is the chief beneficiary of prohibition, these views have a pragmatic appeal. Researchers disagree about the validity of such theories, and political bias all too often prevents a rigorous evaluation of comparative drug law enforcement strategies, but policy-makers are gradually realizing that the urgency of the drug problem calls for all the available options to be studied.

## Drug trafficking and Eastern Europe

Drug trafficking trends for the foreseeable future will crucially depend on how the beleaguered Eastern European nations confront this challenge. The relaxing of frontiers between the CIS republics to both East and West has opened a multitude of new drug transit routes which are being fully exploited. Whereas in 1989 drugs intercepted were counted in grammes, nowadays seizures of dozens and even hundreds of kilograms are not uncommon. In February 1993 a single consignment of one metric tonne of cocaine, worth at least US $100 million dollars, was seized in Russia close to the Finnish border – it had come through Finland from Colombia, and was probably en route for a destination outside Russia.

Judging by the arrest figures, 70 per cent of all Russian drug trafficking is in the hands of Azeri groups, but Chechens and Jewish mafia-type organizations are also active. According to the Russian Ministry of Security, the ultimate beneficiaries reside in Moscow, the USA and Israel. Drug abuse, addiction and AIDS are rising rapidly in CIS countries, with an estimated 1.5 million regular narcotics users in Russia alone. At present the demand for drugs in the former Soviet Union is covered by domestic production of opium poppies and cannabis in Uzbekistan, Tadzhikistan, Kazakhstan and Azerbaiijan, with processing plants situated closer to the big industrial cities, the primary areas of consumption. However if reports of an Afghani bid to set up a permanent production base in Tadzhikistan are correct, a sizeable surplus could be created. This could have significant consequences both for aggravating CIS drug problems and for making more drugs available on the Western European market.

The Russian Interior Ministry reports that 531 organized crime groups were operating in the first six months of 1993, of which 83 had inter-republican links. Many Chechen, Azeri and Georgian criminals have been arrested in Poland, Hungary and the Czech Republic.

The impact of Eastern European organized crime groups is also being felt in the West, especially in Berlin and the *Länder* of former East Germany. The deputy assistant commissioner of the Metropolitan police warned an international police conference in June 1993 that Eastern European crime syndicates would be supplying arms and drugs to the inner cities of Britain within five years.

**Other illicit traffic**

Warnings that illicit trafficking in arms, counterfeit currency and even nuclear components could be taking place from the former Soviet Union to Western Europe and to Third World countries have been borne out. Authorities in northern Italy have uncovered a network through which sales of plutonium, caesium and unenriched uranium from deposits in Russia are handled by Italian, Swiss and Austrian middlemen on behalf of purchasers in Iraq and Libya.

The privatization of former state industries in the former Eastern bloc, together with the precarious economic conditions and the absence of sound, well regulated financial institutions, offers considerable scope for money launderers wishing to conceal illicit capital and invest in lucrative new projects. The mushrooming of joint venture projects and investments in import/export businesses, tourism, casinos, property and financial services by suspect Italian and South American sources is thought to be linked to the presence of organized crime groups. Russian authorities claim to have evidence of formal agreements between Russian and Colombian drug traffickers; it is believed a series of meetings took place in 1991 and 1992 in Prague, Warsaw and Moscow between Italian and Russian organized crime groups, resulting in a pact to expand and protect illicit trafficking routes through the former communist countries of Central Europe.

**Conclusion**

The future is hardly rosy. Europe's defence against drug trafficking and terrorism is only as good as its weakest link which, as the studies presented in this volume and subsequent developments indicate, is somewhat flimsy. Western Europe has a pressing duty to help its less experienced neighbours for both selfish and altruistic reasons. The recent and still inadequate cooperation between East and West against organized crime and terrorism must be intensified. Within the new European Union, officially 'born' with the ratification of the Maastricht Treaty on 1 November 1993, priority should be given to resolving judicial discrepancies between member states. Yet, as Juliet Lodge suggests, the quest for legislative uniformity is doomed as long as the Union has neither a supranational political authority nor a legal base for intervention on criminal law matters.

The Brussels summit of 29 October that preceded the entry into force of Maastricht put flesh on the bones of a more united Europe, in particular with the agreement on the timetable for a single European currency and economic union, and with the choice of Frankfurt as the home of the European Monetary Institute. The establishment of The Hague as headquarters of Europol – initially a non-operational European Drugs Intelligence Unit – and of Lisbon as host to the European Observatory on Drugs should significantly boost cooperation in tackling the supply and demand sides of the drug equation respectively. The Brussels summit also gave the British prime minister, John Major, and the Irish Prime Minister, Albert Reynolds the opportunity to exchange ideas on the future of Northern Ireland; their meeting concluded with a joint pledge to seek urgently a formula for peace in Ulster.

The summit began acrimoniously but ended on a note of optimism. It remains now for the fine words pronounced in Brussels to be translated into action – political sincerity alone will not determine the extent and reality of European unity.

**Alison Jamieson**

# [1]

# Technology and Civil Liberties

## *Richard Clutterbuck*

Before 1989, an average of 100,000 people were arrested every year at West German Frontier checks, about 50,000 of them spotted from wanted lists, the other 50,000 questioned on hunches by frontier staff. After 1992, these people will remain at large unless they are arrested on external EC frontiers or at police spot checks in Germany or elsewhere in the EC. Any terrorist, criminal, drug trafficker or illegal immigrant, having crossed the Mediterranean and landed in a rocky inlet in Italy or Spain, will be free to move to Frankfurt or Paris or London (via the Channel tunnel) without passing any of the normal immigration or customs checks.

### COUNTER TERRORISM AFTER 1992

Paradoxically, the removal of internal borders may encourage EC police forces to improve their co-operation in order to make these spot checks effective. The Single European Act will allow greater latitude for hot pursuit into neighbouring countries, but there are differences in their laws – for example, France and Belgium have lax gun laws, whereas those of the Netherlands, Germany and Britain are much stricter. On the other hand, the Dutch are more permissive than their neighbours in controlling drug traffic, especially in soft drugs. Judicial systems also differ; the Dutch do not have trial by jury. Though laws and procedures should be harmonised as far as possible, it will be quite acceptable for EC countries to retain their laws and traditions provided that they all accept the principle that a citizen of any EC country who is accused of committing an offence in Country A against the laws of Country A must be extradited for trial in that country according to its laws and judicial procedures, even if the offence is not an offence in the country from which extradition is demanded; and the courts must have power to sub-poena witnesses from any other EC country. This already works well between England and Scotland, which have different systems of prosecution and trial; accused persons are arrested and witnesses called quite freely between them. And the British Government readily extradited British football hooligans to stand trial in Belgium after they had caused violent deaths in the European Cup Final in the Heysel Stadium in 1986.

Countering terrorism depends on the rule of law. This in turn relies on highly practical things like intelligence, security of access to likely targets and sensitive premises, identification and the prevention of impersonation, detection of concealed guns and explosives, arrest, interrogation and trial. Emerging technology can assist in all these tasks, but it can be abused. A balance must be struck between using the most effective means of enforcing the law and applying them in such a way as to result in unacceptable curtailment of civil liberties.

3

## Intelligence

Some of the most significant technological advances are in the field of intelligence. Computers can instantly spot and reveal links between apparently unconnected facts. If, for example, a police officer finds a note of a telephone number in an arrested man's pocket, the National Police Computer (NPC) can immediately call up every police report in which that number has occurred. Police officers can be issued with personal computers programmed as "expert systems" enabling them to carry out logical interrogations on a variety of subjects, each answer prompting the next question. This gives them access to a far wider range of expertise than any one officer could hope to carry in his head. A pocket computer the size of a Walkman cassette recorder can carry in its own memory as much as a 300-page reference book; one the size of a telephone answering machine can hold as much as the Encyclopaedia Britannica. If the information is still not available, it can activate the main computer at headquarters to provide it.

Within the EC, most NPCs are now linked and there is continual improvement in their harmonisation. Human intelligence, however, is ultimately more important than technological intelligence, because the decisive information is that which indicates likely future intentions. This can only come from people within the terrorist organisation or who live and move in the same environment as the terrorists. The task of an intelligence organisation is to identify people who have knowledge of the terrorists, to obtain background information against which to interrogate them, to encourage them to speak and to provide confidence that they will thereafter be secure.

## Identification and anti-impersonation

To combat terrorism and crime, the police need the power and the capability to check people's identity. In some countries (France for example) they have the power to demand proof of identity from anyone leaving the scene of a crime, and to detain anyone failing or refusing to provide such proof. With open internal frontiers, the power to check identity will be essential if terrorists or criminals, whether on wanted lists or not, are to be found by questioning at spot checks. This power, like any other power, can be abused or applied oppressively, and safeguards against this will be discussed later. There is, however, no fundamental civil right to conceal identity, and impersonation is an abuse of other people's civil liberty. Few people need to conceal their identity for any honest purpose, and liberty to do so must not be preserved at the expense of more fundamental liberties.

All the major EC countries except Britain, Ireland and the Netherlands require their citizens to carry identity cards (ID cards). The German government has a system of machine-readable ID cards in readiness, but has not yet put it into operation. When issued, these ID cards will be able to activate the National Police Computer.

After 1992, there will be strong pressure from all EC countries to issue ID cards and for their systems to be harmonised to enable a person's identity to be checked in any of the 12 countries. The only way to do this will be for the

## Technology and Civil Liberties 5

cards to be machine-readable – that is, to contain magnetic or electronic data such as is already recorded on every bank or credit card. It will also be necessary to harmonise the visa system so that anyone not holding an EC ID card can be identified. Machine-readable visa cards would provide the simplest answer. Every ID and visa card should contain biometric data to ensure that the person presenting it is in fact the person to whom it was issued.

There are currently some non-EC countries which have customs unions and non-visa agreements with EC neighbours – e.g. Norway, Sweden and Switzerland. There is every likelihood, however, that these countries will wish to join an enlarged EC after 1992, and a number of East European countries are also likely to apply, so further harmonisation will be needed.

There are now many means of digitally recording unique biometric data to prevent impersonation, all of which are much more reliable than a simple photograph or signature. Though the initial cost of the equipment to record and then to identify the data is high, economies of scale would make it relatively cheap if it were part of a universal ID or visa system.

Digital recording of fingerprints is currently used for forensic work, and also in the USA for access control. The fingerprint characteristics are digitally recorded by a scanner, and can be stored either in a computer data base (for example an NPC) or on a microprocessor printed on an ID card (a "smart card") or on both. If this data were recorded on everyone's machine-readable ID card or visa, a police spot check could be equipped with a simple portable terminal having a fingerprint scanner and a slot for the card. This would reveal (in a few seconds) whether the person was the rightful owner of the card. Immediate access to the NPC would further reveal whether the card was forged and whether the person had any other data recorded on the NPC – for instance on a wanted list.

The pattern of the retina is as unique as a fingerprint and can be read by an infra red camera pointing into the eye. There is some consumer anxiety about this, but less psychological resistance than against the recording of fingerprints, with their criminal connotations.

Hand geometry is more user friendly, cheaper and has very low false acceptance and false rejection rates. The geometry of the hand is recorded by a few seconds exposure on a screen and this data, again, can be recorded both on a machine-readable ID card and on a computer data base. A police spot check terminal with screen, card slot and access to the NPC data base would weigh less than 5 kg, and accept or reject the match in a few seconds.

Voice matching is also cheap. Selected words can be digitally recorded and an imposter who is asked to repeat these words will be unmasked. The vein pattern on the back of the hand is also as unique as a fingerprint, and can be digitally recorded and read like a bar code on a jar of sauce in a supermarket; there are still some problems to be solved before this is a commercial proposition, but it might well emerge as the best system in a few years time.

"Genetic fingerprinting" (analysis of DNA in body fluids) is valuable for forensic use but too slow for spot checks or access control.

Effective measures to safeguard civil liberties will be essential to ensure against harassment of victims of prejudice such as ethnic minorities, immigrant workers, and so on. Again, modern computers with their vast capacity of small interlinked memories, can provide these safeguards. Each spot-check computer and each policeman or official can have a code, without which it will not work, and each check can be recorded. In the event of a complaint of harassment, these checks can be accessed and their circumstances investigated. If no access were called for, they would be "washed off" after a certain period – just as the everyday mass of fingerprints on the furniture in a room are never used unless it becomes the scene of a crime.

Given such safeguards, there is no more to fear from ID cards than from the mass of bank and credit cards, all linked to computers, which almost every citizen now carries from choice.

## Detection of explosives

Another important area of technological development is the detection of explosives – which can also be applied to drugs and many other contraband materials. This poses no threat to civil liberties but some radiation techniques could cause health hazards if they were used carelessly.

Metal detection, by X-rays or magnetometers, is no longer enough. Guns can be made almost wholly of plastic. Bomb firing mechanisms are often incorporated within the ordinary wiring circuits of electrical appliances such as radios and cassette recorders. So intensive research is now going on into the detection of explosives. X-rays can be designed to display different colours for different materials; organic materials such as explosives, for example, show up as orange. There is, however, a lot more research needed before this can be relied upon to provide an adequately high detection probability (DP) and an adequately low false alarm rate (FAR).

The detection of vapour from explosives through the use of sniffer dogs has been a well-known method for half a century. A dog's nose can be a million times more sensitive than human noses, but its sense of smell can become fatigued and neither the dog nor its handler may be aware how far this fatigue has gone. Furthermore, certain military plastic explosives (such as Semtex) emit very little vapour, and vapour can be largely contained by hermetically sealing the explosive charge in several layers of polythene.

There are various forms of chemical or spectrographic vapour detector ranging from hand-held sniffers which give an instant signal if there is more than one part of explosive vapour in 100 million parts of air. These can cost from £2,500 to £10,000. More sensitive vapour detectors require the air to be sucked into a sampler which has then to be taken to a mobile analysing plant. This process may take from a few seconds to two minutes but can take longer still if there is a backlog of samples awaiting analysis. These plants may cost between £25,000 and £250,000 but can be a million times more sensitive than the simple hand sniffers, detecting as little as one part in 100 million million.

Various forms of neutron detector are also under development. These can rely on detection of hydrogenous material which includes explosives but may also give false alarms from other materials. Others detect nitrogen compounds, but these too can give an unacceptably high rate of false alarms. The simplest neutron detectors are hand-held and cost around £10,000. A cobalt source projects neutrons through any material, however solid, and the explosives (and "false alarm" materials) cause a backscatter of gamma rays which the equipment detects. More complex systems, such as Thermal Neutron Analysers (TNA) can cost £500,000 or more.

**Airport security**

Hijacks, though rare and not usually lethal, have a disproportionate power of political blackmail and aircraft bombs, though even rarer, can cause horrific loss of life. The defeat of both depends largely on strict access control and the detection of weapons and explosives.

There are in general three routes whereby hijackers or bombers can get access to civil aircraft: through the activities on the ramp including cargo-handling, refuelling, servicing and administrative services such as catering and cleaning; through hold baggage checked in by passengers; and through passengers (criminal, treacherous or naive) and their cabin baggage.

The ramp should be the easiest to control, since only staff employed or specially authorised by the airport should have access. All such staff should be vetted and should carry reliable means of identification which ought in future to include biometric means of preventing impersonation as described above (digital fingerprinting, retina-scanning, etc). Cargo, kitchen, toilet supplies and so on should be strictly controlled and subject to explosive detection.

Lax security of checked-in hold baggage has been the probable cause of the worst air disasters, including the loss of 329 lives when an Air India aircraft blew up over the Atlantic in 1985 and of 270 lives when a Pan-American aircraft was bombed over Lockerbie in 1988. Tight procedures to ensure that no aircraft carries a bag without its owner is the most important precaution. If the threat justifies it, detailed interrogation of passengers and hand search of baggage can be done, as it is by El Al, but this requires a three hour check-in time, which is not practical for all air traffic. Security would be greatly improved if all baggage were checked on a continuous-flow belt passing through multiple checks – not just X-rays but vapour and neutron checks too. No single one of these tests has a 100 per cent DP, but no bomb or gun is likely to pass undetected through all of them. This would require some reconstruction in airport terminals, plus extra staff and equipment, which might cost in the order of 10 dollars per passenger passing through. The acceptance or objection to this would depend on the public perception of the threat.

Secure handling of embarking passengers with cabin baggage depends on a "leakproof" corridor, including departure and boarding lounges, from the moment they are searched until they have entered the aircraft door. It is equally important that the corridors for embarking and disembarking passengers are insulated from each other, to prevent a would-be hijacker receiving a gun by arrangement from an accomplice arriving from an airport with low embarkation security. The simplest and most secure is for the detailed search of passengers and hand baggage to take place at the door of the boarding lounge exclusive to one specific aircraft, as at Singapore airport, but this is expensive in staff and equipment. Ideally, cabin baggage should be subject to a similar series of multiple checks to those proposed for hold baggage.

Any procedures introduced at airports must, however, be economically realistic and such as will secure staff and passenger co-operation. Adding 50 per cent to the current check-in times would paralyse busy airports. A five or 10 dollar "security surcharge" could pay for the extra staff and equipment for the multiple checks described, but no airport or airline could afford to do this for long unless its rivals were compelled to maintain similar standards by a higher authority having effective power of enforcement. The best body to set and monitor security standards would be the International Civil Aviation Organization (ICAO) and this could be provided with teeth if the Group of Seven (G7) countries agreed in advance to boycott any airport or airline which failed to rectify any shortcomings revealed by regular ICAO monitoring. These G7 countries (Canada, France, Germany, Italy, Japan, UK and USA) control 80 per cent of the world's civil aviation so, if they all carried out the threat of a boycott, it could be devastating. If they were joined by other big airlines – Aeroflot, KLM, Swissair, and so on – better still.

Though every passenger and every bag should be subject to search, any system is more effective if most effort is devoted to those which constitute the greatest risk. Various means of profiling have been used – picking out for special attention, for example, passengers of young or early middle age who have bought their tickets for cash. El Al subject passengers to at least two interrogations and concentrate selectively. A possible system within the EC would be to issue Air Travel Permits to regular travellers who voluntarily subject themselves to vetting by their national police and carry a machine-readable permit which includes biometric data which can be checked against the person (e.g. fingerprint) *and* against the linked EC PNCs. The incentive to seek such a permit could be, for example, later check-in and priority seat allocation. This would leave airport staff more time to concentrate on higher risk passengers.

Other procedural improvements are also needed. At intermediate stops, all transit passengers should be required to disembark with all their cabin baggage. Under current procedures, a disembarking passenger can leave a hand bag containing a bomb aboard, which will be assumed to be that of a transit passenger. This was almost certainly the cause of a cabin explosion in a Cairo-Athens-Rome shuttle in 1986 which cost four lives, though the pilot miraculously landed the aircraft safely.

In the medium term, airports should be redesigned so that embarking passengers are issued with boarding cards *after* passing a "passengers only barrier", after which they should have no possibility of return or exit other than onto the aircraft on which they have been allocated a seat. As they go through passport and immigration checks, all their baggage should pass through a continuous flow multiple check system as described. Passengers should then be held in a baggage search hall in which any suspect bags should be hand-searched in their presence. An electronic code on the boarding card and baggage labels could ensure that no bag was loaded without its accompanying passenger. With continuous flow, the throughput of bags per minute would be as fast as if each had a single X-ray check. Provided that the false alarm rate (X-ray, neutron, etc) did not exceed 5 per cent in all, the hand search should impose no more than five minutes extra on check-in time. The extra manpower and equipment could all be covered by a 10 dollar airport security surcharge which, provided that it were universally enforced, would be acceptable.

## Justice and videotapes

Many convictions have been made on the evidence of confessions during police interrogation which have later been challenged as unfair and quashed by the Appeal Courts. In many countries jury trial for terrorist offences has been suspended, for example in the Republic of Ireland (1962), Northern Ireland (1973) and France (1986), because intimidation of juries made it impossible. There have been many cases of juries and witnesses being bribed as well as intimidated both by criminal gangs and by terrorists. All of these things can make liberal processes of law unworkable, and that is sometimes their wider purpose. All these evils could be curtailed by widespread use of the video camera.

In all political terrorist cases and serious criminal cases, police interrogation of the accused should be video-recorded, and a copy of the entire videotape handed at once to the accused or his lawyer. The caution at the start of the interrogation should be reworded: "You are not obliged to say anything, but this interview is being recorded. You will receive a copy of the tape, and you and the prosecution will be free to show any part of that tape as evidence at your trial." This would provide powerful protection against improper questioning or the fabrication of confessions. It would also enable the jury to place their own interpretation on the fairness of the interrogation, the demeanour of the accused or of refusal to answer questions – exactly as they put their own interpretation on those of a witness in court, which is the cardinal feature of trial by jury.

In most European countries, the USA and many others, jury trial is regarded by the public as the fairest form of trial, though a few countries prefer a "professional jury" of, say, six lawyers or junior judges – for instance in the Netherlands and in France (for cases involving terrorism or national security). Jury trial could, however, be made workable even in the face of organised intimidation or bribery, by preserving total anonymity of the jurors through use of video cameras. The jury needs to see the witnesses, accused, counsel and judges, but does not need to be seen – any more than a politician needs to see the audience he is trying to convince on television.

In cases where intimidation or bribery is a serious risk, the judge should have power to order the jury to sit in a different building. In the jury room there would be five video screens, showing the accused, the witness, the prosecuting and defence counsels and the judge. There would be *no* camera of any kind in the jury room and its location would be unknown to anyone involved in the case. To ensure (and let it be seen) that the jury is not "packed" or prejudiced, its members should be selected from a panel and interviewed by an independent judge, assisted by two lay assessors.

The only "liberty" eroded would be that of a counsel to object to individual jurors, but this is a liberty more often used to pack juries with prejudiced members than otherwise, so the transfer of this responsibility to the independdent judge and assessors would on balance improve the fairness of trial by jury.

In extreme cases it might also be necessary to afford similar protection to witnesses (by placing them behind a screen, as is done in terrorist trials in Northern Ireland). Video protection would be better than the screen, though both erode the quality of trials more than the anonymity of juries. This erosion, however, is far less than the erosion of judicial processes by intimidation or bribery of witnesses and juries.

## The ultimate civil right – to live

Terrorism, whether carried out by a state or by its opponents, pursues its aim by killing or threatening to kill, and is incompatible with liberty and the rule of law. So are intimidation and bribery. Modern technology now provides means of curbing their effects. This same technology, like any other, can be abused to erode civil liberties. Technology also, however, provides means to prevent or detect such abuse. By using the power of technology to the full, we can curb both terror and the abuse of civil liberties in defeating it. But we must never allow a self-claimed right to kill to override the ultimate civil right to live.

# The Italian Experience

## *Alison Jamieson*

Terrorism in Italy is associated for most people with the Red Brigades, and Italian democracy's 20 year battle against this form of political violence is considered exemplary. In the course of the 1970s and 1980s some 3,000 left wing terrorists and their supporters were identified, arrested and tried. Despite the terrorists' efforts to disrupt court trials by murdering judges and lawyers and attempting to intimidate witnesses, trial by jury in open court by democratic laws was never abandoned. The last Red Brigades action of any significance was the murder of a Christian Democrat Senator almost three years ago, and all those responsible are safely in prison. Nowadays there is no popular consensus for political violence as preached by the Red Brigades: a success story for democracy, by any standards.

But Italian terrorism neither begins nor ends with the Red Brigades.

### A CLIMATE OF TERRORISM

In all, 425 people have been murdered in attacks described as terrorist since 1969 – 150 were the work of the far left, but almost as many – 148 – are attributed to the far right. International terrorism has caused 68 deaths, the rest are unattributable.

Left wing terrorism in Italy has always aimed at the individual representative either of a hated sector such as advanced capitalism, or of a state institution, with the aim of unmasking for the benefit of the masses the hypocrisy behind apparent attempts to democratise. The far right, on the other hand, has generally targeted as wide a range of victims as possible by planting bombs in public places such as trains or railway stations. One aim of the indiscriminate massacre is to terrorise the civilian population into relinquishing certain rights and liberties in the interests of law and order, so that a strongly authoritarian, even military government will appear acceptable. The rationale behind this form of terror was evolved in the mid 1960s and is known as the **strategy of tension.** It began with a bomb explosion in a Milan bank in December 1969 which killed 17 and injured 88. There have been nine separate judgements in the course of the last 20 years for this attack, from which numerous guilty verdicts have been handed down, only to be converted into acquittals on appeal or to be judged technically invalid by the Supreme Court. At this moment, there are no culprits, and the chances of finding any in future trials are fading fast.

After more than a decade and two trials there are no culprits for the bomb that exploded in Bologna station in August 1980, when 85 died and 200 were injured. In fact, out of the seven indiscriminate massacres attributed to the far right, in only one case has a definitive verdict of guilty been reached –

13

and that only thanks to the confession of one of the participants.

## The Mafia

It was the Red Brigades who coined the phrase "bring the attack to the heart of the state" but ironically those who have come closest to doing so are the Mafia, who in the space of three and a half years assassinated the nine senior political, institutional and judicial representatives of state power in Sicily, including General Carlo Alberto Dalla Chiesa, Prefect of Palermo. In this case, where the Red Brigades had tried and failed, the Mafia succeeded.

Organised crime and terrorism are generally held to be quite distinct, but what would you call a secret society which murders, extorts, intimidates and uses the power of its illicitly acquired wealth to further political and economic objectives? The Mafia does not aim to overthrow democratic institutions but to corrupt and subvert them – in the long term more dangerous for democratic stability than the full frontal attack of the Red Brigades.

In 1989 there were 328 mafia murders in Sicily alone – 186 in Calabria and 230 in Campania – last September there were 15 murders in 48 hours – five of them were of children. During the run up to administrative elections held in May 1990, six candidates were murdered in the urban area of Reggio Calabria, where the Parliamentary Antimafia Commission estimates that up to 90 per cent of all economic activities are in the hands of organised crime.

At this moment there are seven kidnap hostages being held in Italy – they are almost certainly all in the mountainous Aspromonte region of Calabria. Some of them have been there for nearly two years, sold from clan to clan in a grotesque trade of human life for drugs. Last September in Locri, the Aspromonte town at the heart of the kidnap industry, the front of the town hall was spattered with machine gun fire in broad daylight, as inside councillors were meeting to discuss the spiralling violence; a few days later. a zealous carabinieri officer investigating kidnap trails was shot dead. The bishop of Locri, outspoken in his denunciation of violence, travels with armed bodyguards in a bullet proof car. The administration of justice is so paralysed by lack of funds that in one southern city the chief prosecutor's armoured car was off the road for months – there wasn't enough money to pay the road tax. This is another battle that Italian democracy is certainly not winning.

## The Aldo Moro affair

Left wing terrorism put down its roots in a young democracy whose political stagnation and moribund bureaucracy were completely inadequate to cope with the rapidity of Italy's social and economic transformation. The ever-present fear of a fascist revival, combined with the momentum of student revolution and of industrial unrest, encouraged the Red Brigades to believe that the state could be toppled by a proletarian revolution led by an armed vanguard. Their political analysis was naive, their assumptions about the Italian working classes were mistaken and their evaluation of their own capacities were grossly exaggerated. This is what we – and they – say now, but in the Spring of 1978 that handful of would-be revolutionaries had the entire world watching as they dangled Aldo Moro's life on a thread for 55 days. The issue was a classic one in the lexicon of terrorism – the sovereignty of democracy pitted against the political recognition of a terrorist organisation. Reality, as usual, is somewhat more banal: I have talked several times to two of Aldo Moro's kidnappers – when I asked them what they felt immediately after the kidnap they said – "well, naturally, there was a feeling of elation at having brought the whole thing off, but the strongest feeling was 'My God, what do we do now?'"

Italy was totally unprepared for an attack of this nature, even though the Red Brigades had been shooting, killing, kidnapping and issuing documents of responsibility and intent for years, particularly against Aldo Moro's Christian Democratic party.

Moro was a creature of habit and rarely altered his timings or routes; his car was not bullet proof, his five bodyguards were unrehearsed and unprepared; on the morning of the kidnap, police crisis procedures began with the activation of a national crisis plan which turned out to be familiar only to the Sardinian police force; a political crisis management team was set up but its meetings dwindled away to nothing. In a Red Brigades base discovered during the course of the kidnap – occupied as it happened by its organiser – no finger prints were taken. No assistance to the police or judiciary came from either of the two security services which had been reorganised the year before. Rivalry between state police and *carabinieri* further depleted the efforts of the judge in charge of enquiries, who was neither relieved of his routine work nor allocated extra staff; he had no telephone in his office and had to use a pay phone in the corridor outside.

In contrast, the Red Brigades moved around the country almost undisturbed – in the course of the kidnap they delivered 26 letters from Moro to family and colleagues in Rome; issued nine printed communiqués in four cities, carried out two murders, six woundings and six property attacks before finally dumping Moro's body half way between Christian Democrat and Communist party headquarters.

This was the desperate position from which Italy began to fight back. How on earth did it win?

## WINNING THE WAR AGAINST TERRORISM

First and most important factor – **the rejection of violence by the mass of Italians.** This came rather belatedly in the sense that until around 1977, perhaps even 1978, the Red Brigades were seen as fighting some of the battles that others did not care or dare to enter – against state corruption, social injustices, authoritarian and inhumane management in the large factories. There was an attitude, surprisingly prevalent, of sitting on the fence and saying – "neither with the state nor with the Red Brigades." This changed after the murder of Moro's five bodyguards and his own undignified end 55 days later. The rejection became almost total after two more murders in early 1979 – the first of a judge whose integrity was bringing too much credibility to the Red Brigades' image of a corrupt state – and the second of a Communist party worker and trade unionist. Then it sunk in that the victims of this terrorism were the reformers, the democrats, the peacemakers – and the tide turned.

A second factor was **conflict within the Red Brigades** – although from the technical point of view the Moro affair had been handled brilliantly, its outcome was bitterly criticised within the organisation. The lack of any real political gain from the kidnap, together with dissent over future strategy and tactics, began a process of fragmentation which in turn created distrust and disillusionment.

This was accentuated by a third factor, namely a dramatic increase in the **efficiency of the police and intelligence services and improved co-operation between the two.** Money was poured in to overhaul training and recruitment and to provide improved communications and information systems. For the first time the counter-terrorist effort was handled at national rather than regional level and its overall direction entrusted to one unit, run by General Dalla Chiesa. His lack of accountability caused some concern, and also resentment within the other police forces, but this was largely mitigated by the speed and efficiency of his counter-terrorist operations.

Another factor was the establishment of an **informal but extremely effective collaboration between judges** in various cities who began to pool information and ideas on a regular basis, thereby overcoming the limitations of a territorially structured judicial system. The "pool" format was adopted successfully for a number of years by antimafia judges in Palermo, but sadly has now virtually collapsed.

Italian anti-terrorist judges were greatly assisted in their task by the passing of **two groups of laws,** the first essentially repressive – known as the "emergency laws" – and the second two premium laws which favoured collaboration and rehabilitation.

The most important features of the emergency laws are as follows:

- For crimes bearing two new aggravating factors – "association with the aim of terrorism and of subversion of the democratic order" and "attack for subversive or terrorist purposes", prison sentences were increased by a half.
- For such crimes pre-trial detention was increased by a third, making it possible to spend 12 years in prison without a definitive verdict.
- Police powers were extended to stop, search and question on suspicion, to order telephone taps, to search buildings.
- Police could hold suspects for up to 48 hours without informing the judiciary.
- Property owners were compelled to report details of all rental or sales agreements from 1977 onwards to local authorities. According to the brigadists themselves, this turned out to be one of the most effective of all the anti-terrorist measures, and caused many bases to be abandoned.
- Premium laws were introduced to create specific legal incentives for

collaboration, given that the constitutional obligation in Italy to prosecute every crime committed does not permit the granting of immunity.

**1) The "Penitence law"** of May 1982 ran for nine months. It did not require proof of "repentance" in any moral sense but insisted on:
"full confession" and an "active contribution" to the cessation of terrorism: in other words – the betrayal of former companions. In return, life sentences were reduced to 10–12 years; other sentences were cut by a half, but not to exceed 10 years. If the contribution were considered "of exceptional relevance" the prison sentence could be further reduced by a third.

**2) The "Dissociation law"** of February 1987 ran for one month only.
This law required:
abandonment of the terrorist group; confession of all the activities undertaken; formal renunciation of violence as a form of political struggle, and behaviour compatible with the foregoing.

In return, life was cut to 30 years, sentences for crimes of bloodshed reduced by a quarter, for less serious crimes by a third and for crimes of association by a half.

**Effects of the legislation**

The legislation just described has both positive and negative aspects. Its greatest single virtue is that it undoubtedly saved lives; it helped bring criminals to justice and contributed to the breakup of entire terrorist structures. Confessions helped towards an understanding of ideology and motivation, thus the phenomenon was easier to combat.

On the negative side, the lengthening of pre-trial detention up to 12 years was a reflection of an antiquated and underfunded criminal justice system rather than a serious response to terrorism. The severity of conditions in some of the maximum security prisions removed almost every trace of human dignity, and violence on and between prisoners was widespread and often unchecked.

Many were caught under generic terrorism charges who had little to do with terrorism but who would leave prison hardened and genuinely criminalised.

The premium laws benefited the terrorist leaders more than the followers, and certainly had more to do with pragmatism than justice – several so-called "repentant" multi-murderers are free whilst over 100 left wing prisoners remain behind bars with no blood on their hands.

Perhaps the most important aspect of these laws, and the final contributing factor to the defeat of left wing terrorism, is that they were passed, admittedly amidst controversy, but by a **substantially united political front** which placed traditional adversaries side by side in the common defence of democratic institutions.

**Problems in combating right wing terrorism**

Why then has Italy been unable to achieve the same results against right wing terrorism? The premium laws for example, should have been equally effective against the neo-fascists. A partial answer lies with ideology. The Red Brigades needed the support of the masses to bring about their wishes for revolution and when that support simply did not materialise, all but a handful would eventually acknowledge the collapse of a myth. The far right has never sought consensus and therefore despite the failure of their projects, its militants have been able to preserve a form of ideological integrity – if one can apply such a term.

But this is only a tiny part of the story – the rest is still shrouded in mystery. There are however two elements present in the right wing massacres **and** in the unresolved political and institutional murders carried out by the Mafia – **corruption in the Italian security services** and **membership of the now outlawed masonic lodge Propaganda 2** (P2). The Bologna – Palermo axis is weighed down with subversive linkages. The security services have been implicated in various ways in all the indiscriminate massacres and it is a fact that the *only* guilty verdict involving direct responsibility for the Bologna station bomb has been the confirmation that the deputy head of the military security service and *his* deputy, both P2 members, attempted to deflect enquiries by laying a false trail of evidence. Who they were protecting and why has not been established.

Left-wing terrorism was politically defeated largely due to the rigour with which all the political parties repulsed the assault on democracy. The Red Brigades were a young, identifiable, external enemy that could be fought with hands free. The Mafia has been around for over a century and has steadily penetrated the political and economic establishment to the point at which the ability – and sometimes even the will – to fight back have been eroded. The problem may be most evident in the south of Italy, but its solution depends on Rome. There is a direct contradiction, not to say hypocrisy, when political parties that promise greater commitment to law and order and the fight against the Mafia allow members facing serious criminal charges to stand for local elections under the party banner. Political protection of ambiguous behaviour, whether in the form of overt support or the more subtle failure to condemn undoubtedly wins votes but is a luxury the decaying morality of Italian politics can ill afford.

Where then, with a view to post 1992, does all this lead?, What horrors will be unleashed from Italy once the European barriers fall?

## THE THREAT TO THE EC

On the far right, it seems that the tactics of mass slaughter have gone out of fashion, for the time being at least. The last was the bomb on the Naples – Milan express train in December 1984 and even that now looks to have been a Mafia ordered operation. However recent evidence, if corroborated, shows that the P2 lodge not only was more powerful than was originally thought, but that it is very much alive and kicking. The President of the Parliamentary

Commission of Enquiry into P2 continues to make public warnings about the destabilisation potential of a secret organisation with political protection at the highest levels.

As far as left wing terrorism is concerned. I mentioned that the Red Brigades have been silent for nearly three years. But in April 1990 three presumed Red Brigades members were arrested in the company of a Palestinian from the Abu Nidal organisation, arrested back in 1985 at Frankfurt airport with 10 kg of Semtex, extradited to Italy and subsequently released. In their possession they had plans relating to possible attacks on Israeli and American diplomats in Rome. If the Red Brigades have any life force left, I believe this can only come from cross frontier collaboration.

A relatively new phenomenon and one which so far defies the label "right" or "left" is that of so-called "eco-terrorism." There were 35 attacks on high voltage electricity pylons in the course of 1989, many of them linked to chemical or nuclear-related sectors of industry. Animal rights protestors have likewise undertaken actions against property and, in common with the other "eco-terrorist" groups, are believed to have some international co-ordination.

Overall, I believe that the greatest immediate threat for the EC comes from the economic and territorial power of the Mafia. The bloodbaths in southern Italy described earlier are spreading northwards and patterns of territorial control such as exist in Calabria have been noted in the Milan hinterland. They stem from a problem that affects us all – control of the drug supplies and routes used to distribute heroin and cocaine throughout Europe.

The Home Office estimates that the annual revenue from drug trafficking in Britain is around £1.8 billion (three billion dollars) – in Italy the figure is £22.5 billion (37.5 billion dollars). America is saturated with cocaine – in the last 10 years wholesale prices have dropped by 80 per cent and purity has quintupled. When the street price of one gramme of cocaine in the United States dropped to as little as 10 to 15 dollars in 1988 the UK price was 90 to 188 dollars. The attractions of a barrier free Europe are positively dazzling for the drug barons, as is becoming evident from the seizure figures.

About 95 per cent of all drugs seized in Britain are discovered at ports or on the high seas. In 1988 48 per cent of cannabis resin and 36 per cent of cocaine seized came from or through another EC country. If border checks are abandoned it will be harder to detect drug consignments before they are broken up for distribution inland. For this reason the British government intends to maintain selective checks on passengers and freight at ports, airports, and at the Channel tunnel terminals. and unless external EC barriers are considerably strengthened. other European countries may end up doing the same.

Italy launched a serious counterattack on illicit financial accumulation in 1982 with an anti mafia law which permitted asset investigation; several EC countries have introduced money laundering provisions in harmony with the UN Vienna Convention and with the declaration of principles signed by the central banks of the G10 countries. But so far only a tiny proportion of illicit funds are trapped by this legislation because investigations often come to a halt at national boundaries. Without legislative harmonisation. the liberalisation of capital and reduction of trade barriers can only make life easier for the money launderers.

The instruments and the organisations for combating this are available if the political will is there. But now more than ever before, terrorism and drug trafficking can only be fought effectively by a sincere and dedicated commitment to international co-operation.

# Frontier Problems and the Single Market

## *Juliet Lodge*

The realisation of the Single Market (SEM) by 1993 raises many issues relating to internal and external security. When the EC Commission first presented its 1985 White Paper on completing the Internal Market the wider implications of the "Four Freedoms" were hardly recognised. The SEM's accomplishment depends on the removal of intra-EC technical, physical and fiscal barriers to realise the Four Freedoms of movement of: goods, persons, services, and capital. That the newly created SEM was to have a reinforced "external frontier" – a *cordon sanitaire* to keep out terrorists, international criminals, refugees and unwanted immigrants – initially eluded attention.

Facilitating the freedom of movement of persons was seen largely in narrow labour mobility terms. Consequently, the wider implications remained obscure. The UK, for example, focused on social security matters, the Social Charter and low key political issues. Only in the annex to the Single European Act is there a hint that the UK was concerned about terrorism and international crime. Even then, officials tended to ignore the wider import of the Four Freedoms. Problems arise, however, because even though the EC Court of Justice has recognised a distinction between border controls and police controls, the freedom of movement of persons is inextricably linked to criminal matters over which the EC arguably has no jurisdiction. Operationally speaking the distinction is not watertight.

The situation is complicated by the fact that questions concerning the freedom of movement of persons cross two sets of decision-making procedures. Issues central to labour mobility are dealt with according to the EC's normal legislative procedures. In many cases decisions are taken by a majority vote in the Council of Ministers and the outcome is binding on all the member states irrespective of whether or not they have approved the legislation.

This contrasts markedly with the decision-making practice relating to what might loosely be called **criminal aspects** of the freedom of movement of persons and goods. Much of the work in this category was not seen as a legitimate concern of the EC until the mid 1970s. Even then, EC involvement started largely as a result of the desire to combat terrorism. In 1976, Interior and Justice Ministers of the EC met for the first time and adopted a resolution leading to the establishment of four consultative groups, three of which were working parties and one involved the director generals of the various ministries. Since then they have intensified co-operation to combat terrorism; narco-terrorism and drug-smuggling; to regulate and harmonise different immigration rules across the Twelve; and to devise the requisite implementing measures. (See Table 1.)

Significantly co-operation on most of these matters follows different rules to those governing EC policymaking and the SEM. Most of the work is done

**TABLE 1**
**Treaty Ratification by EC States**

| EC State | European Convention on Extradition 1957 | | European Convention on Mutual Assistance in Criminal Matters 1959 | | European Convention on Suppression of Terrorism 1977 | |
|---|---|---|---|---|---|---|
| | Signature | In-force Ratification | Signature | In-force Ratification | Signature | In-force Ratification |
| Belgium | 1957 | — | 1959 | 1975 | 1977 | 1986 |
| Denmark | 1957 | 1962 | 1959 | 1962 | 1977 | 1978 |
| France | 1957 | 1986 | 1961 | 1967 | 1977 | 1987 |
| Germany | 1957 | 1977 | 1959 | 1977 | 1977 | 1978 |
| Greece | 1957 | 1961 | 1959 | 1962 | 1977 | 1988 |
| Ireland | 1966 | 1966 | — | — | 1986 | 1989 |
| Italy | 1957 | 1963 | 1959 | 1962 | 1977 | 1986 |
| Luxembourg | 1957 | 1977 | 1959 | 1977 | 1977 | 1981 |
| Netherlands | 1965 | 1969 | 1965 | 1969 | 1977 | 1985 |
| Portugal | 1977 | 1990 | 1979 | 1984 | 1977 | 1982 |
| Spain | 1979 | 1982 | 1979 | 1982 | 1978 | 1980 |
| UK | — | — | — | — | 1977 | 1978 |

*Source: House of Commons Home Affairs Committee, Vol. 1, 1990, p. xxxi.*

in an intergovernmental framework not *formally* subject to the supranational rules and obligations of the EC. Much has been accomplished within working groups of European Political Co-operation (EPC) and the Council of Interior and Justice Ministers. EPC is *not* subject to the intervention of the European Court of Justice. EPC decisions are subject neither to compulsory majority voting nor to the co-operation procedure with all that implies for intervention by the European Parliament.

It is not appropriate to put a sinister interpretation on this firstly because early on not only did the EC not have a defined interest in security matters and foreign policy broadly conceived; but secondly, the EC was not seen as being concerned with criminal law. The EC's aim was to create "an ever closer union" among its members and to realise a common market.

Co-operation has grown in tandem with European integration and member states gaining the habit not only of using the EC to advance national goals but of thinking in European terms. Since the 1970s, they have increasingly sought EC backing for or acquiescence in international *demarches*. Faced with the need to combat indigenous European terrorism and international terrorism on European soil or against European targets outside the EC, the case for greater co-operation among EC states seemed compelling. The difficulties in securing and implementing effective international measures to combat terrorism also persuaded the EC's then Nine member states of the desirability of trying to succeed within the tighter body of the EC.

The groundwork for intergovernmental *co-operation* (not supranational

*Frontier Problems and the Single Market*    25

*integration*) on "criminal" matters had been laid well before 1985. The Council of Europe was instrumental in pursuing European-wide action against terrorism. Informal links between police forces were set up in 1978 in part to improve the exchange of information and to track down terrorists[1]. To some extent, the push to realise a seemingly exclusively economic goal – the SEM – led to a *qualitative change* in, and raised the status of, such co-operation. The goal of *eliminating* internal *physical* barriers to freedom of movement (e.g. customs posts and systematic border controls) and *reinforcing* the EC's *common external border* raises sensitive political and legal issues.

## THE MEMBER STATES AND BORDER CONTROLS

EC states differ widely over the respective competences of border control posts. The police presence varies. For example, **Germany** has a heavily armed federal border guard (the *Bundesgrenzschutz* whose role developed at a time when Germany was neither part of Nato nor expected to develop a military capacity); **France** has a special division of the *Police Nationale*, the *Police de l'air et des frontieres*, for both border policing and immigration control; and in the **UK**, border control work is shared by the police, HM Customs & Excise and HM Immigration Service[2].

Matters relating to controlling the movement of persons, and particularly of "undesirable" persons, was addressed not so much in internal market forums (such as the Commission and Council of Ministers) but in those connected with the Council of Europe, and more importantly EPC: the **Trevi** and, for drugs matters, the **Pompidou** working groups[3]. A European Committee for the Fight Against Drugs (CELAND) was set up after the Strasbourg 1989 European Council. Its task is to formulate a Euro-plan to combat trafficking. It comprises drugs co-ordinators and the relevant Commission official responsible for the internal market. It reports regularly to the European Council.

A plethora of groups work on the criminal side to the removal of internal EC borders. Co-ordination is weak and no clear hierarchy of authority exists. In practice reports tend to filter up to the European Council (an intergovernmental body that parallels the EC institutions and was first mentioned in the treaty through the Single European Act). At a political level, the EC Council of Ministers favours close co-operation between the EC and Pompidou group whereas a stricter division seems to obtain in respect of the EC and Trevi. Internal market issues are treated by too many separate working groups[4].

### TREVI (*Terrorism, Radicalism, Extremism and International Violence*)

Trevi was set up as an intergovernmental forum in 1976 independent from the EC though limited to EC members and, in a loose sense, paralleling it and EPC[5]. Even after the December 1990 Intergovernmental Conferences (IGCs), EPC's status remains somewhat ambiguous and pressure is growing for it to be fully integrated into the Community system. Trevi's goal is to facilitate co-operation at a practical, operational level against terrorism, drug-trafficking and other serious crime and public order problems. Trevi is divided into working groups.

*Trevi I:* on terrorism – the European Liaison Service of the Metropolitan Police Special Branch is involved in this.

*Trevi II:* on public order issues, football hooliganism, forensic science etc. (and also police training).

*Trevi III:* on serious and organised international crime, principally drug-trafficking.

*Trevi 92:* on police and security issues of the free movement of people, including compensatory measures to combat the relaxation of intra-EC border controls. Senior officials prepare reports for European Councils on policing matters (e.g. May 1990 Dublin summit) and report upwards to another group: *the Group of Co-ordinators* on the free movement of people set up by the 1988 Rhodes European Council.

Trevi lacks a permanent secretariat even though it has an ambitious programme of action. It has been derided by the Spanish police forces. Even though its concerns overlap with those of the EC Commission, the Commission is not involved in its work. This creates problems because the Commission is directly involved in customs but not police management of frontiers. Trevi has links with the Customs Mutual Assistance Group 1992 (MAG92), the Ad Hoc Working Group on Immigration and its sub-groups, the working group on judicial co-operation and the European groups of drugs and border co-ordinators. Moreover, measures taken to realise a European legal area, resulted from EC initiatives in the mid-1980s – some of which grew out of EPC reaction to the US Libyan raid – to build on the Dublin Agreement[6].

## The Group of Co-ordinators

Consisting of national representatives, this group worked on the complexities of eliminating individual border checks and intra-EC borders and finalised a report known as the Palma report (after a special meeting held in Palma in early June 1989) which it presented to the July 1989 Madrid European Council. The Group of Co-ordinators cannot take decisions itself. It acts as honest-broker and tries to co-ordinate the work of other relevant bodies including, according to the matter at hand, the EC Council, EPC, Trevi, Pompidou Group, the ad hoc immigration group, MAG92, etc.

The Group of Co-ordinators identified the following areas as being of particular concern:

- terrorism, drug trafficking and other illicit trafficking;
- improved police co-operation;
- legal co-operation in criminal matters and reviewing the possibility of approximating certain provisions;
- controls on "elements" accompanying travellers – veterinary controls; plant health controls; protection of endangered fauna and flora; weapons; drugs; art smuggling; exchange and tax controls;
- family problems – treatment of minors, "legal" kidnapping of children.

The Group stressed that the external frontier must be strengthened in a way that gave all member states confidence in the type of external control being operated by their partners. It highlighted the need to regulate the entry of third country nationals to the EC, including visa policies, a European visa, and the drafting of a common list of undesirables, and the right of asylum and the status of refugees, taking into account member states' obligations under the Geneva Convention and the New York Protocol.

The Group drew attention to the financial implications for the implementation of a common policy and stressed that traditional values specific to member states had to be respected, and that strengthened controls at the EC's external frontier should not exceed what is strictly required to ensure states' security and public order.

The Palma document took these issues a step further and tried to distinguish between measures that were essential – such as common immigration and computerised information control and surveillance systems – and those that were desirable as intra-EC borders were lifted and the external frontier consolidated. Deadlines for taking the appropriate decisions in time for 1993 were set. Many have been met.

## SCHENGEN

The Schengen group comprised Belgium, the Netherlands, Luxembourg, Germany and France ("the Five"). Italy, refusing to accept the Group's *acquis*, was denied membership. The aim was to show that a core group of states committed to deeper integration could remove internal barriers well before the end of 1992 even if the EC's least *communautaire* states wished to postpone the SEM. They signed an agreement to this effect on 14 June 1985, that is before the Single European Act had been concluded.

Early optimism over the Five's ability to solve seemingly intractable problems regarding the reinforcement of the external frontier gave way to disgruntlement in December 1989 when signature of an additional convention was postponed. Fears grew lest the Schengen agreement fail to come into force before the end of 1992 and lose its demonstration effect on the Twelve with potentially damaging consequences.

### What were the problems?

The chief obstacles arose out of first, government reservations and second, German unification. The Dutch were anxious about the right to exile; visa requirements and individual liberty. Belgain MPs objected that the computerised information system envisaged (SIS) was likely to compromise individual liberties in a country lacking data protection legislation. However, shortly before the scheduled signing of the convention, Belgium dropped all its reservations providing that the agreement's ratification was "accompanied or preceded by bills on weapons, the protection of privacy and control of police and information services." A condition for Schengen's ratification is Belgium's ratification of the Council of Europe's Convention on Data Protection.

On 15 December 1989 the FRG requested a postponement of the signing of the convention on three grounds:

(i) *the opening of the FRG-GDR border* (and hence the extension of the Schengen external border and the implications for its policing);

(ii) *the right to asylum.* This reservation against harmonisation was a red herring in that Ruud Lubbers (the Dutch Presidency) assured Bonn that contracting parties would be able to treat asylum requests in specific cases in accordance with national practice. (This was a particular bone of contention in the Twelve with Denmark raising numerous objections.)

(iii) *tax harmonisation* and mutual legal help in the case of tax fraud. Luxembourg resisted its inclusion in the convention although the Five had agreed to it in principle *in extremis.*

The FRG undertook to reopen the Schengen process after the GDR elections on 18 March 1990.

EUROCARITAS (the secretariat liaising between the EC and NGOs Caritas Catholica) argued that the Schengen convention compromised refugees' and asylum seekers' rights and wanted the convention to be postponed indefinitely. An annex on security safeguard measures to the convention (supposedly secret but published in the Amsterdam weekly *Vrij Nederland*) listed **45 countries** whose nationals would be **subjected to border controls** when entering Schengenland. Identified as posing risks to the Five, they included: *Arab states, East European countries (including Yugoslavia), Turkey, South Africa, Zaire, the Sudan, Ethiopia, Colombia, Surinam, Afghanistan, Cambodia, Pakistan and Taiwan.*

Significantly the Commission officially expressed "great regret" over the delay. It doubted the validity of German objections and reservations against the SIS. Moreover, ratification of the convention and SIS's setting up were likely to take some 18 months: thus Schengen could not enter into force more than six months before the SEM. The Commission rightly feared that delay would imperil wider discussions on freedom of movement within the Rhodes Group. Many issues raised at this stage in the Schengen context were discussed in parallel by the Twelve's various working groups (e.g. The SIS system and the Twelve's talks on computerised information exchange). Similar objections surfaced on both. The guns versus drugs lobbies epitomised national divisions (eg France and Belgium were seen as being "soft" on hand guns à la US; the Dutch lenient on drugs). Compromises had to be found.

Failing this, and given entrenched national reservations, rather than protract deliberations well beyond 1992, the Five decided to set out principles and signed the additional convention on 15 June 1990.

**What was the crux of the problem?**

There were two key inter-related areas of dispute: the first concerned Germany, the second civil liberties. The Five hesitated given rapid change in Eastern Europe. The Dutch Presidency in February 1990 supported a postponement of the signature of the agreement ostensibly pending the outcome of the GDR elections on 18 March. The result was not in question. The meaning of the EC's commitment to reinforcing its external frontier was, however, given Chancellor Kohl's equivocal statements on Germany's eastern border and the associated Two Plus Four talks.


## THE GERMAN QUESTION

Franco-Dutch Prime Ministerial talks in early April led to senior officials resolving outstanding issues on the basis of a German note requesting a softer line on the visa issue and the monitoring of Central and East European nationals. Franco-Belgian anxiety that the Five could not control the vulnerable and leaky East German border (whose precise location was still to be fixed) deterred them from removing their borders with Germany. When the FRG said it would guarantee the border and they suggested extending Schengen to the GDR, agreement swiftly followed on excluding East Germans from visa requirements. By May EC Ministers had agreed to sign the GDR agreement before the end of the summer, in parallel with the German unification process, so giving Schengen and the EC a new external frontier: the Oder-Neisse.

The Four insisted that the FRG provide information and confirmatory evidence as to the fulfilment of the terms of the agreement. They shared EC reservations that the FRG was insufficiently forthcoming and objected to the lack of consultation. This was an important point because the Commission official initially responsible for both internal market matters, the EC response to the GDR, and for sitting in on some, but not all, Schengen meetings was German.


### The State of Play

By November 1989 progress had been made on the draft convention on visas at external borders; on the right of asylum (designed to ensure that a request refused by one member state is not accepted by another); on the transmission of repressive procedures (to foster judicial co-operation, ease extradition procedures); on strengthening of police co-operation (within Trevi); and on data protection. By the end of 1990, *four draft conventions* lay before the Twelve on:

- crossing of frontiers and visas;
- determining the state responsible for asylum bids;
- transmission of criminal proceedings;
- recovery of maintenance for children.

However, it was clear that operationalising many of the issues identified was going to prove far from easy.

## Lack of co-ordination: a recurrent problem

The lack of co-ordination between the various working groups continued to give concern. Quiet diplomatic and political initiatives to try and convince national police authorities of the desirability of greater co-operation only slowly yielded results.

In August 1988, the International Union of Police Federations declared its opposition to the SEM by one vote. The UK and Denmark were the chief opponents to the opening up of internal borders. From then on, political pressure grew. In October 1988, Chancellor Kohl told a conference on Franco-German relations that it was essential to set up a Euro-police force along the lines of the FBI because existing co-operation was inadequate to combat terrorism, drug-trafficking and major international crime[7]. In March 1989, the Spanish President of the Trevi Group, Interior Minister Mr. Corcuera proposed the creation of a permanent secretariat as a kind of embryonic EC police force[8]. This idea was also raised by the Italian and German governments. In May 1989, a compromise was reached on setting up a permanent team of five high-level officials responsible for following up Trevi group work. The team meets regularly but does not have a permanent headquarters or budget[9]. Simultaneously, all bar the UK, Ireland and Germany, agreed on expediting extradition demands and signed a special convention on this on 26 May 1989 in San Sebastian[10].

While Trevi groups met regularly, almost monthly, during the last half of 1989 under the French Presidency, and achieved a good deal of progress, police co-operation remained such a sensitive subject that the possibility of the EC convening a special IGC on police co-operation to give *political legitimacy* and impetus to the process was discussed[11].

The Group of National Co-ordinators, for its part, issued a first stage report in which it tried to define the precise parameters for cross-EC police co-operation. It highlighted: exchanges of experts; external border controls; establishment of joint units along common border zones; the right of hot pursuit across borders (à la Schengen which referred to the "depth" (by km) of hot pursuit to be allowed); some harmonisation of radio bands and equipment (where actual arrest by non-indigenous forces was not permitted) and a common computerised system of information and research on serious crime. The Trevi Ministers adopted a political statement on political co-operation in December to expedite progress between then and 1993[12].

However, advances in some areas exposed gaps in others. By mid 1990 judicial co-operation lagged behind police, customs and administrative co-operation (the latter having been fostered through the MAG and its study of measures to complement the Naples Convention) and police co-operation having grown through the work of the separate Police Working Group on Terrorism, modelled on Trevi[13]. The lack of concrete proposals to rectify the situation owed as much to vast discrepancies between the Twelve's legal systems and the continuing sensitivity over policing and judicial control issues and the lack of links between them as to political fears that the 1992 enterprise could be endangered by a full-blown public row over the issues raised. (See Table 2.)

*Frontier Problems and the Single Market*                              31

## TABLE 2

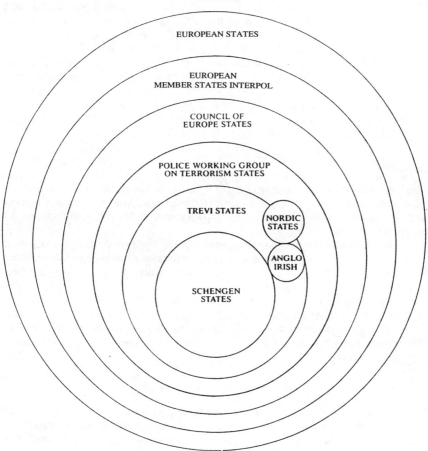

Schengen States: **Belgium, France, Germany, Luxembourg, Netherlands**
Trevi States (non Schengen): **Denmark, Greece, Ireland, Italy, Portugal, Spain, UK**
Police Working Group on Terrorism (non Trevi): Finland, Norway, Sweden
Council of Europe (non PWGT): **Austria, Cyprus, Iceland, Liechtenstein, Malta, Switzerland, Turkey**
Interpol (non Council of Europe): **Andorra, Bulgaria, Hungary, Monaco, Romania, Yugoslavia**
Other European States: **Albania, Czechoslovakia, Poland, USSR (the last three are expected to join Interpol later this year)**
*Source: House of Commons Home Affairs Committee, Vol. 1, 1990, p. xix.*

The explosive question of weapons in particular led to heated debate in the European Parliament. MEPs stressed that the right to have a weapon did not confer a right to carry or use it especially when crossing the (eliminated) internal borders. Acquisition and ownership of weapons requires licences in some states whereas it is relatively easy to buy them in others.

The Commission proposed in summer 1990 that the movement of firearms between states be prohibited unless specified procedures of authorisation and declaration are met. Its proposals were designed to oblige member states to adopt minimum EC checks. They may adopt stricter rules if they wish. This means that states with lax provisions (ie that permit firearms to be freely acquired without licence) will have to tighten their rules.

**Implications**

The removal of internal borders and steps to facilitate the freedom of movement of persons embrace myriad technical obstacles and require a good deal of co-operation among agencies often accustomed to untrammelled independence.

The wider political context within which this co-operation unfurled impeded progress. The highly contentious, sensitive political implications of the enabling legislation provoked several states, and notably the UK, into calling for less integration and more independence.

The fear that the EC would delay progress on the SEM in order to accommodate recalcitrant members led five states to form a core group (known as the Schengen group) committed to realising the goal of an internal barrier free zone in pursuit of European Union. Their efforts, as the 1992 laboratory, provide a salutary tale.

## THE COMMISSION'S VIEW

Having initiated the SEM and being responsible for drafting the enabling 1992 legislation, the Commission had an interest in the Schengen group's progress. While it did not have a direct role in it, its expertise was often needed. On some issues, it was given observer status. On others, it was invited by one of many of the working groups dealing with the most sensitive issues.

The Commission expected the removal of intra-EC borders to be complemented by the strengthening of the common EC external border and tighter controls on non-EC air traffic; and by enhanced co-operation between the member states (traditionally mutually suspicious) police and immigration authorities[14]. It drafted legislation accordingly and immediately came up against national interests. Its first draft directive on "Easing of Controls at intra-Community frontiers" was produced in response to a request from the European Parliament in January 1985. The Council limited the directive's applicability to land frontiers, and excluded the German–Danish border (because Denmark belongs to the Nordic Passport Control Agreement) and the Chunnel (subject to an evolving bilateral regime)[15].

Widely different asylum and immigration rules also held up progress.

German rules were deemed too liberal and the Italian too lax, notably in Sicily. The contentiousness of these issues was heightened owing to the pre and post-unification influx of East Germans (with automatic rights throughout the EC as "German nationals") and the host of non-German nationals working in the former GDR. Now part of the EC, derogations from EC law apply to the GDR for a limited time only[16].

Immigration and asylum problems raised the question of the status of an asylum-seeker. The Twelve generally agree on treating terrorist offences as criminal not political acts even though fugitive terrorists may seek political asylum. Laborious co-operation by the Twelve has met with some success in respect of extradition and international crime. However, differences in states' provisions on asylum and immigration have led would-be applicants to apply either to several states simultaneously or to the most lenient with a view, after entry, to moving freely around the EC. Not until 1990 did the Twelve agree that the first state approached should assume responsibility and co-ordinate things.

A final complicating factor lies with internal problems of communication and co-ordination within individual member states. Little headway will be made unless those at the sharp edge of eliminating intra-EC border controls and continuing security checks co-operate effectively. Inconsistencies could multiply if bi- or multi-lateral accords grow in default of a common set of goals. The question of who has ultimate authority in border control matters remains. Direct experience of chaos led Franco-German authorities in 1984 to sign the Saarbrücken pact to ease formalities on their common border. Within months this was extended to the Benelux[17].

## THE PROBLEM OF PROTECTING INDIVIDUAL LIBERTIES

The question of individual liberties proved explosive. While it was generally agreed that exchanging information was desirable in terms of the pursuit and apprehension of suspects, MEPs objected to the "secrecy" surrounding the Schengen deliberations. National parliaments were alerted to gaps in domestic provisions on data protection. Parallel discussions were pursued by MEPs concerned with promoting a *European Bill of rights* and a *Residents' Charter* to guarantee individuals' fundamental liberties. By the December 1990 IGCs, this had become submerged in the Spanish advocacy of EC "citizenship" but not before a lot of agonising in the interim over Schengen and SIS.

Trevi Ministers at their December 1989 Paris meeting tried to allay fears with a political declaration to the effect that Trevi, far from being a threat to civil liberty, sought to safeguard public security. It recalled the Twelve's commitment to individual and collective freedom, human rights and democracy[18]. However, Hans Neusal, (German State Secretary for the Interior) was the subject of a failed Red Army Faction (RAF) terrorist attack in summer 1990. The RAF accused him of being the motor behind Trevi and initiatives to intensify repression with the French Interior Minister[19].

The National Co-ordinators Group, on the initiative of the French presidency, submitted a report to the Strasbourg European Council on: *Common*

*Principles for the Protection of Individuals in the Use of Personalised Data Banks*. This set out guidelines and noted the desirability of member states ratifying the parallel Council of Europe convention of 28 January 1981. It recalled the recommendations of its Ministerial Committee of 17 September 1987.

The report stressed that access to computerised information should be limited exclusively to public authorities concerned with freeing the movement of persons[20]. The FRG wanted to include non-computerised information given its access to Stasi files on international terrorist attacks (eg in Berlin) and on Stasi who connived in their transmission. Italian Socialist MEPs asked the Italian Council Presidency in July 1990 to ask the new democracies of Eastern Europe to open their archives on international terrorism.

The SIS is limited in scope and, in practice, its operation will depend on whether or not national police authorities think it desirable or otherwise to divulge information to their counterparts on a "need to know" basis. MEPs insisted that Interpol should not have access to SIS and successfully won an undertaking to be regularly informed about SIS use. National security services may request information and seek to have it placed within SIS on condition that "concrete proof makes it possible to suppose that the information to be acquired is necessary for the prevention of a serious threat to the safety of the state"[21]. This again is highly sensitive in view of the *Berufsverbot*. In practice, SIS information cannot be broader in scope than data already exchanged on a bilateral basis.


## SCHENGEN LESSONS FOR THE SINGLE MARKET

Ultimately, legislative uniformity can only be sought when the EC has first, confirmed the source of supranational political authority; and second, determined the legal base for EC intervention (criminal law matters are excluded from its jurisdiction although the Commission has investigative powers notably in respect of agricultural fraud and the abuse of competition rules).

In the short run, steps will probably have to be taken to encourage closer approximation of national laws. This should allow members to appreciate each other's systems and discourage them from taking up entrenched positions early on likely to prevent subsequent agreement. The Schengen "laboratory" serves as a cautionary tale. It demonstrated how, given political will, sensitive issues can be successfully attacked. However, legitimate doubts as to Schengen's impact on the democratic deficit have been raised. Operational matters often require secrecy but the broad principles could have been openly discussed. Fears that Schengen might exacerbate divisions among the Twelve are exaggerated: the Five concluded in one agreement what might otherwise have demanded ten conventions. Schengen-type provisions will have to be extended throughout the Twelve. This inevitably means that even more issues will have to become subject to EC level rules.

## FUTURE ISSUES: POLITICAL AUTHORITY AND CONTROL

Responsibility for advancing the SEM lies primarily with the Commission. Commissioners principally responsible for freedom of movement of persons logically must confront related criminal issues. However, giving the Commission a central, co-ordinating or policy initiating role in these matters may not be the most appropriate solution to problems of co-ordination. It would be politically controversial and probably unacceptable to the member states and to the Commission itself. The Commission is not equipped to deal with such issues. Giving the Commission such responsibilites might alter the nature of the beast and undermine its relative openness.

Whatever formula is adopted, close co-operation with national authorities is essential. The Commission and member governments, through the working parties, would have to assume responsibility for goal setting. Implementation would have to be given to local bodies.

In brief, the Schengen and 1992 processes place demands on bodies unused to transfrontier consultation, co-ordination and co-operation. The issue of crime-related matters raises a whole gamut of problems ranging from police co-operation to differential penalties for crimes. In addition, it raises the grander issue of what structures, institutions and safeguards are needed to realise the SEM and a democratic political European Union.

Since sensitive issues are at stake, including the locus of political authority, the EC will have to advance European Union by defining the parameters of internal and external security. If authority for them is to be shared between EC authorities and the member states on the basis of subsidiarity, or if it is to be given exclusively to the EC, proper political controls must be put in place. Agonising over whether or not this moves the EC towards a federal entity, is a secondary issue to the one of ensuring that the EC, in the post 1992 era, functions effectively, efficiently, transparently and democratically.

---

### NOTES

[1] His Excellency Mr. Frederick Korthals Altes, Minister of Justice, speech to the AEGEE conference on "Towards a European Response to Terrorism: National Experiences and Lessons for 1992," University of Leiden, 16 March 1989.

[2] F. Gregory, "The Evolving European Community: An Agenda for the 1990s," paper presented to the Public Administration Committee Conference, York, 1990.

[3] The Pompidou Group is known as the Co-operation Group to Combat Drug Abuse and Illicit Trafficking in Drugs but is outside the scope of this discussion.

[4] *Agence Europe*, 6/7 November 1989.

[5] EPC was, until the Single European Act that came into effect in July 1987, parallel to but not fully integrated into the EC with its legally binding structures even though the EC Commission increasingly played a central role in it.

[6] For details see J. Lodge (ed.), *The Threat of Terrorism*, Wheatsheaf, Brighton, 1988: pp. 229–264.

[7] *Target*, July 1988.

[8] *Agence Europe*, 13–14 March 1987.

[9] *Agence Europe*, 16–17 May 1990.

[10] *Target*, May 1989.

[11] *Agence Europe*, 14 December 1989.

[12] *Agence Europe*, 18–19 December 1989.

[13] House of Commons Home Affairs Committee, *Practical Police Co-operation in the European Community, Memoranda of Evidence*, 18 April 1990, London, HMSO, 363–i.

[14] See House of Commons Home Affairs Committee, Seventh Report, *Practical Police Co-operation in the European Community*, Vol.1, 20 July 1990, London. HMSO 353–I.

[15] *COM(89)446. fin.*

[16] *Bulletin of the European Communities*, Supplement, April 1990.

[17] Initially this meant that cars crossing Schengen's borders were subjected to random checks if they displayed a green disc confirming that all passengers were EC nationals obeying duty free and currency rules. This has never worked effectively. *Financial Times*, 19 June 1990.

[18] *Agence Europe*, 14 December 1989.

[19] *Agence Europe*, 1 August 1990.

[20] *Agence Europe*, 1 January 1990.

[21] *Agence Europe*, 29–30 May 1990. On Interpol problems see M. Anderson, *Policing the World*, Oxford, Clarendon Press, 1989 and R. Clutterbuck, *Terrorism, Drugs & Crime in Europe after 1992*, London. Routledge, 1990.

# [2]

# The Modern Mafia: Its Role and Record

## *Alison Jamieson*

*Reputation of power, is Power; because it draweth with it the adherence of those that need protection.*

*Also, what quality soever maketh a man beloved, or feared of many; or the reputation of such quality, is Power; because it is a means to have the assistance, and service of many.*

*Affability of men already in power, is increase of Power; because it gaineth love.*

*The Value, or WORTH, of a man, is as of all other things, his Price: that is to say, so much as would be given for the use of his Power: and therefore is not absolute; but a thing dependent on the need and judgement of another.*

**Hobbes,** *Leviathan.*

## THE TRANSFORMATION OF POWER – RURAL MAFIA TO URBAN MAFIA

The development of the Sicilian mafia is primarily a study of power – not power as a static form of fixed control or dominion, but power as a constantly shifting, dynamic series of elements, often in conflict with each other, used and manipulated in ways ranging from the most primitive and brutal to the most subtle and sophisticated.

In Italy the word "mafia" is used as a generic term for organised crime, however its legal definition is quite distinct: an association consisting of three or more members is "of a mafia kind" when

"those who form it make use of the power of intimidation provided by the associative bond and of the state of subjugation and of criminal silence (**omertà**) which derives from it to commit crimes, to acquire directly or indirectly the running or control of economic activities, of concessions, grants, contracts and public services in order to realise illicit profits or advantages for themselves or for others."

Organised crime in Italy is traditionally categorised by three groups, each with quite separate, clearly identifiable geographical and historical characteristics: the **camorra**, centred on the city of Naples but extending throughout the surrounding region of Campania; the **'ndrangheta** (ndr) which operates throughout the region of Calabria, and **Cosa Nostra**, the Sicilian mafia. Each group has a different form of power base and a different relationship to state power, but in common are their two principal sources of profit – drug trafficking and the control of public works contracts via the infiltration and/or corruption of local administration. In the latter case the fight to win contracts for road, bridge, hospital or school building, for drain

1

and sewage maintenance, for irrigation, public lighting, and a wide range of other public works is usually conducted at local or regional level between companies affiliated to mafia clans in competition both with each other and with "clean" companies. The Sicilian mafia has always dominated the internal heroin traffic, although not the importation and distribution of cocaine, which is fought over at local and clan level.

### The *mafioso* as power broker

What differentiates the Sicilian mafia from the rest of organised crime in Italy is the nature and diversity of its power. Unlike the *camorra* and *'ndrangheta*, both rooted in the fight for survival of the poorest and most deprived social classes, *Cosa Nostra* emerged in the 19th century as a middle class, rural phenomenon whose function was to mediate between the feudal landowning and the peasant classes.

Skilful exploitation of this function gave the *mafioso* power over both and established a system of mutual favours and protection between himself and his employer with whose power he became identified. Not then, the *mafioso* as protector of the poor or as victim of an oppressed class, but the *mafioso* as power broker – a role carefully honed during more than a century of practice into an instrument of keen precision.

The power of *Cosa Nostra* has four components: human resources – literally, man-power; the power of violence; political power and financial power. Whether employed singly or in conjunction, the manipulation of such variegated power makes it not only **anti-state** – able to put its own authority against that of a democratic society; **state within a state** – complete with government, army, financial resources and territorial competence in which it operates with relative impunity; but even to **be** the state: *Cosa Nostra* has been represented in local and national government, in the judiciary, the police forces, in public corporations, on the directorial boards of banks, hospitals, and business enterprises.

In early 1988 a Rome government minister was forced to resign after an informer revealed his long-standing mafia associations; a few months later the mayor of Palermo warned that the mafia had taken on "an institutional face". In November, Domenico Sica, High Commissioner against the mafia, commented, "in certain areas of Sicily, Calabria and Campania territorial control on the part of organised crime is total". Shortly afterwards the President of the Sicilian Region admitted "in many town halls and health authorities the mafia is in charge".

Such control simply could not exist without the co-existence of the four forms of power outlined above. Clearly wherever the line between legal and illegal, state power and criminal power becomes blurred to this extent, the problem of combating organised crime becomes infinitely more difficult. The "state" cannot fight organised crime effectively when from laziness, greed, convenience or fear, state illegality has become endemic.

*The Modern Mafia* 3

### Organisational structure

The casual observer frequently regards the mafia as an over-romanticised myth – a "state of mind" or a "way of behaving" born from an obsessive emphasis on honour, courage, the power of silence, the protection of the family and its territory. In other words, that as an organisation the mafia "does not exist". In the first place these values were not created by the mafia, they are traits deeply carved in the Sicilian character as a whole which the mafia has deliberately exaggerated, distorted and manipulated. *Cosa Nostra's* current sophistication and astonishing adaptability may seem incompatible with retention of these superficially anachronistic principles but in reality they have been a vital factor in the acquisition and conservation of power. They help not only to create a profound sense of brotherhood and mutual loyalty but also to reinforce the power of the **capi** over the soldiers.

**The pyramid shows the rigid hierarchy which rules the mafia. The families are grouped under the control of the** *cupole* **(one for every Sicilian province except Messina and Syracuse). These are in turn dominated by the** *supercommissione*, **presided over by the "chief of chiefs" who is known to very few.**

Secondly, judicial investigations, considerably amplified by the information provided by informers or **pentiti**, have shown that far from "not existing", *Cosa Nostra* is a tightly structured, hierarchical organisation whose human resources are deployed in specific areas and with specific responsibilities. Multi-layered and multi-faceted, it operates in both the legal and the illegal economy, with criminal activities covering the pettiest of extortions to the systematic murder of internal and institutional opponents.

The Sicilian journalist Giuseppe Fava – murdered by the mafia for his investigative intuition – simplified mafia functions down to three – "the killers, the thinkers and the politicians".

It was the *pentito* Tommaso Buscetta who in 1984 provided the first full description of the internal structure of *Cosa Nostra*, which is best understood in the form of a pyramid. At the base were the **soldati**, or simple "men of honour", each of whom belonged to a clan or **famiglia**. A family varied in size but on average had 50 members. Over each group of ten presided a **capodecina**. Every family was governed by an elected boss or **capo**, also known as a **rappresentante** who was assisted by a **vice capo** and by one or more advisers or **consiglieri**. Three families together covering a specific geographical area comprised a **mandamento** from which one was elected (usually the head of the largest family) to the **commissione**, or commission, which governed for three years. The commission was responsible for all the most important business and criminal decisions. If for arrests or other reasons a *capo* could not be elected the commission appointed a **reggente**, or regent until proper elections could be held. There were regional commissions for different areas of Sicily, but the Palermo commission or **cupola**, also known as the **regione**, had absolute authority.

Admission to the "honoured society" was by recommendation, and the applicant carefully scrutinised beforehand. He had to be of proven courage, ruthless and decisive, of a "respected" family, maintain "correct" relations with women (it was considered acceptable to have mistresses, but not to leave one's wife); and could have no friendship or blood relationship with the police. The only permitted recourse to state justice was the reporting of car theft, otherwise justice was exercised according to the leaders' decisions. Each family controlled a clearly defined area and had to be consulted on all relevant activities within it. In the case of murder, not only the **capofamiglia** but the whole commission had to give its approval.

No one was a true man of honour until he proved his courage by committing murder, which "was not an exceptional event or one requiring justification for *Cosa Nostra* but the ordinary means for the realisation of the purposes of the organisation and for the affirmation of power".

Entry to the organisation was by formal, secret ritual in the presence of at least three members of the family to which the newcomer would belong. He had to swear to tell the truth to other members of *Cosa Nostra* about matters concerning the organisation, to respect the code of moral conduct already described, and that of silence or *omertà*. He was then instructed in the use of certain code words and forms of conduct intended to protect *Cosa Nostra* from infiltration and arrest. (If imprisoned, men of honour were not to try to escape, given the inevitable repercussions on other prisoners; an alternative and encouraged ruse was the feigning of madness or illness.) The ceremony ended when the novitiate, having pricked his finger to make it bleed, took a religious image in his hand, smeared it with blood, set it alight and held it until it burnt to ash, swearing, "My flesh will burn like this image if I do not maintain faith with my vow." He was then a man of honour for life.

These rituals were observed at least until the mid 1980s, when the mafia

Clan "map" of Palermo area (reproduced from Calvi, *La Vita Quotidiana della mafia dal 1950 ad oggi*; Biblioteca Universale Rizzoli; Milano 1986).
1. Ciaculli: Greco
2. Corso dei Mille: Marchese
3. Palermo centro: Noce, Borgo, Calatafimi clans
   Porta Nuova: Calò, Buscetta and Alberti most important families
4. Santa Maria di Gesù: Bontate
5. Passo di Rigano/Uditore: Inzerillo
6. San Lorenzo: Giacolone
   Resuttana: Madonia

*pentiti* began to talk. Since the arrests that followed and the maxi-trial of 1986–87, Sicilian judges believe that a number of modifications have taken place, which are discussed later.

Fundamental to control of the human resources in *Cosa Nostra* is the concept of territory. The absolute jurisdiction of a family within a geographical confine is held sacred, and if violated results in drastic consequences. A family may physically control entry and exit from its own area and even evict undesirable residents if they happened to belong to the wrong clan. This occurred in the Ciaculli district of Palermo controlled by the Greco clan where two families were given a date by which they were "strongly advised" to have moved out of the area or suffer the consequences. Common criminals may and often do operate in areas controlled by *Cosa Nostra*, but only with its permission and under strict supervision, and, naturally, only if such activity ultimately serves mafia interests.

**The birth of the modern mafia**

The birth of the modern mafia can probably be dated to a series of circumstances which occurred in the years 1956–58. The introduction of **soggiorno obbligato** or compulsory domicile in 1956 was a measure which compelled many of the bosses of *Cosa Nostra* to take up residence outside Sicily. The forced expatriation was turned to good advantage for the mafia as the post war economic boom and consequent acceleration in the demand for consumer goods offered plenty of black market opportunities, particularly in the industrial centres of Milan, Genoa and Turin. American cigarettes became an emblem of the new-found prosperity with a consequent boost to the tobacco smugglers operating around Naples, another major host city for the Sicilian exiles.

It is believed that at least three groups within the Sicilian mafia were dabbling in the drugs traffic throughout the 1950s, but only in a secondary capacity, and always in a subordinate role to the Corsicans operating from Marseilles. However two meetings in the autumn of 1957, one in Palermo, the other in Appalachian, New York State, were decisive. Present at the Palermo meeting were representatives of the most powerful US mafia families who, together with their Sicilian counterparts, addressed four vital issues: how US financial resources could best be combined with Italian networks to maximise profits from the narcotics traffic; how to guarantee continuity with the suppliers in the areas of production; the maintenance of quality control and the recycling and reinvestment of financial profits.

The New York State meeting was broken up by the police who made many arrests, but the essential decisions had been taken – heroin rather than cocaine was to be the principal drug activity of *Cosa Nostra*, and Sicily the ideal geographical staging post, half way between areas of production and distribution.

The late 1940s and early 1950s were turbulent years in Sicily – 90 per cent of local administrators appointed by the allied occupying forces were representatives of landed interests who remained in control even after the

## The Modern Mafia                                                                7

granting of the Statute of Sicilian autonomy in 1946. Land reforms intended to break up the big estates were evaded, and in many cases property was simply divided up amongst family members. Protests and land occupation by the peasants were dealt with harshly as once again the mafia did the dirty work on behalf of the landlords. Absentee landlords and feudal conditions had severely retarded the development of Sicilian agriculture, which suffered even more in the immediate post war period as farm workers deserted the land in favour of the cities. Many moved to the northern triangle of Milan, Genoa and Turin where the economic boom offered the prospect of certain work and wages. Thousands more headed for Palermo in search of work on roads, building sites, in the docklands and in the wholesale markets. Between 1951 and 1961 the percentage of agricultural workers in Sicily fell from 51 to 41 per cent, whilst in the same period the population of Palermo grew by 100,000.

The rush to the city and the expanding consumer markets turned Palermo into the new, fiercely contested ground for wealth and power. The immediate provision of new housing was imperative, given the devastation wrought by war-time bombing and the expanding urban population. Quick profits could be made by buying up land on the periphery of the city, beginning the construction of huge apartment blocks and then selling again before completion of work. The "garden mafia" on the outskirts of Palermo tried to protect its citrus fruit groves and found itself continually opposed by the new urban mafia of land speculators. Bitter struggles broke out for the purchase of construction sites, for control of the food markets, of the outlets for consumer goods and most of all for public works contracts.

In order to win control of these activities the urban mafia had to learn a new kind of power game. Building licences had to be granted, surveys approved and political blessing given to development projects. Mafia power no longer came from the mediation between two sectors of society but from the integration of interests between the mafia and local politicians, public administrators and the professional classes – architects, surveyors and engineers.

In the course of the mid-1950s a new political class emerged, replacing the landed gentry with a more dynamic, forward-looking generation intent on modernisation and industrial expansion. Its leaders, Christian Democrats Giovanni Gioia, Salvo Lima and Vito Ciancimino, were quick to take advantage of the powers devolved to the region by the statute of Sicilian autonomy: the regional government had responsibility for all the island's natural resources (with the exception of oil), for economic incentives, primary education, tourism, public services and transport. It could authorise the setting up of bank branches, approve loans, appoint tax collection agents, acquire rural and urban property and had complete discretion over the generous sums allocated by central government for rebuilding and development projects. Naturally an army of civil servants and officials were required to staff the regional offices, the banks and the twelve public corporations set up to administer the multiple regional interests. Between 1953 and 1959 the number of employees taken on by the Sicilian Region increased by 137 per cent, of which 90–95 per cent were hired without any form of selection process.

Convicted criminals, relations of *mafiosi* and even those suspected of being actual members of the mafia were given jobs. On the very day he applied for the position, the brother of a well-known *mafioso* was appointed managing director of a public corporation.

Vito Ciancimino began his career working in Rome in the Transport Ministry under fellow Sicilian Bernardo Mattarella; he moved back to Sicily in the early 1950s, and, by faking a series of documents, won a contract for the transportation of rail freight. From 1954 until 1970 he was Christian Democratic party counsellor, from 1959 to 1964 was the regional deputy responsible for the assessment of public works and was mayor of Palermo from October–December 1970. Ciancimino never canvassed or held election meetings yet had consistent electoral success. His period of public office coincides exactly with the period of maximum building speculation known as the "sack of Palermo" – the ruthless tearing down of once-fine old buildings and their replacement with vast estates of flimsy, hideous apartment blocks built fast and carelessly. It has been proved that of 4,000 building licences granted by Ciancimino 3,500 nominally went to three old age pensioners who had little or nothing to do with the construction industry, men of straw behind whom lurked an array of unscrupulous speculators. Ciancimino and Gioia set up an estate agency with the mafia builder Vassallo for whom particular favours were granted, whilst Ciancimino's wife sat on the board of two credit institutions. Even when he came under direct suspicion in the early 1970s and was obliged to leave public office, Ciancimino was still a powerful influence on Palermo political life. When he was finally arrested in 1984 and his finances investigated it was discovered that he had over seven billion lire (over three million pounds) deposited in bank accounts in Lugano, Lausanne and Montreal, and that despite being officially unemployed, he had an annual income of around 700 million lire (£315,000).

Salvo Lima became Christian Democrat (DC) mayor of Palermo in 1958 thanks, according to a later police report, "to the help of the La Barbera brothers (prominent *mafiosi* ndr) who subsequently protected him". Despite his presumed mafia connections (his name was mentioned 149 times in the 1976 report of the first Antimafia Commission) Lima was re-elected mayor in 1960, 1962 and 1964. He was suspended from the post of special commissioner for the Sicilian Agrarian Reform Corporation in 1964 but afterwards became Deputy Director of the Bank of Sicily although he had not worked there for 10 years. He was elected national deputy in 1968 until 1979, when he became Euro-MP for the Italian islands, an office he still holds.

Dr Michele Navarro was not only local mafia boss and wealthy landowner around the town of Corleone, but consultant surgeon, president of the local farmers' association, and director of the irrigation programme for the valley. Another member of Navarro's clan was Luciano Liggio, who in contrast to his boss had the benefit of neither money nor education but had progressed from rural bandit and protector of a feudal estate to landowner in his own right from a lucrative series of interests including construction, farming, grain dealing, cattle rustling and the monopoly control of the slot machines throughout the west of Sicily. Liggio's insatiable appetite for power led him into a direct challenge to his boss, when one day in the summer of 1958, without asking Navarro's permission he diverted the course of a river to provide drinking water for his cattle. That evening Navarro sent nine men to kill Liggio but he managed to hide from their bullets. The following week, on August 2, Navarro was driving with a young medical colleague when six men armed with machine guns fired 300 shots into the car, killing both instantly. In the weeks that followed, all Navarro's supporters in the Corleone clan were either murdered or fell victim to the **lupara bianca** (literally "white shotgun") – they disappeared, never to be seen alive again. The relentless series of murders that began with Navarro and consolidated Liggio's power in Corleone strengthened his hand when he entered the power struggle for Palermo and in its ruthless tactics, set a pattern for the conduct of future conflict.

**First mafia war**

One of the precipitating factors in what is known as the "first mafia war" came in 1961, when a consignment of heroin delivered by Calcedonia Di Pisa, head of the Noce clan and member of the Palermo commission, arrived underweight in the United States. Di Pisa denied his responsibility but was not believed by the La Barbera brothers of the Palermo *centro* clan. Another incident involving Di Pisa occurred in the summer of 1962 with the marriage of a female member of his family with a young man from the Porta Nuova family. Blood ties dictated he should remain with his original family, Di Pisa claimed he should join that of adoption. Di Pisa was murdered in December 1962, probably by Angelo La Barbera, without prior agreement from the rest of the Commission who then turned against the La Barberas and the Porta Nuova family, intending to expel them from *Cosa Nostra*. 11 days after Di Pisa's murder Salvatore La Barbera "disappeared"; his brother fled to Milan but was shot and wounded there in an ambush laid by his rivals in April 1963.

As the Corleonesi extended their power into Palermo they found allies in the powerful Greco family of the Ciaculli district. Opposition to the alliance led to numerous gun battles between the warring clans. In February 1963 Salvatore Greco, head of the Ciaculli family, narrowly missed being blown up in a car bomb parked outside his house. Transversal clan murders took place throughout May and June. The war finally came to a head on June 30 1963, when an anonymous telephone call to *carabinieri* headquarters warned that a car bomb had been parked in the Ciaculli district. The Alfa Romeo Giulietta was identified and an explosive device attached to a gas bottle on the back seat de-activated. When the boot was opened the car exploded, killing seven soldiers and bomb disposal experts. Whether the bomb was intended for the Grecos originally or whether a last minute change in plans (one wheel was punctured) prompted the phone call and thus a deliberate trap for the authorities, is not certain. However the massacre brought the first decisive crackdown on the part of national government and major repercussions for the Sicilian mafia.

## URBAN MAFIA TO HEROIN MAFIA

Public outrage over the Ciaculli massacre jerked the Italian authorities into the first serious move against the mafia since the war. 10,000 police and *carabinieri* combed Sicily and made 1.200 arrests within 10 weeks. Safe houses and arms deposits full of bombs, firearms and ammunition were discovered. The Parliamentary Antimafia Commission which had been talked about for seven years began to investigate at last.

Some *mafiosi* got away in time, like Salvatore Greco, who dissolved the Palermo commission just after Ciaculli and fled to Venezuela, where he remained until his death in 1971. Another was Tommaso Buscetta who had left for the United States in February, anticipating not only retribution from within *Cosa Nostra* for his suspected support for the La Barberas, but also the arrest warrant for murder which had just been issued in his name. Buscetta had had his passport withdrawn in 1958 after accusations of involvement in tobacco smuggling, but had regained it in 1961 on the strength of a letter to the Palermo issuing authorities from a national member of Parliament.

*Cosa Nostra* kept its head down for the next few years with so many of its members either in prison, abroad, or else quietly consolidating contacts and networks outside Sicily. A mere 16 murders in Palermo in 1968 set a record minimum.

In the course of 1968 and 1969 two major mafia trials took place in Catanzaro and Bari, transferred from Sicily in theory to provide better guarantees for the carriage of justice. In practice they acquitted more *mafiosi* than they convicted, to the particular benefit of the bosses, who either got off scot free or else received minimum sentences, like Michele Cavatajo and Luciano Liggio. Liggio was acquitted in Bari of nine murders, attempted murder and criminal association, the only restriction on his liberty being to remain at his home in Corleone. Relying on either the negligence or compliance of the authorities, Liggio ignored the court order and left Sicily first for a nursing home in Rome, then, before an arrest warrant could catch up with him, headed for Milan where in November 1969 he set up his new criminal headquarters.

By the end of 1969, *Cosa Nostra* was back on its feet again, but with a difference. The generation temporarily taken out of circulation by imprison- ment was intent not only upon reasserting territorial supremacy but also upon taking vengeance on those perceived as responsible, by their double games and betrayals, for having caused the war and the damage inflicted on *Cosa Nostra*. This second factor was the motive for the ferocious attack in the office of the Moncada construction company in Viale Lazio, Palermo, on December 10 1969, where discussions were taking place between the Moncada brothers, two of their associates and mafia boss Michele Cavatoja, acquitted at Catanzaro of the murders of 10 mafia rivals. Nine assailants disguised as police officers burst in and began to shoot, wounding the Moncada brothers and killing the other three in the office before disposing of a security guard who approached as they made their escape with their own victims – one dead and another dying – whom Cavatoja had managed to shoot before dying himself.

*The Modern Mafia*                                                                11

At the end of 1969 the Palermo Commission was re-established, headed first by Giuseppe Calderone, then by the triumvirate of Salvatore Riina, an ally of Liggio's from Corleone, Gaetano Badalamenti, and Stefano Bontate, heads of the Palermo Cinisi and Santa Maria di Gesù clans respectively. From his hideout in Milan, Liggio began to consolidate a network of national and international contacts, and in particular to organise ways of recycling money from the immensely lucrative kidnap business which he operated with the Calabrian *'ndrangheta*. The Commission had decided to ban kidnaps in Sicily because of the ill-feeling the crime aroused, but Liggio resented the ruling and tried to sabotage it on more than one occasion.

A critical change in mafia fortunes in the early 1970s came about simultaneously with the need to launder the large sums of money from kidnap ransoms, particularly after computer memorisation of serial numbers became a standard form of tracing bank notes. The depositing of considerable sums of small denomination bank notes (the traditional form of ransom payments) was also more likely to arouse suspicion with the increasing automation and sophistication of bank transactions.

In addition, the mounting profits from cigarette smuggling and from the narcotics traffic of which *Cosa Nostra* was by now controlling a vital part not only had to be laundered but also re-invested – to pay costs and expand existing illegal activities as well as reappear in the form of "clean" profits from perfectly regular business transactions. The infiltration and appropriation of the banking sector had become a priority for the men of *Cosa Nostra*.

**Illegal capital transactions**

From humble Sicilian origins, Michele Sindona had built up his career into one of Italy's most powerful private bankers, with finance companies all over Europe, the Caribbean and the United States. Acclaimed "the saviour of the lire" by Giulio Andreotti in 1973, Sindona made maximum use of the privileges and welcome extended to him by prime ministers and presidents of both the US and Italy to provide cover for his corrupt and fraudulent dealings. Through Sindona, *Cosa Nostra* gained access to a channel of communication between the legal financial circuit and that of illegally accumulated capital. The ability to transfer illegal capital between Italy, the United States, the Bahamas and Switzerland, to open bank accounts protected by bank secrecy laws and to pour dirty money into the faceless Eurocurrency market, bypassing currency regulations and avoiding the risky and cumbersome physical transportation of cash (even though this did continue to some extent) was a gift to the mafia money men.

Furthermore the discretion granted to the Sicilian Region in banking matters meant that approval could be given for the setting up of any banking or credit institution unless the Bank of Italy vetoed the application within four months of its being made. Authorisation requests would be accompanied by assurances of electoral support and favourable credit terms, whilst oversight or overwork meant that Bank of Italy inspectors rarely checked the backgrounds of the proposed bank directors or used their power of veto. Bank branches opened up in Sicily at double the national rate; Sindona opened up 20 branches of his **Interfinanziaria Spa** in the small town of Agrigento, offering as enticement double the usual rate of interest. But the mafia did not have to own a bank to dominate it – sometimes physical intimidation of bank personnel was enough; on other occasions the threat to withdraw huge sums of capital and thus bring a bank to the brink of collapse would guarantee instant compliance.

Another bridge between political/financial circles and that of the mafia was built by the cousins Nino and Ignazio Salvo, proprietors of two revenue collection companies, whose fortunes had risen in line with those of the DC team of Lima, Ciancimino and Gioia on whose behalf the Salvos had political control over a large area around the town of Trapani. Their financial power was impressive: their companies drew a 10 per cent commission from revenue collection compared to the standard 3.3 per cent and they received considerable sums from national and regional corporations for use in development projects whose distribution they could delay at their discretion. Despite questions raised about their dubious associations by the first Antimafia Commission in the early 1970s, their membership of *Cosa Nostra* would not be revealed until over 10 years later.

### "Strategy of tension"

It began to seem as though the ruthlessness with which the mafia had resolved its internal problems was being applied equally to the protection of its power from external threat. In September 1970 the Sicilian journalist Mauro De Mauro was kidnapped and was never seen again. Some believe his investigative work had taken him too close to discovering either the location of the bases used for drug trafficking in the Mediterranean, or else the whereabouts of Luciano Liggio and the complicity on which he had relied, first for his acquittal and then for his escape from house arrest.

Public prosecutor of Palermo, Pietro Scaglione, the judge responsible for Liggio's restriction order and in some eyes negligent for not enforcing it, was murdered in May 1971 whilst making his daily visit to his wife's grave. Scaglione may have decided to "get tough" with the mafia after a period of intimidation or compliance, or he may have possesed information that made him dangerous. A different version of both these crimes comes from the mafia *pentito* Antonio Calderone, who claims that they formed part of "a more complex terrorist project" whose aim was to create social alarm and terror by means of demonstrative actions in order to provoke an authoritarian reaction.

If this were so the murders would fall in line with the aims of the neo-fascist "strategy of tension" which resulted in a series of indiscriminate bomb explosions in public places carried out between 1969 and 1974 and revived with the bombs at Bologna station in 1980 and on the Naples–Milan express train in December 1984. There is evidence and in one case proof, that the interests of the mafia and of the far right have coincided to the point of co-ordinating politically subversive activities. Buscetta and Calderone have referred to discussions held between Prince Valerio Borghese and mafia leaders (including Calderone's own brother, then head of the Commission)

## The Modern Mafia     13

for a proposed *coup d'état* in December 1970. *Cosa Nostra* was apparently divided over whether or not to provide military support for the *coup*, but withdrew when Borghese insisted that the men of honour should submit a written list of those participating and wear visible identification.

Throughout the 1970s and until his arrest in 1985 Pippo Calò, head of the Palermo Porta Nuova family, cultivated close contacts with prominent neo-fascists in Rome and Milan, as well as with highly placed members of the P2 masonic lodge such as Michele Sindona and Roberto Calvi, President of the Banco Ambrosiano. In February 1989 Calò, together with fellow *mafioso* Cercola, *camorra* boss Missi and two neo-fascists were found guilty of organising the 1984 train bomb, and were sentenced to life imprisonment by the Florence Court of Assizes. The mafia–political terrorism equation was upheld for the first time ever with the confirmation of the aggravating factor, "an attack with the aim of terrorism and the subversion of the constitutional order".

### Narcotics trafficking

Cigarette smuggling continued to thrive uninterruptedly in Campania in the 1960s and 1970s largely thanks to lackadaisical application of inadequate legal restrictions. Between 1963 and 1971, 78 ships were impounded with contraband goods on board, but given the impossibility of prosecution without proof of the guilt of the ship's owner, in almost every case crews were exculpated, vessels released and at worst, modest fines paid. The combination of the experience and international contacts of Neapolitans Zaza, Bardellino and Nuvoletta with the input of Sicilian cash and organisational skills was formidable. According to Buscetta, where once a consignment of 500 cases of cigarettes at a time was considered large, by the peak year of 1973, each shipload would amount to 35–40,000 cases. It has been estimated in 1976 that one in every eight packets of cigarettes smoked in Italy was illegally imported.

The United States was first to recognise and take legal action to curb the narcotics traffic, prompted not only by increasing addiction and drug-related criminality from imported drugs but also by the proportion – estimated as high as 15 per cent – of its GIs returning from Vietnam as heroin addicts. The RICO (Racketeer Influenced and Corrupt Organisations) law passed in 1970 provided for prosecution of the members of any organisation "whose purpose was to further its activities by extortion, intimidation and violence." In 1971 the Nixon government persuaded Turkey to ban the cultivation of opium in exchange for subsidisation of alternative crops, and put similar pressure on Paraguay and Bolivia as regards the coca plant, although with less success. In the same year an official agreement was reached with the French to crack down on the extensive heroin trafficking network based in Marseilles accompanied, apparently, by an unofficial grant of 100 million dollars for the physical elimination of the principal traffickers.

The result of these measures was a major reorganisation of the heroin traffic: Turkey was replaced as chief supplier of heroin and morphine base to the West by the "golden triangle" of Thailand, Burma and Laos and the "golden crescent" of Pakistan, Iran and Afghanistan. The break-up of the Marseilles drug ring allowed the Italians not only to protect and control one stage of the heroin route, but to take over a significant share of the entire market, using the extensive network already in place for contraband tobacco. French Connection chemists instructed the Sicilians in the techniques of refining from morphine base to heroin, and the first refineries went into production around the mid 1970s. A period of relative peace ensued, as the settling of internal conflict was subordinated to a greater common goal – the accumulation of financial profit.

According to Tommaso Buscetta the decline of tobacco smuggling and the mafia's "massive entry" into heroin came about in 1978 at the instigation of Nunzio La Mattina who already had contacts with sources of drug production. The Neapolitans were co-opted as honorary members of *Cosa Nostra* to ensure three essential elements – their co-operation, their loyalty and their subservience to *Cosa Nostra's* rules. La Mattina, Tommaso Spadaro and Giuseppe Savoca began to import morphine base and to refine in Sicily, each working within his own organisation. The heroin exporters were those families with North American contacts, such as the Cuntrera and Caruana families to Canada; the Bono, Spatola and Inzerillo families to the US, where the latter could rely on their cousins, the powerful Gambinos in New York, for distribution. Three Palermo clans dominated the market – the Badalamenti family, the Inzerillo/Spatola/Bontate group and the Grecos of Ciaculli. Buscetta claims virtually all the Palermo families were involved in heroin in some way, although some contributed financially rather than actively, thereby sharing the risks and the profits.

Raw opium would be transformed into morphine base either in the areas of production – usually under the control of ethnic groups such as the Chinese in S.E. Asia, the Kurds in Iran and the Pathans on the Afghan/Pakistan border, whose bonds of kinship and territorial protection in many respects resembled those of the Sicilians – or in Middle Eastern countries such as Lebanon, Syria, Iran and Turkey. From there the product would travel by a variety of means – car, train, sea or (especially) Tir haulage truck to Ankara, Istanbul and through the Balkans. Passage through the Middle East was frequently smoothed by compliant government and military officials.

After the morphine base had been through the Sicilian refineries there were two options – each family could find its own means of transportation and distribution or else contribute to larger consignments exported to the US by air or sea, in which case each "lot" would be identifiable by special marks and symbols. The second method involved both greater profits and greater risk.

By the end of the 1970s the Spatola/Inzerillo group alone is estimated to have been making 600 million dollars worth of profits each year. With five refineries working at full production in Sicily, that is around 50 kilos per week, shipments of 20–100 kilos of heroin at a time were going to the US, each transaction being worth between four and 20 million dollars.

The ability to refine morphine base into heroin was the factor which transformed mafia finances. The Swiss dealer Eric Charlier who worked with

*The Modern Mafia*　　15

*Cosa Nostra* in the early 1980s told judge Giovanni Falcone that a kilo of morphine base bought in Afghanistan for 2,000 dollars would cost 3,500 dollars in Turkey, 8,000 in Greece and 12,000 in Milan. Once refined it would fetch profits of between 1,000 and 2,000 per cent. Thus a kilo would cost 250,000 dollars on the US wholesale market and between 120,000 and 150,000 dollars in Europe. In the early 1980s it is believed that the Spatola/Inzerillo, Gambino, Bontate and Badalamenti families were responsible for 30 per cent of all the heroin introduced into the United States.

### Financial organisation

Switzerland was the financial centre of mafia operations in the late 1970s and early 1980s, the pivotal point of money movement between West and East. Banking secrecy was inviolate, currency exchanges could be effected without questions being asked and anonymous companies could operate under cover of fictitious economic activities. Whatever methods were used to move illegal drug profits around the globe, they nearly always passed through Switzerland. In the case of the Italian "pizza connection" operated by the Sicilian families mentioned above, money from the sale of heroin in the US was deposited into a branch of Chemical Bank in New York, transferred to an account in Handelsbank in Zurich, and from there to the account "Wall Street 651" in Credit Suisse in Bellinzona.

Sometimes money was physically carried from the US to Nassau, deposited into the **Banca di Svizzera e d'Italia** and from there transferred by cheque into Swiss bank accounts. Between 1981 and 1983 900 billion lire was paid into the Credit Suisse in Lugano for heroin supplied by Tommaso Spadaro. After the drug profits had been laundered through Swiss accounts, tax havens or other off shore banking methods there were basically three options open to the financiers of *Cosa Nostra*:

to return illegal profits back to the illegal economy, for example to pay middle men and couriers, to purchase more heroin or morphine base; to acquire arms and ammunition, usually through the same channels as those for drugs;

to place the profits in overseas bank accounts, in tax havens, in overseas holdings or in the Euro-currency market, from which money could then be transferred and invested in property or business activities anywhere in the world;

to invest illegal profits in the Italian legal market – in the purchase of property, company shareholdings, or in private business enterprises – especially those which satisfied four conditions: high return on investment; low risk; absence of control and fast movement of money.

The Bontate and Gambino families, for example, owned 11 separate companies (in the construction and service industries), the Badalamenti family 10, the Inzerillo and Spatola families 23 between them. In each case control remained with a tiny number of the most trusted members of the family, and conventional activities ran parallel and complementary to the illicit recycling of drug profits.

The result in Sicily of the continual distortion of the legitimate economy by the dual operating level of the mafia enterprise was that the latter, flush with illegal profits, unhesitating in its use of coercive powers and territorially omnipotent, succeeded in retarding or suffocating entire sectors of legitimate business activity. The mafia mediator had become mafia entrepreneur.

## WAR ON ALL FRONTS

In 1974 Michele Sindona's financial empire crashed on both sides of the Atlantic, leaving even his influential friends powerless to save him from the charge of fraudulent bankruptcy. In the same year Luciano Liggio was finally run to ground in Milan and was replaced as head of the Commission after a two year gap by Gaetano Badalamenti. That Liggio's Corleonesi were allying themselves with the Grecos of Ciaculli against the Badalamenti–Bontate families became apparent in the late 1970s. Stefano Bontate had his authority eroded first in 1975 by the kidnap of Luigi Corleo, father-in-law of the revenue collector Nino Salvo, a good friend of Bontate; then by the murders in 1977 of police officer Angelo Sorino, and of the *carabinieri* official investigating the Corleo kidnap, Giuseppe Russo. Quite apart from the personal interest in the kidnap, these actions were open challenges to the unity of the Commission – kidnaps had been banned in Sicily, and murder was only supposed to take place with the permission of all members of the Commission – Bontate was not informed about either, nor was he given a satisfactory explanation afterwards when he confronted Michele Greco. Although it seemed as though the Commission was blatantly disregarding its own rules, this was not the case – the rules were still rigid, but were being re-written with a formal justification – distrust of the Bontate–Inzerillo group and fears for their supremacy in heroin.

Another member of *Cosa Nostra* who objected strongly to the Russo killing was Giuseppe Di Cristina, boss of the town of Riesi, district of Palermo and also a close friend of the Salvo cousins. Not a Commission member and therefore more vulnerable than Bontate, Di Cristina's first warning not to interfere came with the murder of his bodyguard. Di Cristina realised that the alliance of Grecos and Corleonesi was conspiring to rid the Commission of its opponents and that his own life was in danger. In early 1978 he went to the *carabinieri* and began to talk, incriminating his principal enemy as deeply as possible. He warned that Luciano Liggio was planning an escape from prison, that he intended to murder Sicilian judge Cesare Terranova; that drugs were stored in one of Liggio's fruit farms and that Liggio had personally killed judge Scaglione.

Di Cristina's revelations ended with his assassination on May 30 1978. The district of Riesi went into full mourning: "Schools, offices and shops remained closed; flags flew at half mast from Christian Democratic headquarters, whilst all the local administrators and politicians walked at the head of the procession which took the beloved boss to his last resting place."

In circumstances which are still obscure, Gaetano Badalamenti was expelled

*The Modern Mafia*                                                                17

from *Cosa Nostra* in 1978 and his position as family head taken by his brother. Michele Greco became the new head of the Commission and Badalamenti's place was taken by Pino Greco, a distant relative of Michele with a reputation as an ace marksman and ruthless killer.

## Attacks on representatives of the state

In the period 1979–83 *Cosa Nostra* made the Red Brigades' triumphant claim to have "brought the attack to the heart of the state" pale into insignificance: in the course of three and a half years each of the most senior political, institutional and judicial representatives of state power in Sicily was assassinated – the Christian Democratic party secretary; the head of the Palermo Flying Squad; the chief examining magistrate of Palermo, the President of the Sicilian Region; the *carabinieri* commander; the chief prosecutor of Palermo; Communist party MP and regional opposition leader; the Prefect of Palermo and another chief examining magistrate.

In May 1989 no definitive legal verdict had been passed on any one of these deaths; numerous trials have taken place but convictions in the Court of Assizes have been overturned either in the Appeal Court or by the Supreme Court, whilst others are in progress at time of writing.

Unlike the Red Brigades, the mafia had and has little interest in attacking state representatives for their symbolic value *per se*, and only risks repressive repercussions when the target represents a particular danger to the organisation and its continuing financial prosperity. *Cosa Nostra's* massive show of force against the state took place because its victims were working to combat the mafia with such dedication either in the investigative or political field that if successful, the colossal influx of profits from the heroin traffic would be imperilled. It has also been suggested that each victim had or was about to discover extensive links between politics and mafia.

DC Provincial Secretary Michele Reina had argued strenuously for the reorganisation of the means of allocating public works contracts; he was murdered shortly after proposing the freezing of 750 billion lire destined for the reconstruction of the centre of Palermo.

On July 11 Giorgio Ambrosoli, government-appointed receiver for Sindona's **Banca Privata Italiana** was murdered in Milan a few days after a meeting with Boris Giuliano, head of the Palermo Flying Squad. Ambrosoli had just uncovered the connections between Sindona's Swiss banks and the Italian and US mafia organisations. Under Giuliano's direction the Palermo police had begun to investigate the mafia's heroin involvement and its network of connections in Italy and the US through the most prominent mafia families. Giuliano was murdered ten days after Ambrosoli.

A mere fortnight after the elimination of his two principal adversaries, Michele Sindona jumped bail in New York and, making a detour via Vienna and Athens, arrived in Sicily as guest of Rosario Spatola, prosperous mafia boss and drug trafficker. Spatola's political credentials were impeccable however; in the spring of the same year he had organised election dinners for Christian Democrat Minister Ruffini. Sindona arranged the action to look like a terrorist kidnap by the far left, with the delivery of letters to his associates and family and a photograph of himself taken against a revolutionary banner. For greater authenticity he even had himself shot in the leg in Spatola's house near Palermo. Trying to frighten his former political protectors, he gave details of the incriminating information his captors required of him as a condition of his release.

Sindona returned to New York on October 13 where he remained for three days with Rosario Gambino, a member of one of the five top New York mafia clans. He then "reappeared", ostensibly to collect the documents his kidnappers required. The kidnap story, which quickly broke down under questioning, was replaced with another – Sindona claimed his fear of a Communist-run Italy had led him to try to organise a separatist uprising in Sicily, to be followed by its eventual annexing to the United States, and that he had returned to Sicily to seek military support for his coup. It is more likely that he knew the extent of his criminal activities had been laid bare by Ambrosoli and was playing a desperate card of blackmail in order to win his freedom. Sindona was subsequently extradited to Italy where he was convicted by a Milan court not only of financial and fraud charges but sentenced to life imprisonment for ordering the murder of Ambrosoli. (A few days after the verdict he died in Voghera top security prison after drinking a cup of coffee laced with cyanide.)

As public prosecutor, Cesare Terranova had convicted some 50 members of *Cosa Nostra* in the western province of Marsala. He realised in the early 1970s that the mafia was moving increasingly into drugs, that legal measures to trace the movement of capital were essential, but that unless he had jurisdiction over Palermo he could not touch the nerve centre of *Cosa Nostra*. He resigned as magistrate, stood for national Parliament and won a seat for the Independent Left on the Communist party ticket. He entered the all-party Justice and Antimafia commissions and helped prepare a draft law whose most important provisions were those designed to investigate and seize the assets of individuals and companies suspected of mafia activities. When in 1979 the post of chief examining magistrate in Palermo fell vacant as he knew it would, he applied and got the job. On September 25, within days of taking up his new post, he and his driver were murdered. The warning given by Di Cristina 18 months previously had been in vain.

In January 1980 the President of the Sicilian Region, Christian Democrat Piersanti Mattarella was assassinated in the centre of Palermo. Like Giuliano, like Terranova, Mattarella had placed himself in the front line of the antimafia struggle at the cost of denouncing corruption and collusion within his own party and trying to ensure that public funds were kept out of mafia hands. Current enquiries suggest that he was murdered by right wing terrorists as a favour to the mafia, or to a mafia-linked sector of Sicilian politics, in exchange for the mafia's help in facilitating the escape from prison of a neo-fascist leader. In May, *carabinieri* captain Emanuele Basile was murdered in the course of investigating the intricate financial threads partially unravelled by Boris Giuliano.

## PRINCIPAL MAFIA MURDERS

| | |
|---|---|
| 2/8/58 | Dr Michele NAVARRO |
| 30/6/63 | "Ciaculli massacre" of seven bomb disposal experts, carabinieri |
| 10/12/69 | "Massacre of Viale Lazio" (five dead) |
| 16/9/70 | Journalist Mauro DE MAURO |
| 5/5/71 | Pietro SCAGLIONE, Public Prosecutor of Palermo |
| 20/7/77 | Carabinieri colonel Giuseppe RUSSO |
| 30/5/78 | Mafia boss Giuseppe DI CRISTINA |
| 9/3/79 | Michele REINA, secretary of Palermo DC |
| 21/7/79 | Boris GIULIANO, head of Palermo Flying Squad |
| 25/9/79 | Cesare TERRANOVA, newly appointed chief examining magistrate for Palermo, with driver Mancuso. |
| 6/1/80 | Piersanti MATTARELLA, President of Sicilian Region |
| 3/5/80 | Emanuele BASILE, Carabinieri captain |
| 6/8/80 | Gaetano COSTA, Public Prosecutor for Palermo |
| 23/4/81 | Mafia boss Stefano BONTATE |
| 11/5/81 | Mafia boss Salvatore INZERILLO |
| 30/4/82 | Pio LA TORRE, PCI national deputy, with driver Di Salvo |
| 16/6/82 | "Ring road massacre" of three carabinieri, driver, Alfio FERLITO and relative during prison transfer |
| 3/9/82 | General Carlo Alberto DALLA CHIESA, wife and driver of escort vehicle |
| 25/1/83 | Giacomo "Ciaccio" MONTALTO, Deputy Prosecutor of Trapani |
| 28/7/83 | Rocco CHINNICI , chief examining magistrate, Palermo (three others killed and 19 injuries) |
| 5/1/84 | Giuseppe FAVA, journalist |
| 23/2/85 | Roberto PARISI, business man, and driver |
| 2/4/85 | Attempted assassination of deputy prosecutor of Trapani, Carlo PALERMO; instead mother and six-year-old twins were killed. |
| 28/7/85 | Giuseppe MONTANA, police commissioner |
| 6/8/85 | Antonio CASSARA, deputy head of Palermo Flying Squad, and escort ANTIOCCHIA. |
| 12/1/88 | Former mayor of Palermo Giuseppe INSALACO |
| 14/1/88 | Policeman Natale MONDO |
| 25/9/88 | Antonio SAETTA, President of Palermo Court of Appeal, and son. |
| 26/9/88 | Mauro ROSTAGNO, leader of drug rehabilitation centre, Trapani |
| 28/9/88 | Giovanni BONTATE and wife |
| 14/12/88 | Luigi RANIERI, building constructor |

**Factions in conflict**

Inside *Cosa Nostra* tension was mounting between the Corleonesi/Greco faction and the Spatola/Inzerillo group. Badalamenti fled abroad, commuting between the US, Brazil and Spain where he continued to hold the reins of his heroin traffic and set up a complementary network for the importation of cocaine from South America to Europe. Within the Commission, Stefano Bontate and Salvatore Inzerillo became increasingly isolated. The Terranova, Mattarella and Giuliano murders had all taken place without the prior knowledge of Bontate and Inzerillo. In defiance, Inzerillo had Palermo public prosecutor Gaetano Costa murdered as "proof" of the power of his own family. Costa had also issued arrest warrants for both Inzerillo and Bontate and was working on the Sindona/*Cosa Nostra* connection.

Tommaso Buscetta, extradited from Brazil to Italy in 1972, left prison in Milan at the end of 1979 under conditions of "supervised liberty" which nonetheless allowed him to make frequent journeys to Sicily to see his old friends. He was struck by the ostentatious wealth which the men of honour paraded and was tempted to stay in Sicily rather than leave for Brazil as he had planned. Pippo Calò urged him to remain, promising that with the imminent arrival of thousands of billions of lire for the reconstruction of Palermo city centre there would be even more opportunities for gain, in particular thanks to Vito Ciancimino, who, he assured Buscetta, "was in the hands of the Corleonesi."

Once again Buscetta was caught in the middle of two factions in conflict. For the time being both the Greco/Calò/Corleonesi group and the Bontate/Inzerillo/Badalamenti opposition trusted him. But being an accomplice had its problems. Stefano Bontate told Buscetta he was going to kill Salvatore Riina, information which alone endangered Buscetta. He tried to make peace between the two sides, and arranged for a meeting between Inzerillo, Bontate, Calò and himself at a service station on the Rome–Naples motorway which ended inconclusively. Buscetta remained in hiding in Sicily for the Christmas/New Year period of 1980–81, staying with his family in a villa owned by Nino Salvo. He might have stayed on had it not been for a dirty trick played on him by Pippo Calò, who first accused Buscetta's son Antonio of owing him money, then pretending to forget the debt, handed him a wad of several million lire. Antonio was arrested when the notes turned out to have come from a kidnap ransom payment. Recognising the warning, Buscetta decided to leave for Brazil immediately, and so avoided being caught in the crossfire of the second mafia war, as he had done 18 years before with the first. The second would prove to be even more ferocious, with 400 dead on the streets and 600 vanished victims of the *lupara bianca*.

Once again, the catalyst for the war was suspected financial deceit. Recycling funds through gambling casinos had proved to be a relatively simple means of laundering dirty money. The construction of the huge Atlantic City complex in New Jersey was planned to combine this need with a lucrative new source of income. The families of *Cosa Nostra* formed an investment society with 30 per cent control of the total project into which each contributed. The disappearance of 20 billion lire from the society's funds in February 1981 was attributed to Stefano Bontate and Salvatore Inzerillo, who owned up when confronted, but claimed the shortfall would be made good with the imminent arrival of money due on a heroin transaction. A second meeting was set up at Inzerillo's house, ostensibly to hand over the money, at which Inzerillo hoped finally to trap and kill his rivals. But they smelt deception and sent henchmen in their place. Revenge was not long in coming: Bontate was murdered after leaving his house on the night of his 43rd birthday. Inzerillo thought he had time on his side, since he still owed Riina a large sum of money. He was wrong: he was gunned down on leaving his mistress's house early in the morning of May 11. Next on the hit list was Salvatore Contorno, who was pursued by Pino Greco's assassination squad through the streets of Palermo in broad daylight but managed, despite being wounded, to return fire at his assailants and drive to safety. In the spring and summer of 1981 Palermo averaged an assassination per day.

Virtually all the Inzerillo family fled to America after the death of the family boss, although his 16 year old son remained, determined to avenge his father. He confronted Pino Greco in a hotel and spitting in his face, accused him of murdering his father. His body was found a few days later, one arm physically wrenched from its socket.

With the decimation of the rival faction, the Corleonesi, aided by the Greco (Ciaculli), Calò (Porta Nuova) and Marchese (Corso dei Mille) families had won total control of *Cosa Nostra*. Their strength was further consolidated by the support of the most powerful clan in Catania led by Nitto Santapaola.

**Action against the mafia**

Public outrage at the bloodshed in Sicily made action against the mafia an imperative. A law was presented to Parliament under the joint names of Communist deputy Pio La Torre and DC Interior Minister Virginio Rognoni. It was based partly on the US RICO law, partly on the recommendations of the Antimafia Commission which had presented its conclusions in 1976, but most of all on the advice and experience provided by Sicilian experts such as the murdered Terranova and La Torre himself. On April 30 1982 La Torre and his driver were murdered in Palermo.

Early in 1982 General Carlo Alberto Dalla Chiesa had been invited to leave his post as deputy national Commander of the *Carabinieri* to become Prefect of Palermo, the direct representative of the Interior Ministry and thus the most senior government official on the island. His investigative skills and intuition during a previous posting in Sicily in the 1960s and 1970s had already shown him to be a serious adversary for *Cosa Nostra*, but his subsequent success against the Red Brigades had transformed him into a mythological god of state retribution.

Prior to accepting the position, Dalla Chiesa had been anxious to clarify his powers of operation and co-ordination and above all to seek reassurances of total backing from Rome. In early April he wrote to PM Spadolini asking for a demonstration of "declared and precisely phrased" support – in other words that guarantees given him in Rome would be publicly confirmed, such that his prestige and authority would be fully understood by those awaiting his arrrival. This was extremely important because, he warned, "it is equally certain that I am destined to experience actions of subtle or brutal local resistance, if not actual rejection, on the part of the famous Palazzi".

The murder of La Torre precipitated Dalla Chiesa's departure for Sicily and prevented the clarification that he had sought so anxiously – he flew to Sicily the same day, to the chilly reception he had predicted. In contrast to his anti-terrorist efforts, which he felt had had unconditional public and political support, Dalla Chiesa confided to his son the impression that "the local DC politicians were putting pressure for him not to be granted the powers he considered essential for fighting the mafia". In an interview given to the journalist Giorgio Bocca in August he commented, "I think I understand the new rules of the game: the powerful man is killed when a fatal combination occurs – he becomes too dangerous, but he can be killed because he is isolated. Costa became too dangerous when, against the majority in the prosecution office, he decided to incriminate the Inzerillos and Spatolas. But he is isolated, therefore he can be killed, cancelled out like a foreign body."

In the space of five days that August, 11 cross-clan murders took place in the notorious "triangle of death" close to Palermo. Two of the bodies were left in the boot of a car outside the Palermo *carabinieri* headquarters, its presence announced by telephone as the start of "operation Carlo Alberto". On September 3 Dalla Chiesa and his young wife had just left the prefecture and were driving to a restaurant for dinner when they and the driver of the following escort vehicle were riddled with Kalashnikov bullets.

Eight months afterwards 14 arrest warrants were issued by the Palermo judiciary – they amounted to a "radiography" of the winning mafia – Michele and Pino Greco, Totò Riina, a number of other Palermo bosses and, significantly, Nitto Santapola and three of his men. The examining magistrates concluded that the murders "followed the logic of the winning faction in *Cosa Nostra* which saw the general as a serious and very dangerous obstacle to the consolidation of the hegemony won with the murder of Bontate, Inzerillo and their allies." It was equally certain, they concluded, that the murder was decided with the agreement of the entire organisation, given the certainty of the repression to follow.

Ballistic evidence was crucial in following this trail: Nitto Santapaola's main rival in Catania, Alfio Ferlito, had been murdered in June along with three *carabinieri* and a driver in a spectacular ambush on the Palermo ring road whilst Ferlito was being transferred from one prison to another. At least one of the Kalashnikov rifles in this attack was used shortly before Bontate's murder against the window of a jeweller's shop to test its power – nothing was stolen; for the actual murder of Bontate; almost certainly for Inzerillo's murder; in the attempted murder of Contorno and in the Dalla Chiesa murder. Evidence from the *pentiti* supports the view that the Ferlito murder was done by the Palermitani as a favour to Santapaola, who then reciprocated with the Dalla Chiesa murder, using men who were not known in Palermo to watch the General's movements. Furthermore Dalla Chiesa, like the institutional victims before him, was breaking new ground – a report had been compiled on the activities of 162 Palermo *mafiosi* considered the most dangerous; the Greco family were included and an arrest warrant had been issued for Michele, head of the *cupola*. Also under scrutiny were the links between the Palermo and Catania clans of *Cosa Nostra*, as Dalla Chiesa had revealed, announcing in his interview with Bocca: "The mafia as geographically confined to western Sicily is finished. Nowadays the mafia is also strong in Catania, it's actually moving in on Palermo from there. With the permission of the Palermo mafia the four biggest Catania construction companies are now working in Palermo. Do you think they could be doing that if there weren't a new map of mafia power?"

Dalla Chiesa's reference to the companies run by Catania's four most prosperous businessmen had caused a sensation, and after his death there was speculation that one of them had commissioned it. The activities of the four **cavalieri di lavoro** ("knights of industry") of Catania are being investigated at the time of writing, although to date none has been formally incriminated.

Nitto Santapaola was certainly well connected and protected. Although his bullet-proof car was discovered close to the site of the Ferlito murder and he himself went into hiding for three weeks afterwards, when he reappeared he was detained briefly and then released. A photograph exists of Santapaola sitting around a restaurant table with other *mafiosi*, a Social Democrat member of the Regional Parliament, the then DC President of the Catania provincial administration, the then mayor of Catania, the Director of the Health Board of Catania prison, a doctor who had recently been accused of arms and drugs traffic and Carmelo Costanzo, wealthiest of the four *cavalieri di lavoro*. It is impossible that Santapaola's dinner companions could not have known of his powerful mafia status.

## The "Rognoni La Torre" law

10 days after the Dalla Chiesa murders the "Rognoni La Torre" law was rushed through Parliament. Its principal provisions are:

1. "Association of a mafia kind" (as described earlier) is punishable with between three and nine years imprisonment;

2. A public prosecutor or questor may authorise investigation into the provenance of income and the tax situation of anyone suspected of mafia association and the members of his family, and may request such information from any public administration office, public or private credit institution. Unless the suspected person is able to prove the legitimate source of his assets they may be impounded and subsequently confiscated.

3. If illegal behaviour has been proven the guilty party loses all rights to apply for contracts, is struck off any official roll of professional category and is banned from ever holding a licence for public services, as are the members of his family.

4. The production of an "antimafia certificate", issued by the Prefecture is required before application can be made for public works contracts, which testifies that the individual or company has no relationship with the mafia and

that its directors have no disciplinary or court proceedings past or pending; it is illegal to allocate such work to companies not possessing such a certificate.

Despite the mafia's best efforts, investigations into the heroin trade had begun to bring results. In 1979 a suitcase opened at Palermo airport containing 600,000 dollars gave a clue to the kind of profits being made. In May 1980 a Belgian courier was arrested at Rome airport in possession of eight kilos of heroin and gave police full details of his accomplices; in August the first Sicilian heroin refinery was discovered. In November 1981 an Italian courier was arrested at Orly airport en route between Bangkok and Rome with four and a half kilos of pure heroin. He, too, collaborated with the authorities and further arrests followed. In May 1983 a Greek ship, the Alessandros G, was impounded in the Suez Canal with 233 kilos of pure Thai heroin and a consignment of arms destined for Rosario Riccobono in Palermo. The captain had first flown to Zurich to pick up the cash for payment.

In January 1983 the deputy prosecutor for Trapani, Giacomo "Ciaccio" Montalto was murdered. One of Montalto's colleagues, deputy prosecutor Antonio Costa, would later be sentenced to three years imprisonment for corruption and illegal detention of arms. His suspected collusion with the Minore clan, heavily involved in the arms traffic, is believed to have facilitated the murder of Montalto.

One link between the mafia and arms traffic in the Middle East was the Lebanese Bou Chebel Ghassan, who was also playing a double game as police informer. In July 1983, two weeks after chief examining magistrate Rocco Chinnici had issued arrest warrants for the Dalla Chiesa murder, Ghassan telephoned the Palermo Flying Squad to warn of an impending attack – he mentioned the names of examining magistrate Giovanni Falcone and Dalla Chiesa's successor, De Francesco. He also warned that the murder would not be in the usual mafia style but in the form of a car bomb, and that two members of *Cosa Nostra* were currently in Milan collecting the explosives. Security measures for the two named targets were stepped up but otherwise nothing was done. Three days later a car bomb exploded outside Rocco Chinnici's house just as he was arriving home from work, killing him, his two bodyguards and the concierge of his apartment block. Like Dalla Chiesa, Chinnici had kept a diary; like Dalla Chiesa he frequently wrote of his isolation. In it he noted his suspicions of some members of the Palermo judiciary and their relations with the economic and political forces in Sicily. Amongst the names of those he suspected were the First President of the Palermo Court of Appeal, the Salvo cousins and their lawyer. "If anything happens to me", he wrote, "go after them."

The enquiries into Chinnici's murder were handled with lightning speed and determination – within 40 days arrest warrants had been issued for the presumed killers and their instigators. Despite six separate trials for this case and the three life sentences passed against Michele Greco and his cousin Salvatore, in December 1988 the Supreme Court annulled the latest verdict on the grounds that the evidence of the double agent Ghassan had been contaminated by his contacts with the police.

The Modern Mafia 25

## Judicial crackdown

An immediate consequence of the Chinnici murder was the setting up of a "pool" of examining magistrates in Palermo to handle mafia cases. In the future a murdered magistrate would not take his entire store of knowledge and experience to the grave, nor would *Cosa Nostra* be able to select a single identifiable target whose elimination would halt enquiries and protect its activities.

The mafia war continued throughout 1982, with 30 deaths within a few days at the end of the year as Pino Greco sought indiscriminate revenge for an attack on his own life. Although Tommas Buscetta had saved his own skin by fleeing to Brazil, his continuing contacts with Badalamenti in Brazil and his former friendship with the losing faction meant he was a direct threat to the Corleonesi. With Buscetta himself out of reach, seven of his relatives were killed in the space of four months.

Buscetta was finally arrested in Brazil in October 1983 and extradited to Italy in July 1984. After a failed suicide attempt before leaving Brazil, he took his last chance to save himself and his family, and entrusted the task of "consuming his vendetta" to the Italian judiciary. As soon as he arrived in Rome he asked to talk to judge Giovanni Falcone, a dialogue which continued for the following two months. On September 29, 366 arrest warrants were issued on the strength of his information.

Despite his years overseas and in prison, Buscetta was completely conversant with *Cosa Nostra* activities from the early 1950s onwards; his full description of the organisation and structure of *Cosa Nostra*, its activities and its internal conflicts helped the Palermo judiciary to compile a proper map of the organisation for the first time. Although insisting on his own extraneousness to the drug traffic (about which there is considerable scepticism but no concrete evidence to the contrary), Buscetta supplied a wealth of information about its operations and those involved. In America his information was largely responsible for the arrests in the famous "Pizza Connection" case – a complex, five-year-long operation involving the export of heroin from Sicily to the US with a total street value of 1,650 million dollars, so-called because of the Sicilian-run pizzerias used as distribution centres.

Gaetano Badalamenti was arrested in Madrid in the autumn of 1984 and extradited to the United States; in May 1985 the entire New York Commission was arrested, again largely thanks to Buscetta. Benefitting from the US Federal Witness Programme, Buscetta was granted protection for himself and his family and immunity from prosecution. In the years that followed others have followed his example. The positions held by the different *pentiti*, the nature and the overlapping periods of their activities have contributed to a reasonably comprehensive picture of *Cosa Nostra* up to the mid-1980s. Antonino Calderone, arrested in Nice in 1987, has been the first to provide incriminating information on the political influence and contacts of *Cosa Nostra*: he implicates ex-mayor Lima, the Salvo cousins and former government Minister Gunnella, by name; he claims that the family of Santa Maria di Gesù (Bontate) had 200 men of honour, each of whom could rally

40–50 votes which in almost every case went to the DC. Petrol coupons and packets of pasta were distributed as extra enticements to vote. Calderone confirmed that on the strength of the approximately 30 mafia families in Palermo the voting power of *Cosa Nostra* was 180,000 strong (in a city of 700,000 inhabitants). Palermo prosecutor Giuseppe Ayala accepts the estimate, and is convinced that "whoever wins these votes cannot be unaware of their provenance – otherwise from the mafia point of view there would be no point – the equation of reciprocal favours would not balance."

Another group of *pentiti* revealed an extensive mafia network stretching from Catania through Calabria to Turin. Amongst the 198 arrests made in December 1984 were the President of the Catania Court of Assizes, the President of the Appeal Court and the former *carabinieri* commander of the city, all accused of favouring the mafia. The charges faced by the other defendants included drug trafficking, racketeering and 30 counts of murder. The trial concluded in November 1988 with 26 life sentences and 130 convictions – including the three institutional representatives.

**Mafia retaliation**

The intensive police and judicial crackdown did not prevent the mafia from retaliating. On April 2 1985 a car bomb intended for the deputy prosecutor of Trapani, Carlo Palermo, missed its target but blew up a young woman and her six-year old twins instead. Judge Palermo had recently requested a transfer to Trapani from Trento in the north of Italy, where he had been investigating an arms/drugs/mafia network operated through Bulgaria. 28 days later a heroin refinery was discovered at Alcamo, in the province of Trapani. Also found were newspaper cuttings describing judge Palermo's investigations in Trento; a high pressure filter pump (Bulgarian made) and 22 jute sacks emptied of morphine base marked in cyrillic script. Had the pump been put to use it is estimated that the maximum output from the refinery would have been increased from 25 kilos of heroin per week to 80.

In the summer of 1985 the mafia tried to sabotage investigations again – in July police commissioner Giuseppe Montana, working to hunt down the several hundred mafia fugitives presumed still to be in hiding in Sicily, was assassinated. Antonio Cassarà, deputy head of the Palermo Flying Squad was murdered with his bodyguard in August. He had been investigating the recycling of dirty money, illegal export of funds and suspected collusion between *Cosa Nostra* and a number of prominent Palermo business men. Amongst the suspects were Count Arturo Cassina, whose company had had a monopoly of drain and sewer maintenance in Palermo for 36 years, and three brothers of the wealthy Fiorentino jewellery family, associates with Cassina in the **Banca Industriale di Trapani.** Cassarà suspected the Fiorentinos of falsely inflating invoices for jewel transactions in Malta as a means of recycling mafia profits, and had had the brothers arrested on the charge of currency law violation just three months before he was killed. In the days following his death, more than half the Flying Squad agents asked for and were granted transferral to other posts.

Buscetta's evidence, particularly that relating to the structural shape of *Cosa Nostra* and the decisional supremacy of the Commission, gradually convinced the Palermo judiciary of the necessity to unite the major crimes of the 1970s and early 1980s under one umbrella. The result was the start on February 10 1986 of the first "maxi-trial", in which 475 defendants were accused on 436 separate charges. A bonus for the prosecution came with the arrest on February 20 of Michele Greco, boss of the Commission and accused of 78 murders. Greco was betrayed to police by one of his henchmen who was later murdered.

The trial ended in December 1987 with 19 life sentences, 342 other convictions and 114 acquittals. Luciano Liggio was exonerated on all counts, his only definitive conviction at time of writing being the murder of Michele Navarro in 1958, the catalyst of the great mafia transformation. Nino Salvo had died early in 1986 but his cousin Ignazio was convicted of mafia association and sentenced to seven years. Of those sentenced to life, Nitto Santapaola, Totò Riina and Bernardo Provenzano were convicted in absentia – in May 1989 they are still at large.

During the course of the maxi-trial the mafia stayed silent, partly to protect and keep peace amongst the prisoners, partly in expectation of the verdict which would determine the future shape of the organisation.

## THE MODERN MAFIA TODAY

The maxi-trial over, *Cosa Nostra* began immediately to eliminate anyone considered treacherous, unreliable or a threat to the organisation. One of the acquitted defendants was murdered within two hours of leaving Palermo's Ucciardone prison; by May 1989 the total had reached 14. The mafia war and a settling of accounts against the *pentiti* have continued relentlessly, as for example with the double murder of Giovanni Bontate (brother of Stefano and brother-in-law of the *pentito* Contorno) and his wife in September 1988 and the killing of a further two relatives in July 1989. Contorno's alliance with the losers in the war together with his collaboration have cost him the lives of 19 relatives.

The most conspicuous change in the power structure of *Cosa Nostra* since the trial has been the split between the Corleonesi and the Greco families and the progressive casting off and elimination of the latter: Michele is elderly and will never be released from prison; Pino Greco, who was on the run at the time of the trial, is presumed dead; Mario Prestifilippo, another notorious killer of the Greco clan, has been murdered as have other lesser figures. There has been a systematic expurgation of the Marchese family, who also sided with the Corleonesi during the second mafia war, and were subsequently judged untrustworthy. The result has been a consolidation of the power of the Corleonesi under the leadership of Totò Riina, a fugitive from justice for over 20 years. Opinions differ as to whether Luciano Liggio still commands *Cosa Nostra* from prison through Riina, or whether there has been a split between the old allies.

The internal shape of the organisation has also been modified – to tighten the hold of the ruling faction over the rest, and to ensure that no future *pentito* will have the knowledge to inflict the harm done by those in the past. Some believe that the *cupola* has been abolished altogether, and that instead of having elections, *Cosa Nostra* has become a dictatorship. It is thought the initiation ceremony and swearing of vows still take place, but in the presence of fewer witnesses.

According to judge Giovanni Falcone, *Cosa Nostra* 1989 is run by "a strong, compact nucleus, absolutely impenetrable from the outside". The organisation is "more tightly knit, more hierarchical and more closely controlled at the top. There still exists a strong local autonomy but I believe there are regents in each zone, men trusted at the top who are directly answerable to the top level. Much more prudence is used and there is a greater compartmentalisation. News doesn't travel the way it once did."

This stripping down of *Cosa Nostra* is described by Sicilian judges as an "implosion" or "simplification" of the organisation, determined to get rid of dead wood and anyone whose alliance with the winning faction may have been for opportunist motives.

**The drug war**

Compared with the past, Sicily now plays a minor role in the international narcotics traffic. This is due to three main factors: the growth of the cocaine market (outside Sicilian control) in parallel with and in some areas displacing the heroin trade (in part due to fears of AIDS); the preference for new drug routes and increased competition from other criminal organisations, in particular the Colombians, the Chinese and the Turks. The principal zones of heroin production are still the "golden triangle" of Burma, Laos and Thailand and the "golden crescent" of Pakistan, Afghanistan and Iran, but different routes are being taken to reach America and Europe. Whereas in the early 1980s 30 per cent of the heroin seized in the US had come from Italy, the figure stands currently at only 5 per cent.

According to the United Nations Fund for Drug Abuse Control (UNFDAC) both heroin and cocaine are increasingly passing through African countries where there is less resistance from authorities who may be more corruptible and less experienced in dealing with the phenomenon. Some have actually asked for UN help to combat it, and positive results have been achieved.

According to Pino Arlacchi, Turkey is returning as a major supplier (although not producer) of heroin to Europe – he notes that in 1988, 50 per cent of European heroin and almost all that seized in Italy came from Turkey, and that 90 per cent of the major distributors in Verona, Turin and Milan are supplied by Turkish, Syrian and Lebanese wholesalers at the average price of 60 million lire per kilo.

UNFDAC Director Giuseppe Di Gennaro considers that Sicily has very little influence in the heroin traffic nowadays, and that Colombia not only controls most of the world cocaine market but the heroin market and the ever-increasing production of synthetic drugs as well, with the Caribbean as heart of the financial empire.

## The Modern Mafia                                               29

However two joint US/Italian police operations in the spring and autumn of 1988 involving nearly 200 arrests proved that *Cosa Nostra* is still highly active in heroin. They also gave the first proof of parallel trading – the exchange of cocaine for Europe with heroin for the US at a ratio of four to one. The arrest of 52 Calabrians in the spring operation suggested that Calabria was being used at least as a transit and distribution zone and probably a refining base as well. The autumn operation, codenamed "Irontower", showed that members of the Inzerillo and Spatola families, the "losers" in the mafia war, were back in circulation on the basis of their valuable US connections, and that albeit under strict supervision from the Corleonesi, had been given back limited control of their Palermo districts.

*Cosa Nostra* has also put down firm roots in the UK, initially through the Sicilian families Caruana and Cuntrera, whose home town of Siculiana was once dubbed "the Wall Street of the narcotics trade". The clan is currently based in Caracas but has extensive links in Canada. Francesco Di Carlo took over the UK operation, covering his illegal activities with a wide range of apparently legal ones – he owned a hotel, a wine bar, an antiques business and a travel agency. Di Carlo imported cannabis from Kashmir and heroin from Thailand, usually concealed in furniture which would arrive by sea at Southampton or Felixstowe. Part was then unloaded for the UK market, the rest shipped on to Montreal. Arrested in 1985 in possession of 35 kilos of heroin, Di Carlo was given a 25 year prison sentence at the Old Bailey in March 1987.

In January 1987 Detroit financier David Medin was arrested in London with 2 suitcases containing 36 kilos of pure cocaine (with a £10 million street value). The operation, financed by the Detroit mafia, involved the sending of cocaine from Bolivia to the UK via Buenos Aires or Rio where it would be packed into heavy plant machinery and sent air freight. Four groups were to see to distribution in the UK, one in Holland and one in Italy. Companies trading in computer parts had been formed in London and Jersey to launder an expected 3 billion dollars of profits each month. With the US market virtually saturated, the UK has clearly been an attractive target for the cocaine dealers, as shown by the statistics of seizures – 98 kilos of cocaine in 1986–87, and 484 kilos in 1987–88 – an increase of 391 per cent.

Although Italy's strategic importance in the narcotics trade may have declined, drugs are still the single most important source of income for the Italian mafia. The amount of heroin seized in Italy rose between 1987 and 1988 from 322 kilos to 576; of cocaine from 327 kilos to 611. The rule of thumb estimate is to multiply by 10 for the amounts actually imported, although even this is often considered a gross underestimate. The figures give an alarming indication that the enormous increase in cocaine demand has not reduced the demand for heroin, but that the two markets continue to grow in parallel.

A report produced by Italy's Superior Judicial Council reported that at the end of 1988 there were approximately 300,000 heroin addicts and 50,000 cocaine addicts in Italy. The rate of heroin addiction has tripled since 1981, and is the highest in Europe, as is the number of drug-related AIDS deaths.

The rate of death from overdose rose in Italy between 1987 and 1988 from 518 to 792 and in 1989 had reached 400 by the end of June. The overall revenue from the drug traffic in Italy in 1988 was estimated at 40,000 billion lire – equivalent to one third of the entire national public deficit.

### Mafia infiltration of business

The Sicilian mafia's diminished control over the international drugs traffic has coincided with a renewed attention to public works contracts, in particular to subcontracting work. 51 Sicilian businessmen were murdered between 1978 and 1988, 12 of them between 1986 and 1988 in Palermo alone. And whereas once the murdered Sicilian businessman was likely to have had some suspect dealings with the mafia, nowadays the targets are those with impeccable records. This is probably an unfortunate byproduct of the otherwise highly-praised *Rognoni La Torre* Law. Previously, the mafia extorted money from clean enterprises in exchange for protection and perhaps the imposition of a few employees such as building site guards, but were able to run their own businesses alongside their clean competitors. Since mafia individuals and companies have been liable to financial scrutiny they have found it necessary to infiltrate clean companies in order to operate in the legal market. Where there was once a clear-cut line between victim and extortionist, the *mafioso* now has every interest in winning the victim over as an accomplice, to the point at which the mafia takes over the company behind an apparently innocent front. The blurring of the distinction is a subtle process – the victim may resent having to pay out his **pizzo** or hush money every month, but may eventually come to enjoy the privilege of working in peace, having no labour problems (forcefully dealt with) and having his competitors suitably harassed.

The next stage, when the reluctant accomplice turns into an active one can be short, especially with the carrot of financial incentive dangled in front of him. This process of victim→ accomplice→ *mafioso* has been proved in several Sicilian trials and is generally acknowledged as one of the most delicate and serious problems the judiciary must deal with, especially since extortions are rarely reported to the authorities. Judge Falcone explains: "They are almost never reported, it's true, but on the other hand I don't see why they should or could be reported when to do so involves a series of reprisals which at best involve the cessation of the ability to go on working. The state simply does not have the fundamental capacity to guarantee the security of those who decide to collaborate. Even supposing someone does want to collaborate he often puts up with the lesser evil, but the lesser evil is often transformed into advantages."

When businessman Luigi Ranieri was murdered in December 1988, Falcone refused to accept that the motive was his refusal to pay extortion money, and believed the cause was much deeper rooted. Ranieri had been head of a co-operative of 19 firms with responsibilities for allocating large sums of public money for reconstruction and development in Palermo. He had resigned as chairman of the co-operative some months before, retaining only his own company directorship. His murder may have been the result of his refusing to allow mafia penetration of the co-operative.

The number of murders in Sicily in 1988 – 298 – indicates that a major reorganisation of the *Cosa Nostra* is still underway. There were 72 murders in Palermo, of which 40 were mafia executions; 84 in Catania, 24 in Gela. The small town of Gela on the southern coast had in June 1989 reached a total of 50 murders within 18 months, largely due, it seems, to the battle to win contracts for the elaborate dam building/irrigation programme for which large sums of public money have been allocated.

## Political links

The situation regarding mafia/political links is still largely unclarified. The conclusion of the judges in the first maxi trial was that "in order to obtain certain benefits the mafia needs the keys of power. Unfortunately we did not have the means of identifying the keys or those who possessed them." The quest is still on.

The murder of former mayor of Palermo Giuseppe Insalaco in January 1988, followed days later by that of police officer Natale Mondo, are still under investigation, but may be linked to a particular line of political/mafia investigation. Insalaco had kept detailed notes on 20 years of Palermo life and intrigue, a diary with information about politicians, building contractors, judges, the Palermo "Business Committee" and on the influential group the **"Cavalieri del Santo Sepolcro"** whose members included former Palermo prefect De Francesco, an ex-questor, several generals and Count Arturo Cassina, described by Palermo magistrate Di Pisa as "one of the pillars of mafia power in Palermo". After a spot of dubious property speculation in the 1970s for which Insalaco had been incriminated, he had begun to oppose mafia power directly, and had given evidence of political corruption to the Parliamentary Antimafia Commission shortly before his death.

At the time of the "illustrious corpses" there was much talk of a mysterious "third level" – an occult force at an elevated but removed political distance which manipulated even the highest echelons of *Cosa Nostra*. This theory has been thrown out by all but a few, although its most distinguished proponent is none other than current High Commissioner for the mafia struggle, Domenico Sica, who believes that a form of "terrorism committee" has operated in Italy since 1980 whose main preoccupations have been to protect the arms and drugs traffic by selective use of terrorism, extortion, bank robbery and the gangsterism of common crime.

Others believe that the key to the political/mafia connection is to be found in the Italian Freemasonry. According to the *pentito* Calderone, plans were under way as early as 1977 to create a masonic lodge especially for *Cosa Nostra* members, and that subsequently Stefano Bontate and Michele Greco had become masons. The secret Propaganda 2 (P2) lodge run by grandmaster Licio Gelli was outlawed in 1981 after its membership list proved to contain several government ministers, numerous high ranking members of the armed forces, judges, chairmen of private and public companies and newspaper proprietors. Court trials have incriminated Gelli in direct and indirect support for right wing terrorist activities.

In 1981, the year the P2 scandal broke, five lodges were founded at Trapani under the collective name of "**Circolo Scontrino**" and another was subsequently founded at Mazaro del Vallo. Gelli was guest of honour at the opening of the *Circolo Scontrino*. A frequent guest of Giovanni Grimaudo, founder and Grandmaster of the *Circolo*, was the Bulgarian Ambassador to Italy who in turn invited Grimaudo and the DC assessor of Trapani for a week's trip to Bulgaria. The power of the *Circolo* grew rapidly, to the point at which it was able to influence the major economic and political decisions in the area.

All ran smoothly until 1985 when a diligent flying squad chief ordered a search of the premises. He was transferred to another post the following day. In 1988 Grimaudo was imprisoned on charges for fraud but has not yet come to trial. The Bulgarian connection, the drugs/arms traffic, the evidence that two lodge members ran the heroin refinery at Alcamo, near Trapani, the murder of Montalto in 1983 and the attempted murder of Carlo Palermo in 1985, the contacts with the P2 lodge, Licio Gelli and thus with right wing subversion may not add up to any "third level" nor do they prove that the *Cosa Nostra* Commission was subordinate to any political direction. (On this point Giovanni Falcone is most insistent.) Nonetheless Grimaudo's trial ought to shed some light on what was at the very least an important point of contact between two secret fraternities. "If it doesn't," admits Palermo prosecutor Giuseppe Ayala, "then I'll feel I have been working for nothing."

## Financial resources

Of the four elements of mafia power already described there is no doubt that the greatest threat now and for the future comes from the immense financial resources available to organised crime. The problem is both national and international, and one whose potential repercussions have only belatedly been realised. Crime arouses less public indignation when it violates laws rather than human lives, disseminates wealth rather than death.

In 1984 for example, the first fully effective year of the *Rognoni La Torre* law, 402 billion lire worth of assets were seized in Italy, but by 1987 the total had dropped to less than 100 billion. Given the certainty that the quantity of illegal money in circulation had not dropped, there could be only two answers: firstly that the criminal organisations had found other ways of recycling money out of the reaches of the *Rognoni La Torre* law and secondly that the time-consuming and extensive investigations necessary to examine the income and tax position of mafia suspects and their families was an excessive work burden for the finance police, which had neither the training nor the legal means to identify and deal with the sophisticated techniques of money transfer and laundering being used. It has become apparent that the mafia, whilst still using the conventional banking system, also recycles profits through leasing firms, usury, casinos and private finance companies, of which over 200 have sprung up in Sicily in recent years. There is proof of illegal activities at the

## The Modern Mafia 33

casino of Saint Vincent, whilst 52 suspected *mafiosi* have been sent for trial for the attempted takeover of casinos at Campione and San Remo.

Proof of fraudulent use of EC funds and the imminent abolition of the European frontiers after 1992 have intensified concern in the banking sector. Michelangelo Ajello, former DC mayor of Bagheria, near Palermo, arranged the fictitious export of citrus fruit to three non-existent companies in London "owned" by his accomplice, Raymond Kingsland. The "business", which within a few years had turned over some £10 million, was protected by the finance company Italtrade, part of the government redevelopment office for southern Italy, and heavily subsidised by EC agricultural funds. Between 1983 and 1984 Kingsland paid 1,392,196 dollars from his Palermo current account into Ajello's Swiss and Palermo bank accounts.

All European countries have laws which punish drug trafficking but few penalise the recycling of profits derived from it. Both the Governor of the Bank of Italy and the *Guardia di Finanza* have issued stern warnings that mafia penetration of financial institutions may be extensive and that through shareholdings, bank investments and manipulative deposits or withdrawals, criminals have a potential stranglehold over the national economy. In a report of April 1989 Governor Ciampi warned: "the danger of contamination of the financial structure on an international scale is derived largely from the link which has been established between consumption, traffic and distribution of narcotic substances on the one hand and the activities of organised crime on the other." A confidential report compiled by the *Guardia di Finanza* in March 1989 identified the recycling of illegal capital as "the meeting point between criminality and the legal economy and marks the entry of mafia power into the world of business, especially those areas characterised by weak barriers to entry of a technological variety, high profit levels and strong internal competition.

The report analysed five methods of recycling:

**1.** Physical transportation of capital via courier.
**2.** "Circular cheques" or cheques made out to the bank account of the bearer who will be a professional courier. This avoids the physical movement of cash.
**3.** Via casinos both in Italy and abroad.
**4.** Use of the national banking system with deposit accounts in the name of fictitious persons.
**5.** Fictitious business transactions with overseas countries.

The same report observed that illegal capital passes not only through banks but through the stock exchange, leasing companies, estate agencies, credit institutions, and government bonds. Small companies with clean front men provide an apparently legal front for these kinds of financial transactions. Money is recycled through tax havens, in particular Panama, Singapore, the Bahamas and Hong Kong. Profits tend to be invested in two main ways – in gold and in property, especially in Italy, Spain and South America.

It has been proved that four senior staff members of the **Bank of Credit and Commerce International,** a Luxembourg bank with branches in 72 countries, laundered large sums of dirty capital. Enquiries are being pursued in Switzerland into the activities of a Turkish-run company called Oden AG, suspected of co-ordinating extensive drugs, arms and currency fraud operations with the possible involvement of the country's three top banks. Even the once-indifferent Swiss have become alarmed at the potential destabilisation effects of the mass movement of illegal capital which flows, inevitably, to areas of least resistance.

Two meetings in December 1988 laid important foundations for greater international co-operation in fighting the drugs traffic and its profiteers. The Declaration of Basel, signed by the central banks of Switzerland, Belgium, Canada, the UK, the USA, France, West Germany, Japan, Italy, the Netherlands, Sweden and Luxembourg, commits banks in these countries to taking steps to identify clients and the sources of their funds, to refuse transactions of suspect legality and to co-operate with judicial enquiries. The United Nations Vienna Convention, once ratified, will bind each signatory nation to much more rigorous controls on the apprehension and treatment of drug traffickers, the seizure of their assets and mutual judicial assistance.

The moves are to be applauded, but it must be stressed that neither has the force of law and in the case of the UN convention, several years will have to pass before all the signatory countries have ratified it. Given the ambivalence of countries like the United States whose fight against communism has tended to prevail over that against drug trafficking, the power of the drug barons in Latin America, the lack of foresight on the part of western economies in tackling the financial power of organised crime and the woeful inadequacy of resources allocated to fighting the drugs scourge at an international level, the outlook is far from bright. These were the conclusions which emerged from a major conference on the international drugs traffic held in Florence in May, 1989 chaired by UNFDAC Director Di Gennaro and addressed by experts from West Germany, Spain, Switzerland, Italy and Canada. In the words of General Pietro Soggiu, Director of the Italian National Anti-drug Unit, "It's not that we have lost the war, we simply haven't begun to fight it".

## CONCLUSION

The prospects for defeating the Italian mafia are scarcely more encouraging. *Cosa Nostra*'s move from "heroin mafia" to "finance mafia" has reinforced it economically and has ensured its continuing predominance over the other organised crime groups whose power bases are less secure. However, many of the problems of response are as applicable to Calabria and Campania as to Sicily: they are the areas of worst housing, unemployment, health care, educational standards and general lawlessness. Despite the often repeated calls for "emergency measures" the most immediate need at national level is to restore "normality" to the southern regions, to inspire public faith in the state's ability to guarantee justice, honest government and the rule of law. These are achievable goals if the political will is there.

Delays in criminal trials due to inadequate judicial resources and manpower result in known *mafiosi* being released from prison; the Supreme court overturns verdicts on purely technical grounds – the lack of one defence lawyer's signature on a court document has caused a whole trial to be rerun. In April 1989 the Palermo Court of Assizes overturned the theory of the unified structure of *Cosa Nostra* in the third maxi-trial and acquitted 80 of the most notorious mafia bosses. In the meantime intimidation and violence against the judiciary continues – the magistrate who was to have presided over the Appeal trial of the first maxi-trial was shot dead with his handicapped son in September 1988. Immediately afterwards requests for transfers to other posts followed from his colleagues.

In June 1989 Judge Falcone and two Swiss colleagues meeting to discuss mafia money laundering in the tranquillity of the judge's seaside villa would have been blown sky high had it not been for the vigilance of Falcone's two bodyguards. An inconspicuous-looking beach holdall left carelessly on the rocks below the house proved to contain 23 kilos of TNT, meticulously prepared with timer device and remote control detonator. Falcone, whose promotion a few days later to Assistant Prosecutor of Palermo the mafia had tried to prevent, is in no doubt that further attempts on his life will follow.

In the Palermo area alone, 854 fugitives are thought to be hiding out, including the *Cosa Nostra* "government" of Totò Riina, Nitto Santapaola and Bernardo Provenzano. Police resources have never recovered from the decimation that followed the murder of Cassarà: the Flying Squad has had eight heads in nine years and a continuous turnover at other levels. In Gela, whose police commissioner was arrested in 1987 on charges of corruption, there was no town council for almost a year – it was dissolved because of electoral irregularities – and unemployed youngsters are being recruited as murderers for 200,000 lire.

The government attitude to the mafia struggle has varied between complacency, inertia and knee jerk reaction. In April 1988 Interior Minister Fanfani admitted that the mafia was "not his greatest problem"; in July his successor Gava and the national Police Commander Parisi promised that there was "nothing to worry about" and that all was "under control". An outcry from the Sicilian judiciary followed by 16 murders in the space of five days that September changed their minds, and prompted Parliament to appoint a new High Commissioner against the mafia, Domenico Sica, whose wide-ranging powers of investigation and co-ordination have yet to bring positive results.

The absence of legislation to protect and provide adequate financial provision for the *pentiti* and their families has caused acute problems: there has been an almost total drying up of information from inside the organisation whose members have no incentive to collaborate. In June 1989 the almost unbelievable happened – resentful and destitute, Salvatore Contorno was re-arrested with two cousins near Palermo in the midst of a cross clan battle zone. Despite the contract out on his life, he had returned to Sicily to offer and claim the only help on which he knew he could rely – that of the family. In the days following his arrest the contradictory statements made by the authorities, some professing "utter amazement" and others admitting with some embarrassment they had known of his presence in Sicily for several weeks, served merely to make the state look ridiculous and hopelessly incompetent.

To sum up, there is little doubt that *Cosa Nostra* is stronger and more compact than it has ever been, that it is continuing to exercise its four powers to the full, and that the myth of invincibility dented between 1984 and 1986 has begun to return.

Endless political bickering, three changes in government and four months of total parliamentary paralysis within the space of two years has prevented the passing of laws urgently needed to deal with drug trafficking, witness protection and money laundering. In one third of Italy murder is virtually a daily event; kidnaps and intimidation continue unabated and courtrooms sag under the oppressive backlog of civil and penal cases. Only individual acts of desperation seem to shame the authorities into action, as when the mother of a 19 year old kidnap victim chained herelf up in a tent in the village square of an *'ndrangheta* stronghold in protest againt the state's inability to safeguard its citizens.

I leave Judge Giovanni Falcone to provide a final, frustrated conclusion: "No one will understand that we are facing a phenomenon so serious, so deeply rooted in the social fabric of our society and so much a part of the system that it is impossible to expect tranquillising answers within a short period. That should be our starting point".

---

## AUTHOR'S INTERVIEWEES

Guiseppe Ayala, deputy procurator of Palermo.
Giovanni Falcone, examining magistrate, Palermo.
Piero Grasso, judge for the first maxi-trial in Palermo.
Senator Ferdinando Imposimato, member of the Parliamentary Antimafia Commission.
Deputy Luciano Violante, member of the Parliamentary Antimafia Commission.
Paolo Borsellino, public prosecutor of Marsala.
Signora Giovanna Terranova, widow of judge Cesare Terranova.
Luigi Colajanni, Sicilian Regional Communist Party Secretary.
Journalists on Palermo daily paper "L'Ora".
Giuseppe di Gennaro, Director General of the United Nations Fund for Drug Abuse Control.
Pino Arlacchi, sociologist.

## REFERENCES AND
## RECOMMENDED READING

Giuseppe Fava: *Mafia Da Giuliano a Dalla Chiesa*; Editori Riuniti/Politica e società, Roma, 1986.

## The Modern Mafia 37

*Mafia: L'atto d'accusa dei giudici di Palermo*; a cura di Corrado Stajano: Editori Riuniti; Roma, 1986.

Luciano Violante: *La Mafia dell'Eroina*; Editori Riuniti; Roma 1987.

Raimondo Catanzaro: *Il Delitto come Impresa – storia sociale della mafia*; Liviana Editrice; Padova, 1988.

Majority conclusion of the *Commissione Parlamentare Antimafia, Atti Interni Documenti Vol XXXVI no XXIII-2, Senato della Repubblica, VI legislatura, 1972–1976*.

Tim Shawcross, Martin Young: *Mafia Wars: the confessions of Tommaso Buscetta*; Fontana/Collins; Fontana paperbacks, 1988.

Pino Arlachi: *Mafia Business: the mafia ethic and the spirit of capitalism*; Oxford University Press, 1988.

Fabrizio Calvi: *La Vita Quotidiana della mafia dal 1950 ad oggi*; Biblioteca Universale Rizzoli; Milano, 1986.

Anton Blok: *The Mafia of a Sicilian Village 1860–1960*. Polity Press; Cambridge, 1988.

Sergio Turone: *Partiti e mafia dalla P2 alla droga*; Laterza, 1985.

Micromega: *le ragione della sinistra* 4/88.

*Stato e mafia oggi*: dalla legge La Torre al "pentitismo"; a cura di Carlo Smuraglia; supplemento al numero 6 novembre–dicembre 1985 di Democrazia e Diritto.

Address given at conference "L'Europa e la droga" organised by FEDRO (Federazione Droga), Palazzo Vecchio, Florence, 19/20 May 1989.

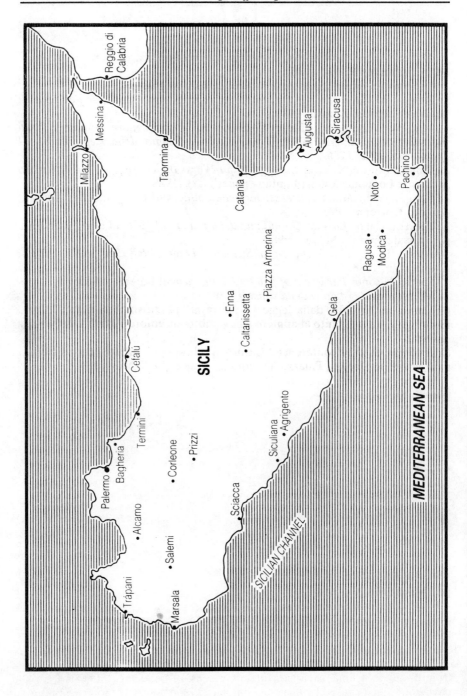

# [3]

# Global Drug Trafficking

## *Alison Jamieson*

The aim of this study is to provide an analysis of the illicit world drugs traffic with special reference to heroin, cocaine and derivatives (but excluding psychotropic drugs, marijuana and cannabis); of its operations and operators, of the production and distribution in sample countries; of the techniques used to launder illicit profits; of the measures which have been taken to counteract the effects of drug trafficking in terms of prevention and repression; and of the successes and failures of such measures and likely future developments in European and global terms.

## BACKGROUND AND CHARACTERISTICS OF THE WORLD ILLICIT DRUG TRAFFIC

On 28 September 1989 the world's largest single cocaine seizure was made in Los Angeles. A simple six dollar padlock was all that protected the inconspicuous warehouse from detection, yet the 21.4 metric tons of cocaine hydrochloride stored inside had a street value of around six billion dollars – more than the gross national product of 100 sovereign states.

Interpol's report on the illicit traffic in narcotic drugs for 1989 provides a useful introduction to the dimensions that the world market has assumed:

> . . . more drug contraband was produced and sold than in prior years; drug addiction is on the rise; the streets of our cities are becoming more violent; the loss of lives resulting from drug trafficking and abuse is increasingly evident . . . there is substantial evidence that Chinese syndicates are regrouping in the Netherlands, the United Kingdom, Belgium, France, Spain and the Federal Republic of Germany. . . . All trend indicators point to: ample supplies of opium throughout 1990; continued clandestine conversion of opium into heroin, and an increase in smuggling activity from South West, South East and Middle Eastern source areas to Western consumer markets. Chinese syndicates are expected to continue their control of the North American and Australian markets and in addition become much more visible in Europe. It is anticipated that Turkish, assisted by European based organisations, will continue to move large shipments of South West Asian heroin into Europe via the Balkan route.

### The cultural tradition

For centuries the opium poppy and the coca plant have occupied a central role in the primitive agricultural societies of South America and Asia as integral elements of a cultural tradition which respected the plants' curative, life-enhancing properties. Consumption within the context of tradition created a stable pattern of supply and demand and rarely led to abuse or addiction.

Towards the end of the 18th century the British began to export opium from India to China as a convenient means of reducing the balance of payments deficit caused by large tea purchases, and continued to bring opium

1

2                      *Research Institute for the Study of Conflict and Terrorism*

into the country in defiance of a ban imposed by the Chinese authorities in 1800. Chinese insistence on observance of the ban and the British desire to expand trading outlets led to the Opium War of 1839–42 which ended in victory for the British, the cession of Hong Kong to Britain and the opening up of four more Chinese ports to foreign trade in addition to Canton. The opium trade continued to flourish with Hong Kong at its centre to such an extent that until 1886 when restrictions were first introduced, the British were selling 200,000 cases of opium per year to the Chinese, whose addiction rate rose to over 100 million.[1]

In 1898 the German pharmaceutical company Bayer launched heroin as a new analgesic 10 times more effective than morphine and without its addictive qualities. The new drug was widely acclaimed and distributed, particularly in the United States, where it could be obtained without prescription.

A German scientist was the first to refine cocaine hydrochloride (cocaine HCl) from the coca leaf in 1862. Within a few years cocaine became renowned both for its pleasurable effects and for medicinal purposes. It was the primary ingredient of an elixir made by a Corsican chemist called Angelo Mariani, whose "vin Mariani" won a devoted following and testimonials of praise from artists and composers, religious and world leaders.

Sigmund Freud was an early advocate of cocaine, recommending the drug in a paper of 1884 as a stimulant, for digestive disorders, as a local anaesthetic and as a cure for alcohol and morphine addiction. Admitting that prolonged or excessive use could cause "weakness, emaciation and intellectual decadence" he concluded that cocaine was "more likely to promote health than impair it". The following year the pharmaceutical company Parke Davis announced cocaine to be "the most important therapeutic discovery of the age", and in 1896 Coca Cola was introduced as a "tonic for elderly people who were easily tired".[2] Adverse affects were noted almost immediately by the American Pharmacological Association which harshly condemned the product and its manufacturers; in 1905 the coca was officially removed from the cola.

The earliest forum on international action to limit the distribution of opiates came in 1909 with a 13 nation conference at Shanghai known as the Opium Commission. The outcome was the International Opium Convention signed at The Hague in 1912, the first binding instrument of international law to control the production and manufacture of narcotic drugs. The US quickly followed up with the Harrison Narcotic Act of 1914 which outlawed the use of heroin and cocaine outside strictly controlled medical usage. International conventions in the 1920s and 1930s attempted to suppress opium smoking and introduced severe punishments for the trafficking of a range of illicit drugs.

**Areas of cultivation**

The opium poppy is cultivated in two main areas – the "golden crescent" of South West Asia consisting of Afghanistan, Iran and Pakistan and the "golden triangle" of Thailand, Myanmar (formerly Burma) and Laos; Lebanon and Mexico also produce, but in much smaller quantities. Heroin destined for the

*Global Drug Trafficking* 3

United States comes in equal proportions from the two source areas: 80 per cent of the heroin reaching Europe is produced in South West Asia or the Middle East and 20 per cent from South East Asia (DND). World opium production is approximately 4,000 metric tons (mt), which after refining amount to roughly 400 mt of heroin.

Peru, Bolivia and Colombia supply almost all the world's coca leaves – an estimated 238,000 mt for 1989. Had the entire production been converted to cocaine HCl the total refined would have been around 700 mt, but losses from seizures and from crop eradication, plus local consumption in less refined forms reduces the estimate to 566 mt (INSCR).

Arrests and drug seizures in the late 1980s prove that South American drug cartels have reached agreements with organised crime groups in Europe for the sale and distribution of cocaine. With the US market virtually saturated and retail price per gramme down to 10 to 15 dollars, the attractions of Europe, where a gramme of cocaine still costs 90 to 188 dollars (UK) or 80 to 112 dollars (Italy) are obvious. In January 1990 278 kilos were seized in a single haul in Spain and 14 Colombians arrested. A Sicilian mafia "supergrass" arrested and convicted in Miami has given details of a 600 kg consignment sent to Sicily in January 1988 from the Caribbean island of Aruba for distribution by *Cosa Nostra* – a trial run for intended future shipments of 1000–2000 kg.

Cocaine only fully "took off" in the early 1980s, yet within a decade the national economies of a number of South American countries have themselves become drug-dependent. The illicit cocaine traffic has increased by 400 per cent in recent years[3]; world seizures have risen over 90 times in the last 15 years (DND) but even the most optimistic view puts seizures at between 10 and 20 per cent of the real total. European cocaine seizures almost doubled from 3,970 kg in 1987 to 6,994 kg in 1988 (DND). Importantly, the supply and demand for cocaine have not reduced the demand for heroin but have grown alongside it: in 1987 for the first time European cocaine seizures surpassed those of heroin; the trend became even more pronounced in 1988 (see table 1) (1989 comprehensive European data not available). Britain followed the same pattern: 425 kg of cocaine were intercepted in 1989, an increase of over 50 per cent from 1988, and exceeded those of heroin (332 kg) for the third year in a row (Home Office).

## Economic and political factors

According to UN analysts, economic factors have been crucial in paving the way for a thriving parallel market:

> These bellwethers of the world economy in the 1980s – debt, falling commodity prices, poverty and drug trafficking – are interconnected and mutually reinforcing. The decline of prices for commodities like sugar (by 64 per cent), coffee (30 per cent), cotton (32 per cent) and wheat (17 per cent) between 1980 and 1988 motivated farmers to turn to cash crops like the coca bush and the opium poppy to avoid economic ruin. At the national level the export of illicit drugs often took up the slack of foreign exchange depleted by falling prices for agricultural goods as well as for minerals, including tin (down by 57 per cent in 1980–88 period), lead (28 per cent), crude oil (53 per cent) and iron ore (17 per cent).[4]

Political instability is a major factor in the growth of the illicit drugs trade and is one of the biggest obstacles to combating it. In the last 20 years the drug producing countries of Latin America and of Southern Asia have all experienced one or more of the following – *coup d'etat,* revolution, tribal tensions, violent ethnic and/or religious protest, invasion, intensive guerrilla warfare. In materially impoverished, politically turbulent parts of the world, drugs have become the principal currency for the purchase of weapons and, as has been proved, the human and organisational structures for the one illicit trade have come to overlap or coincide with the other.

## Global competition

At an international level no single organisation has overall control of the illicit drugs traffic; different groups tend to dominate in particular areas at different times but ruthless competition is constant and intense, and in a business with no recourse to written rules or courts of law, the use and maintenance of power by corruption, intimidation and violence determines today's, if not tomorrow's victor. In global terms the four main competitors are the Japanese *Yakuza,* the Chinese *Triads,* the Colombian cartels and the Sicilian mafia. Turkish crime groups have a virtual monopoly of the distribution routes from South West Asia to Europe.

It is clearly impossible to gauge the number of participants in any illicit market, but some educated guesses have been made. In 1977 it was estimated that 20,000 were involved in the drugs trade in New York (Kaplan); in Los Angeles in 1989: 10,000 (Interpol); in Italy in 1985: 20,000–30,000 (Martinoli); in Bolivia 500,000, or 30 per cent of the working population, and in Peru 10 per cent of the workforce (UN).[5] Political scientist Ethan Nadelmann's 1986 study of the Latin American cocaine trade estimates that for every 300 cocaine exporters there are 222,000 coca farmers, 74,000 paste processors, 7,400 paste transporters and 1,333 refiners, adding up to a total of 1.5 million drug employees.[6]

Two other points worth noting are the speed and ease of international communications and the multiracial diversity of western industrialised society. The migratory flows of the 20th century have led to large diasporas of ethnic colonies in stragetic parts of the globe which in some cases have been activated, in others have settled deliberately, to exploit the trust formed by blood ties to the homeland with the commercial opportunities offered by economic prosperity in the adopted country. Thus regular flights between South American and Spanish cities, human and financial transfers between the United States and Sicily, the activities of closed Chinese communities in large western cities – afforded cover by the overwhelming majority of their law-abiding countrymen – have provided protection for what is currently the world's most profitable and most truly multinational activity, whose annual takings – estimated at 500 billion dollars – surpass world oil revenues and are second only to those of the arms trade.

## PRODUCTION AND DISTRIBUTION – HEROIN

"Opium poppy" refers to the plant of the species *Papaver somniferum L.* "Opium" refers to the coagulated juice of the opium poppy. "Poppy straw" refers to all parts (except the seeds) of the opium poppy after mowing (*Single Convention on Narcotics Drugs, 1961*).

The dependence-creating and medicinal properties of opium are derived from its two main constituents, morphine and codeine. Opium contains 10 per cent morphine which may be extracted directly or from poppy straw. Heroin can be produced by relatively simple processes from morphine base.[7] The colour of heroin varies from white to brown, the whiter the colour the greater the purity. The consumer's dose is never pure, but is "cut" or adulterated with other substances which in themselves can be harmful. When cut, a gramme of pure heroin provides up to 40 doses. Heroin acts on the central nervous system and on the gastro-intestinal system, it reduces the ability to feel pain, causing sleepiness and euphoria. Withdrawal symptoms usually begin after a few hours in the form of sweating, trembling, back and leg pains, sometimes accompanied by diarrhoea, vomiting and spasms.

### Chronology of heroin trafficking

A description of the illicit heroin traffic falls roughly into three time phases: the period from the 1930s to the end of the 1960s when exportation from the production zones was in the hands of the Turks, with refining and distribution predominantly controlled by the French; the 1970s until mid 1980s, when Turkey ceased to produce opium but maintained its distribution network, whilst the "French connection" run by the Corsicans was destroyed and replaced by the Sicilian mafia; and the present situation, in which the Sicilian element has fluctuated in importance, redefined by the lacerations of cross-clan warfare, arrests and trials in Europe and the United States, the consolidation of the Colombian drug cartels and intensified activities on the part of the Chinese and Japanese, especially in moving heroin across the Pacific to the US and Australia.

Until the 1950s the United States consumed between 10 and 13 mt per annum of heroin of which 80 per cent was sent via the "French connection" – the Marseilles criminal organisation dominated by the four Corsican families Venturi, Francisci, Guerini and Orsini. Their monopoly was dented after two important meetings held in 1957 in Appalachian, New York State and Palermo, Sicily between the Italian *Cosa Nostra* and the US mafia, after which the Italian involvement in heroin grew rapidly.

In the early 1970s the Marseilles ring was smashed by the French under pressure from the United States, and control passed to the Sicilian clans of Bontade, Spatola, Inzerillo, Badalamenti and Gambino whose family networks spanned the Atlantic and safeguarded supply and distribution routes. Although overall supervision came from the top level of the *Cosa Nostra* hierarchy, each family or clan could act on its own behalf, using men and means as deemed suitable. Numerous individuals were active in the trade who were not sworn mafia members – couriers, transporters, chemists and financiers.

Four heroin refineries were operating in Sicily in the mid 1970s, each with the capacity to produce around 50 kg of heroin per week. By 1980, when the first laboratory was discovered, it is believed the Sicilians had supplied the US with between 4 and 5 mt of pure heroin, approximately 30 per cent of the country's consumption. The net profits would have been around 700–800 billion lire per annum (at 1990 exchange rates £350–400 million).[8]

A four-city study involving New York, Naples, Paris and London identified six main links in the heroin distribution network. These were:

- importers of quantities in excess of 10 kg
- wholesalers able to purchase quantities from 2–3 up to 10 kg and who resell in much smaller denominations (usually under one kg) to
- intermediate distributors
- dealer/traffickers "by weight" who purchase small quantities and resell even smaller – from 10 gm downwards to
- street dealers and
- consumer/dealers – both these last two categories buy on average two grammes at a time both to finance and satisfy their own addiction.

The authors of the Naples study classified the profit margins made by the six categories as follows – importers: 370 per cent; wholesalers: 135 per cent distributors: 90 per cent; dealers "by weight": 40 per cent; street dealers: 54 per cent; consumer/dealers: 12 per cent.[9]

One of the main suppliers of morphine base and heroin to the Sicilian mafia was a Singapore Chinese based in Bangkok named Koh Bak Kin. He first came to police notice when he was arrested in Rome in 1976 in possession of 20 kg of heroin. On his release in 1980 he returned to Bangkok and from September 1981 began supplying the mafia families with whom he had made contact in prison. From this time onwards many of the important heroin seizures made in Europe involved couriers and drugs supplied by Koh Bak Kin.

After police had located three heroin refineries in the Palermo area in 1980, the mafia began to increase the quantities purchased of refined heroin relative to morphine base. The drug would be brought into Italy by air via Stockholm or Copenhagen and stored prior to distribution in suitcases in Rome or Florence railway stations. For larger consignments ships were used: in May 1983 the Greek registered ship Alexandros G was impounded in the Suez Canal with a consignment of arms and 233 kg of pure Thai heroin on board.

The mafia set up an important structure in Britain in 1976 under the supervision of Altofonte boss Francesco Di Carlo. Officially Di Carlo ran a travel agency, an hotel, a bureau de change, a wine bar and an antiques business, all of which he had paid for in cash. Unofficially he trafficked in marijuana from Kashmir and heroin from Thailand concealed in furniture imports to the UK and sent on to Canada. He was joined in 1983 by Alfonso and Pasquale Caruana, prominent members of the Caruana/Cuntrera clan from the southern Sicilian town of Siculiana, who bought luxury mansions close to Di Carlo's opulent home in Woking.

Investigations began with the discovery by Felixstowe customs officials of

*Global Drug Trafficking* 7

£750,000 worth of cannabis hidden in desks. The crates were repacked and delivered to a Mitcham transport company where the Sicilians awaiting their arrival were arrested. Checks at the intended final destination of Montreal led investigators to mafia-run companies in Canada and the UK. In May 1985 Customs officials at Southampton discovered 60 kg of pure heroin also en route for Canada, carefully built into items of furniture. Again part of the consignment was repacked and sent on, permitting the arrest in Canada of three Sicilians, including one of the Caruana brothers, Gerlando. Di Carlo was subsequently arrested in possession of 37 kg of heroin and sentenced to 25 years' imprisonment by an Old Bailey court, but Alfonso and Pasquale Caruana escaped to Caracas, where they continue to supervise their multinational drug trafficking and money laundering interests under the benevolent eye of the Venezuelan authorities.

According to a study by Arlacchi and Lewis,[10] the town of Verona, in North East Italy was the nerve centre of a complex drug trafficking network extending through seven European and Asian countries. The principal components of this network were:

- A group of six wholesale morphine base and heroin suppliers resident in Syria, Southern Turkey and in towns close to the frontiers with Iran, Afghanistan and Pakistan.
- Eight transporters, partly answerable to the suppliers and partly to a Yugoslavian crime organisation which guaranteed delivery of the drug to the Sicilians and to Verona, Bolzano and Trento – feeder markets for Northern Italy and Germany.
- Eight "custodians/mediators/distributors" based in Verona, Bolzano, Trento and Milan consisting of ex-smugglers and con men with long experience of illicit trade between the Middle East and Central Europe.

This network was able to import about four mt of morphine base and heroin (50:50) per annum to the two principal Italian centres of Milan and Palermo. The same structure was used for the clandestine export of arms bought in Italy and sent back to terrorist or nationalist groups in the Middle East. The system worked successfully for 10 years thanks to the low criminal profile of most of its operators, skilful mediation between the Italians and the Middle Eastern crime organisations, and a low violence level which kept them out of public and police attention.

Arlacchi and Lewis estimated that annual heroin consumption in Verona was 72.75 kg of heroin at 80 per cent purity (compared with their previous studies of Naples (1984) – 74 kg and Rome (1986) – 87 kg). The average Verona drug addict, they concluded, spent 15.6 million lire a year (£7,800) to maintain the habit.

## THE GOLDEN TRIANGLE

1988 illicit opium production: 1,298–1,833 mt; 1989: 3,050 mt (INSCR).

8                    *Research Institute for the Study of Conflict and Terrorism*

**Thailand**

Estimated illicit opium production 1988: 23–33 mt; 1989: 50 mt; hectares cultivated 1988: 4,604; 1989: 4,795.

Thailand outlawed the cultivation of the opium poppy in 1958, although until the mid 1970s approximately 150 mt of opium was produced per annum. Cultivation takes place almost exclusively in Northern Thailand by Highland tribes of mainly Chinese or Burmese origin in mountainous, jungle covered areas almost inaccessible by road. The opium specialists are the Meo tribes, numbering about 60,000, who devote themselves almost exclusively to poppy production. Growers make little more than subsistence living since farming methods are primitive and offer little protection against disease and weather. The planting season for the poppy is staggered: it begins in late August or early September with harvesting between December and March.

The next link in the chain, the opium dealers known as the *Haw*, are Chinese emigrés of many generations from the Yunnan province. The *Haw* go to deal directly with the growers, often paying in advance for the opium, and sell or barter primary goods such as salt, sugar, tea and shoes. They are also usurers, lending money at rates of 10–20 per cent per month. They see to the transportation of opium down to the plains where they either refine the drug themselves or resell it at 100 per cent profit.

Overall supervision of the drug in transit is in the hands of Chinese syndicates or *Triads*, originally from the Swatow region of China. The dominant figure in the golden triangle is currently believed to be a certain Chang Chi Fu, usually known as *Khun Sa* ("Warlord"), a native of Taiwan, who allegedly collects taxes, bribes important officials – especially in Bangkok and Hong Kong, where sectors of police and local administrators have been corrupted – and organises the marketing of the product. *Khun Sa*'s army of 10,000 men, fully equipped with the latest weaponry, provides armed escorts for the opium caravans which leave from March to June for the refineries on the Thai/Myanmar border or for those in Myanmar itself.

With its excellent air and road links, Thailand is currently the main country for South East Asian heroin going to international markets. The drug is transported by air on passenger or cargo flight, by sea in passenger ships, container cargoes or fishing boats, and over land by haulage truck. Although the greatest quantity of heroin leaves Thailand by air and sea, Chinese reports of large seizures of Thai heroin suggest that land routes are increasingly being used. India and Malaysia are other major transit countries. Some refining is done in Thailand, but less than in Laos or Myanmar. Precursor chemicals manufactured in Europe enter Thailand through its southern border although it is reported that traffickers have been able to produce acetic anhydride from chemical substances readily available at local markets.

In recent years the Royal Thai government has put considerable effort into its anti-drugs commitment but this has been hindered by widespread corruption at lower police and administrative levels. Although Thailand has severe laws against consumption and trafficking, its penal code does not include the concept of conspiracy, thus making it difficult to prosecute without the physical presence of drugs. Crop eradication began in 1984/85 and in the course of the 1988/89 growing cycle it is estimated that 37 per cent of total planting was destroyed. Seven major traffickers were arrested in 1989 and eight refineries discovered and destroyed (INSCR/UN).

Drug abuse and the spread of AIDS also cause concern – Thailand has between 100,000 and 300,000 addicts who inject pure heroin in doses which would be fatal for the western consumer; the first HIV positive cases were reported in August 1987 but by 1989 between 30 and 40 per cent of addicts tested proved to be carriers.

The Japanese *Yakuza* feature prominently in the Thai drugs trade, especially in Bangkok, where in the early 1980s they took over clandestine gambling dens, night clubs, prostitution rings and other illegal rackets. Yet not only do they not traffic heroin back to Japan but apparently make active efforts to prevent it from entering the country. Japan has no real narcotics abuse problem because the *Yakuza* believe the government is right to forbid trade in these substances. The consistency of views between official culture and deviant culture extends to an ambiguity regarding psychotropic drugs, widely and increasingly abused in Japan. Although trafficking and consumption of narcotic and psychotropic drugs are punished equally, the *Yakuza* appear to have benefited by endorsing official moral disapproval of the former and exploiting unofficial tolerance of the latter.

## Myanmar (formerly Burma)

Myanmar is currently the world's largest producer of illicit opium. 1988 production: approx 1,280 mt; 1989: 1,650–2,625 mt. Yield: approx 12 kg per hectare (INSCR).

The 1989 crop was especially fruitful thanks to excellent weather and to increased cultivation. Excesses in production in any given year cause no problem for opium producers and traffickers since the crop can be stockpiled and held in reserve for leaner years.

Cultivation takes place in small fields, especially in the east and north of the country in remote zones of the Shan, Kachin and Kayah states. The Shan plateau, at an altitude of 1,000 metres, is considered the world's prime growing area for the opium poppy. The tropical climate ensures a mean annual temperature of 80 degrees Fahrenheit, while the rainy season from June to October provides about 90 per cent of the yearly 80 inch rainfall. The cultivation areas are populated by ethnic minorities such as Karen (7 per cent), Shan (6 per cent), Indian (6 per cent) and Chinese (3 per cent) and have a long tradition of hostility and opposition to the Burmese (72 per cent) domination. The seizure of power by General Ne Win in 1962 aggravated the grievances of independence movements in these areas and was also bitterly opposed by the Burmese Communist Party until its dissolution in March/April 1989.

Officially poppy cultivation has been banned since independence in 1948 but this has only sporadically been enforced, thanks to central government fears of provoking an intensification of ethnic resentment. Since the uprising of September 1988 it is believed that the government is more anxious to maintain the *status quo* than to fight the drug traffickers. US sources believe that the regime now tolerates the activities of the *Shan United Army*, the most powerful drug trafficking organisation, and has reached agreements with the *Wa* and *Kokang* organisations (INSCR).

Myanmar has long borders with China, India and Thailand through which the drug is trafficked, although it is believed that increasing amounts are going through Laos, Cambodia and Vietnam. US officials estimate that between 105 and 175 mt of refined narcotics were produced in refineries in Myanmar from the 1989 opium crop, of which approx 40 per cent came from the northern Shan state refineries and 60 per cent from refineries along the Myanmar/Thailand border. Acetic anhydride is imported from China, India and Malaysia (INSCR).

### Laos

Laos is currently the world's third largest producer of opium. An estimated 255 mt were produced from the 1988 yield, and this figure rose to 375 in 1989. Much of the yield from Laos is controlled by Chinese *Triads* who take the drug to small mobile refineries on the Lao/Thai border from where Hong Kong transporters take it to Australia, Da Nang (Vietnam) and to Hong Kong itself.

The country's efforts to combat opium production and heroin trafficking were considered patchy until 1988 when anti-narcotics legislation was introduced and international assistance was requested to deal with trafficking and drug abuse problems.

### THE GOLDEN CRESCENT

Illicit opium production 1988: 1,090-1,420 mt; 1989: 1,015 mt. Hectares cultivated 1988: 36,296; 1989: 25,510.

### Pakistan

Opium production in Pakistan increased throughout the 1980s until 1985, then declined in 1987/88 to 205 mt and in 1988/89 to 130 mt. This was due partly to poor weather at planting time and partly to crop eradication. Estimates for the 1989/90 crop after eradication are predicted to be 118–128 mt.

The principal areas of production are remote, inaccessible mountain areas of the North West Frontier Province and the Afghanistan/Pakistan border. It is estimated that around 100 mobile, primitive refineries for the conversion of opium to morphine base and from morphine base to heroin are operating in the border zones, particularly in the Khyber Agency next to Afghanistan and close to the main highway connecting the Khyber to the rest of the country. This is the chief production zone for injectible heroin, or heroin No. 4. The seven million tribal inhabitants of the area are virtually a law unto themselves. Most of the opium grown here is taken over the border into

Afghanistan by Kurdish or Pathan tribesmen; from there a proportion goes to Iran for domestic consumption, some is taken on to Istanbul by Kurds and some is loaded on to small boats in the Persian Gulf or the Gulf of Oman and taken to Dubai. A frequently used trans-shipment point is Karachi, also a stage on the Eastern route to Hong Kong and Singapore.

Pakistan has been jolted into tackling drug trafficking not only by international pressure but also by the country's own spiralling drug problem. In the space of 10 years Pakistan went from having no drug misuse problem at all to a heroin addiction rate of 700,000, a figure which was revised up to 1.2 million in 1989.

## Iran

Opium production estimates for both 1987/88 and 1988/89: 200–400 mt.

Despite an official ban on production since 1980 and death penalties for traffickers and for those in possession of 30 grammes or more of heroin, Iran has a severe abuse problem estimated at almost two million heroin addicts. Domestic production is not enough to meet internal demand and opiates are imported from Afghanistan and Pakistan. However a proportion of the Iranian production is exported from Iran with Afghan and Pakistani heroin to Turkey or other Middle Eastern countries such as Lebanon and Syria, where it is transformed into morphine base. Some is destined for the European market, some is sent on to the United States, in particular to California, where drug traffickers have been active within the large Iranian communities (DEA). Once again, refining and distribution appear to be controlled by ethnic minorities: principal laboratories are situated in the Kurdish controlled sectors of North West Iran and in the Baluchi tribal sectors of the South East.

## Afghanistan

Opium production estimates: 1988: 700–800 mt; 1989: 585 mt.

Afghanistan is currently the world's second largest opium producing country. Opium poppy cultivation has been officially banned since 1957, but weak administration, the inaccessibility of the production areas and their domination by tribal forces made the ban ineffectual even before the Soviet invasion drove the resistance commanders to finance their struggle by exchanging drugs for arms.

Over 80 per cent of opium is grown in the northern province of Nangarhar and in the Helmand Valley in southern Afghanistan. The ethnic link between Baluchi tribesmen on both sides of the Afghan/Iran border provides the transitional link which safeguards the traffic. Although the Kabul government has promised a commitment to fighting the drugs traffic, the prospects for this being effective in the short term are poor, given the continuing ethnic/religious tensions and the disastrous state of the country's economy, for which a thriving drugs trade is likely to be a major incentive.

**Transit countries**

Routes used by traffickers to transport drugs are continually being modified. In general however, the most favoured itinerary from South West Asia has been through Turkey (via Istanbul and Ankara) through Bulgaria and Yugoslavia to Italy and Austria–the so-called Balkan corridor. Other routes from Bulgaria via Hungary and Rumania to Austria are of secondary importance.

The United States pressurised Turkey into ceasing opium poppy production altogether in 1971 after official reports that 80 per cent of heroin in the US came from Turkey via France. Since Turkish opium is of an extremely high quality and much valued by the pharmaceutical industry, the ban was modified in 1974 to allow introduction of the concentrated poppy straw method by which codeine and morphine can be extracted.

Despite the success of the poppy growing ban, Turkey continues to occupy a pivotal role in illicit traffic thanks to the organisational network set up during the producing years. This established an important two-directional conduit for both drugs and arms between the Middle East and Western Europe and found cover in the presence of thousands of Turkish immigrants in Western European cities.

The predominantly Kurdish town of Baskale, near the Turkish/Iranian border is an important transit point for heroin going westwards. In this area primitive refineries convert opium into morphine base ready for transportation by lorry to Istanbul. A courier will be paid 150 dollars to bring one kg of heroin into Turkey from Iran; from the Turkish border to Istanbul payment rises to 300 dollars. As the risks increase so do the wages, and on the next stage of the route from Istanbul via Bulgaria to the Yugoslav/Italian border drivers are paid 1,500 dollars per kilo transported.[11]

74 per cent of all the opiates seized in Europe transit through Turkey and Turkish nationals were involved in 70 per cent of all drug arrests and seizures in Europe in 1989. From the marked increase in seizures of acetic anhydride, it appears that more opium and morphine base are being processed before shipment than was once the case, due perhaps to the greatly diminished refining activities of the mafia. Laboratories for the conversion of morphine base to heroin have been discovered in Eastern Turkey and also in Istanbul. Most are small, primitive and mobile.

Until recently, frontier controls at the Turkish/Bulgarian and Bulgarian/Yugoslav borders were negligible. Duty free whisky, western cigarettes, coffee and hard currency would fend off awkward questions, and loads were only checked following specific customs indications. The situation has improved slightly since 1988 with the implementation of a control point on the Bulgarian/Yugoslav border at Gradino and the formal commitment of the Balkan countries to collaborate in the repression of drug trafficking; however with 1,000 TIR lorries using the Balkan corridor each day much remains to be done.

In recent years West Africa has become one of the favoured transit routes for Asian heroin, especially through the airports in Benin, Nigeria and Togo, and there are indications that traffickers may also be operating in Cameroon, Chad, Congo and Zaire (INCB). The drug arrives from Pakistan, India and Thailand.

Nigerian courier organisations are very active, and at least seven have been identified. Drugs are carried on or in the body, in special capsules produced by a Nigerian factory which escape airport security detection and allow the drug to be swallowed in safety. Tamils also find employment as couriers, bringing morphine base and heroin to Europe as a means of financing their independence struggle in Sri Lanka, assisted by the presence of some 10 million Tamils in India.

## PRODUCTION AND DISTRIBUTION – COCAINE

"Coca bush" means the plant of any species of the genus Erythroxylon. "Coca leaf" means the leaf of the coca bush except a leaf from which all ecgonine, cocaine and any other ecgonine alkaloids have been removed (*Single Convention on Narcotic Drugs*, 1961).

Cocaine is an alkaloid agent derived from coca erithroxylon and from other species of plant from the same family. It originates in western South America where it is chewed by between four and five million peasants to combat fatigue and hunger. It is legally grown in Peru and Bolivia; illegally grown in Peru, Bolivia, Colombia, and to a lesser extent, Ecuador and Brazil. It is a hardy and productive evergreen shrub which yields up to four crops per year. 500 kg of dry coca leaf produce 2.5 kg of coca paste, a product of about 25 per cent purity. Coca paste is then transformed into cocaine base: ivory coloured granules of 75 per cent purity which are then dried. The refinement from cocaine base to cocaine hydrochloride involves a further process. The end product is a white powder – cocaine HCl. This is cut or diluted for the consumer market.[12]

Cocaine can be inhaled through the nostrils, smoked or injected. It provokes excitement, loquacity, lack of inhibition, mental stimulation and a lessening of a sense of fatigue. It can cause heart problems, irregular breathing, dilation of pupils, diarrhoea and vomiting. Inhalation over a long period can cause erosion or rupture of the nasal membranes. Cocaine does not cause physical dependence, thus there are no withdrawal symptoms, but psychological dependence can be very strong. Cocaine HCl is water soluble and can be injected; when combined with heroin this is called speed ball. Cocaine freebase is obtained through another process. "Washing" this produces pure cocaine crystals which are smoked or vapourised in a pipe.

Crack first appeared in the Bahamas in 1981. It is a form of cocaine free-base which is sold in the form of pills or "rocks" of 1/4 to 1/5 gramme and is the smallest unit of cocaine available. Its cheapness relative to cocaine has caused its widespread diffusion and popularity – in 1989 crack cost £10–£15 per gm compared with cocaine HCl at £80–120 per gm (NDIU). Crack is usually smoked in a small glass pipe or in a cigarette and has a rapid and intense effect, 10 times more powerful than that of cocaine.

Colombian black marketeers led the cocaine revolution in the early 1970s.

| **Worldwide Production: 1986 1990** | | | | |
|---|---|---|---|---|
| Country | 1990 (Metric Tons) | 1989 (Metric Tons) | 1988 (Metric Tons) | 1987 (Metric Tons) | 1986 (Metric Tons) |
| **Opium** | | | | | |
| Afghanistan | 500–800 | 585 | 700–800 | 400–800 | 400–500 |
| Iran | 200–400 | 300 | 200–400 | 200–400 | 200–400 |
| Pakistan | 118–128 | 130 | 190–220 | 190–220 | 160–160 |
| Total SW Asia | 818–1,328 | 1,015 | 1,090–1,420 | 790–1,420 | 740–1,060 |
| Myanmar | 2,780 | 2,625 | 1,065–1,500 | 925–1,230 | 770–1,100 |
| Laos | 300–450 | 375 | 210–300 | 150–300 | 100–290 |
| Thailand | 40 | 50 | 23–33 | 20–45 | 20–25 |
| Total SE Asia | 3,120–3,270 | 3,050 | 1,298–1,833 | 1,095–1,575 | 820–1,415 |
| Guatemala | 6 | 14 | | | |
| Lebanon | 45 | 45 | | | |
| Mexico | 85 | 85 | 45–55 | 45–55 | 35–50 |
| Total | 136 | 144 | | | |
| Total Opium | 4,074–4,734 | 4,209 | 2,433–3,308 | 1,930–3,050 | 1,595–2,525 |
| **Coca** | | | | | |
| Bolivia | 64,000 | 65,998 | 57,445–78,355 | 46,000–67,000 | 44,000–52,920 |
| Colombia | 33,360 | 33,487 | 19,000–24,200 | 18,000–23,000 | 12,000–13,600 |
| Peru | 108,544 | 123,828 | 97,000–124,000 | 98,000–121,000 | 95,000–120,000 |
| Ecuador | 170 | 270 | 300–500 | 400 | 1,000 |
| **Total Coca** | **206,074** | **223,583** | **173,745–227,055** | **162,400–211,400** | **152,000–187,520** |

Source: INSCR.

From a dominant position in illicit emerald smuggling and then in marijuana trafficking, they were encouraged by a series of factors to switch over to cocaine: marijuana was easily and increasingly grown in the United States; a series of FBI raids on US amphetamine laboratories had caused prices to rise, availability to fall and consumption to be more risky; cocaine was rapidly becoming the vogue drug for the trendy rich who believed it was non-addictive and loved the intense high it produced; profit margins were higher than for marijuana, and international marketing possibilities apparently limitless.

The South American move from marijuana to cocaine follows a similar pattern to that which occurred when first the Corsican/French and then the Neapolitan/Sicilian crime organisations expanded from cigarette smuggling to heroin. In each case illicit structures of individuals, transport and finances were already in place; accumulated profits from the previous activity permitted a qualitative leap to make new investments for the streamlining and greater impermeability of the network.

### Colombia

Illicit cultivation of coca bush: 33,487 mt. An estimated 566 mt of cocaine were refined or distributed in Colombia or by Colombian organisations in

1989 compared with 508 in 1988 (INSCR). Most is refined from coca paste or cocaine base originating in Peru and Bolivia. Colombia is the third largest coca producer although the leaf grown here is less valued since it has a lower cocaine alkaloid content and therefore requires a higher proportion of leaves to make a single kg of cocaine. 65 per cent (173 mt) of cocaine base produced in Bolivia is refined in Colombia or else refined into cocaine HCl in Bolivia and then distributed through Colombia. 90 per cent of Peruvian cocaine base (335 mt cocaine HCl) is refined in Colombia (INSCR).

The most prominent trafficking organisations in the Andean region are based in the Colombian cities of Medellin and Cali. Between them the two cartels account for approximately 60 to 70 per cent of all Andean cocaine traffic, the remainder being shared out between another 50 smaller organisations. It is estimated that the Cali and Medellin cartels take four billion dollars annual revenue, of which one billion dollars remains in Colombia, the rest goes abroad. The profit margin over the entire production/distribution chain ranges from 6,000 to 10,000 per cent.

The Cali cartel is headed by the brothers Gilberto and Miguel Angel Rodriguez Orijuela and Jose Santacruz-Londono; Medellin is controlled by Pablo Escobar Gaviria and the brothers Jorge and Fabio Ochoa. Gonzalo Rodriquez Gacha, known as "the Mexican" was another leading member of the Medellin cartel, but was killed by police along with his son and 11 bodyguards in December 1989. In general terms, it is throught Gacha was responsible for the supply of coca base and cocaine paste to the refineries, Escobar supervised production and the Ochoas took care of the financial side and of distribution.[13] Wheras the Cali cartel leaders tend to be middle class, discreet and keep a low profile, the Medellin leaders have varied backgrounds, have almost all had spells in prison and until recently, have publicly and ostentatiously enjoyed the trappings of great wealth. From petty thief and small-time trafficker Pablo Escobar rose in less than 10 years to being the 14th richest man in the world outside the United States.

Although cocaine trafficking is a generally disapproved-of activity in Colombia, the cartels have gained some public support amongst the poorer sectors of the population for their philanthropic gestures: houses, schools, hospitals and sports grounds in Medellin owe their construction to cocaine profits. Escobar's philosophy, on which he bribed and threatened his way into election as congressman in 1982, was that coca production was a source of pride and wealth which could guarantee widespread prosperity for Colombia and liberation from the tyranny of the United States. His rhetoric had some appeal; Colombia's economy is thriving in comparison to its South American neighbours – it is the world's second largest coffee producer and is fourth in gold production – however the stability of the coffee price depends upon the United States' adherence to an international coffee agreement from which it broke away in 1988. Estimates of the loss to the Colombian economy vary from 400 to 1,000 million dollars. Colombia is also a country of great social inequalities – 4 per cent of the population own 68 per cent of cultivatable land whilst out of a population of 28 million, 13 million live in conditions of abject poverty.[14]

Another factor which distinguishes the Colombian cartels is the way in which they exercise violence: the Cali cartel has conducted fewer attacks against state representatives, possibly due to its infiltration of state power at a higher level than its rival. It is reputed to have the support of certain sections of the military who protect or collude with some of the 140 paramilitary groups of the far right in carrying out assassinations of left wing politicians or supporters. The Medellin cartel is more openly vindictive and posits itself in blatant opposition to democratic forces. Public criticism brings fatal consequences: the two policemen who arrested Pablo Escobar in 1976 were later murdered, as was the judge who tried him. On Escobar's election to Congress the newspaper El Espectador published a photograph of his arrest; the paper's editor was murdered in 1986. In the course of the 1980s more than 50 judges were killed by narco-traffickers or those working on their behalf; between 1985 and March 1990 2,011 members of the police and armed forces were killed and 3,384 injured.[15] In one of three attempts on the life of the Director of Colombia's security police force (DAS), Brigadier Miguel Alfredo Maza, a bomb explosion in DAS headquarters killed 70 and injured many more, although Maza, secure in his fortified office, was unhurt.

The fundamental issue over which the Medellin cartel challenges the democratic state is that of extradition, and in particular the 1979 treaty with the United States which has periodically been exhumed, activated and dropped. Justice Minister Rodrigo Lara Bonilla promised tougher action against drug traffickers on assuming office in August 1983 and ordered the re-opening of the Escobar case after his election to Congress: he was assassinated in April 1984. In November 1985 the Colombian Supreme Court was about to deliver its verdict on the validity of the extradition treaty when the Palace of Justice was occupied by the M-19 guerrilla group with the backing of the Medellin traffickers. The building was stormed and over 100 were killed, including all the 15 judges present. During the hiatus of the next two years one major Colombian trafficker, Carlos Lehder Rivas, was extradited in record time to the United States but in June 1987 the treaty was declared unconstitutional. Commitment to its revival, promised by presidential candidate Luis Carlos Galan, was the cause of his assassination in August 1989.

Far left terrorist formations and far right paramilitary groups have seriously undermined the Colombian fight against drug trafficking, the far left by using it as a tool of revolutionary struggle, the right by direct collusion with the traffickers themselves. Of the 50 or so Marxist groups active in the 1970s and 1980s it is believed only five still operate. The oldest and most proficient is FARC (Colombian Armed Revolutionary Forces) which still has around 5,000 members, active mainly in rural areas. M-19 began discussions with government authorities at the end of the 1980s and formally laid down arms in September 1989; FARC is reportedly thinking of doing the same.

Opposition to the Marxist guerrillas in the 1970s led to the formation of a "national defence movement" known as MORENA based in the central Colombian area of Middle Magdalena, where its links with narco-traffickers have been proven. This organisation is believed to be responsible for some

400 murders of left wing sympathisers in 1988 and for the murders in March 1990 of presidential candidate Bernardo Jaramillo, leader of the left wing party Unione Patriotica, and of former M-19 leader Carlos Pizarro in April, whose canditature in democratic elections a month before had brought him 8 per cent of the popular vote. Foreign mercenaries and experts such as former Mossad General Yair Klein have been brought in to train the paramilitary squads on behalf of the cartels. Another unholy alliance may have been formed with the Basque independence organisation ETA, whose responsibility claim for the explosion aboard a Colombian civil airliner in November 1989 which killed 111 people was given credibility by the use of the explosive Semtex to which ETA is known to have access.

With the run-up to the presidential elections in May 1990, terror tactics continued, designed to intimidate the electorate and sabotage the election of those committed to continue the war against the narco-traffickers. In May 1990, Colombian police reported 8,831 murders and 86 kidnaps since the start of the year. 130 policemen were killed in Medellin alone.[16]

Despite the strength of the forces arraigned against them, Colombian anti-narcotics efforts have brought notable successes: cocaine seizures soared from just over 3 mt in 1986 to 30.6 in 1989. In the same year 3,607 arrests were made and 452 laboratories destroyed (Colombian government statistics).

## Peru

Peru is the world's largest producer of coca leaf. INSCR figures put total cultivation area of coca bush (licit and illicit) at 120,415 hectares of which approximately 10,000 is for licit production, but this figure is considerably lower than the 200,000 hectares reported as under cultivation by the Director of the Anti-Drugs Police of the Peruvian Interior Ministry.[17]

Estimated illicit production 1988: 97,000–124,000 mt; 1989: 123,828 mt. An ideal Peruvian conditions one hectare can produce up to 120 kg of coca leaf every 3 months.

65 per cent of all the coca grown in Peru is produced in the Upper Huallaga Valley. Chemicals such as kerosene, sulphuric acid, potassium permanganate and ammonia are all produced domestically and have too many commercial uses to be controlled. There are official government controls over ether and acetone but these either escape detection during the various stages of distribution or else are smuggled into Peru by river and road routes. The refining of coca leaves into paste takes place in small, well-equipped laboratories from where the drug is taken to Colombia, usually in illegally registered small planes.

Peru has a national plan for eradication which has led to the voluntary destruction of some 18,000 hectares but development programmes involving crop conversion have been hampered by economic instability and a soaring inflation rate which in 1989 was 2,600 per cent. Corruption within the poorly paid categories of the police and judiciary is a continuing problem, according to the US State Department.

A series of anti-narcotics operations were conducted in Peru between

August 1985 and October 1988 during which 850 mt of coca leaf and 106 mt of cocaine were seized, 183 clandestine airstrips detected, 76 cocaine laboratories destroyed and 1,325 arrests made (DND).

Anti-narcotics efforts have been severely contested by the Maoist group *Sendero Luminoso* (Shining Path) whose guerrilla warfare against the state since 1980 has directly favoured the drugs traffic. In 1987 the organisation moved into the Upper Huallaga Valley where it exploited local anti-government feeling provoked by crop eradication efforts and began a self-interested defence of the coca-growing *campesino* livelihood. It entered into separate agreements with both traffickers and *campesinos,* and extorts an estimated 30 million dollars per year from the former in exchange for protection of production areas and transit routes.[18] Obedient silence and non co-operation with government are expected of the *campesinos,* in return for which *Sendero Luminoso* negotiates a guaranteed minimum selling price for coca.

Between February and September 1989 a concentrated assault by *Sendero Luminoso* brought anti-drug efforts to a virtual standstill. In retaliation against the use of the herbicide Spike, the *senderos* surrounded a 50 man garrison in the town of Uchiza, forced its surrender and shot the officers. The presence of 300 to 500 guerrillas in the Santa Lucia area induced the Peruvian government to declare the Upper Huallaga Valley a military emergency zone under the control of a zone commander.

In late 1989 a joint Peruvian/US military base at Santa Lucia was reinforced both as an anti-guerrilla outpost and as an anti-narcotics base. A number of laboratories were destroyed, equipment and weapons were seized, arrests were made and 179 clandestine airstrips were discovered and blasted with dynamite. Nonetheless the twin aims of severing the links between traffickers and guerrillas and that of the eradication and interdiction of drugs has caused an overlap between police and military roles in the area and tension between the two forces – to detrimental consequences for both objectives. Prior warning required by the zone commander before interdiction raids take place suggest he is prepared to tolerate trafficking activities in exchange for intelligence on *Sendero Luminoso* from the traffickers and peasants. As in Colombia, traffickers have set up social centres for the benefit of the *campesinos* to win their loyalty and set them against the authorities.

**Bolivia**

Bolivia is the second largest world producer of coca, with a cultivation area of approximately 53,920 hectares in 1989, a 9.2 per cent increase in hectarage over 1988. Coca leaf production for 1988: 57,445–78,355 mt; 1989: 80,004 mt of which 65,998 mt was converted into 261 mt of cocaine HCl (INSCR).

The main coca growing area of Bolivia used to be the lower Andean foothills of the Yungas region but nowadays 70 per cent of the crop is grown in the semi-tropical lowlands of the Chaparé province. Since the leaf in this area is unsuitable for chewing the entire production is presumed to be given over to the export market. Some 30 organisations buy up most of the coca production of the Chaparé Valley and either process it themselves or sell on direct to Colombian traffickers. Precursor chemicals are smuggled in from neighbouring countries. A proportion of Bolivian coca paste is refined into cocaine and distributed through Argentina and Brazil for the European market and a significant amount also goes directly to the United States.

Bolivia's 189th *coup d'état* in 1980, encouraged and financed by drug baron Roberto Suarez Gomez, gave a major stimulus to the growth of the coca trade. Although General Luis García Meza remained President for only one year before being deposed, he and his Interior Minister, Luis Arce Gomez (Suarez's cousin), devoted most of their efforts to promotion and protection of the cocaine traffic.

Other contributing factors were economic, as a UN study shows:

> The coca leaf boom took off in 1982–83, at the same time that economic recession and a severe drought brought havoc in the rural highlands. Bolivia's gross national product declined by 17 per cent between 1980 and 1985, per capita consumption fell by 30 per cent, per capita income by 20 per cent and unemployment doubled. Terms of trade for farmers suffered from inflation of 2,800 per cent in 1984 and 10,000 per cent in 1985. In 1985, producers of coca leaves could earn 9,000 dollars from 2.2 acres, while those growing the next most profitable crop, citrus fruits, were averaging only 500 dollars from plots of the same size.[19]

Between 1985 and 1988 Bolivia increased coca production by 107 per cent despite government efforts to combat it. A four month joint exercise was carried out in 1986 by the US military together with Bolivian police known as "Operation Blast Furnace" whose aim was to find and destroy drug processing laboratories. In 1987 the Bolivian government presented a three year project which envisaged the eradication in 1988 of all the plantations in the Chaparé region and 80 per cent of those in the Yungas region, but the plan failed since it was dependent upon US subsidies which came nowhere near making crop substitution a viable alternative.

With the support of the United Nations Fund for Drug Abuse Control, economic development and crop substitution programmes have been introduced with some success, especially in the latter half of 1989. Corruption continues to be a major problem in the judiciary, the police and the military although law enforcement has been improved with UN and DEA assistance: Roberto Suarez was arrested in 1988 and is still in prison; Luis Arce Gomez was extradited to the United States in 1989 on trafficking charges; during the first few months of the year approximately 760 cocaine laboratories were dismantled (DND).

**Distribution and Transit**

Intensified law enforcement activities on the part of the Colombian government since August 1989 and the greater commitment in general demonstrated by Peru, Bolivia and Colombia to fighting drug trafficking have deflected some trafficking activities to neighbouring countries such as Ecuador and in particular Brazil. Brazil is now not only a major transit country between South America and African countries but is believed to produce coca in 12 of its 23 states.[20] Four processing laboratories were discovered in the second half of

1989 in the Amazonian jungle, each capable of processing 200 kg of cocaine HCl each day.

Ghana, Kenya, Madagascar, the Ivory Coast, Mauritius and Nigeria also give cause for concern: once these were used simply as transit countries but in recent years serious drug abuse problems have arisen and UN assistance has been requested.

The principal routes taken from the cocaine refining laboratories in Colombia to the main consumer markets are shown in the diagram of The Cocaine Trail. The DEA reports that 50 per cent of all US cocaine is now distributed through Los Angeles, the rest via Mexico and Florida. If it is carried overland from Mexico the courier or "mule" may expect to receive 1,000 dollars per journey. A pilot flying a load of cocaine in an unregistered plane from Colombia into the US by night without the assistance of lights or radar may earn between 250,000 and 500,000 dollars.

The DEA maintains that the Cali cartel takes a larger share of the US cocaine market than its rival Medellin thanks to a network of 10,000 nationals working on its behalf around the country. However the pattern varies from city to city. According to Colombian sources, New Orleans is run by Medellin; Miami is shared amongst Medellin, Cali, Cubans and Puerto Ricans; Cali controls San Diego with the Mexicans; Los Angeles is split between Cali, Jamaicans and Haitians; New York is also Cali territory, divided up with the Sicilian Mafia.[21]

Crack tends to be distributed in America by West Indian nationals. Jamaican groups (allegedly with some political cover) have the largest share in the American East and Midwest – New York, Kansas City, Denver and Maryland. Haitians control Florida, Georgia, the south of Delaware, the east of Maryland and New York State, and hold the dubious honour of being the only producers of crack in rectangles or "french fries". The Dominicans run Connecticut and Rhode Island whilst crack in California north of Los Angeles is monopolised by black criminal groups from LA.[22]

The scattered archipelagoes of the Caribbean are vitally important both as money laundering centres and as transit points for drugs going to the US and to Europe. Islands having colonial links with France, Holland or Great Britain are frequent departure points for drugs leaving for those countries, concealed in consignments of regularly traded items.

British born Colombian resident Alan Knox skippered a Chilean registered ship which left Aruba in December 1987 with 600 kilos of cocaine hidden amongst an official load of fertiliser for delivery to a Spanish wholesaler. His route took him via Gibraltar to Castellamare del Golfo on the north west tip of Sicily where it was received in early January by Mafia importer Francesco Madonia. According to the detailed accounts kept by Madonia's son Antonio which were discovered during a police raid in Palermo, the Sicilians paid the Colombians 20,000 dollars per kg of cocaine; it was then resold to other mafia clans for sums ranging between 33,300 and 85,000 dollars per kg depending on the closeness of the relationship between the Madonias and the buying family.[23] As part of the deal the Mafia apparently insisted that all future deliveries were to be made in large consignments by sea and not by Colombian

*Global Drug Trafficking* 21

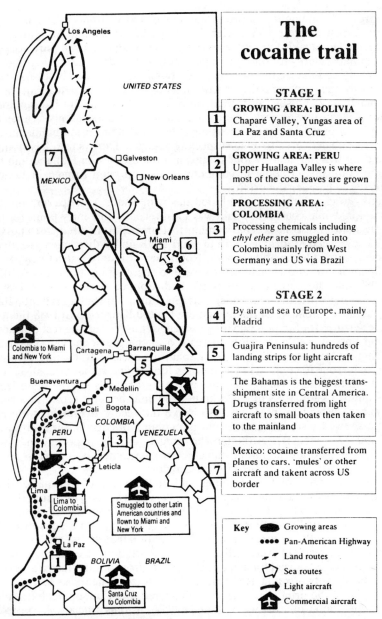

# The cocaine trail

## STAGE 1

**1** **GROWING AREA: BOLIVIA**
Chaparé Valley, Yungas area of
La Paz and Santa Cruz

**2** **GROWING AREA: PERU**
Upper Huallaga Valley is where
most of the coca leaves are grown

**3** **PROCESSING AREA:
COLOMBIA**
Processing chemicals including
*ethyl ether* are smuggled into
Colombia mainly from West
Germany and US via Brazil

## STAGE 2

**4** By air and sea to Europe, mainly
Madrid

**5** Guajira Peninsula: hundreds of
landing strips for light aircraft

**6** The Bahamas is the biggest trans-
shipment site in Central America.
Drugs transferred from light
aircraft to small boats then taken
to the mainland

**7** Mexico: cocaine transferred from
planes to cars, 'mules' or other
aircraft and takent across US
border

Key
- Growing areas
- •••• Pan-American Highway
- Land routes
- Sea routes
- Light aircraft
- Commercial aircraft

Reproduced by kind permission of *The Guardian*

couriers, whom they threatened to kill, and that ships making the return journey were to be loaded with heroin.

A three-way smuggling network was uncovered in London in early 1987 with the arrest of Detroit financier David Medin, caught on his way to the Dorchester Hotel with two suitcases containing 36 kg of almost pure cocaine. Medin collaborated with police and gave details of a drug trafficking organisation set up in 1986 by the Detroit mafia family Giacaloni. The cocaine was supplied by the Lopez family in Cochabamba, Bolivia, sealed inside heavy plant machinery and sent air freight via Buenos Aires and Rio De Janeiro to London's Heathrow airport. The cocaine in Medin's possession when he was arrested was part of a consignment imported to Britain inside bulldozer and JCB parts and delivered to an unsuspecting garage in Derbyshire. Distribution of the drug was handled by four groups in London, one in Holland and one in Italy; companies trading in computer parts had been formed in London and Jersey to launder the profits.

Thanks to close linguistic and blood ties with South America and most of all to a 4,000 mile coastline, Spain was until recently the entry point for half to three quarters of all cocaine coming to Europe. Both Medellin and Cali cartels established Madrid bases in the mid 1980s under their most prominent members, Jorge Ochoa and Gilberto Rodriquez-Orejuela respectively. However Spanish law enforcement efforts were so successful in the course of 1988 and 1989 that the percentage of traffic had dropped by the end of 1989 to around 30 per cent, the remainder entering Europe through Holland, Italy, the Federal Republic of Germany and the United Kingdom. In 1988 the total cocaine seizures for Spain – 3.45 mt – exceeded those for all the rest of Europe together and showed a threefold increase over the previous year (DND); In 1989 there were over 2,000 arrests in Spain for cocaine trafficking involving individuals from 70 countries, but seizures for the first six months of the year went down to a mere 640 kg. Seizures in the Netherlands, on the other hand, rose from 517 kg in 1988 to 1,425 kg in 1989 and the 3 mt seized in a single haul near Amsterdam in March 1990 broke the record overnight.[24] Overall, Europe showed a six-fold increase in the volume of cocaine seized between 1985 and 1989 (INCB). Although the drug is usually imported in a fully refined form, laboratories for the manufacture of cocaine have been discovered in France, Spain, Italy and the United Kingdom.

Further examples of transit routes and of the value of international co-operation in disrupting them came in 1989 with two Anglo/Dutch/Belgian operations codenamed "Tropical" and "Equator". "Tropical" began in June when the Tilburg Police Force, working with the narcotics section of the Belgian National Police force, received information that three Dutch nationals and a Belgian resident were active in the importation of cocaine, and that plans were well advanced for a cocaine shipment from South America through the ports of Antwerp and Rotterdam. The Dutch police also learned that some 20 kg of the drug were due to be delivered to a London dealer. At this point "Operation Equator" was initiated by UK customs officials. A controlled delivery of 12 kg of cocaine with a street value of almost £3m was intercepted at Harwich in August but police made this appear the work of a sniffer dog to avoid alerting other members of the group. The trick was successful, and across the North Sea the Dutch traffickers continued their activities. After a surveillance operation of some weeks police raided the homes of 11 suspects and a warehouse in the village of Wovw. 100 kg of high purity cocaine were concealed in 21 out of a total of 1,600 barrels of tar imported from Venezuela via the Belgian port of Antwerp.

By early 1989 the UK traffickers had reorganised and had access to a source of cocaine direct from Colombia. In February 1990 34 kg of cocaine hidden in a box of worthless brassware were delivered to a warehouse 45 miles north of London. The consignment had come on a direct flight from Bogotà to Heathrow the same day. The street value of the drug was in excess of £8 million. Seven arrests were made in addition to the organiser of the importation of the 12 kg intercepted in August. In all, the joint operations had led to the arrest of 20 drug traffickers and the seizure of 136 kg of high purity cocaine with a street value of over £30 million in the UK.[25]

## THE FINANCES OF ILLICIT DRUGS TRAFFIC

Illicit drug trafficking generates an annual income of over 500 billion dollars of which as much as 250 billion may be net profit.[26] In the UK, the Home Office reckons drug trafficking to be worth £1.8 billion per year, (3b dollars); Italy's High Commissioner against the Mafia, Domenico Sica, estimates that illicit drug revenues in Italy are 45,000 billion lire or £22.5 billion (37.5b dollars).

Profit margins are colossal, and all the more so because untaxed. The 1988 wholesale price of one kilo of heroin in Thailand was 3,400 to 5,600 dollars; the same kilo would have cost the British wholesaler 45,000 to 51,000 dollars, a US wholesaler 70,000 to 200,000 dollars, depending on purity levels and on the area purchased (near Mexico, for example, the price drops considerably). In the same year the retail price of one gramme of cut heroin, that is diluted to anything between 5 and 70 per cent purity was 112 to 225 dollars in the UK and 90 to 200 dollars in the US.

The Bolivian wholesale price of a kilo of cocaine including base and paste ranged in 1988 from 300 to 2,500 dollars. US and UK wholesalers paid 35,000 to 42,000 dollars and 47,000 to 57,000 dollars respectively. The street price for one gramme of cut cocaine in the same year was around 5 dollars in Colombia, 90 to 188 dollars in the UK and 10 to 15 dollars in the US. Varying purity levels account for wide price ranges at retail level. Comprehensive details of 1989 prices were not available at time of writing but indicate for cocaine at least, decreasing prices with increasing purity levels.

Estimates of the value of cocaine revenue in relation to the revenues of legal trade in the Andean countries vary considerably. The UN figure puts 1987 illicit cocaine exports for Bolivia, Peru and Colombia at 75 per cent, 14.5 per cent and 13.5 per cent of those countries' legal exports respectively; however Peruvian journalist Gustavo Gorritti suggests that the percentage is much higher: he claims that with an illegal drug revenue of one billion dollars, Bolivia's illegal earnings exceed those of the legal economy; that for Peru cocaine exports are 1.5b dollars against 2.5b dollars of legal exports, and that for Colombia the figure may be as much as 2 to 4 billion dollars of illicit revenue over 1987 official exports of 5.25 billion dollars.[27]

In contrast, money recovered from this enormous traffic has been derisory: assets to the value of 895 million dollars have been seized in the United States[28]; since the UK Drug Trafficking Offences Act (DTOA) came into force in January 1987 around £16 million has been confiscated (Home Office) despite evidence that over 50 million dollars has been laundered through London banks (INSCR); of the 1.6b dollars laundered in the famous "Pizza Connection" case only 60m has been traced.

Yet these profits have a corporeal existence and therefore cannot disappear altogether – they may be transferred secretly, disguised and re-invested but they do exist and therefore in principle are traceable. More than 100 billion dollars of drug trafficking profits are laundered each year, according to the financial experts.[29] Therefore the questions to be asked are:

- How are the profits from the illicit drugs traffic laundered?
- How are they used?
- Why, since the world must be awash with dirty money, has it been so difficult to find and prosecute the money movers?

## How drug profits are laundered

Money laundering has as its objective the securing of access to channels which conceal the illegal source of funds, make "dirty" money appear clean, and permit reinvestment in either legal or illegal activities. The financial cycle thus falls into three stages: accumulation, transformation and reinvestment of capital. The principal money laundering methods used, as proven by European and US judicial enquiries, are as follows:

- **Physical transformation of cash by courier**

- **"Compensation" system:** this operates through the use of trade accounts in more than one country. Thus a million dollars deposited in a company's trade account in New York would be available to the same company in its account in a Swiss branch of the bank. The advantage of this system to the money launderer is that since the money never physically moves, it is not subject to currency or customs controls.

- **Gambling/lottery:** large sums of small denomination bank notes can be exchanged for gambling chips or winning lottery tickets, then turned in for clean notes.

- **National banking systems:** current and deposit accounts are opened; these can be either in the name of fictitious persons; or in the name of accomplices whose business enterprises involve the rapid movement of large sums of cash; or in the names of front men who may have no other involvement in illicit trade. Until the mid 1980s almost all the profits from drug trafficking passed through official banking channels; however since the introduction of patrimonial enquiries and the obligation of banks to identify their clients and the source of their funds, banks are increasingly used only at an advanced stage of money laundering.

• **Fictitious commercial operations or inflated invoicing:** two cases are worth noting, both Sicilian. One involved the non-existent export of citrus fruit from Bagheria, near Palermo, by a former mayor of the town, Michelangelo Aiello, to an equally fictitious fruit juice manufacturing company in London run by one Raymond Kingsland. The only part of the transaction that was real was the 46 million dollars that finished up in Aiello's bank accounts in Sicily and Switzerland, almost certainly the product of heroin trafficking by mafia boss Leonardo Greco with whom Aiello was a business associate. Aiello also used his account with the Union des Banques Suisses in Bellinzona to invest on the Italian stock exchange.

The second case concerns three brothers of the wealthy Palermo jewellery family Fiorentino, arrested in 1985 for illegal exportation of funds totalling 30 billion lire. Before his murder the same year, Palermo Police Questor Nini Cassarà found evidence indicating that as well as violating Italian currency laws, the brothers were using inflated gold and jewellery invoices to a Maltese jeweller to launder drug profits on behalf of *Cosa Nostra*. The question of whether the family were victims or accomplices of the mafia was complicated by the 22 month kidnap of one of the brothers, released after ransom payment of 3.6 billion lire (£1.8m; 3m dollars). Rumours circulating after his release held that the kidnap may never have taken place and that the "ransom" may either have been pure extortion or alternately another means of laundering mafia money.

• **Exportation of currency to overseas banking institutions:** for instance to fiscal havens, especially those with politically corruptible or tolerant regimes and/or a high density of cash-intensive activities such as tourism and casinos.

• **Fictitious hire purchase/leasing contracts**

• **Formation of shell or façade companies:** these are particularly convenient wherever corporate and banking secrecy apply, for example in Liechtenstein, or on the island of Aruba, where since July 1988 the only requirement for setting up an Aruban Exempt Corporation (AEC) is 5,000 dollars of capital. The owner's identity may remain hidden by the issue of anonymous bearer shares (INSCR).

Façade companies are also popular with seasonal enterprises which use a "black" or clandestine workforce. In order to pay employees in cash, façade companies make up false invoices which apparently justify the exit of funds. The false invoices are paid for by cheques which are re-cashed in liquid form. An example of this was found in France, where an extensive network of 20 false companies employing "black" labour had a turnover of more than 20 million FF. In another case an important French bank opened a branch which specialised in the repatriation of savings of immigrant workers. It transpired that a number of drug traffickers had accounts here and that 7.5m FF worth of false entries for salaries had been passed through 80 suspect account holders.[30]

• **Formation of finance or other para-banking companies:** these are particularly prevalent in Italy where the area is subject to few regulations.

• **Manipulation of the stock exchange** (for example through insider trading), or of **other legitimate banking and intermediary financial services:** this may involve buying into common investment funds – certificates are made out to the bearer and can be sold as cash instruments. Another method discovered in Italy is the purchase of atypical stocks: for instance sharing partnership certificates; trust company stocks; shares of property investment funds and mixed stocks. This form of transaction is partially or totally unregulated.[31]

Several million Italians use Treasury Bonds (BOT) as a means of saving, and money launderers hide amongst them; in 1984 the Italian Finance Police confiscated 600 million lire (£300,000) in Treasury Bonds and 300 million in atypical stocks from one individual.

• **Foreign exchange bureaux:** used especially in large cities such as London, Miami and New York where they may escape the notice of the banking authorities.

• *Hawala:* Some forms of money laundering completely bypass conventional financial channels and are therefore particularly hard to detect. One is the primitive, totally informal system of *hawala,* meaning 'truth' in Hindi. This method was evolved and is used in perfect legality by Indians and Pakistanis but has been abused by drug traffickers. It relies on a system of trust between families or ethnic groups who may be thousands of miles apart, between whom a half playing card or a bus ticket can be a binding instrument of exchange for cash.

**Heroin trafficking: The Pizza Connection**

The Pizza Connection case of 1985 revealed the methods used by the mafia to repatriate profits derived from heroin trafficking between the golden triangle of South East Asia and North America. It was one of the first thorough investigations into money laundering techniques. Enquiries began in 1979 with the opening of a suitcase at Palermo airport containing 600,000 dollars. Further arrests of drug and money couriers, the discovery of five heroin laboratories in Sicily between 1980 and 1982 and the pooling of knowledge between magistrates investigating arms and drugs traffic in Sicily and in North East Italy with colleagues in the US and Switzerland finally put the pieces of the jigsaw together. In its simplest terms, the profits from heroin sold in North America went through bank accounts either in New York or in

Bermuda, were transferred to banks in Switzerland and either held there or moved to accounts in Italy.

One of the Pizza Connection couriers, Franco Della Torre, had the cash delivered in small denomination notes to his room in the Waldorf Astoria hotel in New York. With the assistance of the security staff of the hotel, he carried the money in suitcases to a branch of Merrill Lynch where it was deposited into the account of a company called Traex, officially a property and raw materials company owned by a Swiss national called Enrico Rossini.

Between 27 April and 2 July 1982 Della Torre made seven cash deposits to a total of 5.2 million dollars. The quantity of small denomination notes and his reluctance to enter the bank vaults where security cameras were installed alerted a Merrill Lynch employee and the bank made enquiries about the Traex account with its Zurich branch. Despite Swiss reassurances, Della Torre was asked to close the account, but simply transferred it to E. F. Hutton. Between 6 July and 27 September of the same year Della Torre made 11 more deposits with E. F. Hutton totalling 8.5 million dollars into the account of the Acacias Development Corporation; other deposits were on the account of PGK Holdings. Suspicions were also aroused in Hutton's legal department but a government plea for discretion was ignored, Della Torre's Swiss lawyer was informed and October 1982 the PGK Zurich account was closed. [32]

Salvatore Amendolito, another mafia money launderer turned informant, has described how he was brought money in suitcases so heavy that the car into which they were placed visibly sank under the weight. He organised the payment of around 10 million dollars into bank accounts in New York, from where it went by bank draft or cheque to Nassau or Bermuda. Important terminals of the Pizza Connection were Chemical Bank in New York, Handelsbank in Zurich and Credit Suisse in Bellinzona, where the account "Wall Street 651" was held by industrialist and mafia financial "counsellor" Oliviero Tognoli. Tognoli's iron and steel business with offices in Brescia and in Switzerland gave cover for the 20 million dollars he laundered in the space of a few years. Banks in towns on the Swiss border such as Chiasso were also used.

Whereas once sworn mafia members only would handle the most delicate financial transactions, the sheer volume of cash to be laundered and the degree of sophistication required in the manipulation of accounts meant that the financial complexities of the drugs business increasingly had to be entrusted to accountants and financiers outside the organisation. The need to rely on outsiders who had not sworn life-long allegiance to *Cosa Nostra* and who tended to collaborate if arrested was a fatal flaw in the mafia's impermeability, as is now acknowledged. [33]

An important figure in the Pizza Connection and one involved in subsequent money laundering cases was the Turkish arms and drugs trafficker Yasar Avni Musullulu, owner of a Zurich-based shipping company called Oden A.G. Musullulu is currently on the run with arrest warrants issued by the Turks for arms trafficking and by the Italians for the smuggling of 2 mt of morphine base to the mafia between 1981 and 1983. Musullulu was paid a total of 55 million dollars via accounts in Lugano and Zurich, although on at least one occasion was paid in cash in Bulgaria. He ceased supplying the Sicilians in 1983 after a disagreement over payment. [34]

The Lebanese brothers Jean and Barkev Magharian are currently in prison in Switzerland accused of laundering 1.5 billion Swiss Francs through their accounts with Switzerland's three biggest banks, the Union des Banques Suisses, the Societé des Banques Suisses and Credit Suisse. A further 1.3 billion SF were allegedly recycled through a precious metals company called Shakarchi Trading on the pretext of gold purchases for Lebanon. The case came to light after the arrest of two Turks in possession of 10 kg of heroin and details of payments to Shakarchi. An associate of Yasar Musullulu is known to have made 31 separate deposits into Shakarchi's account with UBS in Lugano. The matter was complicated by the fact that the Vice President of Shakarchi Trading until October 1988, a week before the scandal broke, was lawyer Hans Kopp, husband of the Swiss Justice Minister. Enquiries are in progress to establish the degree of responsibility, if any, the three Swiss banks bear for the activities described above.

### Laundering cocaine profits

Cocaine profits go through equally convoluted laundering techniques. Officially a dealer in Colombian coffee, Edoardo Orozco used 11 different banks to recycle 151 million dollars worth of narco profits between 1978 and 1982, taking care not to use small denomination notes or to make deposits of more than 10,000 dollars at a time (when documentation was necessary) and by the formation of fictitious companies. In fact four of the banks he used closed his account and refused to do further business with him but only one, the Marine Midland in Jamaica, actively moved to report him.

In October 1988, after 30 months of investigations in six countries involving the infiltration of several money laundering groups working for the Medellin cartel, 43 employees of the Luxembourg-based Bank of Credit and Commerce International were arrested, ten of whom were senior managers. BCCI initially defended its staff but finally admitted in January 1990 that some 32 million dollars had been laundered through its branches. The pivotal office was located in Tampa, Florida, which distributed the money via other BCCI branches to New York, Luxembourg and to London, where it was invested in 90 day deposit certificates. General Noriega had 23 million dollars deposited in various branches of BCCI; indeed the ex-head of the Panama branch, one of the accused employees, used to claim he was Noriega's personal banker.

Banks can be used unknowingly as money laundering vehicles, as happened with Philipp Bros in London, exonerated from all blame for the 250 million dollars of cocaine profits it recycled between 1987 and 1989 in the form of gold sales and purchases on behalf of the Medellin cartel.

### How drug profits are used

Drug profits once laundered can be returned as investments in the trade from which they emanated – that is, in the purchase of more drugs or in payments of overheads such as couriers and transportation costs. They may be used more generally to strengthen the power of the organisation through intimidation or elimination of competitors; bribery of government or military officials; arms for self defence or for aggressive purposes. In this context it is worth noting the discovery by Colombian authorities in March 1990 of 10 French-made surface to air missiles which would have certainly have marked a qualitative leap in the traffickers' military capacity.

But because laundered money has no "smell" it can equally well be re-invested openly – in property, in ordinary stocks and shares, or in business activities such as restaurants, hotels and tourism. Naturally the form of investment varies according to the level at which the trafficker operates. Pablo Escobar bought a huge ranch to which he imported giraffes, Indian elephants and hippopotamuses; the Medellin cartel owns property, radio and television stations and at least six of Colombia's professional football teams. Preferred investments in the UK are property, antiques and fast food outlets (NDIU). US traffickers frequently put their money into beauty parlours, petrol stations and launderettes. The most attractive from the launderer's point of view are businesses which have a high cash turnover, weak technological or regulatory barriers to entry and are strongly competitive.[35] The construction industry in Italy has long been under pressure from the mafia and has been infiltrated not only in Sicily but also in the north, especially Lombardy, where in 1988, according to the President of the Milan Chamber of Commerce, income from criminal activities was around 15 per cent of the GNP of the Region.[36]

At the simplest level, drug traffickers may use their profits to buy themselves a life of luxury, as did Ravi Sharma, a 44 year-old London housewife convicted in 1989 of smuggling 30 kg of heroin through London to the United States. The heroin originated in Pakistan, was purchased in India and was smuggled by courier to London before being taken on to New York, where Sharma's husband handled distribution. Sharma was responsible for organising the couriers and the laundering of the profits through Swiss bank accounts in her and her husband's names. In addition to her nine year prison sentence the court ordered that Sharma's house, her Mercedes and her jewellery be confiscated. The case was the first conviction in British legal history for a drug smuggling charge when no drugs had been seized in Britain, and the first to prosecute a money launderer for recycling the profits of a drug network in which Britain was merely the conduit rather than the final destination of the drug.

Whereas in the early to mid 1980s most drug trafficking profits finished up in tax havens in Europe or the Caribbean, the trend changed in the latter years of the decade, with more and more money being repatriated to the drug production zones where alternative money laundering structures have been set up.[37] Non-monetary instruments are increasingly used instead of cash.

**The problems of detection**

Economic impreparation and political complacency are amongst the principal reasons why drug revenue has escaped detection for so long. With the exception of the United States, whose 1970 law introduced mandatory documentation on all financial transactions over 10,000 dollars, few countries have exercised adequate control over their financial markets. Although drug trafficking has long been an offence, until recently no European country penalised the laundering of profits made thereof: Britain and the US did so in 1986; France with laws in 1987 and 1988; Luxembourg and Italy in 1989; Switzerland did so as of July 1990 but only after a long political battle, probably only won thanks to the fall from grace of Justice Minister Elizabeth Kopp. Legislation in Spain and Germany is still being formulated.

Italian banks are subject to regulations imposed by the Bank of Italy yet inadequate controls of para-banking institutions such as investment management, insurance and finance companies, hire purchase companies and of the stock exchange have created conditions of financial anarchy which legislation is only now beginning to tackle. In April 1989 there were 50 leasing companies and 600 finance companies in Sicily; the Sicilian province of Trapani, one of the lowest income areas of Italy, had 102 finance companies and 23 banks with a total of 142 branches. Anyone can form a finance company, and even setting up a bank in Sicily can be done with the approval of the Sicilian Region unless the Bank of Italy vetoes the project within four months of application.

Naylor[38] considers that two other factors have particularly favoured money launderers: the growth of the Eurodollar market – an electronically integrated international system which guarantees anonymity and instant transfer at the touch of a computer key — and the rise of the service component of a country's economy, the aptly defined sector of "invisible exports".

A major problem in identifying criminal funds is that of separating "black" or "dirty" money from the "hot" or the "grey" – that is, capital in flight for fiscal reasons – tax evasion or tax avoidance. Switzerland has an estimated 150 billion SF of tax evaders' money;[39] economists at Chase Manhatten Bank reckon that 30 to 50 per cent of money entering Hong Kong's banks from abroad is capital in flight.[40] What Naylor calls "creative accounting" allows tax exiles and international companies to live on an ill-defined border between the legal and the illegal which makes investigation and control extremely difficult. Banks have legitimate but nonetheless strong commercial interests in economic diversification and maximisation of profits, and are rarely challenged by national governments as long as they fall in line with political choices. The attraction of opening branches in tax havens such as the Bahamas, Panama, Hong Kong and the Channel Islands and the extension of financial services to countries where banking and corporate secrecy are protected is obvious. Banks benefit from the high liquidity which permits further investment whilst host countries may compensate for otherwise unproductive economies by the lucrative provision of commercial services. Even assuming that the large banking institutions conduct their business correctly, the sheer volume of financial activities and the impossibility of verifying every transaction has led to abuse by criminals using well camouflaged laundering techniques, by competitors in the credit market prepared to tolerate and/or benefit from illegal flows of money and by unscrupulous employees in the banks themselves. White collar crime is notoriously difficult to detect because it involves no blood, no obvious "victims" and is committed by individuals who use positions of power and privilege to protect their activities.

Future prospects for successful identification of drug money movement have been boosted by national and international agreements which are discussed later. The *Declaration of Principles* signed in Basle in December 1988, the financial clauses of the UN Convention of the same month and the setting up of a 15 country Financial Action Task Force in July 1989 are indications that financial crime, and in particular that deriving from the illicit drugs traffic, is being taken seriously at last.

## RESPONSES – NATIONAL AND INTERNATIONAL

Legislation regarding the possession, consumption and trafficking of narcotic drugs is gradually being harmonised throughout the world. It is not within the scope of this study to evaluate and compare drug laws in each producer and consumer country, but to give a background to the instruments available for combating illicit trafficking and where possible to give an overall assessment of their effectiveness.

### National measures

Holland and the United States embody the two extremes of western consumer drug "philosophy". The United States has rigorous drug laws imbued with a fervent moral tone which unequivocally set the drug consumer in the criminal class. The Dutch on the other hand regard criminal law and its enforcement as tools to reduce the supply of drugs, not to criminalise their use. "The function of Dutch criminal law is an instrument of social control rather than an instrument for expressing moral values. Our primary aim is to protect health and social well-being and to reduce the harm and risks associated with drug use. Criminal proceedings against consumers would not solve the problem but aggravate it".[41]

The self help and education programmes initiated by the Dutch government have been effective in Holland – the number of deaths from overdose is stable at about 60 cases per year and addicts represent 0.1 per cent of the population. Welfare programmes for addicts are free, have no waiting lists and are easily accessible.

The United States' attitude can be summed up by the "zero tolerance" approach: "We have served notice that drug use will no longer be tolerated, and that those who use illegal drugs will be held accountable. We are building more prisons, and we are trying to create true disincentives for drug use and distribution by ensuring that for those involved, punishment is more certain. . . . The media has joined force with the government (and with) influential members of the entertainment, movie and music industries to depict drug use as it really is – destructive, vile and weak."[42]

According to the 1989 *National Household Survey on Drug Abuse* the number of *frequent* (once or more per week) users of cocaine in the US increased between 1985 and 1989 from 600,000 to 1.2 million, although the estimated number of persons abusing *any* drug on a *current* basis (i.e. at least once in a 30 day period) has dropped 37 per cent (INCB), a sign that repressive measures and social stigma have had the desired effect on the casual or "yuppie" user. Yet the overall picture of the US drugs problem is bleak: an estimated 6 per cent of US citizens are drug addicts; since 1984 there has been a 28-fold increase in hospital admissions involving the smoking of cocaine which is now the prime cause of drug-related death; between 1986 and 1988 the number of babies born with birth defects linked to cocaine abuse tripled; 60 per cent of homicides in Washington DC are drug-related. New York police made 90,000 drug arrests in 1988, the equivalent of one every six minutes (Interpol); of all arrests made in the city, only 10 per cent have no trace of drugs in their bodies.[43]

To draw from this the superficial conclusion that all countries ought to follow the Dutch model would be an error: factors such as national character, geographical location and size, social factors, historical, cultural and criminal tradition are all crucial in determining a country's legislative evolution and will continue to undermine the notion of universal judicial harmony. The futility of making simplistic equations between repressive legislation and success in combating drug demand and trafficking is further demonstrated by the case of Italy.

Between 1975 and 1990 the severity of Italy's drug laws lay somewhere between the Dutch and the American, yet amongst European countries it has had the highest overall rates of drug abuse, seizures and deaths from overdose. In the course of 1989 there were 680 kg of heroin seizures, 667 of cocaine and 970 deaths from drug overdose[44]; there are an estimated 300,000 to 500,000 drug addicts. The controversial new law which came into effect in July 1990 has abolished the formerly permitted "modest quantity" of any drug for personal consumption and has changed the legal perception of the drug addict from victim to criminal; its effects will not be evident for some years.

Possession, consumption and trafficking of narcotic drugs are theoretically illegal in all EC countries, where the real differences lie in discretional application of the law. In some countries, first time users caught with small amounts of drugs for personal consumption are merely cautioned, with recidivists punished by a graduated series of sanctions. Most operate a distinction between "hard" and "soft" and the quantities of drugs found. Holland rarely punishes consumption at all and tolerates dealing in soft drugs if done in small quantities and unostentatiously. Prison remains an option for courts sentencing drug abusers but many countries see this as compounding the problem and hold it as a last resort. Some offer to suspend prison sentences for consumers if disintoxication therapy is followed. In Italy there is a constitutional obligation to prosecute when a crime has been committed, therefore every infraction is codified and discretion severely limited.

## Global Drug Trafficking 33

The United States pioneered legislation to prevent the flow of illicit profits with the requirement from 1971 for documentation of all financial transactions of over 10,000 dollars by means of Currency Transaction Reports (CTR). This was incorporated into the Money Laundering Control Act of 1986; in 1989, a federal law was introduced which permits the government to track and to claim ownership of laundered drug money. Pre-trial freezing of the assets of suspected drug dealers pending judicial forfeiture procedures is also permissable.

In terms of financial asset verification, the British 1986 Drug Trafficking Offences Act (DTOA) has taken a different path, namely the obligation on the part of anyone handling finances on behalf of a third party – solicitors and accountants as well as banks and financial institutions – to disclose suspicious transactions, overriding any confidentiality imposed by contract. Both systems have their advantages and disadvantages: the US mechanism operates automatically without having to rely on the suspicions or alertness of banking staff, yet the very automation of the reporting procedures creates a mountain of paperwork in which illicit transactions can undoubtedly be concealed.

A House of Commons Home Affairs Committee report on the effectiveness of the DTOA indicated that the disclosures system worked reasonably well as far as the major banks were concerned: by November 1989 suspicions had been reported on approximately 1,000 occasions. However smaller financial institutions, banks and building societies and foreign banks operating in Britain were felt to be less co-operative. One weakness that emerged was that of inadequate feedback between banks and the police – after reporting their suspicions banks are not always informed about the progress of the enquiries, thereby causing uncertainty and difficult relationships between bank and customer.

Another reported loophole is the status of the *hawala* system which, whilst not officially deemed to be banking under the Banking Act of 1987, is nevertheless subject to the DTOA.

An apparently slight but important difference regarding the tracing, freezing and confiscation of assets in the UK and in the US is that whereas in the US the crime of money laundering involves concealing the source or origin of money derived from *unlawful activity,* the offence in British law has to be traced to *a particular unlawful act.* This partly accounts for the greater difficulty of prosecution in Britain, as the report explains: "There have been few prosecutions of money laundering offences under Section 24 (of the DTOA), despite investigations identifying individuals whose conduct falls within the section. The lack of prosecutions arises from: difficulty in proving the drug trafficking origin of the assets; frequent lack of evidence relating to the *mens rea* of the launderer – knowing or suspecting the origins of the funds; in some instances, difficulty in proving actual "retention or control" of the funds."[45]

Italy has had legislation permitting the investigation of financial assets and their preventive seizure since the innovative *Rognoni La Torre* law of 1982. 402 billion lire of assets were seized in its first year of implementation but by 1987 the total had fallen to less than 100 billion. Since more, not less, dirty money had to be circulating in the economy it was apparent that criminals were recycling their profits in subtler ways. Modifications to the law in 1990 have extended the powers of patrimonial investigation and criminalise "whoever substitutes money, goods or other assets derived from crimes of aggravated extortion, kidnap for ransom or from crimes concerning the production or the traffic of narcotic or psychotropic substances with other money, goods or assets, or else hinders the identification of their provenance from the above crimes."

But Italian as well as British legislators feel that criminal organisations have anticipated their every move. The RLT law omits reference to the handling of fraudulently obtained EC funds, of profits from the illict arms traffic, from casino fraud or from illegal gambling. The difficulty of penetrating the multiple layers of corporate and financial protection which separate the criminal from his profits has not been adequately tackled and has prompted the suggestion that preventive seizure of assets should be permitted without proof that a crime has taken place.[46]

National anti-drug legislation in producing countries has met obstacles of a different kind than in the predominantly consuming countries and these have been outlined in previous sections. In South East and South West Asia control of production and traffic is in the hands of groups operating outside the reach of governmental power, or occasionally in collusion with it. In South America the narco-traffickers and the extreme left and paramilitary right wing groups have exploited political and economic instability in the attempt to discredit the institutions which oppose them; in Colombia this has taken the form of direct blackmail by the threat and use of violence, alternating with promises to cease all trafficking activities in exchange for judicial immunity. A major challenge came with the murder of Senator Luis Carlos Galan on 18 August 1989, to which Colombia responded with enormous courage and decisiveness. The terms of the Emergency Power decree enacted the same day by President Virgilio Barco and his Council of Ministers were as follows: the article of the Penal Code requiring the application of an international treaty in order to extradite a Colombian citizen was suspended; a provision of the Constitution whereby the Council of Ministers could order the arrest and detention of suspected dangerous criminals (relieving the judges of this responsibility) was enforced; preventive seizure of assets of suspected drug traffickers was permitted and serious penalties for those who assisted them to conceal their illicit profits were introduced. Suspected drug traffickers or terrorists could be held incommunicado for up to seven days; more protection and resources were allocated to the judiciary; juries were abolished where intimidation was likely and ambulatory judges were appointed with territorial jurisdiction.

These emergency measures had immediate effect: between 18 August 1989 and 20 March 1990 15 drug traffickers had been extradited and a further 12 were awaiting extradition; 11,500 arrests had been made; 1,800 weapons were seized, 300 aeroplanes grounded, 1,370 properties occupied. Large quantities of cocaine, cocaine base and precursor chemicals were seized and hundreds of laboratories destroyed. 80 per cent of all world cocaine seizures for 1989 took place in Colombia itself.[47]

*Global Drug Trafficking*    35

The repercussions were felt immediately in Peru and Bolivia, where coca prices plummeted. The farmer who had been paid 100 dollars for 100lbs (45.34 kg) of coca leaf began to receive a mere 10 dollars for the same quantity. Peru suffered from an acute dollar shortage and the exchange rate soared.

## International measures

*The United Nations Single Convention on Narcotic Drugs* of 1961 aimed to codify all the existing multilateral treaty laws, streamline the control machinery and extend this to include the cultivation of plants that were grown as the raw material of natural narcotic drugs. It also established or maintained certain national monopolies for the production of drugs for medical and scientific purposes, and introduced guarantees for the treatment and rehabilitation of addicts. It prohibited the practices of opium smoking and coca chewing and the use of the cannabis plant for non-medical purposes, but allowed those countries in which the practice was a long standing tradition to introduce these bans gradually. The Single Convention was amended by the *1972 Protocol* which reinforced efforts to prevent illicit production of, traffic in and use of narcotics. The necessity of providing care and rehabilitation facilities for drug abusers was also stressed.

*The UN Convention on Psychotropic Substances* of 1971 was passed following concern at the harmful effects of hallucinogens such as LSD and mescaline; stimulants such as amphetamines, and sedative-hypnotics such as barbiturates. The World Health Organization (WHO) was designated as the agency responsible for deciding whether on a medical basis a new substance should be included in the four Schedules of proscribed drugs. The criteria are:
• the substance must have the capacity to produce a state of dependence and it must stimulate or depress the central nervous system, resulting in hallucinations or disturbances in motor function, thinking, behaviour, perception or mood;
• the abuse of the substance must produce ill effects similar to those caused by a substance already included in one of the four Schedules. The WHO must also establish that the substance is being or is likely to be abused so as to cause a public health and social problem.

*The UN Convention against Illicit Traffic in Narcotic Drugs and Psychotropic Substances* of 1988 imposes the following obligations on ratifying states:
i the provision of adequate sanctions for offences relating to drug trafficking;
ii the identification, tracing, freezing, seizure and confiscation of proceeds and property derived from trafficking;
iii the extradition of offenders for drug trafficking charges (i.e. no safe havens);
iv mutual legal assistance in terms of investigations and prosecutions (banking secrecy not to be invoked);
v other forms of co-operation, especially amongst law enforcement agencies in fields such as training;

**vi** international co-operation and assistance for transit states;
**vii** the law enforcement technique of controlled delivery;
**viii** the monitoring of precursor chemicals;
**ix** prevention of trade in and diversion of materials and equipment for illicit production and manufacture of narcotic drugs and psychotropic substances;
**x** measures to eradicate illicit cultivation of narcotic plants and to eliminate illicit demand for narcotic drugs and psychotropic substances;
**xi** the suppression of illicit traffic by sea, in particular in free trade zones and ports, and by air (UN).

By mid March 1989, 89 countries had become signatories to the Convention; nine countries had ratified.

*The International Narcotics Control Board* (INCB) was established by the 1961 Convention to monitor the licit cultivation, production, manufacture and utilisation of drugs for medical and scientific purposes. Governments are required to report annually on licit and illicit production and the INCB will advise, assist or propose sanctions if countries default.

*The Division of Narcotic Drugs* (DND) analyses and publishes data on the illicit drug traffic, on seizures and trends, advises other UN organisations on drug demand reduction policies, on law enforcement and runs training and information programmes on drug abuse and countermeasures.

*The United Nations Fund for Drug Abuse Control* (UNFDAC), established in 1971, is the only international body entirely devoted to assisting governments in combating the production, trafficking and use of illicit drugs. UNFDAC's brief includes demand reduction, supply reduction, crop eradication and substitution, but most of all the provision of development strategies aimed at helping the producing countries to develop economically viable alternatives to the illicit crop with the maximisation of opportunities for the substituted crop to provide an equal standard of living for the farmer. UNFDAC is funded entirely by voluntary donors who may offer *special purpose funds* designed for a specific project in a particular area, or else *general purpose donations* which UNFDAC uses at its own discretion. The Fund's 1990 budget is almost 70 million dollars to which Italy is by far the major contributor. In 1989 more than 110 development programmes were being implemented in some 50 countries including Pakistan, Thailand, Bolivia, Brazil, China, India, Laos, Peru and Turkey. Additionally, there are 38 regional and global projects underway with broad-based aims such as law enforcement education and training, drug education programmes, rehabilitation of drug addicts and scientific and agricultural training. Since 1982 these broad-based projects have been known as "master plans", a concept which entails a rigorous analysis of the drug problems within a region, an assessment of all narcotics control activities already accomplished, underway or planned, and the identification of new projects to be undertaken (UNFDAC).

A recent proposal conceived by UNFDAC's Executive Director Giuseppe

Di Gennaro is the establishment of regional courts under the jurisdiction of an international pool of judges with experience in the investigation of organised crime and drug trafficking. The premise behind this plan is the vulnerability of the judiciary in the Andean region: inadequate protection, low pay and impossibly difficult working conditions often place a judge before a choice of *plomo* or *plata* – literally "lead" or "silver" – a bullet or a bribe. The actions of the Medellin cartel have shown that the traffickers fear extradition above all else, hence the proposal to take legal decisions regarding the most serious examples of terrorism and drug trafficking away from the individual or identifiable group and put them into the hands of a "faceless judiciary" who would nonetheless remain fully accountable. The idea of an "Andean Judicial Space" evolved out of an earlier model for an *Espace Judiciaire Européen*, inspired by Giscard D'Estaing and elaborated by Di Gennaro and other European jurists during the wave of 1970s terrorism. It already has the tentative approval of Bolivia and further efforts are being made to see how it can be developed and integrated constitutionally into the country's legislative system.

**International banking co-operation**

The articles of the Vienna Convention dealing with the investigation and identification of assets was complemented by a *Statement of Principles* signed in Basle in December 1988 by the heads of the G10 countries' central banks. This declaration commits the signatory banks to taking active steps in the identification of clients and the source of their assets; to reporting any suspicions to the authorities if there are reasonable grounds to believe that clients' assets may be linked to the recycling of illicit funds, and promises full collaboration with police and judicial authorities in patrimonial investigations.

**Other international bodies with responsibilities in combating drug trafficking:**

*The European Committee to Combat Drugs* (CELAD): set up by the Heads of State of the Twelve in December 1989 as a group of ministers with responsibility for co-ordinating the fight against drugs in the EC.

*The Pompidou Group:* includes 20 European countries with the recent addition of Cyprus; is the main policy forum in Europe for all aspects of the drugs problem from law enforcement to illicit traffic and demand reduction policy. It meets at senior ministerial level every six months. It is hoped that three or four East European countries will join in the near future.

*Interpol:* has a sub-division dedicated to the collection and diffusion of information on drug trafficking activities.

*Customs Co-operation Council:* its 104 member states aim to harmonise and standardise customs laws and regulations; it circulates information regarding drug trafficking and promotes collaboration in law enforcement.

*Financial Action Task Force* (FATF): set up in July 1989 by 15 major industrialised countries whose aim is to make a practical study of money laundering, to review national strategies to counter this and to make recommendations for national and international instruments to combat it.

### Bi- and multi-lateral agreements

Outside the scope of international organisations and formal treaties, a number of bilateral and multilateral agreements contribute to the fight against illicit drug trafficking, for example that signed by the Interior Ministers of Turkey, Bulgaria, Austria, Greece, Yugoslavia, West Germany, Italy, France and Switzerland on 17 March 1990 to suppress the supply of drugs brought through the "Balkan corridor". Agreement was reached on the need to exchange information, co-ordinate police activities, exchange staff, establish more effective frontier controls and collaborate generally in the implementation of the Vienna Convention.

In March 1990 Italy and Spain became the first countries in the world to abolish maritime territoriality in drug trafficking investigations: their agreement permits the pursuit, search, seizure, arrest and prosecution of vessels or individuals of either country without recourse to extradition procedures.

The British-inspired *Memorandum of Understanding* (MOU) can be an agreement either between governments or between customs administrations, and may cover co-operation in one specific area, for example the MOU on co-operation signed in October 1989 between the UK and Bulgaria, or on a broad range of activities such as that signed with the US relating to all customs matters. Britain also collaborates on maritime and aerial surveillance with France, Spain, Portugal, Guernsey, Jersey and the Netherlands.

## CONCLUSION AND FUTURE PROSPECTS

The facts and statistics cited in this study should leave no doubt about the seriousness of the drug trafficking problem in the world today. The supply capacity of the narcotic drug producing countries has not been exhausted nor is it likely to be so in the foreseeable future. Whilst supply and demand for heroin seem to be reasonably stable, with new users taking the place of those who either come off the drug successfully or die from it, the demand for cocaine and its by-products continually increases. Despite record seizures and soaring arrests each year, supplies are not interrupted nor, presumably, is the risk of detection sufficient to deter dealer or consumer. Wholesale cocaine prices in the US have fallen by 80 per cent in the last 10 years and retail purity has quintupled from 12 per cent to 60 per cent. Psychotropic drugs, though not the subject of this study, should be mentioned briefly since their growing popularity is of universal concern. The appearance of "designer drugs" such as MDMA or Ecstasy shows how consumer demand can deliberately be created and manipulated where none previously existed. As these drugs are synthetic, new versions can be manufactured every year.

Developing countries are destroying their rain forests, exhausting their soil and polluting their rivers in the rush to produce drugs; African countries face serious epidemics of drug addiction and of AIDS; organised crime and drug trafficking are compounding the desperate problems of the Soviet Union which has neither the know how, the legislation nor the economic resources to confront it.

On paper, the future looks grim. But it is still too early to assess the effects of the international commitments made in the latter years of the 1980s. If these are brought within a solid framework of judicial assistance, information exchange and financial co-operation throughout the industrialised countries and are integrated with carefully planned programmes of development, education and economic assistance to the developing countries, then an effective global approach may yet prove too strong for the drug trafficking organisations. East/West and North/South efforts are already under way in a spirit of cautious co-operation.

It must be recognised that the only possible solution is an international, politically disinterested strategy which puts social and economic welfare above victimisation or national chauvinism. Crop eradication on a mass scale without adequate provision for ensuring an approximate if not identical income from the alternative crop is counterproductive, nor will crop substitution programmes ever work unless transport and distribution facilities exist and unless there is a proven market for the substitute.

The industrialised countries bear considerable responsibility for the initial nurturing of the drugs trade and for not intervening sooner when under-developed nations began to provide new markets for profit-hungry drug companies. The producing countries are dependent on the consuming countries for the chemicals with which drugs are refined, yet President Bush has yet to accuse the chemical giants of undermining his war on drugs. All too often high-flown rhetoric conceals vote-seeking political ambition or hypocritical moral outrage. The most obvious example concerns General Manuel Noriega, whose contemporary activities as drug trafficker and DEA troubleshooter helped him to accumulate millions of dollars in bank accounts around the world. As long as his help was needed to stave off the Communist threat in Central America Noriega was of use and, as former CIA Director Bush must have known when he sent the troops into Panama, he has two signed letters of gratitude from DEA head John Lawn to prove it.

In fairness, credit must be handed to the American President for his February 1990 trip to meet Bolivian, Peruvian and Colombian presidents at Cartagena. The significance of Bush's journey to Colombian territory to meet his South American colleagues went far beyond a diplomatic gesture and an offer of aid: it implied an acceptance of equality and the recognition that the problem of drug trafficking is too serious and too complex to be solved by branding the producing countries as villains and by dynamiting guerrilla headquarters or coca plantations.

Unfortunately, the political finesse which accompanies every international manoeuvre, including action on drugs, means that sincerity can always be questioned. Furthermore, political choices are heavily conditioned by the presence of vested interests such as commercial drug companies and arms manufacturers. Support for an international convention limiting the manufacture and sale of arms might spell political suicide for an American President, but if implemented this would provide an invaluable adjunct to the UN Convention on drug trafficking. A requirement on manufacturers or on governments to register every weapon produced and the possibility that would derive of tracing the provenance of arms seized from terrorists and drug traffickers might reveal some politically embarrassing choices, but would almost certainly reduce the current promiscuity of military hardware on the international circuit.

Politicians must be challenged on the genuineness of their commitment to the welfare of the planet and for once should put politics aside. Unless they put their wallets *and* their hands on their hearts, the "war on drugs" will remain exactly as the phrase appears – empty and lost.

---

## NOTES

[1] Lamour Catherine and Lamberti Michel R; *Il Sistema Mondiale della Droga*, Einaudi 1973, 2nd ed. 1974, p. 52.

[2] Garrett R.C., Waldmeyer U.G., Sernaque V., *The Coke Book: The Complete Reference to the Uses and Abuses of Cocaine*, Berkley Books, New York, 1984, p. 81.

[3] Charles Saphos, Head of Narcotics Section of US Justice Department. quoted in *La Repubblica*, 25 April 1990.

[4] UN Department of Public Information, January 1990.

[5] Kaplan C.D., "The Heroin System: a General Economy of Crime and Addiction". *Crime and Justice* November 1988, quoted in Arlacchi P., *Droga e grande criminalità in Italia e nel mondo*, Salvatore Sciascia Editore. Caltanissetta/Roma. 1988, p. 73. Martinoli, Censis 1985; quoted in Santino U.: *The Financial Mafia, Contemporary Crises 12*: (1988) p. 228.

[6] Gorritti Gustavo: *Atlantic Monthly* July 1989.

[7] Lamour/Lamberti, *op. cit.* pp. 49–50.

[8] Arlacchi P.: "La mafia nel sistema mondiale della droga", in *Morte di un generale*, Mondadori. Milano, 1982.

[9] Arlacchi P., *Droga e grande criminalita* . . . pp. 70–72.

[10] Arlacchi P. and Lewis R., *Micromega* 4/89.

[11] *L'Espresso*, 12 November 1989.

[12] Eddy Paul. *The Guardian*, 5 September 1989.

[13] Eddy Paul, Walden Sarah. Sabogal Hugo, *The Cocaine Wars*, Arrow Books, 1989, p. 340.

[14] *Avvenimenti*, 18 October 1989.

[15] *The Fight Against The Drug Traffic in Colombia*, Office of the President of the Republic, February 1990.

[16] *L'Unità*, 21 June 1990.

[17] Presentation by Juan Zarate Gambini, World Ministerial Drugs Conference, London, 9-11 April 1990.

[18] Dziedzic Michael J., *Survival*, November/December 1989 Vol. XXXI No. 6 p. 542.

[19] UN Department of Public Information, January 1990.

[20] *L'Espresso*, 20 February 1989.

[21] *Corriere della Sera*, 12 June 1990.

[22] *Le Monde*, 7 September 1989.

[23] *Panorama*, 17 June 1990.

[24] *L'Unità*, 5 March 1990.

[25] Presentation by Chief Inspector T. M. Bremners, (Netherlands) and D. Tweddle. HM Customs and Excise. World Ministerial Drugs Conference, London 9 11 April 1990.

## Global Drug Trafficking 41

[26] Statistics from report by SISMI (Italian Military Security Service) quoted in *L'Espresso*, 22 April 1990.

[27] Gorritti, *op. cit.*

[28] Saphos, *La Repubblica*, 25 April 1990.

[29] Presentation by Jacques Genthial, Directeur Central de la Police Judiciare (France), World Ministerial Drugs Conference, London, 9–11 April 1990.

[30] *ibidem.*

[31] Santino U., *op. cit.* p. 224.

[32] "Cash Connection", report presented by Irving R. Kaufman to Presidential Commission on Organised Crime in October 1984, quoted in Violante L., *La Mafia dell'Eroina*, Editori Riuniti, Roma 1987.

[33] Author's conversation with Palermo Public Prosecutor Giuseppe Ayala, Palermo, 25 June 1990.

[34] Stajano Corrado (ed), *Mafia: L'Atto di Accusa dei giudici di Palermo*, Editori Riuniti, Roma, 1986.

[35] Violante L., *op. cit.* p. 66.

[36] *L'Espresso*, 20 November 1988.

[37] Genthial, World Ministerial Drugs Conference. London, 9–11 April 1990.

[38] Naylor R.T., address given at conference "L'Europa e la Droga", organised by FEDRO (Federazione Droga), Palazzo Vecchio, Florence, 19/20 May 1989.

[39] *Financial Times*, 19 April 1989.

[40] Arlacchi P., *La Repubblica*, 9 April 1989.

[41] Presentation by Dr. Eddy L. Engelsmann, Head of the Alcohol, Drugs and Tobacco Branch, Ministry of Welfare, Public Health and Cultural Affairs, The Netherlands' on the theme "Individual responsibility and the role of criminal law", World Ministerial Drugs Conference, London, 9–11 April 1990.

[42] Presentation by Louis W. Sullivan, M.D. Secretary of Health and Human Services, United States of America, to World Ministerial Drugs Conference. London, 9–11 April 1990.

[43] Presentation by Dr. Mark Gold, of Yale University and Fair Oaks Hospital, founder of the National Cocaine Helpline (US) to World Ministerial Drugs Conference, London, 9–11 April 1990.

[44] Italian Ministry of the Interior, published 12 April 1990.

[45] Minutes of evidence, House of Commons Home Affairs Committee, Vol II 5.10 (iv).

[46] Suggestion made by judge Piero Grasso, adviser to the Italian Antimafia Commission, at conference on money laundering held in the Sala del Cenacolo. Camera dei Deputati, Rome, 7 April 1990.

[47] *The Fight Against the Drug Traffic in Colombia*, Office of the President of the Republic, February 1990.

---

## ABBREVIATIONS

DEA: Drug Enforcement Administration (US)
INSCR: International Narcotics Strategy Control Report (US)
DND: Division of Narcotic Drugs (UN)
NDIU: National Drugs Intelligence Unit (UK)
INCB: International Narcotics Control Board (UN)

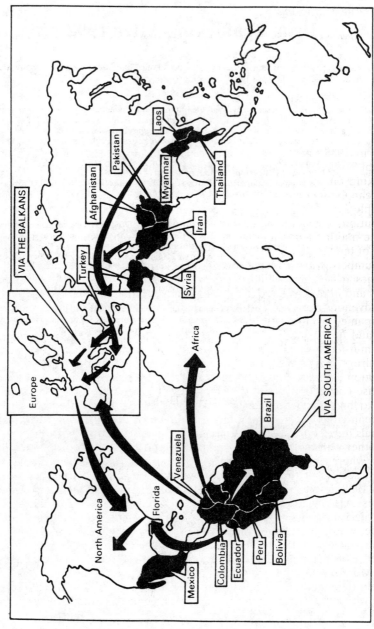

Drug producing areas (in black) and routes for transfer of drugs world-wide to consumer countries.
Reproduced from *La Repubblica*.

# [4]

# Drug Trafficking After 1992

## A Special Report

## Alison Jamieson

When in 1985 the TREVI (Terrorism, Radicalism, Extremism and Inter-national Violence) group of Ministers decided to include drugs and drug trafficking on their agenda along with organised crime and terrorism, the European Community (EC) had no specific brief to deal with either demand or supply-side drug programmes. Yet only a few years on, drug production, distribution, consumption and the laundering of the profits thereof have become major preoccupations of the EC member states as they look to the future of the Single European Market.

A number of factors have contributed to this: the relentless rise in all EC countries in seizures of illicit substances, in drug abuse and consumption figures and in drug-related illness and deaths, in particular those attributable to intravenous drug use and needle sharing. Increased drug abuse has been accompanied by a notable rise in crime of all kinds, ranging from petty theft and fraud to mugging, robbery and, in some countries, significant increases in the murder rate. Although research into the nature of the link between the illicit drugs market and violent crime in Europe is not conclusive, public perception assumes, and an analysis of crime statistics suggests, that there is a precise connection; there is also uncontested evidence that illicit drug use leads to higher rates of acquisitive crime. Public fears that once-civilised European cities are becoming unliveable ghettos of drug addicts and narco-criminals have spurred all governments into taking action.

Another warning for the EC came at the end of the 1980s from the United States, where a crack explosion was spreading rapidly, especially amongst the poorest sectors of the population; cocaine/crack prices reached an all time low in 1988 despite significant rises in border interdiction rates and domestic seizures; AIDS victims were doubling their numbers each year. Officials from the Drug Enforcement Administration (DEA) predicted a similar trend for Europe, whose barrier-free market was seen as offering particular attractions for the cocaine trafficking cartels. In contrast to an almost saturated US market, European consumption of cocaine was still relatively low and prices high. Moreover by the end of the 1980s, US federal drug laws were being severely tightened and drug use repressed with a moral and judicial fervour beside which the tolerant European countries seemed a paradise of *laissez faire*.

## 1. THE EUROPEAN RESPONSE

The EC Commission has contributed to the work of the Council of Europe Pompidou Group, the main policy forum in Europe for all aspects of drugs problems. The Pompidou Group's most recent concern, since the adhesion of several former East-bloc countries, has been with East-West co-operation in drug matters, and a meeting was held in Oslo in May 1991 on this subject.

CELAD, the European Committee to Combat Drugs, was set up by the EC Heads of State in December 1989. Its programme is divided into five action areas:

- co-ordination of anti-drug strategies in member states
- suppression of illicit trade
- demand reduction
- EC participation at a multilateral level
- creation of a European Observatory on Drugs (EOD)

CELAD and the Pompidou Group are working together to extend inter-European collaboration, especially involving Non-Governmental Organisations (NGOs). A European Policy Co-operation Group on Drugs was set up in 1990 to establish forms of co-operation in drug matters with developing countries, in particular drug producing and transit states.

Within the ambit of its Special Co-operation Programme the EC has granted a renewable, four-year "Generalised System of Preferences" to exports from Colombia, Bolivia, Ecuador and Peru. Additionally, the North-South Programme, operational since 1988, has been allocating increasing amounts of financial aid to Latin America to encourage alternative agricultural growth and for the cure and rehabilitation of drug addicts.

The TREVI group has four working groups, two of which have a precise relevance to drugs: Group III is devoted to organised crime and drug trafficking, and Group IV to post 1992 co-ordination.

The EC Commission has elaborated two important statutes concerned with drug trafficking which are binding on member states: the first is a Council Regulation which implements Article 12 of the Vienna Convention by introducing measures to prevent the diversion of precursor chemicals for drug production. It was approved in December 1990 and went into force from 1 July 1991. It calls for strict controls on documentation, identification, importation and exportation of specified chemicals. Each member state is required to report movements of these chemicals to the International Narcotics Control Board annually. The second is a Council Directive aimed at preventing the laundering of drug profits through the financial institutions of the Community. This was approved in Luxembourg in June 1991 and will take effect from 1 January 1993. It is discussed later.

The EC Commission has also been an active participant in multilateral agreements, treaties and conventions to curb the illicit drugs traffic and money laundering: it has supported and ratified the Vienna Convention of 1988, approved the Basel Declaration of 1988 signed by the central banks of 12 countries; its member states adhere without exception to the conclusions and recommendations of the Financial Action Task Force and of the Chemical Task Force, set up by the G7 group of countries. It has been consulted on the terms of the Council of Europe Convention on Laundering, Search, Seizure and Confiscation of the Proceeds from Crime, signed but not ratified to date.

*Drug Trafficking After 1992*     3

The impressive list of achievements briefly described above reveals the high priority and degree of commitment that the EC has shown in tackling the drugs problem in a responsible and comprehensive way. Epidemiological research and demand reduction policies seem likely to be given even greater attention in the coming years, given the AIDS alarm. Once established, the EOD will perform an invaluable function of co-ordination and comparison of research as well as being a centre of documentation and information on all drug issues from seizures, precursor legislation and epidemiological study to national and Community aims and policies.

Nonetheless, a number of unforeseen problems and unresolved areas remain outside the scope of legislation and international action undertaken to date, and these will constitute vulnerabilities within the Single European Market after 1992.

## 2. THE TRAFFIC IN ILLICIT SUBSTANCES – RECENT AND LIKELY FUTURE TRENDS

Recent trends in European drug trafficking show an overall increase in the *variety* of illicit substances being trafficked and in the *frequency* and *quantities* of drugs seized. Estimates of the relationship between seizures and the amount of drugs in circulation vary, but even the most optimistic do not exceed 10 per cent. In Italy, for example the percentage is as low as 3.5 per cent, according to a 1991 government assessment.[1]

### Cocaine

American predictions regarding the targeting of Europe by cocaine traffickers would seem to be borne out, although the use of crack has not to date become a major problem. Ignoring the alleged saturation of the US market, the coca producing countries of Bolivia, Peru and Colombia have all increased the land given over to cultivation. According to the UN Division of Narcotic Drugs (DND), Colombia more than doubled its hectarage in 1989, whilst Peru has increased from 6,000 to 200,000 hectares in recent years. A German intelligence report leaked to *Der Spiegel* magazine warns that the cocaine cartels are building up "strategic reserves" of the drug in Europe, and that during 1990, 180 metric tons were smuggled into EC countries – almost three times the present demand requirements of 67 metric tons.[2]

Although European cocaine seizures represent a mere 3 per cent of the world total, they rose sharply between 1987 and 1989 from 4 to 8 metric tons and in 1990 reached over 14 metric tons, a total which was already recorded in the first six months of 1991. (Interpol)

Increased vigilance and improved efficiency in Spanish interdiction efforts have tended to push sea-borne consignments northwards towards France, Italy, the Netherlands and to the UK, where cocaine seizures rose by 21 per cent in 1990 to 606 kilos. Denmark, and in particular Copenhagen airport, seems to be an important air route used by Lebanese traffickers in transit to Damascus. In 1991 Czechoslovakia seized a quantity of cocaine which had come from Colombia by sea to Poland, where a significant number of Colombians have come to settle.

Both Italy and Spain have noted a shift from illicit importation by air to significantly larger quantities brought in by sea. In January 1988 Colombian traffickers used Italo-American mafia contacts in Florida to arrange the transport of 576 kg of cocaine from Colombia via Aruba to Sicily. The Sicilian mafia does not have a monopoly over the European cocaine traffic as it came close to doing with heroin in the late 1970s and early 1980s, but is highly active, as has emerged from arrests and court testimonies in recent years. The Neapolitan *Camorra* has exploited to the full its traditional cigarette smuggling routes and networks which have been adapted to accommodate cocaine, and has a strong foothold in Spain, in Marseilles and along the Côte d'Azur. In 1990, 474 kg of cocaine seized at Le Havre were due to be taken in sailing boats to Cannes for distribution by the *Camorra*.

## Heroin

There have been a number of significant trends in heroin trafficking in recent years, the first being the involvement of African countries as transit routes and in operating drug courier networks throughout the world. In 1989, 760 West African heroin traffickers were arrested in Europe of whom 636 were Nigerian. (DND) At the end of 1990, 1800 Nigerians were under arrest in the UK on drug trafficking offences.[3] The second trend has been the increased use of the so-called "Balkan corridor" for the transportation of heroin to Europe. Of all the 6 metric tons of heroin seized in Europe in 1990 75 per cent came from South West Asia by this route. (Interpol) The variations are many, but as the bulk of refining takes place in Turkey, most take Istanbul as their starting point; Turkish and Iranian syndicates oversee transport and distribution – usually in road transport vehicles – which pass from Turkey through Bulgaria, Yugoslavia, Hungary and into Austria, or else through Greece and Yugoslavia into Italy. Significant seizures have been made in Romania and Czechoslovakia, confirming that traffickers have taken advantage of greater freedom in Eastern Europe. This is discussed in more detail later.

The main EC transit country is the Federal Republic of Germany (FRG), whose eight European borders present formidable problems of traffic control: 21m road vehicles crossed the Austrian-German border in the first six months of 1990. France has noted a significant increase in heroin seizures sent by mail, in particular from Pakistan. UK heroin seizures rose by 73 per cent to a new record of 609 kg in 1990. In general, Turkish syndicates are becoming more powerful all over Europe, with Hong Kong based Chinese *Triads* digging in more aggressively in anticipation of 1997.

## Cannabis and derivatives

Quantities of cannabis products seized have fluctuated considerably in recent years, although Europe's share of world seizures rose from 38 per cent in 1988 to 54 per cent in 1989. (DND) A single seizure of 45 metric tons of

*Drug Trafficking After 1992*    5

Pakistani cannabis in the Netherlands distorted 1990 figures. Morocco is Europe's main supplier, with Spain and Gibraltar favoured transit routes. Supplies arriving in Spain are frequently carried into France by hired car. Afghanistan and Pakistan are also important source countries; distribution lines continually vary, but a relatively new route was discovered with the seizure at Hamburg of 1.9 kg of Afghanistan cannabis in December 1990, transported by land through the Soviet Union (Interpol).

### Psychotropic drugs

European seizures have risen dramatically both in quantity (dosage units) and weight, particularly in Northern Europe. Hallucinogen seizures, which include MDMA, or "Ecstasy", rose from 6,300 dosage units in 1988 to 938,000 in 1989. Almost all the total, ie 930,000 dosage units, was seized in the Netherlands. 75 to 80 per cent of the amphetamines consumed in Scandinavia, the Netherlands, the UK and France are manufactured in the Netherlands, almost all the rest in Poland. (DND)

### Trafficking – future threats

*(i) Instability in principal heroin source areas.*    Political instability, civil unrest and religious/nationalist tensions within the drug producing areas of South West Asia – Europe's principal supply source – encourage the trading of arms for drugs, as in Afghanistan, or of arms for drug courier services, as is the case with Sri Lankan Tamils. The border areas of the "Golden Crescent" of Iraq, Afghanistan and Iran are controlled by tribes such as Pathans, Kurds and Beluchis whose dislocation on both sides of a border guarantees safe passage across it. These are "grey areas" outside central government control, thus despite government commitments and promises to eliminate opium growth, there seems little likelihood of this happening in the immediate future. There has been increased opium production in another "grey area" – the Syrian-controlled Bekaa valley in the Lebanon where the Italian mafia is providing refining expertise.[4]

*(ii) Instability in principal cocaine source areas.*    All three of the world's main coca producing countries – Peru, Bolivia and Colombia, face economic and social problems at the same time as having to service large external debts. The situation is worst in Peru, where much of the country is under emergency rule and traffickers and guerrillas fight for and occasionally collaborate in control of the coca growing zones. Bolivia and Peru have agreed to accept US military and economic aid for counter narcotics efforts, but the results remain uncertain due to national hostility to such intervention. Colombia has negotiated the surrender of the leading members of the Medellin cartel but on the evidence to date, their "imprisonment" constitutes little more than a sanctuary from which to conduct their operations in greater peace.

*(iii) Impoverished countries service drug traffic.*    According to a British judicial enquiry,[5] most West Africans arrested for smuggling drugs into Britain are

6                    *Research Institute for the Study of Conflict and Terrorism*

driven by poverty rather than greed and are ignorant of the seriousness of their crime and its personal consequences if detected. Nonetheless as long as the consumer market exists there will doubtless be thousands willing to take the risk for a sum that represents several years' legitimate labour.

*(iv) Colombian move to heroin production.*    There is evidence that Colombians are turning to opium growing to augment their financial stake in the drugs trade. The US Justice Department fears that an alliance may already have been made with the Mafia to produce and export heroin to North America and Europe. The Colombian Chief of Police reported in the autumn of 1991 that 2,000 hectares of opium had been eradicated in a few weeks[6]; there may be as many as 25,000 hectares under cultivation in 12 different provinces of the country. The far-left guerrilla group FARC is thought to have an agreement with the cartels to protect the production areas.

*(v) Heroin refining in Europe.*    Major seizures of morphine base and of acetic anhydride near the Iran/Turkish border and on the Ankara-Istanbul highway respectively in 1990 and 1991 (Interpol), suggest that morphine base may be being brought into European laboratories for refining, as was the case in the early 1980s. The seizure of 15 kg of morphine base from a Turkish lorry on the French/Italian border in December 1990 suggests an Italian involvement.

*(vi) Traffickers' perceptions of a "barrier free Europe".*    The much-heralded Single European Market opens up new horizons for drug traffickers when internal border checks are abolished. Given the low prices and apparent reduction of demand in the North American market, the EC will be particularly attractive to the cocaine cartels who have yet to exploit the full European consumer potential.

*(vii) Drug trafficking and the former East bloc.*    The most significant developments in drug trafficking may yet emerge from changing conditions in Eastern Europe and the former Soviet Union. Some relate to capital transfer and investment and will be dealt with later. Other developments could give rise to new drug sources and therefore constitute both a European and a global threat.

It has already been noted that the relaxing of controls in former East bloc countries has led to these countries being used as transit states, in particular for heroin moving westwards along variations of the Balkan corridor. Yugoslavia made Europe's largest opium seizures in 1988 and 1989 but since the outbreak of civil war, consignments have largely been rerouted. It is also possible that now or in the future, drugs may be given free passage in exchange for arms or hard currency.

Many other countries are experiencing a combination of political unrest, economic hardship and an explosion of nationalist/separatist tensions. Not only is it likely that these countries will experience greater abuse problems and related social costs – crime rates in Russia have soared since 1989 as have drug related crimes – but there is a strong possibility that, following the

*Drug Trafficking After 1992*                                          7

Afghanistan model, groups within these countries may try to alleviate economic distress and/or fund nationalist struggle by turning land over to profitable drug production. The Asian republics have the potential for growing cannabis, opium and coca, and with some organisational and technical help, could in a short time be important drug producing countries. There is evidence that Sicilian and Colombian organised crime groups may already be in place: in June 1991 the Czech Interior Minister reported in the course of an interview with the Italian news agency ANSA that the Mafia was trying to establish drug production in the Soviet Union and set up new transit routes via Poland.[7] Polish authorities have reported that growing numbers of Colombians have settled in recent months. In addition, both Czechoslovakia and Poland have large and technically advanced chemical industries whose resources could be diverted into the increased production of existing or new synthetic drugs.

### Trafficking trends: conclusions

*(i) The "external threat".*   It must be pointed out that considerable international attention is being paid to drug problems in the developing nations whose governments are aware of the risks and have sought international assistance: the Pompidou Group, the United Nations, the Organisation of American States (OAS) and Interpol as well as several national drug enforcement agencies are already involved in the provision of expert legal advice, law enforcement training, the supply of drug detection equipment and in offering the basic lessons of experience. However Yugoslavia must be considered out of bounds for drug enforcement monitoring and therefore an important Balkan route initiative started by the Italian government with the collaboration of the United Nations International Drug Control Programme (UNDCP), the Customs Co-operation Council and Interpol cannot proceed as planned. Should the civil unrest in the former Soviet republics degenerate it will become equally difficult to intervene in potential drug production zones. Finally, the prospect of a heroin marketing drive aimed at Europe directed by a Colombian-Mafia alliance is a formidable one, and presents a serious threat to EC stability.

*(ii) The "internal" threat.*   Some observers of the drug phenomenon consider the EC as "under attack" and Europeans as innocent victims of ruthless drug barons from far-off countries. This is hardly accurate. Domestic demand directly stimulates supply, and indigenous trafficking groups are in constant search of new contacts and drug sources. It is generally believed that the quantities of cocaine stockpiled in the Netherlands and in Spain require these countries to be considered as primary producer countries. Rotterdam handles 280m tonnes of goods and 2.5m containers annually. Only 10 per cent of the incoming containers are destined for Holland, the rest are transhipped to other European countries. According to Euro-MP Sir Jack Stewart Clark, out of 6,000 containers arriving each day, only seven or eight are being searched and these are from the 10 per cent destined for the Netherlands. Of Rotterdam's 1,500 customs officers only 150 are assigned to investigative

work.[8] The Netherlands, it will be remembered, is also principal manufacturer of amphetamines for the Community.

It has been officially acknowledged that parts of southern Italy are under the "total dominance" of organised crime.[9] The power of the Mafia is continually being consolidated inside Italy by political influence and territorial control, and outside the country by a powerful influence in illicit drug markets and by penetration of the legal, financial and economic system. Unless firm action is taken in Italy to isolate and prevent the spread of the "mafia model" of corruption and intimidation, and unless EC partners take suitable precautions against it, the security of European financial and economic structures may be compromised.

Links between ethnic groups of Chinese, Turks and Pakistanis with rights of residence within the Community are using the cover of their predominently law-abiding countrymen to run networks of drug trafficking and money laundering systems within and beyond Community borders. Chinese groups based in Hong Kong and Macao are likely to intensify their European bases over the coming years.

In conclusion, the threat from drug trafficking to the Single European Market represents not only a continuation of trends already identified, but new elements which require immediate policy responses and different strategies.

## 3. DRUG LAW ENFORCEMENT POST 1992 – PROBLEMS AND RESPONSES

### Interdiction – general prospects

The trends described above suggest that interdiction efforts, however much they may rise from year to year, are doing little to stop drugs entering or moving around the Community; there is no reason to suppose the situation will improve after 1992. Some experts believe that pouring manpower and resources into interdiction is not cost-effective and may even be counter-productive. It is worth noting in this regard the detailed study carried out in 1988 by Rand Corporation[10] which examined the likely success of attempts to reduce availability of cocaine and cannabis in the US by altering the behaviour of actual and potential traffickers through increases in risks and costs.

According to Rand, interdiction of cocaine supplies had an almost negative impact – impressive rises in seizures inland and in interdiction at frontiers had no impact on the price, which fell steadily during the period examined. Such increased costs as there were had been passed on to final users with little loss of market, indicating that the demand for cocaine was inelastic with respect to the costs of importation. Interdiction efforts with cannabis products were more likely to be successful due to the greater bulk, but in the United States had served chiefly to boost illicit domestic production. The report concluded that unless interdiction severity were increased significantly on all possible routes, price increases in drugs would not be sufficient to deter or reduce consumption.

The geographical size and position of the United States makes some of the premises of the Rand study inapplicable to Europe as far as cocaine is concerned, but the references to demand elasticity and the proximity of land and sea routes linking cannabis and heroin producing countries to Europe may make for a realistic comparison. If so, the outlook is not reassuring.

## External frontiers

According to the principles of the Single European Market, a reinforced external frontier will compensate for the abolition of internal borders after 1992, and fixed customs checkpoints at internal borders will be replaced by mobile, flexible anti-smuggling teams which will increasingly rely on intelligence and on profiling of likely drug trafficking suspects. In practice, external border controls will inevitably vary in their severity and traffickers will quickly learn which entry points to use and which to avoid.

Joint surveillance of common air and sea borders has been a feature of EC co-operation for several years: the UK has Memoranda of Understanding (MoUs) to this effect with Spain, France, and the Channel Islands. For Belgium, France, the Netherlands and the UK, such collaboration is daily routine; mutual border surveillance is enshrined in the Schengen Accord; Italy and Spain have mutual vessel boarding and inspection rights.

In 1989, joint EC operations led to the seizure of 25 metric tons of cannabis, 10 kg of cocaine, 1000 rounds of ammunition, 5 metric tons of cigarettes and 10 vessels. In 1990, eight drug smuggling vessels and 9.2 metric tons of drugs were detected. (Customs & Excise) Yet the limited success of such operations in relation to the amounts actually smuggled through has been achieved in a narrow and relatively well-patrolled maritime area; one must presume that more exposed and vulnerable zones of the outer EC frontier such as Greece and the Baltic will offer more opportunities for drug traffickers. The northern Community seas are dotted with myriads of archipelagos and natural harbours which could afford cover to traffickers; likewise, the southern Mediterranean may become extremely attractive for drug smuggling vessels, particularly in the guise of cruise or pleasure boats. Gibraltar is another weak point on the outer perimeter; its disputed territorial status has prevented the signing of an External Frontiers Convention between member states[11] and makes police co-operation and practices such as surveillance and controlled deliveries of drugs more difficult.

Britain regards its seas as a natural asset, but they also provide drug trafficking opportunities: Customs and Excise list 147 ports in England and Wales for trade statistics purposes: there are at least 150,000 pleasure craft around the shores of the UK; Reeds Nautical Almanac lists over 40,000 berths at 188 marinas and this excludes many yacht clubs and other facilities for portable craft.[12] France and Belgium have compulsory registration of pleasure craft, and the Netherlands is planning to introduce it. Devon and Cornwall Police introduced a voluntary registration scheme in 1986 known as "Operation Boatwatch" which is already harmonised with registration schemes in the Netherlands, Belgium and Germany. Such schemes should be mandatory throughout the EC and technically compatible.

Containers are and will remain a major means of smuggling drugs into the EC by sea and road. More resources and manpower should be allocated to introducing swifter, more efficient means of checking these which will not cause undue delay. The impossibility of carrying out regular, comprehensive physical checks on TIR vehicles is acknowledged (Interpol), yet stricter controls can and should be exercised **a**) by the use of specific intelligence and computerised suspect data bases co-ordinated between neighbouring countries, as envisaged for example in the Balkan route initiative and **b**) by tightening up on the rules for granting TIR licences.

The Customs Co-operation Council (CCC) has made significant efforts in promoting international collaboration between transport associations. CCC's "Carrier Co-operation Initiative', devised to improve and enhance co-operation between customs authorities, private carriers and the international trading community, was approved at the G7 summit in July 1991. This represents an important advance in the fight against drug trafficking and should also be encouraged.

### Internal borders

*(i) Discrepancies.* The flexibility for each EC state to find its own solution to internal border control is enshrined in two policy statements. The first, provided for by the Treaty of Rome Article 36, allows each member state to retain

".. . prohibitions or restrictions on imports, exports or goods in transit justified on grounds of public morality, public policy or public security."

The second is contained in a joint declaration by EC Heads of Government on Articles 13 to 19 of the Single European Act (1985):

"Nothing in these provisions shall affect the right of member states to take such measures as they consider necessary for the purposes of controlling immigration from third countries, and to combat terrorism, crime, the traffic in drugs and illicit trading in works of art and antiques."

Differing interpretations of these clauses has led to some confusion, for example over the EC Baggage Regulation which calls for the abolition of baggage checks on passengers travelling by air and sea inside the Community. Britain initially protested, but has now accepted, that checks on travellers from outside the EC should be carried out at the first point of Community entry only, with all further intra EC travel to be treated as domestic.

In order for this to be effective, common procedures for external border checks will have to be established, and this is indeed one of the goals of the original five, now eight countries party to the Schengen Accord of 1985 (signed in 1990, to be ratified 1 January 1993) which provides for the total abolition of checks on persons at the common frontiers of the participating countries. In compensation, it provides for co-operation on a wide range of subjects including the surveillance of external frontiers, common policies on visa and political asylum, co-operation between police and legal authorities, extradition and the delegation of the enforcement of criminal judgements. It also covers drugs, firearms and immigration policy, and anticipates many of the EC single

*Drug Trafficking After 1992*                                      11

market provisions. Britain has justified its reluctance to follow the Schengen states by citing the evidence of drug seizures: of all drugs seized in the course of 1990, 61 per cent had come from or through another EC country. Police seizures inland were six times as high as those of Customs seizures on the borders, but the latter represented 79 per cent of the total by volume. (C & E) Discrepancies in attitudes towards policing the internal frontiers may yet be a source of friction between Britain and her EC partners when the Single Market becomes a reality.

*(ii) Precursor Chemicals.*   Mention has been made of the EC Regulation on precursor chemicals and its valuable contribution to preventing diversion of chemicals into drug production. Given that many of the chemicals are produced within EC states – France is a major producer of a chemical whose only use is to manufacture amphetamines; the Netherlands produces large quantities of acetic anhydride – attention should be given to intra-Community movements of chemicals as well as to movements in and out of the EC. Chemical profiling of seized substances should be routine procedure for the identification of laboratories and source materials.

**Policing and accountability**

Problems of manning joint frontiers call into question the issue of responsibilities and accountability in law enforcement. British police and customs officers, unlike most of their European counterparts, are not armed except in exceptional circumstances. Most EC police forces are organised nationally and functionally and are often answerable to several ministries, whereas the UK police has no central political direction: the 52 separate forces operate a tripartite system of accountability through the Home Office, the area Chief Constable and local Police Authorities.

The Supplementary Agreement signed at Schengen in 1990 foresees a declaration by each signatory, at the time of ratification, to harmonise procedures for cross border pursuit, rights of arrest, territorial and time limits, and penalties for violation of the agreed procedures. These are important initiatives and are a model for the rest of the EC to follow, but the process is not without problems: French law has hitherto denied the possibility of arrest by a foreign policeman on French territory; hot pursuit is a particularly delicate issue in the UK, given that the one EC land border is between the Irish Republic and Northern Ireland. Nor are matters straightforward even between England and Scotland, where fundamentally differing legal systems apply and there is no automatic reciprocity of powers of arrest or even validity of arrest warrants.

Overall, the potential for an overlap of roles, for conflicts of responsibility and for uncertain accountability make for numerous ambiguities within the otherwise welcome prospect of Community cross-border co-operation.

**Police and customs exchanges – developments**

Progress has been made in nurturing co-operation and understanding within European police and customs forces: since 1984 there have been exchanges of Drug Liaison Officers (DLOs) within EC customs forces and more recently, a number have been posted to East European locations as well as to the producer countries. The Matthaeus Project provides for exchange of customs officers from ports and airports in EC countries for one month postings to observe and participate in similar work in another EC state.

Members of Scotland Yard's European Liaison Section (ELS) have carried out exchanges with other EC countries for periods of four to six weeks. Language training is slowly improving but remains a stumbling block, particularly for the British. It is hard to see how any fruitful collaboration can take place without a mutual language of communication, therefore all such developments should be improved and broadened as far as possible.

**Legal discrepancies**

*(i) Extradition.* Bilateral and multilateral agreements on extradition are in place amongst all EC member states, and all have ratified the 1957 European Convention on Extradition (although Britain did so only in 1991). This means that instead of having to present a *prima facie* case for extradition, parties to the Convention need provide only an arrest warrant and a request for extradition accompanied by a statement of facts and evidence of law and identity. However Dutch police are prevented by law from passing on any information to another country which may result in the arrest of a Dutch national. Any party may refuse to extradite its own nationals and Germany and Greece must refuse on constitutional grounds. Given that extradition is a cornerstone of mutual legal co-operation in the fight against drug trafficking, and that international drug traffickers continually cross national boundaries, any single country's refusal to co-operate will inevitably weaken the chances of bringing them to justice.

*(ii) Disclosure of identity.* There are considerable discrepancies within the EC over the requirement to carry an identity card, for drivers to have their licence and car documents with them, and in obligations for hotels to compile a register of guests and make this available to the police. These can all be exploited by the criminal and make police detection of forged documents and papers more difficult.

*(iii) Law enforcement/drug use.* Although drug law enforcement policies against trafficking are broadly similar within EC member states, the wide disparity of treatment of drug possession and consumption is another obstacle in the way of full European harmonisation. Personal consumption of any drug is rarely, if ever, an arrestable offence in Belgium, the Netherlands, Denmark and Spain. France, Italy and the UK in theory penalise personal consumption and possession although in making an arrest, discretion is used on the basis of the quantity and type of drug found. All countries make a distinction

## Drug Trafficking After 1992                                  13

between "hard" and "soft" drugs but the criteria for distinguishing these vary. The Netherlands is exceptional in that dealing in, possession and consumption of modest amounts of cannabis is never punished and it is sold in public places without interference. Mobile methadone buses tour the cities and distribute quantities of drugs and syringes to addicts. Social services concentrate on harm minimisation and do not emarginate drug users but concentrate on trying to make them behave responsibly. The result is that drug abuse problems amongst the Dutch population have been contained, with a low AIDS and drug-related death rate. Unfortunately, drug users from other countries abuse the regime and cause problems and unwelcome burdens for the Dutch authorities. These are likely to increase after 1992. The ready availability of drugs in the Netherlands will make it more likely that consumers will enter the country, purchase their own requirements and return unhindered to other EC countries with stricter drug controls and higher prices, where they will resell at a profit.

**Problems of non Community nationals**

The collapse of the Communist regimes has led to acute and previously unforeseeable problems of migratory movements. These affect the EC as a whole, but have particular implications for tackling the problem of drug trafficking.

A combination of the perceived attractions of a wealthy Community and the urge to flee from hardship and homelessness, from nationalist or from religious persecution have and will in the future put increased pressure on EC resources. Western European countries with already high unemployment risk exacerbating existing social tensions by allowing in a new tide of immigrants. Opinion polls and electoral trends during 1991 in many EC states have provided alarming evidence of national xenophobia and outright racial hatred.

As far as the drugs market is concerned, there is a risk that those who come and find no work or homes will be easy prey for traffickers looking for a desperate and easily replaceable source of black market labour without papers, residence or legal identity. The most susceptible will inevitably be the young.

A conference of Justice and Interior Ministers of 27 European countries met in Berlin in October 1991 to try to resolve some of the most urgent immigration issues. It was revealed that at least 200,000 illegal immigrants had used Eastern Europe as a springboard into the EC in a single year, most remaining in Germany. Official immigration requests amounted to the same number again, although Soviet authorities warned of 5m potential emigrants with sights set worldwide. The EC Commission reported that the Community had received 169,000 applications for asylum in 1989 and 327,000 in 1990. 60 per cent of the applications were for Germany, 20 per cent for France. It was predicted that some 3m potential immigrants would be knocking on EC doors over the next five years.[13]

Two policy responses were formulated, one to deal with illegal immigration networks and those trafficking in false entry and work documentation, the other to deal with legitimate demands for entry, residence and asylum. The following measures were approved in principle:

(**i**) harmonisation of rights of asylum;

(**ii**) harmonisation of expulsion procedures and of other measures to deter illegal immigration;

(**iii**) airline companies to be asked to refuse boarding rights to passengers without the necessary immigration requirements in the country of destination;

(**iv**) establishment of a data bank which, with the assistance of the Red Cross, would distinguish genuine refugees from fake ones;

(**v**) launching of a new policy to improve settlement and integration of legal immigrants to avoid racism and ill feeling;

(**vi**) provision of economic aid to countries from which most immigrants come, combined with pressure on these countries to discourage emigration.

Further discussion and endorsement of these proposals were expected from the Maastricht summit in December 1991 but a unified Community line was not reached. Henceforth the EC will decide on the list of countries from which visitors will need visas to enter the Community but a decision on asylum policy has been postponed until 1993.

At best, resolution of the immigration problem will be a long, slow process requiring enormous generosity and sensitivity; in the short term, the EC can expect no let up in the pressures upon it, with all the social, political and criminal implications that this entails.

**New structures**

*(i) Europol.*    Following a meeting of TREVI ministers in The Hague on 2–3 December 1991 to discuss the 1992 Programme of Action, a formal agreement was made to establish a European Police Organisation or **Europol**, whose purpose will be to collect and analyse information on cross-border crime, including crime that extends beyond the territory of the Community. The first stage in this process will be the setting up, by the end of 1992, of a European Drugs Unit (EDU) to collect and analyse relevant information from member states relating to combating drug crime at a European level. Europol's other activities will then be extended on a step by step basis, with an operational function envisaged in the long term.

Despite the obvious advantages for law enforcement of a federal-style operational police force, practical problems and political realities make its creation unlikely in the immediate future. Differing judicial systems within EC member states, different attitudes to law enforcement, different languages and cultures, and most of all, the implicit loss of sovereignty that it would entail are the major obstacles. Experience shows that even co-ordinating national forces is not a simple task. In Italy, for example, rivalries within the three main police forces have made the construction of inter-force units a highly-charged political issue and one almost impossible to realise. In the brief 15-month spell that General Carlo Alberto Dalla Chiesa was put in charge of a single anti-terrorist unit with a national remit, he virtually brought the Red Brigades to their knees, but the conflicts and jealousy that arose were only just contained by an awareness of how desperate the terrorist emergency was and by the abandonment of political differences in order to bring it under control. Attempts to repeat this experience with cross-force anti-kidnap and anti-mafia units were begun at the end of 1991 to strong resistance within the *carabinieri*; it remains to be seen whether this can be successfully overcome.

Without diminishing the value of the numerous personal contacts built up over years between individuals in different countries, it must be said that the prospects for overcoming national pride and achieving mutual trust amongst 12 widely-differing nations seem remote. In operational terms perhaps the best one can hope for are implementation of the Schengen objectives such as fuller co-operation in external border surveillance, better internal cross-border assistance and in particular, more operations such as controlled deliveries which permit a longer drug trafficking chain to be detected. This law enforcement technique has proved an invaluable tool, quite independently of EC or Schengen agreements, and is provided for in all recent multilateral treaties and conventions. Its use should be intensified and extended to those countries such as Turkey and Portugal which currently forbid it.

*(ii) Euro-criminal court.*   It has been pointed out that political opposition to loss of national sovereignty has been an obstacle to full European harmonisation. Research is currently going on into the feasibility of a European Criminal Court to judge cases of transnational crime or crimes designated as "international" such as certain drugs and terrorist offences. Although the prospects seem distant at present, it is a worthwhile goal to aim for at an EC level because it would transcend many of the existing legal discrepancies mentioned here. If all member states were duly represented and a common judicial code for certain crimes adopted unanimously, political pressure might in the end be overcome in the interests of perceived benefits and greater justice for all.

**Europol – repercussions**

One of the most important issues to be resolved for the future of European anti-drug efforts is the role of existing information and intelligence structures and how these should best be co-ordinated, particularly in the light of EDU/Europol.

*(i) Present situation.*   Within the EC, TREVI Group III deals with organised crime and drug trafficking, as does the Mutual Assistance Group (MAG) and MAG 92, although these have policy making and strategic functions rather than intelligence gathering. TREVI is apparently considering setting up a centralised data base for all serious crime to which all EC police forces would have access. The eight Schengen countries have set up a Schengen Information Service (SIS) based at Strasbourg which, although to date not fully operational, has a valuable data base on asylum requests to member countries. Schengen aims to set up a common computer-based suspect index but progress on this has been delayed due to differences in data protection standards. The

considerable difficulties posed by varying standards in this area between member states ought to be resolved by 1993 with a Community Directive on data protection, currently being drafted.

The UK has been forced to modernise its police intelligence structure to meet the needs of the Single Market: information and intelligence exchange in the UK has always been hampered by the existence of 52 separate police forces and the lack of a centralised intelligence database. This will be remedied from Spring 1992 by the establishment of a National Criminal Intelligence Service (NCIS) which will unite the information currently held by Regional Crime Squads and will absorb the National Drugs Intelligence Unit and the National Football Intelligence Unit. It will hold data on active travelling criminals and will link up with all Regional Criminal Intelligence offices in the UK via the X25 Police National Network. The question of whether and how this might be linked up with other EC police forces seems not to have been adequately studied, although it has been reported[14] that the new computer system will be compatible with that of the *Bundes-kriminalamt* at Wiesbaden.

*(ii) The role of customs.* The future role of customs forces inside EDU/Europol is a delicate one and is not yet clear. Customs officers in the UK and in Denmark collaborate fully in drugs cases (in National Drugs Intelligence Units) but this is not the case in most EC countries. In the FRG, the *Bundeskriminalamt* seems intent on running antidrug activities to the gradual exclusion of border and customs forces, although this is not admitted officially. There is a risk for those countries where police and customs have built up a close working partnership that drugs may be merged with organised crime and, in losing its "exclusivity", may slip out of customs control for all but interdiction efforts. The Customs Co-operation Council will doubtless continue to serve the needs of its 111 member states through its many activities but its drugs role may be re-defined once Europol becomes fully effective.

*(iii) Interpol.* Interpol has become increasingly involved in collecting inform-ation on drug movements and traffickers, and the rise in information requests of 66 per cent between 1986 and 1989 is due in no small measure to this activity. In 1989 Interpol began the electronic storage of data on Chinese members of organised crime groups in Europe, otherwise known as "Operation Prostar", a data base containing details of some 300 individuals, their associations and their meeting places. More recently, "Operation Probalkan" was set up to collect information and intelligence on Balkan route traffic and traffickers. It includes data on known suspects, associations, vehicles and routes. Special seizures information is collated and working group meetings are held on specific drug syndicates from which important arrests have been made. The Interpol/CCC/UNIDCP/Italian government Balkan route initiative aims to provide a secure communications network to link drug enforcement agencies of the 10 principal countries along which heroin is transported to Europe; the on-line data base should have its terminal in Interpol HQ in Lyon. Cocaine working groups are currently studying packaging and labels

on cocaine seized worldwide to match them up with drug trafficking groups. A data base has been set up to store information on money laundering issues, including a file on money couriers. From March 1992 a new system known as Automated Search Facility will provide direct access to hard core information for each National Central Bureau. Independently of ASF, Interpol operates a three-tier internal data protection system governing the release of information which respects the wish of the originating country to limit the recipients of any information given.

Unfortunately, the international dimensions which make Interpol valuable as a privileged observer of international criminal activities are the very same that are perceived as reducing its effectiveness in terms of speed of response, reliability of security and formality of procedures, and ultimately may jeopardise its future role in European drug monitoring efforts. The location of EDU's headquarters has not yet been decided, although Wiesbaden, Rome and Lyon are all candidates. Regardless of the choice, the originality and breadth of Interpol's achievements in the drugs field should serve as a vital complement to the EDU and should not be replaced by it.

## 4. CAPITAL MOVEMENT

"Those who accumulate profits of thousands of billions [of lire] cannot be without a political project. . . . It is the means whereby they enter the legal market, take over banks or other economic structures; it is the beginning of the transformation from criminal system to political system."[15]

This study is particularly concerned with the issue of money laundering legislation because it represents the spearhead of any successful attack on the business of drug trafficking. The accumulation of illicit profits is perhaps the most politically and economically destabilising element of the international drugs trade: it gives traffickers the means to buy arms, property, companies, political power, protection and of course more drugs. After arms trafficking, drugs turn over more money than any other business – an estimated 500bn dollars per annum. The most dangerous aspect of money laundering lies in its potential for eroding and distorting the legal economies of public institutions and entire national economies. The free circulation of untaxed funds distorts freedom of competition and undermines the autonomy and liberty of legitimate business. Criminal control over large sums of money can be used to condition the liquidity levels of credit institutions, especially small ones, and therefore influence their operational capacity. On a large scale, it can provoke sudden reactions from markets sensitive to movements of a speculative nature and even cause fluctuations in stock market prices, exchange or interest rates.

The purpose of money laundering is to conceal the source of illicit capital, change its form and control its integration or reinvestment in the legal economy. This last stage completes the financial transformation and in turn creates the conditions for another change to take place: the legitimisation of illegitimately acquired capital implies not simply the laundering of criminal funds, but allows criminals to "launder" themselves; to move out of a clandestine underworld into an assumed status of respectability and relative impunity where the criminal is virtually indistinguishable from the honest businessman.

Efforts to curb drug trafficking within the EC after 1992 will depend crucially on international co-operation in the criminalisation of money laundering and the identification, tracing, seizure and confiscation of illicit assets. The European Community is in its relative infancy in this field: a few member states have introduced appropriate legislation in the last three to four years but the majority are only on the verge of doing so. By 1 January 1993 however, all 12 EC member states will be bound by the provisions of the EC Commission Council Directive on Money Laundering, backed up by appropriate national legislation.

This section of the report outlines the financial power that drug traffickers have, discusses the international agreements reached to combat money laundering and highlights the problems that two EC states, Italy and the UK, have already experienced domestically and will encounter with regard to European harmonisation.

### Drug profits and Latin America

The power that drug money bestows on the major traffickers has been seen in crudest evidence in Latin American countries. In 1980, a coup d-état in Bolivia encouraged and financed by drug baron Roberto Suarez Gomez established his cousin Luis Arch Gomez as Interior Minister. His spell in office was brief, but it was largely devoted to facilitating the production and distribution of cocaine.

Civil strife in Peru intensified in the mid 1980s when the Maoist revolutionary group *Sendero Luminoso* (Shining Path) took on the "protection" of the principal coca plantations in the Upper Huallaga Valley. Such are their profits from "revolutionary taxes" exacted from growers and traffickers that, according to the US Task Force on Terrorism and Unconventional Warfare, the group has been able to "increase the size of its armed force from 2,000 to 3,000 between 1983 and 1984 to 10,000 by mid-1987, as well as improve the training of its professional units, and support expensive urban operations."[16]

The financial and political power of Colombian cartels has conditioned the exercise of democracy in that country and has imposed a series of political compromises through the force of intimidation and violence.

It has been estimated that Bolivian cocaine exports in 1989 reached approximately 0.8–1.2bn dollars, representing 19 to 23 per cent of gross domestic product (GDP) and 150 per cent of legal exports; for Colombia the figure was 1.5–4bn dollars, 4 to 10 per cent of GDP, 29 to 77 per cent of legal exports. Peru, the biggest coca producing country, earned 1–1.8bn dollars: 38 to 69 per cent of legal exports and 2.5 to 4.6 per cent of GDP.[17]

### Money laundering and Italian organised crime

International attention awoke to the significance of drug money laundering with the Italo-American "Pizza Connection" case that came to trial in 1985.

*Drug Trafficking After 1992*                                                    19

It began in 1979 with the opening of a suitcase containing 600.000 dollars at Palermo airport and led to the arrest of drug and money couriers. the discovery of five heroin refining laboratories in Sicily and a drug trail that began in Thailand and crossed Asia, Europe and North America. The return money trail started in Mafia-run pizzerias in New York and took a different route, passing through Canada and the Caribbean to Switzerland and Italy, and ended up in banks in Hong Kong, Singapore and Bangkok. Of the 1.6bn dollars laundered, only 60m was ever traced.

Nowadays the Sicilian Mafia, or *Cosa Nostra*, no longer supplies 30 per cent of all the heroin destined for North America as it did at the beginning of the 1980s, but still takes a major slice of its income from drugs. as indeed do the Neapolitan *Camorra* and the Calabrian *'ndrangheta*. A recent survey estimates that organised crime in Italy earns approximately 100.000bn lire per year (120bn dollars) from illicit activities, of which 32bn dollars is attributed to drug revenue. In terms of Italian net profits from drugs, guesses vary wildly, but range from 4.8bn dollars per annum[18] to 9bn dollars[19]. In comparison, drug revenue in the UK and in the FRG seems small: the *Bundeskriminalamt* estimates illicit drug sales in Germany to total between 2 and 4bn DMs[20] (approx 1.2–2.4bn dollars) whilst NDIU puts the British figure at around £2.5bn[21] (4.2bn dollars) of which up to half may be profit.

**Global action**

*(i) Basel Declaration.*    The first concerted international action against money laundering was the Basel Declaration of Principles. signed in December 1988 by the G7 countries plus Belgium, Luxembourg, Netherlands. Sweden and Switzerland. It commits central banks of these countries to take active steps to identify customers and the source of their funds, to refuse all transactions of dubious legality and to collaborate with criminal investigations within the maximum limits permitted by domestic legislation.

*(ii) Vienna Convention.*    The UN Vienna Convention, signed the same month and in force since November 1990, compels ratifying nations to introduce the crime of money laundering, to provide means for the identification, tracing, seizure and confiscation of the proceeds from drug trafficking and calls on the removal of bank secrecy for this offence. Ratifying countries must provide mutual legal assistance in drug trafficking enquiries and are urged to introduce techniques such as that of controlled deliveries.

*(iii) Financial Action Task Force (FATF).*    The FATF was set up in Paris in July 1989 after the G7 summit of that month. Composed of the G7 members, the EC. Sweden. Netherlands, Belgium, Luxembourg, Switzerland, Australia, Spain and Austria, its stated tasks were:
● an analysis of the money laundering phenomenon
● an assessment of the international instruments and national programmes already in place
● the presentation of action recommendations.

FATF reported in June 1990. Working on estimates of consumption needs of drug users, of seizures made and of world drug production, it concluded that sales of cocaine, heroin and cannabis were in the region of 122bn dollars per annum in the US and Europe, of which 50 to 70 per cent (85bn dollars) were available for laundering. Global profits at main dealer level (ie those most liable to international laundering) were estimated at about 30bn dollars per annum.

FATF members approved and endorsed 40 action recommendations, subsequently extended to 24 nations. These concentrate on improvements to national legal systems, the enhancement of the role of national financial systems and the strengthening of international co-operation. The enlarged group reported a second time in June 1991 to assess progress and implementation of the 40 recommendations by the participating countries, and to extend participation as far as possible.

*(iv) Interpol.* A special FOPAC (*Fonds Provenants d'Activités Criminelles*) Working Group was formed in 1988 by resolution of the ICPO–Interpol General Assembly. Its aims are:
• to study and develop new mechanisms for the gathering of financial information connected with narcotics transactions and other crimes;
• to develop proposals for the sharing of such information by member countries and
• to develop an implementation plan for the creation of a clearing house for the receipt, co-ordination and execution of requests for this information.

FOPAC has developed a model law which incorporates measures deemed necessary for the identification, tracing, seizure and confiscation of assets of funds derived from criminal activities. It publishes a "Financial Assets Encyclopaedia", a guide for law enforcement officers in their search for financial information concerning criminal organisations. Following a questionnaire sent out to member countries, the 1992 edition will include details of each respondent's confiscation laws, central bank currency regulations and other financial information, and FOPAC will provide regular updates in the form of a newsletter. FOPAC has also set up a data base on money launderers which includes names of individuals, their aliases, their bank accounts and their companies real and fictitious; a special file on money couriers is being developed. This database will provide a valuable input for EDU when it is established.

**European Action**

The first paragraph of the preamble to the EC Council Directive on prevention of the financial system for the purpose of money laundering lays out its essential objective: " . . . when credit and financial institutions are used to launder proceeds from criminal activities, the soundness and stability of the particular institution concerned and confidence in the financial system as a whole could be seriously jeopardised, thereby losing the trust of the public".

The Directive is primarily a proactive tool: that is, it deals with measures to be taken before any crime has taken place. This is a deliberate approach, since the explanatory memorandum states that repressive measures are dealt with by the UN Vienna Convention. In fact, once ratified, the Council of Europe Convention on Laundering, Search, Seizure and Confiscation of the Proceeds from Crime (henceforth known as the Council of Europe Convention) should be more effective still in terms of repression since it covers a whole range of measures from proactive prevention to reactive procedures such as asset restraint, seizure and confiscation and the means by which these should be harmonised between contracting parties. Furthermore ratification of the Convention is not limited to Council member states: Canada, Australia and the United States are likely to sign in the near future and former East bloc countries are being urged to consider doing so.

## International Treaties – definitions

Defining money laundering is a crucial first step: whereas the Vienna Convention limits it to drug related offences, the EC Directive defines it as: "the conversion or transfer of property, knowing that such property is derived from criminal activity or from an act of participation in such activity, for the purpose of concealing or disguising the illicit origin of the property or of assisting any person who is involved in committing such activity to evade the legal consequences of his actions; the concealment or disguise of the true nature, source, location, disposition, movement, rights with respect to, or ownership of property, knowing that such property is derived from criminal activity or from an act of participation in such activity; the acquisition, possession or use of property, knowing, at the time of receipt, that such property was derived from criminal activity or from an act of participation in such activity." Any attempt to "counsel, facilitate or assist the commission of" such actions is also an offence. The required element of knowledge, intent or purpose is to be inferred from objective factual circumstances.

## UK and Italian national legislation – definitions

According to the UK Drug Trafficking Offences Act of 1986 (DTOA), the crime of money laundering is committed when "retention or control" of the proceeds of drug trafficking is facilitated, "whether by concealment, removal from the jurisdiction, transfer to nominees or otherwise" or when funds from drug trafficking are placed at the disposal or benefit of another to acquire property by way of investment, and the person who enters into such an arrangement knows or suspects that the other person carries or has carried on drug trafficking or has benefited from drug trafficking. A similar provision was made in the Prevention of Terrorism (Temporary Provisions) Act 1989 (PTA) which criminalises anyone who facilitates retention or control of "funds which may be applied or used for the commission of, or in furtherance of or in connection with, acts of terrorism".

Although Scotland applies a separate legal system, money laundering provisions are substantially the same as those in the rest of the UK unless otherwise specified.

The Criminal Justice (International Co-operation) Act of 1990 (CJICA) extends the drug-related offence: A person is guilty of an offence if he "conceals or disguises" any property which represents his profits of drug trafficking or "converts or transfers that property or removes it from the jurisdiction". Anyone who assists another in such arrangements or who acquires a given property for no or for inadequate consideration, in either case "knowing or having reasonable grounds to suspect" that it represents another's proceeds from drug trafficking, is also guilty.

Italian law 55 of 1990 punishes whoever "substitutes money, goods or property derived from aggravated robbery, aggravated extortion, kidnapping for the purpose of extortion or crimes concerning the production or trafficking of narcotic or psychotropic drugs," or obstructs the identification of the source of such property, and whoever invests money, goods or property from the afore-mentioned crimes in "economic or financial activities".

Money laundering can thus be defined as a synthesis of three elements: the crime which precedes the money laundering – drug trafficking, terrorist offences etc, otherwise known as the *predicate crime*; the form of *conduct* of the money launderer such as concealment, removal, obstruction; and the degree of *awareness* – knowledge or suspicion – of the criminal origins of the funds. (This is implicit in the Italian criminal code but requires explicit mention in British law.)

As will be seen, there are a number of loopholes which limit the effectiveness of the legislation.

### Principles of national legislation – UK and Italy

The general guidelines that national legislation has established rely on the following principles:
**(i)** reduction of cash flow in the economy
**(ii)** reporting of cash transactions over a certain limit (Italy only)
**(iii)** mandatory reporting of suspicious financial transactions
**(iv)** careful record keeping of financial movements
**(v)** introduction of legal means for identification, tracing, seizure and confiscation of assets.

### Cash and the money launderer

Because money laundering stems from an illicit activity, the process usually begins with a transaction in cash or some other transferable instrument. Cash proceeds from drugs consumed in EC countries may remain in the home country to be laundered – using the legal financial circuit, cash intensive businesses or non banking financial/economic intermediaries – or else they can be transferred outside the financially regulated EC to a less well-regulated area where they will be laundered and then returned for "legitimate" reinvestment.

There are therefore three moments of transformation – the initial entry point of illicit cash into the legal system, the exit from one financial "culture" to another, and re-entry or final integration in the legal economy.

## Italian cash restrictions

Italian law 197 of 1991 contains the most recent anti-money laundering provisions. It forbids all transactions in cash, in foreign currency or in transferable instruments over the value of 20m lire (approx £9,000) except those in traceable form and carried out by authorised intermediaries. The authorised intermediaries must note all such transactions in an appropriate register with full details (name, date of birth. place of residence, profession, reasons for the transaction) of the persons by and for whom the transaction is being performed. From 1 January 1992 the details must include each individual's tax reference number. By the end of 1992 each bank register must be integrated into a computerised archive to be held in the bank's head office. There is no provision for a national database of all large operations. The Italian Exchange Bureau (*Ufficio Italiano dei Cambi*, UIC), may perform arbitrary checks as to the proper functioning of the system, and may carry out statistical analyses of the aggregate data (only) provided by each intermediary to verify possible anomalies in a given geographical region. If anomalies emerge, UIC must inform the Treasury Ministry which in turn will inform the competent investigative authorities.

## Avoidance of Italian cash restrictions

The money launderer wishing to convert cash is unlikely to be deterred by the above provisions, particularly when he is freely entitled to hold bank accounts in any EC country.

(i) He may make use of the money laundering technique known as "smurfing", namely the breaking up of the sum to be laundered into amounts lower than the reporting restrictions, to be deposited in irregular amounts on irregular days. If he wished to make further transferrals into other bank accounts, even in sums over 20m lire, he could do so by simple bank to bank transfer or *bonifico* which is not included in the large cash transactions register. The details of this type of operation are retained by the bank (for whom this is a daily exercise), but not in the "over 20m" register, and therefore are less liable to external scrutiny.

(ii) He could physically carry the cash to a country which does not have reporting obligations and where, if he has a business account and the volume and nature of his business activities were such that cash transactions had an apparently legal justification, he would not provoke a suspicious disclosure.

(iii) He may make use of automatic currency exchange machines which are frequently to be found in airports, main stations and large cities.

(iv) He could employ the technique known as "layering". This involves the multiplication of operations with illicit capital in order to put as many layers or screens as possible between source and final use. Safe placement opportunities might include paying the sum into a variety of nominee accounts or else purchasing shareholdings in corporations where beneficial ownership is disguised. It is not in fact *obligatory* in any EC country except Luxembourg to identify beneficial ownership. The EC Directive has not tried to legislate in this area, and merely states:

"Because of the difficulties which this identification of beneficial owners could involve in some circumstances, credit and financial institutions are exhorted to take 'reasonable measures'."

(v) Even cash over 20m can be laundered without necessarily arousing suspicion. Italy has a deep-rooted cash culture; an innate distrust of central government means that Italians have little faith in the protection of institutions such as banks. Credit cards are still relatively rare compared with some other EC countries, and may be more so after a 1991 budget amendment that imposed a tax on their use. Banks do not formally accept responsibility for customer losses incurred when cheques are stolen or forged, even within the clearing system (as the author knows from bitter experience), thus it is hardly surprising that cash or cash instruments are frequently the preferred option for payment of wages, professional services, and a wide variety of commercial transactions. In general, substantial cash movements are not likely to arouse suspicion in Italy and this will work to the undoubted advantage of the money launderer.

The EC Directive explicitly calls for vigilance over

"professions and undertakings, other than credit and financial institutions, which because of their involvement with cash transaction business, may be particularly susceptible to being used for money laundering purposes."

The FATF made its own extensive list, but did not propose means of controlling these activities. Scrutiny of the non banking sector remains one of the major problems facing all the EC countries in combating money laundering. In Italy, individuals and businesses regularly making cash transactions over 20m lire and therefore likely to be used by the launderer are: bars, restaurants, and fast food venues; casinos, betting shops and all forms of gambling establishment; wholesale fruit, vegetable and grocery merchants; second hand car dealers; antique and art dealers; gold and jewellery dealers. The above are all businesses which *legitimately* turn over large amounts of cash; illicit operations may hide amongst legitimate transactions, but over-invoicing, under-invoicing or completely fictitious invoicing will not arouse suspicion if the nature of the trade apparently justifies the quick turnover of cash.

It is worth noting that invoice manipulation and document falsification are also common practice with French money launderers. In one case a major French bank opened a branch that specialised in the repatriation of savings of immigrant workers. Numerous drug traffickers opened accounts using aliases and were able to deposit and transfer 7.5m FF worth of drug profits on the basis of false salary slips. In all, 80 suspect accounts were identified.[22]

## Cash/UK

The United Kingdom has no reporting obligations for large cash transactions because it does not judge them an efficient use of institutional resources and prefers to rely on suspicious disclosures; France, the United States and Australia operate both systems where it is claimed they are necessary and complementary. Privately, some UK customs officials feel that money laundering will never be defeated without exchange controls or, as in America, civil forfeiture laws, which permit confiscation whatever the origin of the funds if cash transactions over 10,000 dollars are not declared through a Currency Transaction Report. (CTR)

Section 25 of the Criminal Justice (International Co-operation) Act of 1990 has given a useful tool to Customs officers in verifying the movement of cash: it allows the seizure of cash sums carried in or out of the UK of over £10,000 when there are "reasonable grounds" to suspect that the cash represents the proceeds from drug trafficking. The onus of proving the legitimate source of the cash lies with the bearer.

Forfeiture can follow if a court is satisfied "on a balance of probabilities" that the cash directly or indirectly represents a person's proceeds of drug trafficking or is intended for use in drug trafficking. The use of the civil standard of proof here makes an interesting contrast with the criminal standard of proof ("beyond all reasonable doubt") required for confiscation of the proceeds of a convicted drug trafficker. The difference lies in the fact that unlike a confiscation order, Section 25 does not require a defendant.

## Centralised data-banks: opposition

There is no doubt that the financial cost of registering every large cash transaction over a given sum would signify major cost and resource implications for the banks: every large CTR in the US costs 17 dollars, and there are approximately 6m of them per year. (FATF) To make such a system functional would involve the average Italian bank taking on an extra 30 staff at head office alone.[23] In Britain, there are 17,000 bank branches, 70 million bank accounts and 6,000 building societies. It may well be that the reason implementation of an analytic control capacity has never seriously been considered is that it would prove too financially burdensome to be politically acceptable. Alternately, the idea may arouse nervousness because it comes too close to the blurred border line that separates tax fraud from tax avoidance. The head of Italy's *Guardia di Finanza* (Finance Police) reported to Parliament that tax evasion costs the country 200,000bn lire (£90bn, $150bn) per year.[24] Too much availability of financial information may create unease amongst influential sectors of the electorate. The Italian Parliament formally rejected the setting-up of a central databank despite the advice of the *Guardia di Finanza* and of many financial experts – officially on cost effectiveness grounds but possibly more from fears that Italy's thriving underground economy, held in place by a network of political favours and exchanges, might be imperilled. As an eminent professor and legal adviser to the Italian Banking Association commented, "The underground system is an essential co-efficient of our national economy".[25] There can be no doubt that institutional unwillingness to adopt a greater "transparency" throughout the whole spectrum of financial activities gives undoubted advantages to the money launderer.

26        *Research Institute for the Study of Conflict and Terrorism*

**Suspicious disclosures – Italy**

Article 5 of the EC Directive establishes a *mandatory* system (as does the Council of Europe Convention) which requires financial intermediaries to inform the authorities "on their own initiative, of any facts they discover which could be related to a money laundering offence."

This reminds member states of the range of predicate crimes that may be related to money laundering. But in the case of both Italy and the UK, this range is extremely limited, as we have seen.

In Italy the obligation to report arises when "any operation which for its characteristics, entity, or nature . . . may lead to the suspicion (*induca a ritenere*) that the money, goods or property . . . may derive" from one of the above-mentioned four predicate crimes. Yet Italian banking staff, unlike their British counterparts, have not (to date) been given a briefing on what criteria they are to use to make such deductions and their training has largely consisted of reminders to make formal identification of clients.

Suspicious reporting obligations have been opposed by the entire Italian banking sector. A senior Italian banking official criticised the measures as "ill considered" and "dangerous" and a provincial junior manager interviewed for this study found them "laughable and ineffective".

There are several reasons why they are unlikely to work in Italy:

**(i)** The vagueness of the language *induca a ritenere/* may lead to the suspicion, and the difficulty of proving or disproving such a suspicion;

**(ii)** The difficulty of linking the suspicion to one of the four predicate crimes. The absence of guidelines for recognising the characteristics of these crimes means that the average bank clerk has no means of distinguishing the criminal of the four predicate crimes from the arms trafficker, the fraudulent trader or the tax evader.

**(iii)** Reluctance to comply through fear of possible consequences. The procedure of making a suspicious disclosure in a bank involves a chain of reporting that begins with the cashier, passes to the bank's legal representative, who makes an arbitrary evaluation of the disclosure before deciding whether to transmit it to the local police chief, who in turn passes it on to the appropriate sector of the *Guardia di Finanza* or the financial section of the civil police. Although there is legal protection from breach of professional secrecy, anonymity is not guaranteed by law, despite a belated commitment to that effect by the Minister of the Interior. The permeability of Italian institutions is such that no bank personnel, particularly but not exclusively in southern Italy, would feel themselves safe from reprisals were they to collaborate in this form of reporting and it is unlikely under the present arrangements that this situation will change. It should be remembered that criminal vendettas are responsible for a large part of the approximately 1500 organised crime murders in Italy per year.

**(iv)** Privileged treatment of certain clients. Provincial bank managers in Italy may use their power and discretion in banking matters to obtain economic or political favours from important clients. The result is a favours system that entirely bypasses formal banking procedures. Bank staff who try conscientiously to enforce the rules may find their promotion blocked or be unaccountably made redundant.

(v) Italian banks are for the most part publicly owned. The sense of "belonging" is lacking, and staff have a low sense of loyalty, hence the incentive to report is weak, despite the risk of sanctions. Knowledge that the Italian banking authorities oppose the measure is likely to discourage the practice still further. The obligation to report suspicious disclosures was introduced in February of 1991 – at the end of September 1991 the total number of disclosures had reached ten.[26]

## Suspicious disclosures – UK

In the UK, where all suspicious disclosures are sent to the NDIU headquarters in New Scotland Yard, the system works extremely well, according to banks and the NDIU. In 1987, the first year of the DTOA, there were 510 disclosures, in 1989 1,200, in 1990 2,000 and the total for 1991 was expected to reach 3,000. (NDIU) 40 per cent are sent to Customs & Excise, 60 per cent to the police. An average of 20 per cent are described as "useful" and 5 per cent start off new investigations that conclude in seizures, prosecutions or in criminal charges in relation to drugs. Nonetheless the majority, perhaps inevitably, relate to tax avoidance or evasion. Inland Revenue do not have access to the data base on disclosures, held by the National Drugs Intelligence Unit, and this undoubtedly has helped to ensure the co-operation of the banking community.

Despite this, there are still relatively few successful prosecutions for money laundering in the UK, and the situation, according to NDIU, is likely to worsen after 1992. Some of the problems relate to issues already raised, such as fewer controls and more people on the move; greater flexibility in capital transfer; the removal of border controls; problems in information exchange. Others involve the legal dimensions of the crime itself.

## Prosecuting the money launderer – UK problems

By the end of 1990 – four years after the introduction of the DTOA – there had been 17 money laundering convictions and £27.2m ordered to be confiscated. In 1990 alone 47 confiscation orders were imposed totalling in excess of £8.3m and five persons were convicted. (NDIU) These are not derisory figures, but set against an estimated drug revenue of over £2bn per annum, it is clear that drug trafficking profits remain largely intact.

The main difficulties in prosecuting the money launderer are the limitation of the crime to offences of drug trafficking and terrorism, and the necessity to prove "beyond all reasonable doubt" his criminal intent or *mens rea*: that is, that he was aware of facilitating retention and control of property that he knew or suspected was connected to specific illicit activities. The defendant is innocent under the DTOA if he can show that he "did not know or suspect that an arrangement related to any person's proceeds of drug trafficking; that he did not know or suspect that by the arrangement retention or control was facilitated; or that he intended to disclose such a suspicion, belief or matter in relation to the arrangement but there was reasonable excuse for his failure to do so".

The DTOA and the CJICA have undoubtedly tightened the net around the money launderer, but even so, one can imagine that a good defence lawyer would find legal loopholes through which his client could escape prosecution.


### Prosecuting the money launderer – Italian problems

The principal problems of money laundering prosecution are:

(i) Money launderers are invariably people "above suspicion": are likely to be prosperous businessmen or independent professionals, cultured, well connected, respected and with acute financial instincts. They are likely to have flourishing legitimate businesses to provide cover for their illicit activities – as was the case with Giuseppe Lottusi, a Milanese businessman and racehorse owner arrested in November 1991 on charges of having laundered 18m dollars on behalf of the Colombian Medellin cartel. (Lottusi, a "text book study of the perfect money launderer", according to the Italian investigators[27], used back to back loans, offshore companies, casinos, fictitious finance companies and invoice manipulation of fake and genuine companies to spread the financial load and cover his tracks. His arrest – an exceptional achievement – was the conclusion of 18 months of wire-tapping, surveillance and methodical police work. His trial has not taken place at time of writing.)

Italian authorities boast that the crime clear-up rate for kidnaps is 75 per cent, but it is invariably the kidnappers, not the money launderers who are caught. Some 400bn lire (£180m, $300m) worth of ransom money has been paid out for the release of kidnap hostages in Italy in the last 20 years but only 8bn lire worth of banknotes have ever been recovered.[28]

(ii) In Italy the "fishing expedition" to trawl for incriminating evidence of money laundering is limited to **a)** suspicion of mafia association or **b)** the reporting of suspicious transactions by a financial intermediary in connection with one of four predicate crimes. Banking secrecy is protected except in the case of criminal enquiries and thus is lifted only *ex post*, once proof of a crime exists.

(iii) The law links the criminal offence of money laundering to one of four crimes – in reality the launderer may genuinely not know from what particular crime the funds derive, especially if the initial transformation has already taken place. Assisting a criminal to conceal or dispose of illicit profits in general is dealt with by other specific offences such as *ricettazione* (literally, receiving of stolen goods) and *favoreggiamento reale* (aiding and abetting) which are less heavily penalised.

(iv) The operations which legally define money laundering – *substitution* and *obstruction* – are not two complementary halves of a single operation. The act required to complete the cycle is *separation* or *concealment* of the origins of the property.[29]

(v) The reinvestment of illicit gains only refers to "financial or economic activities" which would exclude, for example, the extinction of a debt using illicit drug funds from the scope of money laundering.

**(vi)** Over the last 10 years there has been a notable link in Italy between the growth of small finance companies, trust companies, leasing and factoring agencies and other consumer credit facilities and an exponential rise in criminal activities: at the end of the 1980s there were 50 leasing companies and 600 finance houses in Sicily. Trapani, one of Italy's lowest income per capita provinces, had 102 finance houses and 142 bank branches. Milan, reputed to be the Mafia finance capital of the 1990s, has 8,000 finance houses, and a total of 173,000 commercial companies.[30] Law 197 of 1991 introduced measures to regulate the activities of financial intermediaries but the ambiguities and lack of precise guidelines make its effectiveness extremely doubtful. The text of the law limits itself to the regulation of companies whose "prevalent activity" includes one or more of the following: "concession of finances of any kind including leasing; purchase of shareholdings or of financial interests; currency exchange, cashing of cheques or of other negotiable instruments, payment and transfer of funds including issue and management of credit cards." Such companies must be listed on an appropriate register or face legal sanctions and by July 1993, directors will have to provide proof of due professional and personal propriety. The Bank of Italy and the Consob (Stock Exchange Control Board) are to be responsible for this sector, but how, and with what powers, is not stated. Furthermore since the register only concerns financial companies, commercial trading fronts and other unregulated sectors such as estate agencies will continue to be favoured as money laundering vehicles.

### Seizure and confiscation – the Italian experience

Italy has permitted asset tracing, freezing and confiscation since the passing of Law 646 in 1982, otherwise known as the *Rognoni La Torre* Law. The law was very largely the work of two courageous Sicilians, judge Cesare Terranova and politician Pio La Torre, both murdered by the Mafia for their efforts to identify the process of illicit wealth accumulation. The law applies to those suspected of "mafia association", which exists when

> "those who form it make use of the power of intimidation provided by the associative bond and of the state of subjugation and of criminal silence (*omertà*) which derives from it to commit crimes, to acquire directly or indirectly the running or control of economic activities, of concessions, grants, contracts and public services in order to realise illicit profits or advantages for themselves or for others."

When the assets of a suspected mafioso are seized the burden of proving their legitimate origin is with the defendant. The law also requires any person or company applying for public subsidies or having any dealings with the public sector to produce an "antimafia certificate" issued by the police which states that no suspicions of mafia association exist and that no serious criminal charges have been brought or are pending.

The short term effect of the law was impressive – in 1984 402bn lire worth of assets were seized, but by 1987 the total had dropped to less than 100bn. In 1990, 300bn lire worth were seized but only 9m definitively confiscated.[31]

**Seizure and confiscation – the British experience**

In British law there is no concept of "mafia association" but if there are "reasonable grounds" for suspecting that a person has carried on or benefited from drug trafficking, a judge will issue a production order that compels a financial institution to disclose details of an account. If reasonable grounds exist for believing that property represents the proceeds of a drug trafficking offence, a charging order can be made (on realisable property) or a restraint order (on a person). Property can be confiscated after conviction for a drug trafficking offence if, according to the criminal burden of proof, it represents in part or whole, a person's proceeds of drug trafficking.

The Council of Europe Convention defines proceeds as "any economic advantage from a criminal offence", but the word "advantage" is ambiguous: some countries confiscate the total amount of a drug trafficker's sales, others his net profits. Under British law the prosecution must prove firstly that someone has benefited from drug trafficking and secondly what his proceeds from drug trafficking have been. The defendant need show to the civil standard of proof (on the balance of probabilities) that the sum capable of being realised does not represent his realisable property or is not part of his proceeds from drug trafficking. British law regards all assets acquired during the six years prior to a conviction for drug trafficking offences as proceeds from drug trafficking unless the defendant can prove otherwise. The Home Office Working Group recommended that the six year assumption be extended to any property that might come to light within six years *after* conviction to avoid concealment or removal from the jurisdiction.[32]

Scotland passed a law in 1991 on subsequent realisation which closes one gap: it rules that when realisable property such as a painting, valued at a given price for the purposes of a confiscation order, subsequently realises more than the estimated amount, the courts can insist on retrospective payment of the difference.

Legal difficulties that have emerged in the UK include:
(i) The difficulty of establishing the defendant's benefit from drug trafficking to a criminal standard of proof. (The Home Office Working Group recommended that the civil standard be applied, given the existence of a proven criminal conviction in any confiscation proceedings.)
(ii) The impossibility of enforcing a confiscation order if the accused either dies or absconds before the case comes to court. (This would not apply in Italy where trial in absentia is permitted.) In some cases a confiscation order can be made if a case for conspiracy (and therefore involving other defendants) is proven, but confiscation needs a guilty party.
(iii) The difficulty of realising the amount of a confiscation order: in 1989 confiscation orders to the value of £7.9m were made: of that only £1.1m were realised.[33]

**Money laundering, seizure and confiscation legislation – potential international incompatibilities**

Asset seizure and confiscation orders are not covered by the EC Directive but are comprehensively provided for by the Council of Europe Convention and, for some EC states, by bilateral agreements. The Convention requires a requested state to enforce such orders either on the basis of the order of the requesting state or on the basis of a new order issued by the requested state. A number of clearly defined reservations are permitted. In addition, particular features of national legislation may weaken international co-operation in money laundering cases:

(i) The Council of Europe Convention obliges all states parties to give full faith and credit to foreign confiscation orders, but not all countries (eg the US) authorise this.

(ii) Countries apply differing standards of proof.

(iii) An extradition request might relate to a predicate crime not covered by the offence of money laundering in the requested country (FATF).

(iv) The offence of "mafia association" which is unique to Italy may cause problems for other EC legislations with regard to seizure and confiscation.

(v) There may be confusion over the powers of the requesting authority: for example in the UK only a judge may authorise a production order (compelling banks to provide details of an account); in Italy the judiciary and a civil authority (the High Commissioner for the fight against the Mafia) have this right.

(vi) In some countries (eg Italy) the concept of corporate criminal liability does not exist and in others it is vague. The extent to which this could have been established in the 1990 money laundering trials involving the Bank of Credit and Commerce International (BCCI) was not fully tested since in Florida, BCCI settled out of court; in the UK trial there was not sufficient evidence to prove corporate knowledge or approval of the criminal actions undertaken in BCCI's name. Future legal action against BCCI may test the principle further.

### Good legislation – side effects

*(i) Italy.* An unfortunate side effect of good legislation is that rather than deterring the criminal, it may force him to seek alternative channels for his activities that are even harder to detect. This has been the case in both Italy and Britain. In Italy the asset tracing provisions of the *Rognoni La Torre* law of 1982 made it more difficult for mafiosi to run apparently legitimate businesses in the light of day because they were unable to present the necessary credentials. The result was that mafia pressure on clean businesses and businessmen increased: rather than simply extorting protection money or imposing a few security guards on the "clean" company, the mafia has sought increasingly to infiltrate clean businesses using intimidation and violence to the point that control comes into mafia hands, although the company nominally retains its legitimate front.

Companies are particularly vulnerable to infiltration during periods of economic hardship, as the mafia has discovered. The need for quick cash to save a firm from insolvency may well prove irresistible; companies are taken over, turned around and quickly resold at a profit with the original illegal investment beyond detection.

Alternatively, money to rescue an ailing business can be provided through usury. Not only does this guarantee a high rate of return but is hard to prove and is a lightly punished crime under Italian law – a maximum sentence of two years imprisonment and a maximum fine of 4m lire. There may be some 800,000 usurers operating in Italy, charging an average annual 40 per cent interest rate on loans.[34] Money launderers are thought to be turning to this as a favoured form of recycling illicit drug funds.

*(ii)  UK – Underground or parallel banking.*  A different situation has evolved in Britain, where a tightening up of the conventional banking system has pushed alternative banking further underground. *Hawala*, which means "reference" in Urdu, is a centuries-old Asian banking system relying fundamentally on trust. A merchant travelling overseas took with him a letter of credit issued by a *hawala* banker in his own country known as a *hundi* ("trust" in Hindi) which would be honoured by a *hawala* banker in the other country. The tradition has continued legitimately until the present day and has been particularly used by Asian immigrants in Europe who have used it to transfer their salaries to their families in Pakistan or India. A broadly similar and equally ancient banking system known as *chopshop* or *chitti* banking is operated by the Chinese. (*Chops* are seals which facilitate money transactions; a *chitti* is a colonial expression meaning a promissory note.)

Nowadays *hawala* banking does not necessarily require a letter of credit: a telephone call, fax or any agreed form of recognition in the form of a secret code or simple object such as a playing card may be enough to ensure the transfer.

In Asia and the Far East, parallel banking is often used illegally to avoid exchange controls and in the case of India, to avoid the import ban on gold. British investigators are convinced that *hawala* is increasingly being used for the repatriation of heroin and cannabis profits to producer countries. *Hawala* does not constitute "deposit taking" under the terms of the 1987 Banking Act, and therefore is not subject to Bank of England regulation. It depends totally on cash and leaves no physical record – NDIU reports that millions of pounds can be turned over without trace in three or four days by some *hawala* bankers. Indian delegates to an Interpol conference devoted to underground banking estimated that the system processed between 10bn and 20bn dollars per year.[35] There are believed to be about 1,000 *hawala* bankers in the UK, of whom 12 may be involved in moving drug money. Some work as gold or jewellery dealers or run bureaux de change, others have quite menial jobs with no connection to money. One suspected *hawala* money launderer in London was believed to have handled £5m to £8m per week, but to date no *hawala* bankers have been prosecuted because it has been impossible to prove that they handled the money "knowing or suspecting" that it represented the proceeds of drug trafficking.[36] Attempts have been made to use the Inland Revenue to curb *hawala* activities on grounds of non declaration of commission, but this has had a limited effect.

Nor is the problem confined to the unofficial banking sector – UK investigators also believe *hawala* was used in illicit transactions by official banking institutions such as Johnson Matthey Bank and BCCI. This gives further cause for concern.

## Fiscal havens

There can be no real chance of success against money laundering – even within the EC – as long as offshore fiscal havens continue to facilitate the setting up of letter box or shell companies, offer banking anonymity, unregulated financial transactions, and a not inconsiderable degree of judicial protection. Criminals or criminal organisations can invest in or purchase finance companies, fictitious trading corporations or active interests such as hotel and leisure complexes. The Caribbean is particularly favoured from this point of view since in addition to its many financial sanctuaries, its island archipelagos serve as useful staging posts for cocaine transit from South America to Europe and North America. The Cayman Islands, the Dutch Antilles, Aruba and Santo Domingo have all been used by drug traffickers and money launderers and will continue to do so unless concerted international pressure forces them to change.

But tax havens continue to prosper within and on the periphery of the EC itself: Monaco, Andorra, Luxembourg, Liechtenstein, the Channel Islands, the Isle of Man, Malta and Ireland all offer considerable tax incentives to outside investers. Austria continues to allow anonymous bank accounts, despite being a signatory of the Council of Europe Convention. Gibralter hopes to rejuvenate its economy, once dependent on British military investment, by becoming a modern financial centre with its 25 banks, almost 30,000 registered offshore companies and new financial services complex, "Europot".[37]

The examples of Monaco and of Ireland provide a useful illustration of potential risks.

**(i) Monaco.**  For several years, until at least 1988, Neapolitan *Camorra* clans invested a part of their profits from drug trafficking and cigarette smuggling in private health clinics in Marseilles. Once these came under surveillance from the DEA and French authorities, funds were diverted towards the purchase of financial interests in banks, estate agents and finance companies in Monte Carlo. There are 30,0000 foreign residents and 57 banks in the Principality which afford suitable cover; ownership of a *societé civile privée* – a kind of trust company – requires the cover of a Monegasque resident as front man but otherwise guarantees anonymity.[38] In the late 1980s, two companies were formed with the name of Sofextour, one in Monte Carlo, the other in Menton. Large sums of money were paid in cash to the Monte Carlo company from Italy. The Menton company was formed to bid for the purchase of casinos, initially in Menton and then in Beaulieu, using the apparently respectable company in Monte Carlo as guarantor. The intention was to take over the casinos and build up hotel and tourist facilities around them. In fact the operation was prevented in time thanks to superb collaboration between the French and Italian authorities, but the case illustrates very clearly the problems of having an unregulated sanctuary in the midst of a regulated sector.

**(ii) Ireland.**   Ireland is beginning to arouse concern amongst those involved in combating money laundering: the International Financial Services Centre in Dublin is a city development specially reserved for financial services companies with registered offices on the site; they pay a maximum of 10 per cent tax rate on profits made from a broad range of financial activities. Thanks to an EC Directive, from 1 January 1992 EC companies pay no tax on money repatriated. Doubtless the overwhelming majority of companies registered within the IFSC will simply be availing themselves of favourable investment and financial facilities but it must also be pointed out that such facilities tend to serve as magnets for less desirable business investors and risk being used as cover for the laundering of illicit profits.

The Financial Action Task Force considers the problem of fiscal havens to be one of the most important issues still unresolved; it rejected the idea of drawing up a "black list" of non co-operating nations for the time being although the use of international sanctions remains a last option which may yet be employed. The United States has considered excluding non co-operating states from the US bank clearing system and preventing their banks and registered companies from doing business in the United States. Britain has put pressure on its crown dependencies in the Channel Islands and dependent territories in the Caribbean, as has the Netherlands. All such efforts will be evaluated under the terms of FATF membership over the next few years, by which a board of two members will judge a third on the effectiveness of anti-laundering legislation.

Singapore and Japan, favoured money laundering havens in the Far East, remain formally outside the FATF group of countries but promise to consider money laundering legislation. Hong Kong introduced a Drug Trafficking (Recovery of Proceeds) Ordinance in July 1989 and almost half a million HK dollars were seized in the following year, but the banking sector remains essentially unregulated and tracing funds entering and leaving the country is almost impossible. (FATF) The transfer of drug trafficking funds out of Hong Kong to other destinations is inevitable before 1997.

**The former East bloc**

The potential risk of drug trafficking related to the former East bloc and its consequences for the Europen Community has been discussed earlier. It is the author's view that money laundering from the EC through these countries is no less serious a concern. There are a number of reasons for this:
**(i)** The lack of customs controls inside the EC will facilitate cash movement across the internal borders and, in all likelihood, over the external frontier.
**(ii)** New national and international legislation to protect financial institutions against money laundering will have a deterrent effect. The FATF has already pointed out that the money launderer's percentage has risen from 2 to 4 per

cent in the early 1980s to a current level of 6 to 8 per cent. The money launderer will naturally look elsewhere to maximise his profits and his opportunities.

**(iii)** The former East bloc countries are desperately in need of hard currency for investment and to meet new market challenges; when this is provided they may be more concerned to revitalise their economy than to ask difficult questions about the origin of the funds. Unfortunately, any form of investment made by criminals is unlikely to have long term advantages for the native economy (witness the economic poverty of the mafia-dominated areas of southern Italy) and thus, instead of stimulating the economy, is likely to destabilise it even further.

**(iv)** Organised criminals are skilled at exploiting fragile economic conditions to their own advantage, particularly where the financial system is weak and unstructured.

**(v)** A number of East European countries told FATF that strong bank secrecy was essential to regain the confidence of the population in the new financial system. Under their former authoritarian regimes, a culture of suspicion was encouraged, and it is unlikely that legislators will wish to revive it, at least for the next few years.

## Drugs/political offences – possible conflict

All EC countries have accepted the principle of mutual legal assistance in drug trafficking cases. The Council of Europe Convention states that no drug trafficking offence should be considered "political". Nonetheless it is not hard to envisage a potential clash of interests were the two kinds of offence to overlap. This could occur with IRA or with ETA, whose members are thought to have some dealings with the drugs trade. An extradition request might be turned down if the primary interest were thought to be political. The experience of the 1977 Convention on Terrorism and the problems of extradition between EC member countries show that such fears are not unfounded.

## Recommendations and conclusions

**(i)** All EC countries should ratify the Council of Europe Convention on Laundering, Search, Seizure and Confiscation of the Proceeds from Crime as soon as possible.

**(ii)** Efforts should be made to improve mutual legal assistance in money laundering cases.

**(iii)** Standard procedures should be followed by financial institutions when a client with accounts in more than one country is being investigated for serious crime.

**(iv)** EC countries without provision for corporate criminal responsibility should consider introducing it.

**(v)** Sharing of confiscated assets should be automatic between countries that have co-operated in money laundering enquiries.
(The US already applies this.)

(vi) Other countries' experiences in money laundering legislation should be studied. For example (a) Italy has introduced premium legislation for drug traffickers who collaborate actively in dismantling illegal networks (b) France passed a law in December 1991 which permits undercover drug agents to provide means of communication, transport, storage and even financial assistance to drug traffickers in order to entrap them.

(vii) A central EC data bank on suspicious disclosures should be set up within EDU when it is established.

(viii) Sanctions should be imposed on fiscal havens that do not collaborate in money laundering enquiries.

(ix) Money launderers may exploit the non coincidence of public holidays in EC countries whereby a bank employee may not be available to answer a query from another bank.[39] A system should be developed to deal with this.

(x) Financial institutions should be required to identify and distinguish between account holder. signing authority and real beneficiary.

(xi) The crime of money laundering should be extended to all offences that generate a significant amount of profits.

(xii) The production order, or its equivalent in each EC state, should be extended when appropriate to become a monitoring order. This requires a bank to report all transactions to and from an account during a given period, and is an effective instrument in Canadian and Australian money laundering legislation.

(xiii) Computerised databanks should be built up of precious metals and fine arts transactions above a prescribed limit.

(xiv) A greater awareness of money laundering techniques and their conse- quences should be passed on to all those working in the financial sector.

(xv) Bank secrecy should be abolished for fiscal as well as for criminal enquiries.

There is no reason why the liberalisation of capital movement in the European Community should be incompatible with the implementation of regulatory measures; on the contrary, it should facilitate commercial exchange and create a climate of greater economic and financial stability. If in practice the money launderer will have more opportunities to move his illicit funds after 1992. bilateral and multilateral agreements ought to prevent him from benefiting from his crime. Nonetheless, international treaties will have little effect without sound national laws.

Finally, unless the two fundamental principles of financial accountability and political responsibility are observed, there is little that any well-intentioned legislation can do. The value of 3,000 suspicious disclosures becomes irrelevant when, for reasons of political expediency, an institution like the Bank of Credit and Commerce International, with a proven record of illegality, irregular procedures and improperly audited accounts, not to mention a "criminal culture" well known to the Governor of the Bank of England, continues to trade. Effective legislation against money laundering relies first and foremost on the co-operation of individual citizens; governments can hardly expect observance of laws for which they themselves show scant respect.

*Drug Trafficking After 1992* 37

## NOTES

[1] Report by Minister of Social Affairs Russo Jervolino on application of Law 162/1990, January 1991.

[2] *Der Spiegel*, 6 January 1992.

[3] European Parliament: Committee of Enquiry into the spread of organised crime linked to drug trafficking in the member states of the European Community. Draft Report Part B. PE152.380/B p. 31.

[4] Marie Therese Atallah of the Fédération Internationale "Terre des Hommes", Paris, in talk given to conference "Droga e Sviluppo", Palermo, 8–9 November 1991.

[5] *The Independent*, 18 July 1991.

[6] Andean Commission of Jurists: *Andean News Letter*; Drug Trafficking Update, Lima, Peru. 7 October 1991, Year 2 No. 18.

[7] *La Repubblica*, 26 June 1991.

[8] *Police*: The Voice of the Service, July 1991, p. 9.

[9] Statement made by Domenico Sica, High Commissioner for the Fight Against the Mafia, *Corriere della Sera*, 16 November 1988.

[10] P. Reuter et al: *Sealing the Borders*; (Santa Monica, CA); The Rand Corporation, 1988.

[11] Sir Leon Brittan: "The European Single Market: Implications for Policing"; the Newsam Memorial Lecture, given at the Police Staff College, Bramshill, 1 November 1991.

[12] House of Commons Session 1989–1990, Home Affairs Committee Seventh Report: *Practical Police Co-operation in the European Community*, Vol. II, pp. 71 and 147.

[13] *Le Monde*, 2 November 1991.

[14] *Practical Police Co-operation*, op. cit, p. 148.

[15] Quoted in Antonio Cipriani: *Mafia: Il Riciclaggio del Denaro Sporco*. Casa Editrice Napoleone, Rome, 1989, p. 97.

[16] *Task Force on Terrorism and Unconventional Warfare*; House Republican Research Committee, US House of Representatives, 10 September 1991, p. 5.

[17] Unattributable. Statistics were provided by a South American delegate to the conference "Fighting the Drugs Trade: Prospects for Co-operation between Europe and the Americas," Wilton Park, Sussex, 3–6 June, 1991.

[18] *Il Mondo*, 10–17 June 1991.

[19] A. Lamberti: Il Mercato della Droga, in: *Rapporto 1990 sulla Camorra*, a cura di F. Barbagallo e I Sales, *L'Unità*, 1991.

[20] European Parliament, *op. cit.*, p. 51.

[21] D. I. Tim Wren, National Drugs Intelligence Unit, in talk to conference on International and White Collar Crime organised by the Commonwealth Secretariat, Oxford, 12–16 August 1991.

[22] Jacques Genthial, Directeur Central de la Police Judiciaire (France) in talk to World Ministerial Drugs Summit, London, 9–11 April 1990.

[23] Pietro Barucci, President of Associazione Bancaria Italiana, chapter in *Riciclaggio del Denaro Sporco e Segreto Bancario*; Quaderni del Cordusio, Milan, 1991.

[24] *Corriere della Sera*, 24 November 1991.

[25] Prof. Avv. Giovanni Maria Flick, speaking at conference "Norme contro il Riciclaggio del Denaro Sporco, Ruolo e Compiti della Banca Centrale", Rome, 15 October 1991.

[26] Minister of the Interior Vincenzo Scotti, *L'Unità*, 27 September 1991.

[27] *La Repubblica*, 1 November 1991.

[28] Calabrian Deputy Enzo Ciconte, speaking at Seminar "Lo Stato e le Mafie: Poterie Criminalità nel Mezzogiorno", Rome, 18 October 1991.

[29] Gherardo Colombo: *Il Riciclaggio*, Giuffré Editore, Milano, 1990, p. 86.

[30] Report of all-party Parliamentary Antimafia Commission, June 1990, p. 12.

[31] *L'Unità*, 27 September 1991.

[32] Home Office Working Group on Confiscation: *Report on the Drug Trafficking Offences Act 1986*; May 1991, p. 16.

[33] *Ibid.*, p. 8.

[34] *Il Mondo*, 25 February 1991 to 4 March 1991.

[35] ICPO/Interpol: *System of Illegal International Financial Transactions: Underground or Parallel Banking*, Appendix 2, November 1991.

[36] *Sunday Telegraph*, 14 July 1991.

[37] *Corriere della Sera*, 8 January 1991.

[38] *La Repubblica*, 9–10 June 1991.

[39] *Practical Police Co-operation*, op. cit., Annex A (City of London Police), p. 28.

# [5]

# The Lessons of Lockerbie

## Paul Wilkinson

On the evening of 21 December 1988, 31,000 feet above the small Scottish town of Lockerbie, Pan Am Flight 103, bound for New York, was destroyed by a powerful mid-air explosion, killing all 259 passengers and crew and 11 people on the ground in Lockerbie. It was the worst civil aviation disaster ever in Britain, and one of the worst in the history of civil aviation.

Subsequent investigation by the UK Air Accident Investigation Branch established that the explosion was caused by a terrorist bomb made of Semtex and placed in the airliner's forward cargo hold. The investigator's conclusions came as no surprise to those with specialist knowledge of aviation terrorism and security. Throughout the mid 1980s there had been a series of terrorist sabotage bombings, and attempts to plant bombs, directed at civilian airlines. On 22 June 1985 Air India Flight 182 was blown up over the Atlantic, killing 329. In April 1986 a bomb exploded on board TWA Flight 840 killing four people. Two weeks later a woman attempted to board an El Al jet at Heathrow carrying a bomb in her hand luggage. Nezar Hindawi, the woman's boyfriend, was convicted of duping her into carrying the bomb. Evidence at the trial implicated Syrian intelligence, which had provided the bomb. The following June a bomb in a suitcase, intended to explode on board an El Al flight to Tel Aviv, detonated prematurely at Barajas Airport, Madrid, wounding 11. And on 29 November 1987 Korean Air Lines Flight 858 exploded in mid-air over the Andaman Sea, killing all 115 on board. A woman passenger, who had disembarked with her elderly companion at Abu Dhabi, later confessed that she and her companion had planted the bomb on the airliner when they boarded it at Baghdad. She stated that the operation had been planned by North Korean intelligence officials.

## THE CHANGING TERRORIST THREAT TO CIVIL AVIATION

The statistics on the distribution of Aviation Targets by *modus operandi* for 1987 and 1988 (see Tables 1 and 2) show quite clearly not only that aviation continues to be an appealing target for the international terrorist but also that there has been a tactical shift by the terrorists away from the preoccupation with hijacking, which characterised the late 1960s and early 1970s, and towards other tactics, such as bombings, carrying far less risk of being caught.

As for the experts in aviation security, the ominous significance of the sabotage bombing should have been brought home to them by the Air India tragedy in 1985. Despite the problems stemming from the fact that the wreckage of Air India Flight 182 was strewn over a wide area of the Atlantic, the Indian authorities produced an extremely thorough report on the disaster, showing conclusively that it was brought about by a terrorist bomb, and making many practical recommendations for enhancing security to deal

1

2                    *Research Institute for the Study of Conflict and Terrorism*

with this threat. The Indian Government's findings were made known
to international aviation organisations and governments, but were largely
ignored.

Independent specialists in the study of aviation terrorism and countermeasures also repeatedly warned of the increasing threat of sabotage bombing. In
an interview, published in *International Herald Tribune* in the aftermath of
the Kuwait Airways hijacking of April 1988, the present writer warned that
the greater threat today to aviation is not hijacking so much as mid-air
sabotage bombing and attacks on airport terminals and airline offices. And
in an article in *Airport Technology International*, published four months before
Lockerbie, Frederick Dorey, former chief security manager, British Airports
Authority, argued cogently:

> "Many governments are now implementing strict measures against hijackers, including
> refusing landing permission, and this is one reason terrorists are rethinking their methods of
> attack and increasingly turning to acts of sabotage against airline terminals, airline offices,
> airports and aircraft in the air and on the ground".

### The rise and decline of hijacking

Sadly, these warnings had no discernible effect on aviation security policy in
any major state. And yet it should have been obvious to those familiar with
trends in international terrorism that by the mid 1980s the aviation security
systems established in the early 1970s to deal with the hijacking threat had
become woefully out of date. This was not because political terrorists
had entirely discarded the tactics of hijacking. The pro-Iranian Shi'ite
fundamentalist terrorists of Hezbollah mounted what in their eyes was a
spectacularly successful hijacking of a TWA airline to Beirut in 1985. They
skilfully turned it into a hostage-taking and used it to pressure the Israelis
into releasing over 700 Shi'ites and Palestinians from Israeli prisons. Hezbollah
used the tactic again in April 1988 when they hijacked a Kuwait Airways
plane to Mashad in Iran, to Cyprus, and ultimately to Algeria.

Despite the fact that they had murdered two passengers, this gang succeeded
in escaping justice and returning to their safe havens in Lebanon. It is true
that they did not succeed in their main demand, the release of 17 imprisoned
terrorist colleagues held in Kuwait. But they did demonstrate a new level of
ruthless professionalism and cunning in outwitting the aviation authorities of
successive Middle East governments, and in squeezing the last drop of
sensational publicity for their cause.

Moreover, let us bear in mind that this gang has since been able to pass on
its expertise to other terrorists in its organisation. The 1985 TWA hijack proved
that this tactic could still be hugely successful in compelling governments to
release large numbers of prisoners. Maintenance and regular monitoring and
upgrading of measures against the aviation hijacking threat is therefore vital.
Even though these incidents have declined in number, they still constitute a
danger to the life and safety of passengers and crews. It is worth remembering
that hijacking attempts can, in certain circumstances, lead to large-scale loss
of life. For example, in September 1986 terrorists who attempted the abortive

## DISTRIBUTION OF AVIATION TARGETS BY *MODUS OPERANDI*

*Table 1*          1987

| Modus Operandi* | Name of Target | | | |
|---|---|---|---|---|
| | Airliner | Airline Office | Airport | Total |
| Armed assault | – | 1 | – | 1 |
| Bombing and arson | 2 | 2 | – | 4 |
| Hijacking | 3 | – | – | 3 |
| Kidnapping | 1 | – | – | 1 |
| Sabotage | – | 2 | – | 2 |
| **Total** | **6** | **5** | **–** | **11** |

*Table 2*          1988

| Modus Operandi* | Name of Target | | | |
|---|---|---|---|---|
| | Airliner | Airline Office | Airport | Total |
| Armed assault | 1 | 6 | – | 7 |
| Bombing and arson | 3 | 7 | – | 10 |
| Hijacking | 1 | – | – | 1 |
| Kidnapping | – | – | – | – |
| Sabotage | – | 1 | – | 1 |
| Specific threat | 1 | – | – | 1 |
| **Total** | **6** | **14** | **–** | **20** |

* Incomplete/thwarted incidents are classified according to their intended *modus operandi*.

hijacking of a Pan Am 747 in Karachi turned their guns on the passengers, murdering 21. And the following December an Iraqi airliner crashed in Saudi Arabia following a hijacking attempt, killing over half the 107 passengers on board.

Recent hijackings have also highlighted the major loopholes in aviation security, of a similar nature to those exploited by terrorists using sabotage bombing and other modes of attack. Deficiencies in the screening of passengers and the checking of hold and hand luggage, lack of airport perimeter security and the absence of proper access controls in ground servicing areas, are just a few examples of security weaknesses which assist terrorists of all kinds.

Hence, a tightening of measures against the hijacking threat does have beneficial consequences in strengthening protection against aviation terrorism generally. But anti-hijacking measures will never be enough to meet the newer and rapidly escalating threat of terrorist sabotage bombing. However good the quality of an airport's x-ray machines and metal detecting archways, this technology cannot provide a reliable means of identifying the plastic explosives which have become the stock-in-trade of the world's most ruthless terrorist groups.

**The destructive power of Semtex**

The best-known of these plastic explosives, and one most frequently used by terrorists is Semtex. This Czech-made explosive consists of Pentaerythrite tetranitrate (PETN) combined with mineral oil as a plasticiser. Semtex is odourless and hard to detect by vapour sniffers as it has a very low vapour pressure at normal temperature and pressure. PETN itself is highly sensitive, but this property is reduced by the mineral oil plasticiser constituent, and a powerful detonator is needed to initiate it. Semtex has a velocity of detonation of over 8,000 metres per second. It is more powerful than TNT, widely in use as a military blasting explosive, which has a velocity of detonation of 7,000 metres per second. Most of the energy of a Semtex bomb is used in 'shearing', or the production of high speed fragments. From the bombers' viewpoint the main attractions of this type of plastic explosive are its enormous destructive power, and the fact that it is so malleable and easy to disguise from normal security checks. For example, Semtex can be shaped into the lining of a suitcase or handbag. It could be moulded to be disguised as almost any innocent-looking object, from a toy or a souvenir to a book or a standard piece of personal electronic equipment.

Investigators believe that the bomb that destroyed Pam Am Flight 103 over Lockerbie was made of Semtex explosive and concealed in a radio-cassette player, similar to the type discovered in the possession of PFLP-GC members in West Germany. The bomb found by the West German police when they rounded up members of a PFLP-GC cell, contained a timer and a barometric pressure detonator. It was skilfully designed to defeat the normal aviation security measures operating in major international airports. The West Germans released 15 of 17 Palestinians they had arrested in October, eight weeks before the Lockerbie bombing. Among those they released was Marwan

*The Lessons of Lockerbie*                                               5

Khreesat, one of the main suspects for making the bomb which brought down the Pan Am flight 103. It is believed that Khreesat was found in a car containing a Lockerbie-style radio cassette bomb equipped to explode at altitude, a kilo of explosives and several detonators. The West German police found detonators in a flat used by the Palestinians, but they missed finding three bombs similar to the one which destroyed Pan Am 103.

## Inadequacy of security systems

The West German police and intelligence authorities have been strongly criticised for these blunders, and rightly so. It seems almost incredible that they should release all but two members of a group who were clearly fully equipped to commit major acts of aviation terrorism.

In October 1989 several disturbing reports appeared in the British press claiming that the Bundeskriminalamt (BKA), West Germany's Federal criminal investigation office, had been responsible for major obstructions and delays in the Lockerbie investigation. It is alleged that they delayed six months before sending the Frankfurt luggage loading lists to the Scottish police. It has also been claimed in *The Independent* (30 October 1989) that the BKA "denied access to interrogate suspects and witnesses; had information and documents withheld and had requests to gather evidence denied."

If some or all of these allegations are true one must assume a basic rift between West Germany and Britain over the line of investigation being pursued, and/or that the West Germans do not wish certain details to come out. There is circumstantial evidence to suggest that the West Germans made fundamental blunders in their handling of the investigation into the PFLP-GC cell based in Frankfurt and Neuss. If these reports claiming that the BKA thwarted the international investigation are substantiated they go a long way to explaining why the criminal investigation has got bogged down, despite the best efforts of the Scottish police. These serious allegations should be thoroughly investigated at European level by the Trevi Group ministers, and in West Germany itself by the Chancellor and his Cabinet.

Nevertheless, the West German authorities did have the good sense to give wide publicity to details of the bomb, which they circulated to the police and intelligence agencies of friendly countries. (There has also been considerable controversy about the way the British Department of Transport handled the bomb warnings from West Germany, and in particular the delay in circulating photographs of the device and details to help airline and airport security personnel spot this type of bomb).

It is important to emphasise, however, that even if all the hold luggage, including that originating from Frankfurt, had been taken out and x-rayed prior to departure from Heathrow, and the radio-cassette player had been spotted, the x-ray alone would not have sufficed to identify the Lockerbie bomb.

If security personnel had been able to benefit from the additional detailed description of the West German bomb, (sent out on 19 December by the Department of Transport, but held up by the Christmas post until the New

Year) they might have been able to spot the clue that when x-rayed the radio-cassette player bomb appeared to contain more wiring than normal. But only careful manual inspection would have been able to detect the more obvious clues notified by the West Germans: the aerial jack plug was taped to the side of the radio and there was no wire attached to the jack plug; additional batteries and explosive material were not secured inside the radio-cassette player, and these loose items rattled inside the set if it was rotated. There is only one airline in the world operating the rigorous search methods that would have been likely to spot such a device without any prior warning and briefing as to what to look for and that is El Al. The rest of the world's civil aviation security systems simply do not have the technology or the human skills and knowledge to prevent another Lockerbie from happening tomorrow.

**An African Lockerbie**

Sadly, the failure to take adequate preventive and deterrent measures, and the continuing readiness of fanatical terrorist groups to commit mass murder in the air, were all too vividly demonstrated on 19 September 1989, when UTA DC-10 airliner, flight 772 en route from Brazzaville to Paris, was destroyed in a mid-air explosion above Niger's Tenere desert, killing all 171 passengers and crew. The disaster had all the hallmarks of an African Lockerbie. The pilot gave no warning of anything amiss; the airliner completely lost contact with air traffic control; and the fact that the bodies of victims and wreckage were scattered over a radius of roughly 60 miles suggests that, as in Lockerbie, the explosion was very powerful and occurred at a high altitude. The French investigators have stated that the disaster was caused by a bomb, comprised of a high-performance plastic explosive. If this is the case it is certainly possible that the bomb was similar to the one which destroyed Pan Am 103 above Lockerbie in an estimated quarter of a second.

Two calls were made to UTA in which a person claiming to be from the Islamic Jihad claimed responsibility. A news agency office in London received a call claiming:

"In the name of Allah and Imam Khomeini, the Islamic Jihad issued this statement. We are proud of this action, which was very successful. We would like to say the French are warned not to exchange information regarding Sheikh Obeid and the Israelis. We demand the freedom of Sheikh Obeid, and otherwise we will refresh the memories of bombings in Paris '85 and '86. Long live the Islamic Republic of Iran".

A few days later a note was delivered to a news agency in West Beirut, in ungrammatical and misspelt French, stating:

"The Clandestine Chadian Resistance announces responsibility for the operation of DC-10 UTA flight number 772, on September 19, 1989 between Ndjamena and Paris. The struggle will continue until the complete withdrawal of all military forces from Africa".

This claim is not as improbable as it may sound. A Chadian group claimed responsibility for planting two bombs on a UTA airliner at Ndjamena airport in 1984. The bombs exploded while the aircraft was on the ground, injuring 25. Moreover there is still simmering hostility between pro-Libyan elements in Chad and the Habre government, which has the support of 1.200 French troops stationed in Chad. In view of Qaddafi's humiliating defeat during his intervention in Chad in 1982 there is clearly a real possibility that the Libyans instigated this terrorist attack against a French target. Yet another theory, circulating in some French media and political circles, is that the bomb which destroyed UTA 772 was a fifth bomb from the stock of the PFLP-GC cell discovered by the West German police.

The UTA bombing thus confronts the French and the African governments involved (Congo, Chad and Niger) with a similarly tangled problem of tracing the true perpetrators of this act of mass murder in the air to that faced by the Lockerbie criminal investigation. This African Lockerbie also dramatically highlights the fatal weaknesses in aviation security which are characteristic of numerous airports in West and Central Africa and many other low income countries of the Third World. Many of these airports have no perimeter security whatsoever. The governments and local authorities involved lack the resources to upgrade their security. As one of their officials pointed out:

> "We cannot afford even an extra x-ray machine for the hospital, let alone any new machine for airport security".

It is clear that while such weak links exist in the global aviation-security system, and the terrorist is quite capable of exploiting these, it is no good depending on the efforts of a few wealthy industrial states (e.g. the USA, West Germany and the UK) to transform themselves into shining examples of effective security. The terrorists will find the easy ways to get their bombs, weapons and operatives into the international aviation system.

Terrorist sabotage bombing is preventable. But the modest—and they are only modest—improvements in the security systems of the major aviation states fall hopelessly short of the radical enhancement of global aviation security that is required in order significantly to reduce the threat of mass murder in the world's airways.

## MOBILISING PUBLIC SUPPORT AND POLITICAL WILL

A major weakness of all democratic governments in addressing countermeasures against terrorism is that instead of devising a sensible and rational long-term strategy they become entirely preoccupied with crisis management and political damage limitation in response to the latest outrage. Once the public memory of the outrage recedes, both the general public and the politicians tend to lose interest, and the pressure to make urgently needed fundamental improvements in security tends to fizzle out, only to be promised once more in the context of the next crisis. It is a phenomenon all too familiar to independent specialists in aviation terrorism and security; I would describe it as the "politics of the latest outrage" syndrome.

The brutal fact is that governments lack the will to set aviation security high on the domestic policy agenda, let alone the agenda of international organisations. They lack a clear strategy and machinery to co-ordinate effective international action. It has often been pointed out that it is governments which have the responsibility for enforcing the rule of law within their jurisdiction, and it is governments which are in almost every case the real

8                          *Research Institute for the Study of Conflict and Terrorism*

targets of terrorist groups' symbolic attacks and demands. It is therefore surely primarily the task of governments, both individually and in alliance, to take the necessary steps to keep ahead of the terrorists. Governments are unlikely to get their aviation security policies right if they are failing to combat terrorism. Hence it is to governments, particularly those of the rich OECD states, that the public must look for measures to strengthen the legal framework to ensure that terrorist suspects are brought to justice under the rule of law. It is up to governments, especially those of the powerful industrial countries, to take firm collective action against state sponsors of terrorism. Without state sponsors the terrorists who committed such crimes as Lockerbie and the taking of hostages in Beirut would not be able to operate with apparent impunity. Yet the sad reality is that democratic governments of the West have generally preferred to protect their short term economic interests, such as access to oil, to markets or lucrative arms deals, by quietly permitting business as usual with sponsor states of terrorism. Motives such as the greed of a few powerful vested interests, or sheer fear of retaliation by the state sponsor, have generally triumphed over the greater general good of collectively isolating and penalising the state sponsors of terrorism.

**Lockerbie: a major outrage**

Has the sheer scale and shock of the Lockerbie outrage broken this cycle of the "politics of the latest outrage"? At first it really seemed that it would. The world was stunned by the sheer scale of the outrage. The 270 passengers, crew and citizens of Lockerbie who were killed constituted over 40 per cent of the total fatalities through international terrorism world-wide in 1988. The public was made immediately more aware of the scale of the disaster because, unlike the downing of Air India 192 in 1985, it had taken place over land in an area fully accessible to the army of the world media. Television pictures taken when daylight broke on 22 December showed the incredible devastation wrought on the small Scottish town and the tragic work of recovering the bodies of the victims, involving a huge area of countryside where the wreckage of the place had been scattered. The wings and connecting section of the fuselage had crashed into Sherwood Crescent in Lockerbie, creating a massive crater 30 feet deep and 100 feet long, and destroying three houses. The vast explosion caused by the Boeing's aviation fuel scorched the earth, setting fire to a number of buildings. And reports came in of piles of mutilated bodies, scenes of terrible carnage. It was the most appalling emergency experienced in mainland Britain since the worst bombings of the Second World War.

Initially the media concentrated on the sheer scale of the disaster and the huge task of recovering the bodies of the victims and the forensic evidence from the wreckage in an effort to establish the cause of the explosion. Once the Air Accident Investigation Branch had concluded that the explosion was caused by a terrorist bomb, attention shifted to the criminal investigation set up under the Scottish police to try to discover the perpetrators of this act of mass murder. Attention also focused on the bereaved families and their increasing anger and frustration at finding so many of their questions unanswered. Many of them visited the scene of the disaster and tried to find out what they could from local police and officials. There was anger and frustration at delays in releasing the bodies and possessions of victims to the relatives. A team of senior police officers flew to America and met groups of relatives, and sought to explain the enormous difficulties involved in recovering evidence in a case of mass murder on this scale and the formidable problems faced by the searchers and the police. But the major development which ensured that Lockerbie would be a recurrent concern of the media, the politicians and the public was the setting up of the Victims of Pan Am Flight 103 Group early in 1989. Through their highly articulate and determined leaders and spokesman, such as Bert Ammerman in America and Dr Jim Swire in the UK, the Lockerbie Victims Group has tended to set the pace. They have raised funds to support their campaign. They have initiated legal actions to press for compensation. The Group has sought to give emotional support to the families of the victims.

At the political and security level, however, their most important role has been to try and establish whether there was any negligence on the part of Pan Am and the authorities in their handling of the warnings concerning a possible terrorist attack on Pan Am 103 and the security arrangements for the flight. They have also acted as a ginger group to try to achieve radical improvements in aviation security in order to ensure that in future such attacks are prevented. Their activities spearheaded much of the intense criticism directed at Pan Am, US State Department and the United States Federal Aviation Administration (FAA), the British Department of Transport and Heathrow for their handling of warnings about the bomb threat and at all the governments involved for serious weaknesses in aviation security. There was a political furore in March 1989 when it emerged that the West German Criminal Office (BKA) and the Federal Prosecutor's Office had passed full details and pictures of the radio cassette bomb of the type which blew up Pan Am Flight 103 to the British Government on 18 November 1988, three days after the European Security Meeting in West Germany. The Home Office, it emerged, had passed detailed information to the Department of Transport on 18 November. Mr Paul Channon, then Secretary of State for Transport, stated that the delay in sending out the 19 December circular was unimportant, but the fact is that it gave information to airport security personnel on the tell-tale signs enabling them to discover whether a radio-cassette player contained a bomb. Mr Channon defended himself vigorously in Parliament, but was replaced by Mr Cecil Parkinson in the Summer reshuffle.

As the Minister primarily responsible for aviation security at the time of Lockerbie, Mr Channon did show himself responsive to pressures from the media, the back-benchers, and the Lockerbie Victims Group, for an improvement in aviation security. He joined forces with the US transportation secretary, Mr Samuel Skinner, in launching an initiative through the International Civil Aviation Organisation's (ICAO) Aviation Security Panel, to improve international co-operation against the bombing of airlines.

10                    *Research Institute for the Study of Conflict and Terrorism*

**Attempts to improve security**

The outcome was a modest improvement in the recommendations on security procedures to member states, but as there is no proper machinery for enforcement and inspection to ensure that standards are implemented the effects have been negligible. However, Mr Channon's Department did introduce some useful improvements in British aviation security, such as the introduction of new standards for airside access to employers at UK airports, using computerised systems for automatic checking of security passes. Passes to admit to restricted areas are only to be issued to those whose references have been checked. Staff who fail to wear passes conspicuously will be disciplined, and restricted areas are to be patrolled. Aircraft are to be given security checks before flights, and once the checks have been completed access to the aircraft is to be tightly controlled. Mr Channon also announced a number of broader security objectives which certainly move in the right direction: screening of all hold luggage on high-risk flights, tightening security requirements for mail, cargo, and courier consignments; closer checking of all electronic equipment taken on board aircraft; strict separation of outbound and inbound passengers; and changes to the design and construction of aircraft interiors to make them easier to search for weapons and explosives.

However, it is the Americans who have been more responsive to the air security lobby and the Lockerbie Victims Group. They have been ahead of other countries in Research and Development to produce effective new security technology capable of detecting plastic explosives, and have already experimented with prototype thermal neutron analysis (TNA) machines besides increasing their investment in research.

By contrast Mr Channon announced an increase in the budget for R & D on security equipment from £500,000 to £1 million – still a derisory amount when one thinks of the huge overall cost of civil aviation. In view of the investment required it may be sensible for major industrial countries to club together to produce the best possible new detection equipment, using a battery of the best available technologies. Some of the most promising technologies are discussed later in the report. In Britain there has been one organisational innovation intended to provide better co-ordination between the many agencies and departments with some role in aviation security. The Department of Transport Aviation Security Branch has been replaced by the Aviation Security Inspectorate, increased to 15/16 staff under a Chief Inspector. The new Inspectorate has the tasks of carrying out security inspections to ensure that security is efficient, and as in the case of the American FAA, to test baggage and personnel searches by posing as terrorists and trying to get test devices through the security system. They also have the key job of anticipating future terrorist trends and advising airport managers.

Some security specialists believe that this will not be sufficient to overcome the problems of fragmentation and lack of co-ordination that occur within the system. However as in the case of the other security changes described above, we can be certain that it would not have been introduced if it had not been for the catalyst of Lockerbie and the post-Lockerbie security debate.

Notwithstanding these modest but welcome reforms it is clear that the

*The Lessons of Lockerbie*                                    11

steam appears to be going out of the campaign for improved aviation security. The nightmare of Lockerbie is rapidly receding in the public mind. The downing of the UTA DC-10 in Africa was hardly mentioned in the British media, though it was top headline news in France. Are we so ethnocentric that we only take notice of disasters that occur to our own airlines when considerable numbers of British and/or American passengers are involved? It so happens that there were four British passengers killed on the UTA disaster, besides the wife of an American ambassador, Mrs Bonnie Pugh, yet there has been little or no comment on the uncanny similarities to the Lockerbie bombing or the implications for aviation security.

Few members of the public seem aware that far more people have been killed by acts of aviation sabotage bombing and other bombing attacks on aircraft and air fatalities on the ground in the past five years (1,059) alone than have been killed in the past 50 years through hijacking (638).

Many passengers do not apparently realise that aviation terrorism acts now vie with technical failure and pilot error as a major cause of fatalities in civil aviation. Moreover, when a case of technical failure, freak weather conditions, or pilot error, occurs, there is a real chance of at least some of the passengers and crew getting out alive. Mid-air sabotage bombing at high altitude is a total catastrophe: no one has a chance of getting out alive.

Above all, we should remember that acts of aviation terrorism are premeditated crimes, not natural disaster. The public's instinctive desire for natural justice demands, and in the author's view rightly demands, that society should actively pursue the criminals to bring them to justice. If we abandon this effort we are conniving at the erosion of the fragile structure of international order and the rule of law and if we are to combat the scourge of terrorism ignoring such threats cannot be an option for any responsible government. Governments, aviation authorities, and airlines worldwide must be mobilised to support and implement an effective global strategy for the enhancement of aviation security.

### Obstacles to security strategies

This is of course easier said than done. Many governments that have been fortunate enough to avoid serious aviation terrorism incidents simply are not sufficiently aware of the threat, or prepared to give countermeasures any priority. A smaller number of rogue regimes have been actively sponsoring and using aviation terrorism as a tool of covert action, and they will seek to obstruct any international co-operation against terrorism. A very large number of states, including some members of the Organisation for Economic Co-operation and Development (OECD) and the European Community, are not willing to place commercial deals with state sponsors of terrorism at risk, because they accord more importance to commercial profit than combating aviation terrorism. Others – usually the smaller aviation countries – are afraid to take firm collective measures against terrorist states because they fear they will become targets of a terrorist campaign of retribution. Yet perhaps the biggest obstacle of all to a strategy of international aviation security enhancement is the short-term thinking and sheer complacency of many of the politicians and bureaucrats in positions of responsibility in this field. Bureaucrats and officials tend always to be reluctant to admit any major shortcomings in their security systems in case such criticism threatens their own position. If a crisis or failure does occur they will point to the plethora of other agencies involved and blame someone else. Politicians will be reluctant to override the advice of their own officials and the views of powerful interests in the aviation industry.

In Britain and the United States it must be recognised that the policy of airline and airport deregulation inevitably tends to bring a conflict between the pressures for commercial profit at a time of intense airline competition and the needs of public safety and security. If many of the day-to-day tasks of security are placed in the hands of the same companies which are responsible for the profitability of the airports, airlines and aircraft, there are bound to be those who cut corners in security in order to cut their costs.

One way of dealing with this problem is to create a powerful governmental regulatory agency with real powers to enforce security standards, for example by imposing heavy fines for security failures. The FAA has these powers, and has already taken action against a number of US carriers. In September 1989 the FAA announced that it had imposed fines on Pan American World Airways of 480,000 dollars for security violations committed in London, and 150,000 dollars for violations in Frankfurt, during an investigation conducted between 22 December and 31 January, immediately after the Lockerbie bombing. The FAA stated that the violations included: the use of improper methods to check carry-on luggage of passengers; failure to conduct the required search of cargo areas before loading, and failure to identify passengers for additional screening before allowing them and their luggage aboard the flight. In some cases passengers who had been identified for further checks did not have their carry-on luggage opened for inspection as regulations require, but were merely given a check with a hand-held metal-detector. According to the FAA, Pan Am failed to apply proper procedures to identify 31 passengers before boarding. Five passengers were identified at Frankfurt for further screening, but this was not done. Perhaps most worrying of all was an incident at Heathrow, when a passenger did not board, but his luggage was permitted to remain on the airliner.

If the FAA's report on violations is correct it certainly underlines the vital need of a powerful regulatory agency to monitor and enforce proper aviation security standards.

**Passenger and pilot pressure**

It should not be forgotten also that the travelling public and the aircrew do have a major potential for pressuring governments, airlines, and airport authorities to improve security. If the passengers vote with their feet, as they did in 1985 and 1986 in the wake of the TWA hijack to Beirut, and the explosion on board TWA Flight 840 as it neared Athens, they can inflict huge economic costs on those deemed to be dragging their feet on security. In 1986, US citizens avoided airports, airlines and whole regions perceived as likely terrorist targets inadequately protected. Fear of flying to Europe did considerable damage to the economies of countries such as Greece, heavily dependent on tourism. And the big airlines had mass cancellations.

Furthermore, as can be seen in Table 3, we now have powerful opinion poll evidence based on a survey of 4,800 frequent flyers in ten countries, conducted by *Interavia* and the International Foundation of Airline Passengers' Associations (IFAPA). 62 per cent could see no change in aviation security, despite Lockerbie. No less than 84 per cent were willing to pay a *nominal* security levy on their air tickets for a special fund administered through ICAO to develop high-tech detection equipment, improve training, monitor airport security procedures, and generally upgrade security in all of the world's airports *in a way which will not slow down passage through controls*. And 62 per cent were prepared to check in well before normal time to perform extra security checks.

This is encouraging evidence of public concern about the quality of aviation. But a word of caution is necessary: the survey was conducted between April and June, 1989, that is between four and six months after the Lockerbie disaster. As memories of Lockerbie fade one might expect to see a dramatic decline in concern about aviation security. Secondly, we should bear in mind that the 4,800 frequent flyers in the sample represent the elite of air passengers, those whose business constantly takes them on the world's airways. We might expect them to have an unusually high sensitivity to security issues, and to express a high degree of concern. Would a broader cross-section of the air travelling public demonstrate the same concern? But the passengers are by no means the only non-governmental players who can be mobilised to wrest significant improvements in aviation security from governments. In many ways the most practicable and potentially the most powerfully effective method of pressuring recalcitrant or negligent states into conforming with aviation security norms is for the trade unions and professional organisations within the international aviation industry to impose their own unilateral sanctions.

It is worth recalling the remarkable speed with which an El Al aircraft hijacked to Algeria was released in 1968 when the International Federation of Airline Pilots Association (IFALPA) threatened to boycott all flights in or out of Algeria. The piloting skills and technical services required by modern airliners are so complex that they could not easily be replaced by the boycotted regime. One leading international legal authority, Dr Edward McWhinney, concludes that the threat of such a boycott:

"against a delinquent state remains a reserve control, to be used, if need be, in default of affirmative and effective control by the organised community . . . Its potential effects are immense and relatively immediate. And if there be argued the extra weight of larger and financially far more powerful organisations . . . then the chances of applying effective, if informal, community sanctions against delinquent states seem very real and also immediate". (*The Illegal Diversion of Aircraft and International Law*, Leiden, Sijthoff 1975. p. 76)

While admitting the potential influence of passenger and pilot pressure, however, one must be realistic about its limits. If commercial civil aviation is

14            *Research Institute for the Study of Conflict and Terrorism*

## TABLE 3: RESULTS OF INTERAVIA/IFAPA SURVEY
## WHAT THE PASSENGERS THINK

| Country | CH | F | SC | NL | E | GB | D | I | GR | USA | All 10 |
|---|---|---|---|---|---|---|---|---|---|---|---|
| In general, are you satisfied with security procedures at the airports you fly from? | | | | | | | | | | | |
| Yes | 55% | 50% | 55% | 67% | 49% | 46% | 61% | 46% | 46% | 40% | 52% |
| No | 45% | 50% | 45% | 33% | 51% | 54% | 39% | 54% | 54% | 60% | 48% |
| Are you more satisfied or less satisfied than you were a year ago? | | | | | | | | | | | |
| More | 18% | 24% | 20% | 20% | 18% | 31% | 21% | 25% | 46% | 17% | 23% |
| No change | 71% | 59% | 65% | 62% | 68% | 49% | 66% | 69% | 49% | 65% | 62% |
| Less | 11% | 17% | 15% | 18% | 14% | 20% | 13% | 6% | 5% | 18% | 15% |

Would you be willing to pay a *nominal* security levy on your air ticket for a special fund administered through the International Civil Aviation Organisation to develop high-tech detection equipment, improve training, monitor airport security procedures and generally upgrade security in all of the world's airports *in a way which will not slow down passage through controls*?

| | CH | F | SC | NL | E | GB | D | I | GR | USA | All 10 |
|---|---|---|---|---|---|---|---|---|---|---|---|---|
| Yes | 82% | 82% | 87% | 76% | 86% | 90% | 77% | 91% | 83% | 79% | 84% |
| No | 18% | 18% | 13% | 24% | 14% | 10% | 23% | 9% | 17% | 21% | 16% |

If yes, how much extra would you be willing to pay *per flight*?

| | CH | F | SC | NL | E | GB | D | I | GR | USA | All 10 |
|---|---|---|---|---|---|---|---|---|---|---|---|---|
| $1–4 | 21% | 25% | 18% | 15% | 20% | 18% | 21% | 13% | 22% | 30% | 21% |
| $5–9 | 36% | 39% | 36% | 29% | 34% | 38% | 41% | 42% | 32% | 30% | 37% |
| $10+ | 25% | 18% | 33% | 32% | 32% | 34% | 15% | 36% | 29% | 19% | 26% |

Some airlines require passengers to check in well before normal check-in time to perform extra security checks. By how much *extra* time would you be willing to check in early?

| | CH | F | SC | NL | E | GB | D | I | GR | USA | All 10 |
|---|---|---|---|---|---|---|---|---|---|---|---|---|
| None | 36% | 41% | 44% | 47% | 27% | 36% | 48% | 30% | 32% | 16% | 38% |
| Up to 1 hr | 52% | 48% | 50% | 44% | 68% | 43% | 45% | 57% | 44% | 64% | 49% |
| 1–2 hr | 11% | 10% | 5% | 9% | 5% | 19% | 7% | 11% | 24% | 15% | 12% |
| Over 2 hr | 1% | 1% | 1% | – | – | 2% | – | 2% | – | 5% | 1% |

Would you be inconvenienced if there is a ban on electronic goods that you can carry by air, such as radios, calculators, tape players and computers?

| | CH | F | SC | NL | E | GB | D | I | GR | USA | All 10 |
|---|---|---|---|---|---|---|---|---|---|---|---|---|
| Yes | 53% | 51% | 55% | 47% | 52% | 53% | 47% | 49% | 59% | 45% | 51% |
| No | 47% | 49% | 45% | 53% | 48% | 47% | 53% | 51% | 41% | 55% | 49% |

| | CH | F | SC | NL | E | GB | D | I | GR | USA | All 10 |
|---|---|---|---|---|---|---|---|---|---|---|---|---|
| Number of replies | 119 | 151 | 211 | 86 | 44 | 197 | 155 | 53 | 41 | 128 | 1,220 |

*Notes*: Key to country abbreviations: CH. Switzerland; F. France; SC. Scandinavia; NL. Netherlands; E. Spain; GB. Great Britain; D. West Germany; I. Ireland; GR. Greece; USA. United States. Note also that the total number of responses in the last column (1,220) is greater than the total of responses from the ten countries added up (1,175) because a number of late replies, which had not been allocated to country breakdown, were included in the global total.

*Reproduced by kind permission of Interavia*

going to remain viable it must be geared to maximising the comfort and convenience of the passengers. If all aviation authorities were to introduce military-style security of the type utilised by El Al the whole civil aviation system would rapidly seize up. El Al can operate such a system quite easily because its passengers are fully aware that Israel is still in a formal state of war with most of her Arab neighbours and is a constant target for terrorist attacks by extreme Palestinian groups. It has no short haul flights. Israelis are quite willing to turn up some hours in advance of their long haul flight; and El Al's high reputation for passenger safety and security is a positive attraction for its customers, hence its extremely high load factor on the important trans-Atlantic route.

But let us make no mistake, for the vast majority of the world's airports and airlines the only feasible way to improved security is the design of an aviation security system which does not slow down the progress of the passenger through the controls. Previous experience is very encouraging in this respect. In the late 1960s and early 1970s the US government was desperate to find measures drastically to reduce the hijackings of aircraft originating from US airports. Lt-Gen. Ben Davis, appointed by the President to construct a sound system, hit on a most effective compromise. Instead of going over to the El Al model he adopted a brilliant formula based on a swift and rigorous check of all passengers and their carry-on luggage at the boarding gate. Many thought this would never work, and would cause protest riots by passengers. But it worked superbly, because the scheme was so designed that if any queues did occur they were at the check-in desks and not at the security gates. This policy, in combination with the 1973 US–Cuba Hijack Pact which blocked the escape route to Cuba, was highly effective.

As with the development of successful measures against hijacking, an effective strategy to deal with the newer and more deadly threat of sabotage bombing depends ultimately on sound national aviation security systems. In a world of sovereign states, in which no international organisation has the authority or power to police international crime, national systems must become the building blocks of an improved international response.

## KEY COMPONENTS OF AN EFFECTIVE NATIONAL AVIATION SECURITY SYSTEM

The first essential requirement of any effective security system is the ability to obtain, properly evaluate, and utilise high-grade intelligence. The primary responsibility for this lies with the intelligence services and the police. It is important to bear in mind that national intelligence services vary widely in quality and resources and in the type of constraints under which they operate. The Central Intelligence Agency (CIA), for example, has relatively abundant financial resources, access to some of the best technology for information gathering in the world, and some very highly trained and able analysts and operatives. However, in the wake of the Watergate and Irangate scandals Congress has imposed such tight constraints and oversight on their operations that it has become difficult for them to maintain the secrecy essential for effective covert activity. In other cases, such as Italy in the late 1960s and early 1970s, some elements in the intelligence services appear to have moved beyond the reach of democratic control and accountability, even, on occasion, becoming involved with shadowy conspiracies of the far right against the democratically elected government.

The experience of many liberal states has shown that it is not impossible for secret intelligence services within the liberal state to operate firmly within the framework of the law and the constitution. They can be made fully accountable for their operations to the democratically elected government and through them to the legislature and electorate, despite the fact that most of the information about their actual day-to-day functioning is necessarily secret or under restricted security classification.

**Problems of intelligence gathering**

Gathering intelligence to combat aviation terrorism faces the intelligence services and the police with special difficulties. The archetypal terrorist group is numerically small and based on a structure of cells. These generally exercise a fair degree of operational independence and initiative, and are obsessively concerned with the security of their organisations and lines of communication. This cell structure is designed to enhance secrecy, mobility and flexibility while at the same time facilitating tight overall central control by the terrorist directorate. Experienced terrorists develop sophisticated cover against detection and infiltration. Few security authorities are lucky enough to capture a terrorist red-handed at the scene of the crime. Hence there is a great deal of patient work needed to build up background information about terrorist groups and their members, leaders, aims, motivations, organisation, sources of weapons and funds.

Gathering and evaluating intelligence on aviation terrorism is rendered all the more difficult by the fact that it is an inherently international phenomenon. Data is needed on every terrorist group in the world which has the track record, potential or motivation that suggests it might commit terrorist attacks on aviation. This will include nationalist and religious extremist movements, ideological terrorists, and state sponsors of terrorism. The intelligence services and the police may be fortunate enough to spot the indicators of a possible impending aviation terrorism operation, such as thefts of arms and explosives, the temporary disappearance of known militants, or meetings or communications between members of extremist groups and/or terrorist state sponsors. With really skilled intelligence work it may be possible even to prevent any terrorist attack taking place.

However, even when the intelligence services and the police have succeeded in using good background information to obtain contact information enabling them to identify members of a terrorist organisation, their problems are by no means over. In many countries legal constraints prevent the police from any adequate questioning of the individuals they suspect because however confident they are of the accuracy of their intelligence data, they have not obtained the formal legal evidence to bring charges against the suspect.

Intelligence data should not be confused with legal proof: moreover, if the intelligence service is pressed to provide more detailed information on which their assessment was based, it may lead to the disclosure or destruction of vital sources of covert intelligence. On the other hand, over-zealousness by intelligence services in seeking to protect sources may involve great risks to the public in allowing dangerous individuals to go free. Some believe that the West Germans made a blunder of this kind when they released so many suspects following the discovery of a PLFP-GC cell in West Germany in autumn 1988.

### Co-ordination failures

Another major problem is failure of co-ordination: tensions and rivalries between the various intelligence and police agencies which have bedevilled the tasks of counter-terrorism in many countries. It is therefore vital that there should be one clearly designated lead agency for gathering and evaluating aviation terrorism intelligence, and that this agency should have a national remit. In normal circumstances in a liberal democracy the most appropriate body for this role is the internal security service or the Special Branch of the police, or its equivalent. The routine police tasks of law enforcement and combating crime at every level of the community give the police an unrivalled 'bank' of background information from which contact information can be developed. Yet it is extremely hard to attain the streamlined national co-ordination required. There are so many different police forces and agencies involved, and they all tend to be reluctant to part with key information which might be used to the advantage of a rival agency. In addition they may have sound reason to doubt the capacity of the other agency to keep the information secure. They may not want to risk compromising or destroying vital intelligence sources. Secret intelligence services have traditionally been reluctant to part with information to the uniformed police for precisely these reasons. In the field of aviation terrorism this problem of ensuring the security of sensitive data passed on to other aviation organisations is particularly acute: there may be hundreds of airlines, airports, local police forces, customs and immigration departments and so on, each with a reasonable claim to be informed. But can you afford to pass on sensitive data when, as is often the case, the recipients do not even possess a secure method of communication?

### The international level

The difficulties in intelligence co-operation at national level are of course magnified a hundred fold at international level. This has become all too evident in the welter of international confusion and recrimination over the international hunt for the Lockerbie bombers. Criticism of the West German authorities for releasing 15 of the 17 Palestinians they arrested in October 1988 has been discussed earlier. The Swedish authorities have been criticised by the Americans for their handling of the case of four Palestinians charged with bombing El Al offices and synagogues in Europe in 1985–86. The

Americans believe that the four Palestinians are in some way connected with the Lockerbie case, but they claim that the Swedish police have been unwilling to assist them with their enquiries. This lack of co-operation is both disappointing and potentially counter-productive for the Swedes. They are by no means immune from the spillover of international terrorism. In February 1989 the Swedes announced that they had discovered a weapons cache, including 10 lb of Semtex, pistols, Kalashnikovs, hand grenades and detonators, close to Stockholm. It is suspected that they might have been intended for an attack on Stockholm's international airport. Another clear instance of the problem of international intelligence co-operation over Lockerbie was the controversy between the West German and British authorities as to whether the Lockerbie bomb had been loaded at Heathrow or at Frankfurt. Even among long-standing allies intelligence co-operation against terrorism is often blocked or severely limited as a result of mutual suspicion, national prestige and pride, or widely differing perceptions of national interest and security policy needs.

## Co-ordinating counter-terrorism policy

The second important requirement for a successful national aviation security system is effective co-ordination, command and control of all aspects of counter-terrorism policy. It is painfully obvious that this has not yet been fully achieved in the US, Britain, and many other countries, including those that pride themselves on having good aviation security systems. In the US there are simply too many agencies involved, including the FAA, the Federal Bureau of Investigation (FBI) and Department of Justice, the State Department, the Pentagon, the Drug Enforcement Administration (DEA), National Security Council, and the numerous airline and airport organisations. In Britain the problems of co-ordination should not be so daunting, given our much smaller geographical area and population. Yet we also have a considerable problem. In addition to the role of MI5, Special Branch, and the Anti-Terrorist Squad (SO13) at New Scotland Yard, we also have the provincial police forces with airports in their jurisdiction, the British Airports Authority plc, the Home Office, the Department of Transport, the Ministry of Defence and the airlines themselves, all involved in some aspect of aviation security. Moreover, even with its new Aviation Security Inspectorate, the Department of Transport is singularly ill-fitted to play a lead role in aviation security: it is simply not used to thinking and planning in security terms, and, in the author's view, it is in far too cosy a relationship with vested commercial interests in the transport business for whom all other considerations, including security, must be subordinated to the profit motive. Truly effective co-ordination requires identifying the most appropriate lead agency and giving it real supra-departmental powers to oversee and steer the whole complex business of aviation security. An Inspectorate, with the capacity to do occasional checks and advise on trends and performance is only part of the answer: it does not provide the necessary policy, direction and co-ordinating authority.

**Providing adequate resources**

The third requirement is adequate resources, including appropriate technology and security equipment. Sadly, even in the relatively rich industrial countries, aviation has not been given the kind of resources it needs if it is to keep ahead of terrorist weaponry and tactics. All our current boarding gate search equipment was developed in the 1970s to deal with the hijack threat. Our airports do not have equipment installed which is capable of detecting plastic explosives. This is not because the technology to do this is not available. There are some excellent thermal neutron activation systems in prototype for example. It is because no country, or group of countries, has yet provided mass produced machines, using the latest technology, for all its airports.

Thermal neutron analysis (TNA) machines detect explosives by bombarding baggage with low-energy neutrons and identifying the characteristic signatures emitted by the nitrogen and hydrogen present in all explosive chemicals. The machines have been tested in San Francisco International and Los Angeles International Airports achieving a 95 per cent success rate in detection, and their false alarm rate has been reduced to 2 per cent. The FAA has assisted Science Applications International Corp (SAIC) in the research and development of this machine.

The FAA has also encouraged the development of explosive detectors working on the principle of chemiluminescence, the phenomenon that causes nitrogen compounds to give off a fluorescent glow in the presence of ozone. These machines "sniff" around the luggage and/or passengers for dangerous chemical molecules. For example, the Secur Scan explosives sniffer booth manufactured by Thermedics, surrounds the passenger with warm air for about five seconds and conducts vapour analysis of the air sample. A metal detector can also be incorporated into the booth, which can process 10 passengers per minute.

A third possible technique is dielectric measurement, pioneered by Dr William Gregory in the USA. This is based on the principle of "capacitance" or the capacity of any object to carry a charge. This method helped to defeat the letter bombing threat in the 1970s. It could be adapted to the needs of the aviation industry.

There are also rich possibilities in the development of mass spectrometry techniques. These work by ionizing suspect molecules with a radioactive source, accelerating the ions in an electric field, and then measuring their characteristic arrival times at an endplate.

The available scientific evidence indicates that we should be aiming at utilising a combination of the best detection technologies in our airport search procedures. We should not attempt to rely on any single technology alone, as they all have their weaker spots, which the terrorist will undoubtedly exploit. There is no ground for assuming such multiple checking systems would need to be any more time-consuming and frustrating than current security checks. Moreover, the passenger would have the satisfaction of knowing that safety against plastic explosives and other terrorist weaponry had been greatly enhanced.

The major obstacle to the adoption of these new security technologies is

cost. The American Air Transport Association (ATA) has estimated that to cover the 45 highest-risk airports outside the USA would require 66 TNA machines and 171 vapour detection machines. They claim that the cost of the TNA machines would total 49.5 million dollars (750,000 dollars each) and the vapour detection machines would cost 17.1 million dollars (100,000 dollars each). The total costs seem formidable, and they would certainly be beyond the reach of the low-income countries. For this reason the question of international funding for enhanced aviation security is an important consideration. However, to place the expenditure in proper perspective let us remember that the total costs of this security package to protect aviation at a wide range of international airports is far less than a major aerospace manufacturer would expect to pay out on the development of a single new aircraft type. We are talking about a tiny fraction of the overall manufacturing and operating costs in the aviation industry.

Other technologies are also well worth examining for this purpose. We need a major R & D programme *now* to get the best designed machines with the best performance under stringent tests, into our airport systems. Substantial resources will need to be channelled to the less developed countries in order to enable them to have this latest equipment and the training needed to use it. Indeed much of the increased financial resources needed for aviation security must be spent on enhanced staff quality, training and management. The best equipment in the world will be no good if you do not have bright, highly qualified and well-motivated security staff.

**Basic security procedures**

The fourth prerequisite for effective aviation security is proper basic security procedures. These must cover:

- efficient passenger identification and screening, ensuring that all 'high selectee' passengers are checked out comprehensively before boarding;
- efficient screening of *all* carry-on and hold luggage;
- stringent procedures for reconciliation of every item of baggage carried with a passenger boarded on the same flight;
- efficient screening of all air freight, including diplomatic baggage;
- strict separation of all transit passengers from non-transit passengers and "meeters and greeters";
- stringent airside security, including proper protection of aircraft on the ground, access control, and perimeter protection;
- efficient screening of all electrical equipment carried on board aircraft, and refusal to carry items of equipment which cannot be properly checked.

Most of these procedural requirements are covered in ICAO's own manual of recommended procedures. Sadly these have only the status of recommendations, however. Security-conscious governments should concert pressure on ICAO to introduce a proper international aviation security inspectorate with powers to carry out spot checks on all international airports, and to report back to the ICAO's security committee. Any country that persistently fails to bring its security up to ICAO minimum standards should then be made subject to official aviation sanctions by the international aviation community. The US government has already demonstrated the potential of this kind of pressure when President Reagan issued his "Advisory" warning to US passengers to avoid Athens airport. As a result the Greek authorities made strenuous efforts to try to beef up airport security: they realised they had much to lose by the sudden decline in US tourist visitors.

This brings us neatly to the matter of public information in response to aviation security warnings. Clearly, just as the policy of total freedom of information on threats is untenable and would lead to chaos and panic, so the other extreme, a policy of total secrecy about threats, is also entirely impracticable and undesirable. The fact that the US government has warned US citizens against travel to certain areas shows that they realise that they have a moral obligation to warn their citizens of a threat, when it is founded on usually reliable intelligence and is considered sufficiently specific and serious. Clearly this only applies to a minority of warnings. A good yardstick would be to decide that if the government believes the threat is sufficiently grave to merit warning its own diplomatic and military employees and their families, then the travelling public generally should also be warned. Moreover, if the authorities do decide on issuing a general warning to the public they must ensure that it is communicated *swiftly and efficiently* to all those involved. A situation, as in the pre-Lockerbie warnings, where some aviation and security organisations knew, while others did not, is clearly totally unacceptable. Nor should governments assume that they can easily escape the consequences of legal actions by members of the public, not only those suing the government for failing to take the necessary preventive measures against terrorism, but also for failing to warn the public when they had prior warning of serious threat to life. In view of the scale of loss of life and devastation that would be caused by another Lockerbie, the real possibility of "class" actions in American courts should concentrate the minds of our political masters and encourage them to develop a more defensible and logical policy and procedure for threat evaluation and public warning. Of course it would help enormously if the powerful aviation states of the western world could co-ordinate their policies and procedures on public information and warnings.

## Relationships with the media

Closely linked with the requirement for an adequate policy of public information is the necessity of establishing and maintaining a good working relationship between the aviation security authorities and the media. This is easier said than done. The media have objectives that are fundamentally in conflict with those of the security authorities. The mass media professionals are driven by an insatiable appetite for being first with the news, for drama, sensation and violent action to entertain their audience. The security authorities, on the other hand, have the primary objectives of protecting the public, enforcing the law, and apprehending criminals and bringing them to justice. The mass media often undermine security even if unintentionally, for example by providing terrorists with enormous publicity for their acts of violence and by glamorising or even romanticising their image. But by far the most serious difficulties created for the aviation security authorities by media coverage of terrorism involve hijacked aircraft on the ground. The Kuwait Airliner hijack in April 1988 showed how the TV cameras and the world press monitored every flicker of movement around the grounded hijacked airliner. Even at night they constantly monitored the scene with infra-red cameras. It would have been virtually impossible for a hostage rescue commando to have launched a surprise assault on the plane. Instantaneous media coverage of the scene on the ground could well forewarn the hijackers of any impending rescue attempt as they constantly monitor radio broadcasts. To deal with this impossible situation in the event of a future hijacking a concordat is needed between the world mass media and the aviation authorities. If this cannot be amicably arranged, then the authorities will have to consider a total media ban from the airports and airport perimeter areas where a hijacked airliner is being held. It is far better, of course, to obtain mass media self-restraint by negotiation. The media can and do provide positive benefits for the management of aviation security crisis and threats. Responsible and constructive co-operation is vital, for example, in handling the problem of informing the public when a specific major warning is issued by the authorities.

**Provision of expert negotiators**

A crucial requirement for an effective aviation security system is the availability of expert hostage negotiators and a specialist back-up staff of interpreters, terrorism experts and psychologists, vital in helping crisis managers in hijack or airport hostage-taking situations. No aviation country should be without some trained negotiators for this purpose. Negotiation with terrorists, many of whom are highly trained and experienced in dealing with the authorities, is not a job for amateurs. It is deeply regrettable that many countries have failed to take the business of selection and training of negotiators seriously. The necessary skills take time to acquire, but states with highly experienced police negotiator teams are generally willing to provide training facilities for friendly countries. This form of training is not vastly expensive. In any case the very poor countries should be provided with technical assistance, under the ICAO's existing arrangements, to obtain this training for their personnel.

In most cases it will probably be desirable to use a trained police negotiator. The authorities should always be suspicious of private individuals pushing themselves forward for the job. And even when they are desperate the authorities should avoid handing over the negotiating function to some external body which offers its "good offices". As the Cyprus authorities found in the 1988 Kuwait Airline hijack, the PLO "negotiators" were anxious to use the event for their own diplomatic and public relations purposes. The PLO did not share the same objectives and obligations as the Cyprus government and security forces, and they had their own special relationship with the parties in conflict, which meant that they did not even bring the benefit of credible independent status.

The negotiator should be selected with great care. He must be firm and tough while also being skilled at building up some rapport with the terrorists and using all his bargaining chips to play for time and to coax concessions out of the terrorists. A good negotiator needs considerable courage, coolness and determination to stand up to the bullying and often brutal aggression of the terrorists and to cope with the strain. The job also calls for enormous patience and a high degree of intelligence to spot clues to the terrorists' intentions, motives and inter-relationships and their likely tactics and behaviour.

It is also vital for the crisis management co-ordination fully to understand the limits of the negotiator's role, and to use the negotiator skilfully. The negotiator is not a decision-maker. He must refer the hijacker's requests to his crisis management team for decision. Richard Clutterbuck's incisive observations on the qualities of a good negotiator provide a useful guide:

". . . the negotiator must be willing to do the job, which is exhausting and may place him at risk, and he must have the necessary personal qualities. He must be reliable and discreet and have the determination and the nerve to handle what are often aggressive and very brief telephone calls during which his instant reactions may be decisive. He must be capable of detached judgement. He must have intelligence at least matching that of the (terrorists) (which in the case of some political terrorists is high), patience so as not to provoke them and the initiative to spot, seize and exploit any opportunity, however small. He should not, however, have too cold a personality. A sense of humour and the ability to show warmth and feeling may help him to develop a working relationship with the (terrorists') negotiator, which can greatly facilitate negotiations and may save the victim's life. He must, on the other hand, have the necessary iron in his personality to seize the initiative and dominate the (terrorists) when he senses that they are beginning to become anxious to reach a settlement . . ."

*(Kidnap, Hijack and Extortion*, London, Macmillan 1987, pp 124-5)

## Co-operation with the military

Last, but not least, an effective national aviation security system requires well co-ordinated liaison and co-operation with the military, particularly in the planning, training and deployment of specialist hostage-rescue commandos. It is true that such rescue operations are extremely risky, and under certain circumstances may prove impracticable, but a state needs to have capabilities to mount them as a last resort. The standard of specialist training needed for such tasks is so high that there is much to be gained from encouraging bilateral training and assistance programmes to enable countries with less well prepared forces to acquire expertise from crack units such as the British SAS and the French GIGN. The military can also provide other highly relevant expertise to assist aviation authorities, such as bomb disposal and defence against missile attack. It should hardly be necessary to add that if the value of the military contribution is to be maximised there must be civil-military liaison of the highest calibre, and frequent joint exercises and training at all levels. There are many countries where this regular liaison and co-operation can hardly be said to exist, or even where the military and civil police are bitter rivals.

24                    *Research Institute for the Study of Conflict and Terrorism*

## "INTERNATIONALISING THE RESPONSE"?

Enhanced national aviation security systems must be the building blocks for any improvement in global aviation security. Yet there is a huge diversity in national security standards. A rich and technologically powerful nation like the United States has a leading place in the development of new security technologies, but its airports are full of major security loopholes, such as poor or non-existent baggage reconciliation procedures, and lack of proper passenger screening and questioning. At the other extreme, there are some very poor countries in Africa and Asia where airport security is no more than cosmetic, where there is no perimeter security whatsoever, and they lack the trained staff and equipment to implement even the most basic of the ICAO's recommended security procedures. Yet in an international form of transport such as civil aviation, security will only be as strong as its weakest link. What is the good of building up our national aviation security in the western industrial countries to be shining examples if the terrorists are able to pick on the airport with poor security to gain access to airliners and the rest of the aviation system? In theory we could establish a kind of fortress state military-style security and impose it on all domestic and international carriers operating in the national airspace. But this would be to turn one's back on the rest of the world's aviation traffic. Few countries would welcome such self-imposed isolation, and the costs of such a policy in terms of loss of international contacts, trade and tourism.

Yet the problems of internationalising the response to aviation terrorism are just as daunting as those confronting other areas of international co-operation. Some governments will oppose or work to undermine the international efforts at co-operation because they wish to continue state sponsorship and use of terrorism as a covert weapon. A rather larger number of states will not support improved international measures because they have been lucky and had a quiet life and do not perceive aviation terrorism as a problem. And even those states that do agree that substantial measures are needed will tend to quarrel about what action is needed and who should pay for it.

Even among the members of the European Community, which has a shared experience of modern terrorism in many of its member states, and spilling over from the Middle East, differences in national security policies, legal systems, procedures, jurisdictions, extradition, law and practice and many other aspects constitute major road-blocks in the way of international co-operation in combating terrorism. Even the prospect of 1992 and the removal of internal frontiers has not yet brought about any real degree of harmonisation in such matters as visas, refugees, asylum, firearms laws, extradition, cross-border judicial and police co-operation.

In the light of these inherent problems of intergovernmental co-operation in prickly areas of law and order and security, one should not be surprised that the International Civil Aviation Organisation (ICAO) role has largely been confined to recommendation and exhortation. It is significant that at the specially convened February 1989 meeting of ICAO some members pointed out that poorer countries would not be able to implement effective security

## TERRORIST SABOTAGE BOMBING OF AIRLINERS: MAJOR BOMBINGS AND ATTEMPTS

**1985**     On June 22 **Air India flight 182** exploded over the **Atlantic off Shannon** killing 329

**1986**     On April 2 a bomb exploded on board **TWA flight 840** on its approach to **Athens**. Four American citizens were killed.

**1986**     On April 17 a woman boarding an **El Al jet in London** was found to have a bomb in her hand luggage. The woman's boyfriend, Nezar Hindawi, was convicted of the attempt. Evidence produced at the trial implicated Syrian intelligence, who provided the bomb. Britain broke diplomatic relations with Syria.

**1986**     On May 3 a bomb blew the tail section away from an **Air Lanka jet** preparing to depart from **Colombo Airport**. 16 were killed and 41 injured.

**1986**     On June 26 a suitcase bomb partially detonated at **Barajas Airport, Madrid**, wounding 11. The bomb was intended to explode on an **El Al flight to Tel Aviv**.

**1987**     On November 29 **Korean Air Lines flight 858** disappeared over the **Andaman Sea off Burma**, killing all 115 on board. A woman who had disembarked with her elderly companion at Abu Dhabi, later confessed that she and her companion had planted the bomb on the airliner when they boarded it in Baghdad. She stated that the operation was planned by North Korean intelligence officials.

**1988**     On December 21 over **Lockerbie, Scotland, Pan Am flight 103** was destroyed in a mid-air explosion killing 259 passengers and crew and 11 people on the ground in Lockerbie. Subsequent investigation showed that the airliner was destroyed by a terrorist bomb.

**1989**     On September 19, **over the Sahara, UTA flight 772** was destroyed in a mid-air explosion killing 171 passengers and crew. French investigators are convinced that the cause of the disaster was a terrorist bomb, and have found traces of Semtex explosive. Claims of responsibility have been made by Islamic Jihad and a Chadian group.

without economic and technical help. The final resolution urged members to increase aid to countries that need financial and technical assistance to improve security. But no steps were taken to set up an International Aviation Security Fund, of the type urged by IFAPA. Thus, as was the case before Lockerbie, international co-operation at governmental level remains limited to good will and ad hoc arrangements.

Faced with the snail's pace of intergovernmental co-operation and the giant gulf between the existing outdated and extremely limited provisions of the Tokyo, Hague and Montreal Conventions and what is actually required to enhance international aviation security, one is tempted to despair. Yet the major aviation states must not give up trying to press for improved measures at multilateral level. They must continue to press states that do not yet adhere to the international conventions to do so. Such progress may be painfully slow, but it is in the right direction.

### IATA plan

By contrast the security proposals of the International Air Transport Association (IATA) seem so ambitious that they could easily be dismissed as unrealistic. IATA has put forward a five-point plan entitled 'Internationalising the Response'. This calls for (i) the establishment of an international advisory group which would be immediately available to support governments when a hijacking occurs; (ii) the setting up of an international team of experts qualified to investigate acts of unlawful interference after the event; (iii) the formation of an international force working in conjunction with the International Advisory Group which could provide a military response to an incident, should such an intervention become necessary; (iv) creation of an international court to try any captured hijackers or other persons alleged to have committed acts of unlawful interference; and (v) establishment of an international detention centre where terrorists may be held while serving their sentence.

Some of these ideas have been around a long time. The proposal for an international criminal court to try terrorists was put forward in the 1930s in the wake of the assassination of King Alexander and Louis Barthou. The International Law Association in 1972 devised a statute for an International Criminal Court. The attractions are obvious: it would obviate the need for extradition between the jurisdiction of the states which became parties to the convention; small states afraid of terrorist retaliation if they prosecuted a suspect could pass the problem on to the International Court, which would also take over the burden of arranging the trial and administering the sentence; and, above all, it would be no good the terrorists seeking to intimidate the original target state into releasing the terrorists because, if convicted, he/she would be placed in the custody of the International Court.

Realism suggests that this proposal has very little chance of being adopted generally by the international states system: the majority of states would be unwilling to concede any sovereignty over such matters to an international body beyond their power to control. There may be a better chance of its adoption within the European Community states. They share the experience of working within the framework of the European Court of Justice and the Council of Europe Human Rights Court. A European Criminal Court could be seen as a logical extension of these structures. Moreover, the new Court could deal with other serious international crimes, such as drug trafficking and international fraud and computer crime. In the light of the impending developments of 1992 and the dismantling of frontiers, such an idea might commend itself to European Justice Ministers.

The proposals for an International Advisory Group for the support of governments, and an expert group of investigators seem eminently sensible, but they would need to operate under a clear international authority with the approval of governments. The only intergovernmental body that could provide an adequate international legal status and framework for such advisers and experts is the ICAO, and to date there is no sign that they wish to take these measures.

The idea of an international military force appears the least feasible of IATA's proposal. Many states would immediately suspect it of being a disguised method of intervention or interference in their internal affairs. A more feasible approach is bilateral assistance by a friendly nation, or request, in an emergency. There are already precedents for such bilateral assistance in cases of aviation terrorism. For example, this method was demonstrated very successfully in the British SAS collaboration with the West German GSG9 in 1977 at Mogadishu. Similarly the US Delta force has assisted friendly states such as Thailand and Venezuela. Local or regional assistance arrangements of this kind may be very useful and are more likely to be acceptable than some supersquad with a global remit.

## Self-help for security

In the light of the great reluctance of nation-states to pool even a small part of their sovereignty in the interests of combating terrorism, the world civil aviation community – passengers, aircrew and airlines and airport authorities – should give careful thought to the possibility of taking further measures of self-help, using the channels of their international non-governmental organisations such as IFALPA, IFAPA, and IATA. Consumers and "producers" have a common interest in promoting enhanced security, and they have considerable muscle to pressure governments if they care to use it. There are at least three important opportunities:

- They have a major task in lobbying and educating governments on the security problems and needs of the industry and in pressing for government action to make real improvements.
- They are in a unique position to take the initiative in starting an international aviation security fund. If governments prove unwilling to act there are other ways of collecting and administering the money. IATA and the airlines and consumer organisations should take joint steps to initiate a special passenger levy, to set up an independent body to administer the funds, and to establish and monitor a programme of security technology research and development, enhancement of security

management and training, and a proper international airport security inspectorate. Governments and intergovernmental organisations are not the only bodies capable of performing these tasks. The aviation industry must act itself if governments fail to act.

• There is also scope for the civil aviation industry and the passengers to take another vital measure of self-help. Over 90 per cent of aviation terrorism involves the use of false passports. Governments have done nothing about it. The world's airlines should go ahead and introduce a new high-technology identity document. A computerised air travel permit the size of a credit-card could carry a fingerprint code which could be checked against the bearer, thus preventing the use of forged or stolen permits. The check would take only a matter of seconds for each passenger, and it would circumvent the outdated and unreliable passport document. There is no legal barrier to the industry introducing its own air travel permit system, just as there is nothing to stop banks issuing cheque and credit cards. The advantages of better screening and swifter passenger throughput would soon become evident. Immigration and security officials could then devote more time to checking out those passengers from the few countries refusing to join the scheme – probably a small number of pro-terrorist states.

## THE BROADER STRATEGY

It is clear that there is considerable scope for self-help by the civil aviation industry and the passengers in striving for enhanced global aviation security. One obvious area of concern which will involve intensive lobbying and legal action by the bereaved relatives such as the Lockerbie Victims Group is the battle for a more consistent, fairer and more generous system of compensation. The present system is a hopeless muddle: the amount of automatic compensation depends on where each airline is registered and where it was flying to when the accident happened. It may take years before this matter is put into some kind of order.

It has been the main argument of this study that there are things that both governments and non-governmental organisations can do radically to enhance national aviation security systems. The precedent of the hijacking plague of the late 1960s and early 1970s is encouraging here. By a judicious mixture of new boarding gate searches of passengers and baggage, and legal measures, the hijack threat was very sharply reduced.

Technologies and procedures capable of detecting plastic explosives do already exist and have been tested. It is now a matter of mobilising the political will and resources to make such improved security available to international aviation generally. Enhancement of national systems is a vital first step, but both governments and the industry and passengers will need to join forces to internationalise an effective response to the major threat of sabotage bombing. Urgent steps are needed to raise the necessary funds for this enhancement, and to set up a system for monitoring, inspecting and enforcing proper security standards world-wide.

One major lesson of Lockerbie that has been completely overlooked by

*The Lessons of Lockerbie*                                                    29

many analysts is that we must never again allow our security to lag behind the tactics and weapons of the terrorist. When terrorists find it harder to plant bombs on aircraft they are likely to turn to other tactics such as shooting them down with surface-to-air missiles. We know that some terrorist groups and state sponsors already have such weapons in their possession. We should already be planning effective preventive and counter-measures to deal with such threats. In an age of terrorism, when aviation will continue to be an attractive target of high publicity value to the terrorist, we can never afford to relax our vigilance.

Above all, we should be aware that to be effective any measures against aviation terrorism must be backed up by a firm and effective policy against international terrorism. The general principles of the firm hard-line strategy, which I have long advocated for the liberal state, and which have the best track record in reducing terrorism, are:

- no surrender to the terrorists, and an absolute determination to defeat terrorism within the framework of the rule of law and the democratic process;
- no deals and no concessions, even in the face of the most severe intimidation and blackmail;
- an intensified effort to bring terrorists to justice by prosecution and conviction before courts of law;
- tough measures to penalise the state sponsors who give terrorist movements safe haven, weapons, explosives, cash and moral and diplomatic support.
- a determination never to allow terrorist intimidation to block or derail international diplomatic efforts to resolve major political conflicts in strife-torn regions, such as the Middle East: in many such areas terrorism has become a major threat to peace and stability, and its suppression therefore is in the common interests of international society.

The battle to protect civil aviation passengers and crew can only be won if the liberal democracies have the will and courage to win the broader struggle against the scourge of international terrorism. Our freedom of the airways is ultimately dependent on our ability to preserve the freedom of society as a whole. Dedicating ourselves to the vigorous pursuit of these goals would be the best memorial to the passengers and crew of Pan Am 103 and the thousands of other innocent victims of international terrorist crimes.

---

### GLOSSARY

| | |
|---|---|
| **ATA** | Air Transport Association (USA) |
| **BAA plc** | British Airports Authority plc |
| **BKA** | Federal Criminal Investigation Department |
| **CIA** | Central Intelligence Agency |
| **DEA** | Drug Enforcement Agency |
| **FAA** | Federal Aviation Administration |

30                              *Research Institute for the Study of Conflict and Terrorism*

| | |
|---|---|
| **FBI** | Federal Bureau of Investigation |
| **GIGN** | National Gendarmerie Intervention Group |
| **GSG9** | Grenzschutzgruppen 9 |
| **IATA** | International Air Transport Association |
| **ICAO** | International Civil Aviation Organisation |
| **IFALPA** | International Federation of Air Line Pilots' Associations |
| **IFAPA** | International Foundation of Airline Passengers' Associations |
| **PFLP-GC** | Popular Front for the Liberation of Palestine-General Command (led by Ahmed Jibril, a splinter group which broke away from the PFLP in 1968) |
| **PLO** | Palestine Liberation Organisation |
| **SAS** | Special Air Service Regiment |
| **TNA** | Thermal neutron analysis |

# [6]

# Terrorist Targets and Tactics: New Risks to World Order

## *Paul Wilkinson*

Political and strategic concepts are notoriously difficult to define in a few sentences. Ask any two historians or social scientists to explain what they mean by "war," "insurgency," and "revolution," for example, and you are likely to get two quite different answers. But this does not mean that these terms have no commonly accepted meanings. Scholars concerned with the study of major events in contemporary international politics could not get along without using such terminology.

"Terrorism" is one of the key concepts in the analysis of contemporary international politics. It is true that it is often abused for propaganda purposes, but in this respect it is no different from "democracy," "imperialism," and "national liberation."

Among scholars of all disciplines who have studied political violence it is generally accepted that terrorism is a special form of political violence. It is *not* a philosophy or a political movement. Terrorism is a weapon or method which has been used throughout history by both states and sub-state organisations for a whole variety of political causes or purposes. This special form of political violence has five major characteristics:

- it is premeditated and aims to create a climate of extreme fear or terror;
- it is directed at a wider audience or target than the immediate victims of the violence;
- it inherently involves attacks on random and symbolic targets, including civilians;
- the acts of violence committed are seen by the society in which they occur as extra-normal, in the literal sense that they breach the social norms, thus causing a sense of outrage; and
- terrorism is used to try to influence political behaviour in some way: for example to force opponents into conceding some or all of the perpetrators' demands, to provoke an over-reaction, to serve as a catalyst for a more general conflict, or to publicise a political cause.

As already noted, terror violence can be committed both by *states* and *sub-state organisations*. The activity becomes *international terrorism* when the citizens of more than one country are involved and *internal terrorism* when confined within the border of a single state. In practice, however, it is difficult to find any protracted and intensive terrorist campaign that remains purely internal as, almost invariably, the terrorists will look across their borders for political support, weapons, funds and safe haven. Another key distinction is between pure terrorism used in isolation and terrorism as an auxiliary weapon in a wider repertoire of violence. The terrorism experienced in Western

1

Europe since the late 1960s has been used as the sole weapon of many groups. The "mixed" form of terrorism is the general rule in all major areas of conflict throughout the world. For example, in Southern Africa and Latin America terrorism has been only one strand in conflicts involving rural guerrilla war, economic sabotage and disruption, and wider political struggle.

This study does not aim to provide an in-depth analysis of counter-terrorist strategies for the liberal democracies. I have attempted this in *Terrorism and the Liberal State*, Basingstoke: Macmillan 1986 (second edition). The object of the present essay is to assess the scale and significance of terrorism as a problem in the international system in the light of recent trends.

## THE HISTORICAL BACKGROUND

Terrorism is not a recent invention. It was used by the *Sicarii* and *Zealots* against the Roman occupation of Palestine. In the 11th and 12th centuries it was the chosen weapon of a radical islamic sect, the *Assassins*, in their campaign to overthrow the existing Moslem authorities. Revolutionaries, nihilists and anarchists used the tactics of bombing and assassination in their unsuccessful efforts to destroy autocracy, for example in Russia and the Balkans. And in the 1940s and 1950s terrorism became the primary weapon of movements engaged in major anti-colonial struggles, for example by the Jews against the British Mandate in Palestine, by EOKA against British colonial rule in Cyprus, by FLOSY in Aden, and by the FLN against the French in Algeria.

These examples of anti-colonial struggles are historically significant because they are the only clear instances in modern history where sub-state organisations using terror as their major weapon were able to achieve their long-term political goals, ie the withdrawal of the colonial power and establishment of a form of government favoured by the insurgents. There is no other clear case where such results have been achieved. Moreover, it is foolish to deny that these strategic successes through the use of terrorism have inspired many other groups to emulate these methods, although often with little awareness that the conditions of these anti-colonial examples were uniquely propitious for the terrorist and most unlikely to be repeated. In each case the colonial authorities lacked any substantial support for maintaining their rule both in the colonial territory and among the population of the European colonial power. After the loss of life, destruction, and economic debilitation of the Second World War, neither the politicians nor the general public in Britain and France had any stomach for wars of attrition. They already saw their colonial commitments as liabilities, costly in lives and treasure, to be negotiated away as swiftly and honourably as possible. It should not be forgotten that for the most part the decolonisation process was completed without significant bloodshed, and terrorism played a key role in only a small number of cases. The real burgeoning of modern international terrorism did not occur until the end of the 1960s. International incidents of terrorism have increased tenfold since 1968 and now directly affect, to some degree, over half the countries in the international system. What are the underlying causes and implications of this iniquitous modern form of political violence?

*Terrorist Targets and Tactics: New Risks to World Order* 3

## UNDERLYING CAUSES AND IMPLICATIONS

There is still considerable debate among specialists as to the reasons for the enormous growth of terrorism in the late 1960s and 1970s. The definitive history of 20th century terrorism is still to be written. Nevertheless it is clear that there are some key characteristics of the contemporary international system which are powerfully conducive to terrorist violence. The most important of these are the deep and bitter ethnic, religious and ideological conflicts which remain unresolved and which fester in the international system, spawning many forms of violent conflict including terrorism, and periodically erupting into civil and international wars. By far the most significant of these is the Arab-Israeli conflict: in the wake of Israel's defeat of the conventional military power of the Arab states in 1967 militant Palestinians decided that terrorism – hijacking, bombings, shooting attacks – was their only remaining weapon. This was the catalyst for a whole new wave of terrorist activity emanating from the Middle East or conducted within Middle Eastern countries. Yet it must be borne in mind that other violent ethnic and religious conflicts around the world which have also given rise to a great deal of terrorism are also very far from being resolved. Separatist conflicts of this kind rage fiercely in many parts of the world, from Northern Ireland, Spain and Corsica to the Central Asian republics of the Soviet Union to the Punjab, Sri Lanka and the Philippines.

Decolonisation has not removed these problems: in many ways it has made them even more intractable. New and relatively fragile political systems with weak economies find themselves confronting fundamental challenges to their authority and legitimacy on the grounds that the new state is denying them the right of self-determination. Some new states in Asia and Africa have had more than a dozen movements ranged against them, often waging full-scale insurgencies, and frequently resorting to terrorism.

Another underlying cause has been the global strategic balance which has prevailed throughout the period, from the early 1950s right through to the Gorbachev area. In the shadow of the nuclear balance of terror between the superpowers methods of unconventional and proxy war, such as terrorism, became more attractive as instruments of policy for states and sub-state organisations such as national liberation movements. Such methods are low-cost, relatively low-risk, and yet afford the possibilities of high yield in terms of weakening, penetrating or even gaining control through covert means. Moreover, such methods carry far less cost and less risk of escalation than conventional war. State-sponsored international terrorism carries the added attraction for its perpetrators that it can be carried out secretly, and, if suspicions are voiced, plausibly denied.

This strategic factor has been of particular significance because it is linked to another central feature of the post-war international system; the influence of Marxist-Leninist regimes and their client communist movements, many of which have used guerrilla war, terrorism, and other techniques of revolutionary warfare, on an extensive scale and which have acted as a major conduit for exporting theoretical and practical knowledge of these methods of warfare around the world. It would be foolish to underestimate the long-term influence of the major theoreticians, such as Mao Tse-tung, Vo Nguyen Giap, Fidel Castro, Che Guevara, and Carlos Marighela. The clear evidence of the worldwide decline in the support for communist regimes and movements today should not blind us to the fact that they were enormously influential in the 1950s and 1960s, when they succeeded in disseminating their theories way beyond their own countries of origin. One sees this vividly illustrated in the shift of emphasis from rural guerrilla warfare to urban guerrilla and terrorism among the Latin American revolutionaries. The ideas of the Tupamaros certainly influenced the *Red Brigades* and Marighela's *Minimanual of the Urban Guerrilla* was a strong influence on Ulrike Meinhof and others in the left-wing terrorist movements of western Europe in the 1970s.

The worldwide dissemination of new technology has also greatly facilitated the growth of terrorism. For example, the development of international civil aviation has created new vulnerabilities and lucrative targets for the terrorist to exploit. TV satellites have brought about a media revolution: the terrorists can exploit this by gaining almost instantaneous worldwide publicity for an outrage, thus enabling them to magnify the element of fear and to disseminate awareness of their cause/demands on a scale that would have been unthinkable for the anarchist bomb-thrower or assassin of the 19th century. Modern weapons technology has also proved a great boon to terrorists, providing them for example, with modern plastic explosives such as Semtex and highly accurate lightweight portable firearms such as the Uzzi sub-machine-gun.

Perhaps most important of all the factors encouraging the spread of terrorism has been the sheer success of this method in achieving short-term tactical objectives of great value to the terrorist. For although it is clear that terrorism rarely, if ever, wins strategic political goals it has an impressive record in gaining such things as massive worldwide publicity, extortion of large ransom payments and the release of considerable numbers of imprisoned terrorists.

There are many reasons for the failure of certain states and the international community as a whole to take firm action against terrorists: they include weakness, double standards and outright complicity. Terrorism, like piracy, will not be eradicated unless it is subjected to concerted and determined action by the entire international system. As this appears highly unlikely we must recognise that terrorism will remain a problem for the world community for some considerable time to come.

The problem of terrorism in the international system has serious implications at a number of different levels. It is an intolerable attack on the individual human rights of the innocent. It is true that wars are infinitely more destructive of human life, but the vast majority of fatalities through terrorism are caused by attacks on unarmed civilians who are going about their peaceful and lawful business. What more fundamental attack on human rights can there be than to deprive the innocent of the right to life? Does murder cease to be murder just because the killer believes human life is expendable in pursuit of some particular species of fanaticism?

When terrorism becomes severe and protracted it can also present a serious challenge to the well being and security of local communities or even entire nation-states. For example, in the most severe cases, such as Colombia, Peru, Lebanon, Sri Lanka, and parts of India, terrorism has bred intensified inter-communal conflict and polarisation. It has severely damaged the processes of law and orderly government and threatened the economy by damaging trade, destroying valuable resources, and scaring away investment. In the most severe cases terrorism can render whole areas of a country ungovernable, as in the cases of Lebanon and Sri Lanka for example, and can provoke full scale civil war.

The implications for the international system as a whole can also be far more grave than is generally realised. State sponsored terrorism, or even the mistaken belief that a state has sponsored terrorism against one's own state or citizens may provoke a retaliation which spirals into war. Full-scale military intervention and international war may result from a move to crush terrorist factions in a neighbouring state and/or to establish a secure zone within the territory hitherto utilised by terrorists. These motives, among others lay behind the Israeli invasion of Lebanon in 1982. Sarajevo is the classic instance of an act of terrorism serving as the spark which sets off a giant international conflict.

In less dramatic circumstances terrorism can still present states with major national security problems. When the Iranian revolutionaries held the entire US diplomatic mission in Tehran as hostages, the White House, the National Security Council and the Department of State became so embroiled in the effort to secure the hostages' release that the US administration's capacity to act on wider issues in the Middle East became almost paralysed. And President Reagan was virtually compelled to alter his administration's policy on Lebanon and bring an end to the deployment of the peacekeeping Multi National Force (MNF) following the massacre of 241 Marines in a truck bombing by *Hezbollah* terrorists. In this case the terrorists and their backers in Iran knew that they were using the psychological weapon of terror to reach over the head of President Reagan to the American public. They did so, and Mr Reagan's policy options on Lebanon were drastically narrowed.

## Can terrorism ever be morally justified?

We live in an age when the idea of universal moral standards or principles is under severe attack. According to the sophistry of moral relativism and "situational ethics" almost anything can be condoned. The oft-repeated cry "One man's terrorist is another man's freedom fighter" is but one manifestation of the widespread confusion about the morality of terroristic forms of violence. Even in those clear cases where we may be persuaded that a terrorist group is motivated by a legitimate sense of injustice or grievance and can truly claim to "speak" for a majority of its professed constituency, does this mean we must condone their use of terroristic means? Surely not, for this is to confuse means and ends. Unless one is a pacifist, the use of force can certainly be justified under particular circumstances. But terrorism is a special form of violence involving deliberate attacks on innocent civilians. According to the doctrines of just war and just rebellion against tyranny a righteous cause can never justify the use of evil means. It is no longer fashionable to believe in good and evil. This writer has always taken the position that terrorism is an unmitigated evil. The undoubted fact that many state and non-state belligerents through history have flouted the most basic principles of the humanitarian law of conflict does not provide a moral argument for abandoning such standards completely and making terror permissible. On the contrary, the historical record of modern war and the heightened threat from weapons of mass destruction should spur the international community to greater efforts to impose recognition of the humanitarian law of conflict.

Yet the moral desirability of strengthening the protection of human rights in conflict provides no easy answer to the moral problems inherent in the use of terror. Suppose terror is used on a major scale against your own people, whether by state or non-state perpetrators, can this justify the use of terror as a means of resistance? Are there circumstances when the use of retaliatory terror can be condoned as the lesser evil? When whole groups or societies start a spiral of retaliation and counter-retaliation the danger is that anything becomes "permissible" in the name of resistance.

On a more hopeful note, it is worth recalling that in Eastern Europe some of the most oppressive one-party regimes in modern history were overthrown without even initiating this spiral of terror and counter terror: the liberation of these countries was achieved primarily by the moral and political pressure of internal resistance, by protests and mass demonstrations on the streets and general economic collapse. What is astonishing is that, with the sad exception of the case of Romania, these revolutions from below were remarkably non-violent. It is also significant that there are no historical examples of a modern dictatorship or totalitarian regime having been overthrown by means of terrorism.

There is more general agreement, of course, that terrorism can never be a justified means of struggle within a liberal democracy. A truly democratic political system, by definition, offers numerous non-violent channels of political protest, lobbying, and electoral competition: it is patently a violation of democratic principle when fanatical minorities behave like petty tyrannies, resorting to the bomb and the gun to impose on their fellow citizens what they are unable to achieve through the ballot box.

In liberal democracies even the claim of terrorist groups to speak for the majority of the minority they claim to represent is generally spurious. It is only in democratic societies that terrorist groups have the option of forming political parties and fighting elections. Even when given the chance, few take it, and if they do their election results are generally derisory. However, in the few cases where the pro-terrorist parties manage to gain a more significant minority of votes (eg in Northern Ireland or the Basque region of Spain) this suggests a worrying degree of disaffection from the democratic political system and the relative success of terrorist propaganda. It does not establish the moral legitimacy of terrorist means.

*Terrorist Targets and Tactics: New Risks to World Order* 7

## RECENT TRENDS IN INTERNATIONAL TERRORISM

As one would expect, the incidence of domestic terrorist crimes and the total casualties they cause vastly exceeds the figures for international terrorism: that is, incidents involving the citizens of more than one country. For example in Northern Ireland alone the number of deaths through domestic terrorist attacks in 1989 (62) was over four times the total deaths caused by international terrorism in the whole of Europe in that year. This pattern is repeated in Asia, Africa and Latin America, where casualties and physical destruction caused by domestic attacks far outweigh those resulting from international incidents. However, few databases even attempt to keep tally of both domestic and international terrorist attacks worldwide.

Our data on international terrorist incidents for the 1980s is far more reliable and comprehensive. The total number climbed from over 500 a year in the early 1980s to 600 a year in 1984, rising to around 800 per year in the period 1985–88. Figures for 1989 show a welcome drop in the number of incidents and total casualties, including a marked fall in international terrorist attacks in Western Europe and Asia. The Middle East remains an important zone of terrorism, with over 40 per cent of examples worldwide originating in, or linked with, Middle East conflicts. Latin America also remains a region with a high incidence of international terrorism, with over half the incidents occurring in Colombia and Peru.

However, statistics on the total numbers of examples and their regional distribution can be misleading. Incidents vary enormously in their lethality and overall impact. Sabotage bombing of airliners in flight has been rare compared with more conventional bombings, yet it accounts for a high proportion of the fatalities caused by international terrorism. For example, in 1988 the 270 deaths caused by the terrorist bombing of Pan Am 103 over Lockerbie accounted for over 40 per cent of the total deaths from international terrorism in that year. And in 1989 the terrorist bombing of the French UTA airliner over the Niger desert with the loss of 171 lives and the bombing of the Colombian Avianca airliner with the loss of 107 passengers and crew accounted for 70 per cent of the fatalities from international terrorism for the whole year. This underlines a worrying trend in international terrorism since 1982, and that is the pattern of increasingly indiscriminate and lethal attacks in which ordinary citizens are targeted. One manifestation of this trend is the mid-air sabotage bombings of airliners referred to above. Another is the use of the car bomb in public places with the object of creating maximum carnage. This development has not been confined to the Middle East. Paris experienced a horrifying example during a nine day terrorist campaign in September 1986 which killed eight members of the public and wounded over 150. And in November 1987 the Provisional IRA exploded a bomb at a Remembrance Day service at Enniskillen which massacred 10 people.

How does one explain this increase in indiscriminateness? In part it results from the terrorists' ever more desperate desire for publicity. With the media and the public satiated with reports of violence around the world, terrorist leaders have concluded that they must commit greater atrocities to capture the headlines. Another key factor is the growing attraction of soft targets to terrorists increasingly aware of the greater risks that face them if they seek to attack high prestige targets which have been "hardened" by improved physical protection, such as military and diplomatic installations. Some experienced observers have suggested that another major element may be a shift inside terrorist organisations away from the more pragmatic "politically-minded" terrorist leaders to fanatical hard men, obsessed with vengeance and violence.

A further important development which has stimulated considerable debate among specialists in the study of terrorism is the sharp drop in international incidents in 1989. It this the beginning of a new and encouraging long-term trend, or is it simply a temporary lull in terrorist activity resulting from a special combination of factors? Are the terrorists simply regrouping with the aim of launching new and more destructive campaigns at the next opportunity?

It seems clear that three major developments combined to have a restraining effect on international terrorist activity in 1989. Firstly there were important shifts of policy and activity among the groups involved. In December 1988 Yasser Arafat renounced the use of terrorism, as part of the so-called Geneva declaration designed to create the conditions for formal diplomatic contact between the PLO and the US government. Although it is clear that many Palestinian militant groups did not agree with this line it is certainly true that there was a significant decline in the number of operations by groups under the PLO's umbrella.

Another factor affecting the level of terrorist group activity was severe internal dissension both within and between the various terrorist factions. It is reported that in 1989 over 120 members of one of the most notorious international terrorist groups, the *Abu Nidal* organisation (ANO), died in an internal purge which virtually paralysed the group's activities. The ANO was also hampered by growing coolness on the part of one of its state sponsors, Libya, which was being strongly encouraged to distance itself from the ANO as part of the price for Qadhafi's badly needed improvement in relations with both the moderate Arab states and the European Community. The ANO also became embroiled in the growing inter-factional conflict and "the war of the camps" in Lebanon, as did other Palestinian radical groups. This all diverted their energies and resources away from international terrorist operations further afield.

A further reason for the drop in international terrorist incidents was the shifts in policy on the part of several key state sponsors of terrorism. In 1987 and 1988 the Soviet-backed regime in Afghanistan conducted over 250 attacks in Pakistan, both in the North-West Frontier Province and in cities such as Karachi, Islamabad, Lahore, and Peshawar. Casualties of these bombings were often extemely high. In 1987, 70 people were killed when the crowded marketplace in Karachi was bombed, and 14 died in the bombing at Peshawar in June 1988. In 1989 the Afghan government scaled down its backing for the WAD terrorist campaign, following the withdrawal of Soviet troops from Afghanistan. This had a considerable effect on the global total of international terrorist incidents: there was a sharp decline from over 120 such events in 1988 to around two dozen in 1989.

A third important trend which undoubtedly contributed to the decline of international terrorism in 1989 was the improvement in counter-terrorist measures by many governments and the increasing effectiveness of international co-operation between governments and security services. This has been particularly true in the European Community, where the *Trevi* network and bilateral police co-operation against terrorism has been gradually strengthened in preparation for the dismantling of internal frontier controls in 1992. For example, in 1989 improved European police co-operation led to the arrest of a number of members of terrorist groups including PIRA in West Germany and France, ETA in France, and *Red Brigades* in France, Spain and Switzerland. This strengthening of international police and intelligence co-operation, combined with the greater organisational problems of operating abroad, has tended to discourage international terrorist attacks outside the borders of the terrorists' own country. It has been estimated that in 1989 almost 80 per cent of international incidents worldwide fell into the former category.

One other key trend of the 1980s needs to be highlighted. The problem of terrorism, especially domestic terrorism, has begun to afflict certain third world states on a major scale. It is quite ridiculous to pretend that terrorism is primarily a problem for rich industrial countries. The scale of terrorist lethality and destructiveness in countries such as Lebanon, India, Sri Lanka, Colombia and Peru totally overshadows the levels experienced by West European countries in the 1970s. Yet the third world countries which have been the major victims of this type of violence in the 1980s lack the basic resources to deal with it.

## FUTURE THREATS

Terrorist groups make no secret of their threats: they generally lose no opportunity of putting out their propaganda messages, asserting the righteousness of their cause, the inevitability of their ultimate victory, and the dire consequences that face anyone who stands in their way. There are very few cases of terrorist groups voluntarily abandoning their activities and simply fading away. Some groups have gone under as the result of the death or capture of all their leading figures and cell structure. Others have been curtailed by the action of state sponsors or as a result of internecine strife. But when a terrorist group possesses unfulfilled political aims, leadership, weapons, manpower and access to targets, it is a fair assumption that it will stay in business.

By far the most durable of these groups since the early 1970s have been those with a nationalist or separatist ideology, such as the radical Palestinian groups, the PIRA, and ETA. These groups have larger constituencies of potential recruits, supporters and more political clout and resources than the extreme ideological groups. We can expect them to remain an important part of the terrorist scene. By contrast the ideological terrorists of the extreme left, such as the *Red Brigades*, *Action Directe*, and the *Combatant Communist Cells* have proved more vulnerable and ephemeral. They are a declining threat worldwide. Exceptions include the avowedly Maoist *New People's Army* in the Philippines and the Maoist *Shining Path* (*Sendero Luminoso*) movement in Peru. These both combine terrorism with rural guerrilla insurgency and have the ability to mount major threats to government.

**The Middle East**

In the field of international terrorism the main threats in the future arise from the Middle East, the conflict-ridden region most closely linked with the development of international terrorism ever since the late 1960s. In 1990 a major new risk emerged in the shape of the reappearance of the Iraqi regime as a leading state sponsor of international terrorism. Saddam Hussein has a long record of sponsoring hard-line Palestinian groups and providing them with headquarters, training facilities, the back-up of the Iraqi diplomatic network and weapons and funds. Baghdad provided these services for the *Abu Nidal* organisation until 1983. This terrorist group has been responsible for over 90 attacks since 1974 in which 900 people have been killed or injured. From 1983–87 the *Abu Nidal* group had its base in Syria, and from 1987–89, in Libya. In the context of the Gulf crisis it is particularly ominous that Saddam is once again proffering sponsorship to the *Abu Nidal* organisation and to other hard-line Palestinian Militant groups, including several with a reputation for carrying out deadly attacks on civil aviation targets.

The Iraqi regime also has a history of using specially recruited hit-squads and its own secret agents, usually operating under diplomatic cover, for terrorist operations abroad. For example, in the early stages of the Gulf War, 1980–81 the Iraqis and the Iranians waged a tit-for-tat terrorist war, including hijackings of airliners and attacks on diplomatic targets.

In addition to these directly controlled and client groups we need to take into account a somewhat more unpredictable factor. Since the beginning of the Gulf Crisis Saddam has frequently called on the Arab world to wage a holy war against America and what he terms "the emirs of oil". He has also presented himself as the champion of the cause of Palestinian liberation and the true leader of the Arab nation. Demonstrations in favour of Saddam in places like Jordan, Algeria and Tunisia indicate that at least some of the Iraqi dictator's propaganda is having the effect of stirring up support for his anti-Western stance among Palestinians, Arab radicals and fundamentalists. But whereas Saddam can keep his own secret agents and his client groups in Baghdad under fairly tight rein, it is unlikely that he can really control many of the supporters he has stirred up within the various Arab countries. Some observers suspect that pro-Iraqi militants were behind the assassination of the Speaker of the Egyptian Parliament in Cairo in October. If these suspicions prove well-founded was this the work of a group acting largely autonomously? Or was it directly planned and ordered by Baghdad?

Until the time of writing, in October 1990, all the signs were that Saddam was seeking to avoid doing anything to provoke a full-scale military confrontation with US forces and their allies. As a major terrorist attack might well be traced to Baghdad it is probably safe to assume that Saddam would hold back his terrorist weapon until the outbreak of hostilities. He would then very likely unleash it as a valuable auxiliary weapon to disrupt and demoralise the US forces and their allies, particularly Egypt, Saudi Arabia and the small Gulf states. It would be relatively easy to stage terrorist attacks in neighbouring Arab countries where there is an abundance of targets, including American personnel and facilities. On the other hand we should also be prepared for more long-range attacks, for example against airliners and airports with a view to terrorising Western countries. The security authorities in both the Western and Arab states aligned against Iraq have already given clear warnings of possible Iraqi-sponsored terrorist attacks. They should also be enhancing their preventive security measures and contingency planning for this eventuality.

The worsening tension in the Gulf has coincided with a resurgence of militant Palestinian rejectionism. The Palestinian terrorist groups which have so readily rushed to support Saddam's call for a holy war were always adamantly opposed to Arafat's strategy of seeking a diplomatic and political solution to the Arab-Israeli conflict. For these maximalists all talk of a compromise involving acceptance of the state of Israel's right to exist is a betrayal. They know that Arafat has lost credibility because of the apparent failure of the *Intifada* to achieve political concessions from the Israelis. They know that they can call on the backing of Saddam, dictator of the most militarily powerful Arab state. Thus if hostilities in the Gulf were to break out we could expect the hard-line groups to take advantage and wage a full-scale Palestinian international terrorist campaign of a kind not seen since the 1970s, not simply in support of Saddam, but on their own behalf. Some of the Palestinians' terrorist effort may well be directed at Soviet targets because of their deep anger against Moscow's policy of permitting Soviet Jews to flood into Israel, and thence to Jewish settlements in the West Bank. Ahmed Jibril, leader of the PFLP–GC group, currently based in Syria, has already threatened to mount terrorist attacks against Soviet targets.

A further danger emanating from the Middle East is terrorism stemming from militant Islamic fundamentalist groups. Much of the impetus for these movements grew out of the Iranian Islamic Revolution which came to power in 1979–80. The *Hezbollah* movement in Lebanon and *Al-Dawa*, active in the Gulf states, are examples of Shi'a movements aimed at establishing Iralian-style Islamic republics. But the Shi'a constitute only 10 per cent of the population of the Moslem world. What is not sufficiently well understood is the existence of a strong fundamentalist tradition in many Sunni Moslem communities, for example in Egypt, Algeria, Tunisia, and even as far away as Pakistan and the Soviet Central Asian republics. Among the Palestinian Arabs in the Occupied Territories we have seen a weird alliance arise between Islamic fundamentalists like the *Hamas* group and the radical Palestinian groups such as the PFLP. Such alliances are potentially a powerful challenge to more traditional and moderate Arab political structures and they are capable of developing tactics of extreme violence.

12                          *Research Institute for the Study of Conflict and Terrorism*

### Ethnic conflicts

Middle East conflicts are already closely linked with over 40 per cent of international terrorism. This proportion may well increase in the light of the trends described above. Yet it would be a grave mistake to see the Middle East as the sole source of emerging threats of terrorist violence. The collapse of Communist one-party regimes in Eastern Europe during 1989–90. has brought to the surface many long-suppressed ethnic conflicts and hatreds, many of which hark back to an earlier tradition of terror violence. One has only to refer to the history of Balkan nationalist movements in the 19th and early 20th centuries to realise that most of them are steeped in their own traditions of political violence and terrorism: the Croatian *Ustashi*, the Serbian *Black Hand*, and the Macedonian *Internal Macedonian Revolutionary Organisation* (IMRO) offer ample evidence. There are real dangers that some of the bitter ethnic conflicts that are now re-emerging in Eastern Europe will manifest themselves in full-scale campaigns of terror violence. Extremists may exploit the relative ease of operating in open and vulnerable new political sytems. Is living with high levels of ethnic conflict and spasmodic terrorism going to be a price East Europeans have to pay for their new democratic way of life? We should also remember that the demographic distribution of these East European nationalities is geographically untidy, with every major ethnic group straddling one or more state frontiers. To complicate things still further, many of the ethnic minorities involved have emigré communities scattered in many western countries, and some of these could well be drawn into any fresh outbreak of inter-ethnic conflict. The whole international community has an interest in the peaceful resolution of these conflicts.

The same is even more true of the Soviet Union where so many of the 197 officially recognised nationalities appear disaffected from the Soviet Communist system and wish to attain independence or, at very least, a far greater degree of autonomy. In parts of the Soviet Union – for example, Azerbaijan, Armenia, Uzbekistan and Tadzhikistan – we have already seen Soviet troops deployed in an effort to suppress or head off violent ethnic clashes and confrontations with the authorities. The potential for ethnic terrorism in the Soviet republics is even more evident than it is in the former communist countries of Eastern Europe. And the Russian leaders are well aware that the Soviet Moslem republics are not immune from the fundamentalist and radical movements based on the other side of their southern borders.

## PROBLEMS OF RESPONSE

### The terrorist threat to civil aviation

In Conflict Study 226 *The Lessons of Lockerbie* (December, 1989), the writer argued that, despite the Lockerbie tragedy and two more mid-air sabotage bombings in 1989 over Africa and Latin America, the world civil aviation system had failed to take the long-overdue measures to protect civil aviation against this major threat. It is depressing to report that another year has gone by without any significant improvement in blocking the major loopholes. A number of terrorist groups and their state sponsors with track records of ruthlessness and lethal expertise are well aware of the vulnerabilities of civil aviation. It is a sad fact that very few countries have made any significant improvement in security measures against the sabotage bomber. Another Lockerbie could happen tomorrow and the carnage caused would, of course, be even greater if the terrorists succeeded in destroying an airliner above the residential areas of a major city.

Some countries, such as the USA and Britain, and certain major airlines, have introduced some welcome improvements in aviation security. For example, in Britain the new Aviation and Maritime Security Act gives the Secretary of State for Transport the power to suspend an airline's operations if they fall below required security standards, and has created an aviation security inspectorate with greater powers. These changes, together with improvements in airside security were long overdue but nonetheless welcome.

However, the greatest weakness of aviation security is the failure to instal in the world's airports, explosive detection systems (EDS) capable of detecting plastic explosives. It is true that the US authorities, and, more recently the British, have conceded that 100 per cent screening of all baggage is their long-term objective. But how is this to be achieved? It is clearly impossible for the major aviation countries to adopt the extremely effective El Al security procedures with their reliance on highly protracted check-in periods, physical searches of luggage and intensive questioning of passengers by intelligence officers. This works well for Israel's specialised aviation needs, but it would soon bring world commercial aviation to a grinding halt! Rapid and totally reliable EDS is therefore an essential weapon in beating the aviation terrorist. Yet, although there are many excellent technologies capable of detecting plastic explosives, there has been no real international effort to make them available in airports, and the only country which has invested substantial R and D efforts to develop such equipment is the USA by means of the Federal Aviation Administration's programme to upgrade security.

This is both a technological and a political challenge, because it is crucial to mobilise the political will and resources to make such improved security – including better management, staffing and procedures – available to international aviation generally. Enhancement of national systems is a vital first step, but governments, the industry and passengers will need to join forces to internationalise an effective response. Urgent steps are needed to raise the necessary funds for this purpose, and to set up a system for monitoring, inspecting and *enforcing* proper security standards worldwide, using aviation sanctions as necessary. It is clear that international and national problems of response to terrorism are interwoven. To be effective, action against terrorists must be synchronised at both levels. By tolerating the terrorists' capacity to provoke war the international community is playing with fire. And we have seen how, in severe cases, terrorists confront democracies internally with a ruthless challenge against the safety of their citizens, the security of the state, and the rule of law. Of course the nature of response required will vary according to the severity of the challenge, but it is vital to get it right, because strong national policies to deal with terrorism are the building-blocks of a more effective international response.

### Principles to combat terrorism

In the current period, when Britain, Spain, Greece and other democratic states face continuing campaigns of violence, it is important to reiterate the cardinal principles of an effective liberal-democratic response to terrorism. These are:

- no surrender to the terrorists, and an absolute determination to defeat terrorism within the framework of the rule of law and the democratic process;
- no deals and no concessions, even in the face of the most severe intimidation and blackmail;
- an intensified effort to bring terrorists to justice by prosecution and conviction before courts of law;
- firm measures to penalise state sponsors who give terrorists safe haven, weapons, explosives, cash and moral and diplomatic support;
- a determination never to allow terrorist intimidation to block or derail political and diplomatic efforts to resolve the underlying conflicts in strife-torn regions, such as the Middle East: in many such areas terrorism has become a major threat to peace and stability, and its suppression therefore is in the common interests of international society.

It may be claimed that these principles are of a very general nature, and that most democratic states confronting terrorism have violated some or all of these guidelines in certain circumstances. It is also true that these general assumptions do not amount to anything like a detailed policy on counter terrorism. Such policies obviously have to be developed and co-ordinated covering such aspects as intelligence, crisis management, emergency measures and the development and deployment of specialist counter-terrorist units within the police and armed forces, with the technical resources to back them up.

It is true that some of the most serious failures in counter-terrorism occur at the operational and tactical levels; for example, weaknesses in co-ordination, intelligence failures, or serious gaps in training or logistic support. It is no good taking the trouble to get the general principles accepted if these are not adequately implemented.

Nevertheless, violations of the fundamental principles of the liberal-democratic response have far more serious long-term implications, causing much wider political damage. For example, policies of appeasement, doing "deals" with terrorists, indiscriminate repression, abuses of the legal process, and similar breaches, damage not only the individuals immediately involved, but also the integrity and legitimacy of the entire system, and thus play into the hands of the terrorists. Hence, the liberal democratic principles should never be viewed as being of purely cosmetic or rhetorical significance. They are the very *essence* of democracy, and any severe terrorist campaign puts them to one of their harshest possible tests.

## The key roles of politics and diplomacy

It is of course a dangerous illusion to believe that if only we could alight on the appropriate formula for a diplomatic settlement or political reform, the underlying grievances of terrorists would be met, and all the violence would melt away. The search for the perfect political solution to terrorism is as much of a will-o'-the-wisp as the pursuit of a military solution. The experience of democratic states in the 20th century suggests that what is really needed to curb terrorism effectively is a concerted multi-pronged approach, carefully calibrated to the level required to deal with the scale of terrorism employed, and combining the most valuable elements of political, legal, police, military and socio-economic measures.

Nevertheless, it is the case that the potential role and value of political and diplomatic approaches in the overall context of efforts to defeat terrorists are generally seriously underestimated. Let us take the key example of the Arab-Israeli conflict. Let us suppose that by some miracle the Israeli government was persuaded to sit down at the negotiating table with Yasser Arafat and the leading Arab states, and succeeded in devising a major agreement reconciling the demands of Palestinians for self-determination with the demands of Israel for secure borders.

Of course we know that extremists on both sides would try to wreck the agreement because they would view it as a betrayal of their maximalist aims. Groups such as the *Abu Nidal* group on the one hand, the Jewish extremists, the modern *Sicarii* on the other, would continue acts of terror in a desperate effort to block a settlement. Nevertheless, who can deny that if a major diplomatic agreement could be achieved that satisfied at least mainstream opinion on both the Palestinian and Israeli sides it would have a considerable effect in reducing the amount of violence and would render the terrorist groups far more isolated, weaker and less politically dangerous.

The same applies in the context of the most intractable and bitter internal conflicts. It has been the great strength of Mr. Peter Brooke, the present Secretary of State for Northern Ireland, that he has recognised the crucial importance of achieving *political* progress in the Province. His patient diplomacy almost paid off in the summer of 1990, only to be blocked by the desire of the Dublin government to be in the negotiations from the outset. He deserves strong all-party support for his efforts to revive the inter-party dialogue. If his initiative does get off the ground it will help in several ways to improve the political climate and to further isolate and politically weaken the IRA. Meaningful political co-operation between the SDLP, the major party of the Catholic minority in Northern Ireland, and the Unionists, in the context of a power-sharing system would indeed be major progress towards healing the bitter divisions of the past. Furthermore, such an outcome would once again demonstrate the futility of the IRA's terrorist campaign. As Mr.

Brooke has made clear, the Provisional Sinn Fein will not be able to take part in any key discussions about the political future in Northern Ireland unless it abandons terrorism.

As was noted earlier in the survey of recent trends, the Middle East is far and away the major source of conflicts which spawn terrorism, and the most serious and dangerous of these in the long run is undoubtedly the Arab-Israeli conflict. Sooner or later major efforts must be made both within Israel and among the leading Arab states to reopen serious diplomatic negotiations to find a way of resolving this festering problem. For the Israeli government the prospect of sitting on the powder-keg of 1.5 million Palestinian Arabs for years ahead is clearly incompatible with Israeli security. Other options must be explored as a matter of the greatest urgency.

The IRA is far and away the most dangerous terrorist movement in Europe. In the past 20 years, more than 2,800 people have been killed through the conflict in Northern Ireland. The IRA is responsible for roughly 60 per cent of these deaths, two-thirds of them civilians. Its bombings and shootings in mainland Britain – there have been 13 attacks this year, seven since the beginning of June – have spilled on to the Continent.

The level of IRA activity outside Northern Ireland is higher than at any time since the mid-1970s. The only other European organisation in the same league is the Basque extremist movement, *ETA*, which has killed more than 500 people in Spain over the same period, half of them civilians.

True, the security forces in Northern Ireland have had more success in thwarting attacks over the past two years. A better flow of intelligence and security has enabled them to prevent many explosions and the rate of arrests in the province has gone up dramatically. But on mainland Britain police are facing intensified IRA violence with an enormous handicap: they lack intelligence on IRA operations in Britain – the leaders and cells involved and their logistic support network – which is vital if they are to capture the cells and prevent further attacks.

Why has IRA terrorism proved so intractable? And what lessons could be learnt from the sucess of other European Community countries in tackling internal terrorism?

One reason for the stubborn survival of the IRA is that it draws on the general support or sympathy of roughly 10 per cent of the population in the Province, providing a constant supply of terrorist recruits and collaborators. By terrorist standards, the IRA has a strong financial infrastructure, using racketeering, extortion, smuggling and legitimate business to raise funds. Above all, it has three great assets for mounting terrorist operations.

First, in the Republic, it enjoys logistic support and relative safety from Northern Irish and British justice. Second, from Colonel Qadhafi it has obtained Semtex and other weapons. Third, 20 years of operations against the combined expertise of the Army and the RUC have made the IRA one of the most technically sophisticated terrorist groups in the world.

It is expert not only in bomb-making and operational planning, but in propaganda warfare, especially in its defamation campaign against the Northern Ireland judicial and penal systems. Its members have also proved

*Terrorist Targets and Tactics: New Risks to World Order* 17

themselves capable of adapting their mode of operations on mainland Britain and the Continent to make it far harder for the police to find them. They keep their distance from the Irish community, maintain secure links with the godfathers and show great versatility in striking a wide range of soft military and civilian targets. It is worrying that there have been only six arrests in connection with IRA terrorism in mainland Britain in the past two years.

**Learning from other countries**

By contrast, the threat from domestic terrorist groups in Continental Europe has declined sharply since the mid-1980s. The main internal threat in Italy, West Germany, mainland France and Belgium comes from extreme-left, Red Army-style gangs, generally tiny in terms of hardcore membership. These groups have been far less lethal than the IRA. The *Red Brigades*, one of the more dangerous extreme-left groups, has killed about 150 people since its inception. Nevertheless, at the peak of its strength, in the late 1970s, the group mounted a direct challenge to the Italian Republic, culminating in the kidnap and murder – on 9 May 1978 – of Aldo Moro, a former prime minister.

In West Germany, the *Red Army Faction* has killed 37 people since its formation. It is true that tiny residues of the Red Army-style groups are still at large and there has been a small number of assassinations and attempted killings. After the West German group's abortive attempt on Hans Neusel – the West German state secretary in charge of security at the Interior Ministry, in early August – the terrorists issued a declaration of war against a greater German/West European superpower.

These grandiose threats are oddly reminiscent of the 1985 claim by the *Red Army Faction*, France's *Action Directe* (*AD*) and Belgium's *Communist Combatant Cells* that they were forming a "united guerrilla front" against Nato, an effort that soon fizzled out. The truth is that Red Army terrorism is a busted flush on the Continent: the *AD* has been inactive since its leaders were captured by the police; the *Red Army Faction* has lost its bolt-hole in East Germany, while the younger generation of German radicals views it as irrelevant to the concerns of the 1990s; and Italian police now see the Mafia as their main organised crime problem.

A common factor in the Continent's success in suppressing Red Army terrorism is that all countries have developed strong national anti-terrorist co-ordination. After Moro's murder the Italians appointed General Dalla Chiesa to co-ordinate anti-terrorist operations. He set up his own task force to infiltrate the terrorist cells and helped devise the *Pentiti* law, which gave generous remission to captured terrorists who provided evidence leading to the arrest of their associates. This law led hundreds to collaborate and helped crack open the *Red Brigades'* cells and columns.

In West Germany, the BKA (the Federal Criminal Office) was the leading agency, with powers to co-ordinate anti-terrorism throughout the country. Horst Herold, head of the BKA until 1980, pioneered the use of sophisticated computerised anti-terrorist intelligence data, which he described as "the material which gives us superiority over the terrorists". West Germany's assets in computerised intelligence have greater practical value than ever following the introduction of machine-readable identity cards and passports, which make it far easier for police to trace suspects.

Given the severity of IRA terrorism, and the implications of dismantling the EC's internal borders in 1992, Dublin and London should study the advantages of the co-ordination and computerisation of intelligence and Continental ID card and passport systems.

We could also learn from the experience of improved cross-border co-operation between France and Spain over *ETA* terrorism. Since 1987 there has been a radical improvement, particularly on intelligence-sharing and extradition, with more than 150 suspected Basque terrorists being expelled from France in 1987. The French and Spanish have also set up a joint police liaison office to strengthen co-operation further.

We desperately need more substantial anti-terrorist co-operation with the Republic. Dublin must abide by its new commitment to extradite those wanted on terrorist charges. We must help Dublin improve its intelligence-gathering and policing to enable it to deal with the threat, perhaps through the creation of an EC fund to enhance anti-terrorist resources.

In our increasingly integrated Community we must learn that no member state is an island, particularly in the modern world of terrorism and drug-trafficking. We need to create the understanding that one democracy's terrorist is another democracy's terrorist and devise a Europe-wide criminal justice system appropriate to a Europe without internal frontiers.

We can also learn some useful lessons from the American experience in fighting major crime. The Northern Ireland Office, the Home Office and the security forces in Northern Ireland have shown considerable interest in the US American Racketeer-Influenced and Corrupt Organisations Act, which has been used very effectively against organised crime, especially the Mafia. It has long caused outrage and puzzlement that the godfathers of terrorism in Northern Ireland are able to walk the streets without fear of arrest. The US anti-Mafia-style law would help to put the godfathers behind bars. The purpose of the legislation is to enable the courts to convict individuals found guilty of being involved in or associated with a criminal organisation through racketeering, extortion and so on. In order to gather the necessary evidence to convict, surveillance (including telephone taps) would be needed over a long period. There would clearly need to be civil liberties safeguards. However, there is no doubt that legislation modelled on the US example, would be of enormous value in bringing the godfathers to book.

In addition to cracking down on the racketeering and corruption which helps to sustain the IRA's murder machine, the authorities should make use of the well-tried method of offering substantial financial rewards for members of the public who provide valuable information to the police leading to the apprehension and conviction of terrorists. In many cases members of the public are nervous of coming forward to help the police with their inquiries, and with good reason, for there may well be a substantial risk to them and members of their families. A generous reward scheme would help to give a greater incentive to take those risks. To work effectively such a scheme would

*Terrorist Targets and Tactics: New Risks to World Order*     19

need to be combined with an adequately resourced and professionally organised witness protection scheme of the kind used so successfully in the USA.

## Measures against State-Sponsored Terrorism

There is no doubt that the democratic revolution in Eastern Europe dealt a huge blow against state-sponsored terrorism. All the one-party Communist regimes were deeply implicated in the sponsorship of terrorism throughout the 1970s, certainly with the full encouragement of the Soviet KGB. Information now leaking out from the files of the former security police has already confirmed that thousands of terrorists were trained and helped by Communist regimes, including Palestinian groups, and left-wing groups active in Western Europe. The East Germans helped the *Red Army Faction* by giving them safe haven, cover and new identities. East German training camps like Finsterwalde, near Dresden, were particularly important for passing on techniques of terrorism and assassination. Czechoslovakia was an important source of Semtex and firearms for terrorists. Hungary served as a haven and base for "Carlos," the notorious Latin American terrorist. Poland was for a long period used as a European base for the *Abu Nidal* group. There is a great deal more to come out about these involvements, and it is at least possible that the new democratic authorities, keen to clean the Augean stables, will bring some of the former officials responsible to trial. They should certainly be encouraged to do so.

However, despite the loss of this valuable network of state sponsors in East Europe international terrorists can still look to other states, such as Iraq, Iran, Syria, Libya and Cuba for safe haven and sponsorship. Despite the fact that these states are flagrantly defying international law by organising and participating in . . . "terrorist acts in another state" (the language is taken from the *UN Declaration on Principles of International Law* etc.) very little effective action has been taken by the world community to penalise them.

State sponsorship greatly increases the danger of terrorism to the international community because it provides the client groups with far greater firepower than they would ever be likely to obtain in the normal arms market. An obvious example would be Libya's provision of vast quantities of Semtex and other weapons to the IRA, thus considerably tilting the balance in favour of the terrorists and against the security forces. It is also worth bearing in mind that state sponsors are strongly suspected of involvement in the mass murder of airline passengers at Lockerbie in 1988 and over the Niger Desert in 1989.

What can be done to stop state sponsorship? It is surely time for the powerful industrial nations to combine their economic and diplomatic power to impose harsh sanctions on the guilty states. Under certain circumstances the use of military measures may well be the most appropriate option. The evidence of the effect of the US bombing of Libya in 1986, however, is rather ambiguous. It certainly pushed Qadhafi off balance for a while. But it did not apparently cause him to cease his covert support for terrorist groups, such as the IRA. On the other hand both Syria and Libya may be highly vulnerable to really tough and concerted economic sanctions, as both regimes have major weaknesses in their economies which make them highly dependent on external trade and financial links. It must be admitted, however, that the European Community has been extremely timid in taking economic action. This is yet another instance where the EC lacks clear evidence of collective will and coherent policy.

## 1992: Rising to the Challenge

It is widely recognised among security specialists that the proposed dismantling of the European Community's internal frontiers in 1992 carries a grave risk that terrorists and organised criminal gangs such as the Mafia will take full advantage of the Single European Market.

The principle that the EC needs to strengthen its criminal justice system to compensate for the abolition of internal borders has already been conceded in the terms of the Schengen Agreement (1990) but the additional co-operation proposed between the Benelux countries, France and Germany is extremely modest.

It is unrealistic to assume that terrorists, drug traffickers and other major criminals will restrict themselves to operating within certain national territories of the Single European Market. Surely, far more imaginative measures are needed to create a Euro-wide criminal justice system. It would be foolish simply to wait for the various national legal systems to "evolve" into a more harmonised system. What is needed is a European Community criminal law statute providing for a European Community Criminal Court in which serious crime (such as terrorism, drug trafficking etc.) committed anywhere in the EC could be dealt with. The legal statute should provide for a court to investigate, try and sentence in such cases. The Euro Court would have the enormous advantage of overriding all the tedious and often chauvinistic national arguments among EC states regarding the extradition of terrorists. Terrorists would know that they could not get safe haven simply by moving from one EC state to another. In addition the criminal law statute could provide a proper remit and legal basis for a Euro-style FBI of the kind proposed by Chancellor Kohl in 1989. This should greatly facilitate the fight against serious crime within the Community. Surely this concept of an EC criminal statute and court is worthy of serious study by the EC Ministers of Justice and Interior. In a sense it would be a logical addition to the existing structures of the European Court of Justice and the Council of Europe's Human Rights Court. The absence of a European criminal court from our institution-building in Europe seems a somewhat glaring omission in the light of plans for 1992.

*Terrorist Targets and Tactics: New Risks to World Order*     21

## CONCLUSION

Terrorism is not simply a problem for the richest and most powerful states. It is a challenge which has to be faced by the entire international community. Terrorism is, at the very least, a threat to individual human rights and the rule of law. But at its most severe levels it endangers the stability and wellbeing of whole communities and states and may, under certain circumstances, trigger internal and even international wars.

A key problem in responding to terrorism is to find the right balance, effective and proportionate measures which avoid the evils of both over-reaction and under-reaction. Democratic societies everywhere can take heart from the fact that a number of countries have succeeded in defeating major terrorist campaigns without losing their democratic process and rule of law. The successes of West Germany and Italy in virtually eradicating the threat from *Red Army* and *Red Brigade* terrorists offer two very encouraging examples.

Democracies are important in a more fundamental sense in the long-term battle against terrorism. While it is true that terrorists can exploit the freedoms of an open and democratic society to mount attacks, the very legitimacy of democracy in the eyes of its citizens provides a kind of inner moral strength which helps the system to withstand any attempt to subvert or overthrow it. In the final analysis the battle between democracy and terrorism is a test of moral strength and political will.

It is unrealistic to hope for an international system purged of all tyrannies and dictatorships, at least in the foreseeable future. All experience shows that as long as there continue to be tyrannies, terrorists will find sponsorship, support, succour and safe haven. Yet this should not cause the democracies to sit on their hands and write off any effort to strengthen international co-operation to counter terrorism. Democratic states must work even more closely together for the suppression of terrorism. For it is in their common interests and in the interests of humanity to work together for the eradication of this scourge.

---

## ABBREVIATIONS

| | |
|---|---|
| EOKA | Ethniki Organosis Kypriakon Agoniston |
| ETA | Euskadi ta Askatasuna |
| FLN | Front de Liberation Nationale |
| FLOSY | Front for the Liberation of Occupied South Yemen |
| PIRA | Provisional Irish Republican Army |
| PFLP–GC | Popular Front for the Liberation of Palestine – General Command |
| Trevi | Terrorism, Radicalism, Extremism and International Violence: set up as an intergovernmental forum under the European Political Co-operation (EPC) in 1976. |
| WAD | Afghan Ministry of State Security |

# [7]

# Northern Ireland: Reappraising Republican Violence

## A Special Report

The terrorism stemming from the Northern Ireland conflict since 1969, often spilling over into mainland Britain, the Continent, and the Republic, is the most protracted and intensive terrorist violence experienced anywhere in Western Europe since 1945. Over 2900 of the 1.5 million strong population of Northern Ireland have been killed through the conflict and over 30,000 injured. This is equivalent in proportionate terms to the killing of over 400,000 in the United States or over 100,000 in mainland Britain. Every killing and maiming is a violation of the most basic human rights of the victims and their loved ones.

## 1. THE ROOTS OF AN INTRACTABLE CONFLICT

The wider impact of protracted terrorism on the Province has undoubtedly severely damaged the well-being of both the Protestant majority and the large Catholic minority. The police and judicial systems have been placed under enormous strain, and the general quality of life has inevitably been affected by the stringent and more intrusive anti-terrorism measures adopted to deal with the emergency. The majority and minority communities have been increasingly polarised, creating a ghetto atmosphere of fear and apprehension in the areas of Belfast and Londonderry where the Loyalist and Republican paramilitaries have been most active, and in the rural Border areas many Protestant farming families believe they have been the targets of a campaign of genocide by the Provisional Irish Republican Army (PIRA). Terrorism deliberately aims to destroy the middle ground of compromise and inter-community co-operation which would characterise "normal" politics. Nor should we forget the serious economic damage inflicted by terrorists. Many businesses have been the targets of terrorist attack and much-needed new investment has been scared away. The damage to Northern Ireland's economy and the economies of the UK and the Republic, which have had to bear the huge security costs of combating the terrorism, has never been fully calculated, but it runs into billions of pounds. A recent Bank of Ireland report (1990) estimated that the "Troubles" are costing the UK and Ireland £410 million per year.

Italy and West Germany have both demonstrated that fanatical terrorist groups can be defeated without destroying democracy in the process. And Britain's governmental system and army have long and painful experience of coping with terrorism and insurrection in the period of colonial independence struggles. Why is it that successive British governments have failed to stamp out the flames in their own backyard?

1

One reason is that it is *not* a colonial conflict, however hard the Irish Republican Army (IRA) terrorists try to portray it as such. If the British government and people could divest themselves of the bloody and costly burden of governing Northern Ireland by handing over to some acceptable authority, whether based in Dublin or Belfast, recognised as a legitimate government by a broad consensus in Northern Ireland, they would do so. They are not a colonial elite ready to "withdraw". The first Protestant settlement in Northern Ireland pre-dates the Pilgrim Fathers' first colony in New England (1620). It is as much their homeland as America is to Americans. But there is no simple solution of this kind because the million-strong Protestant majority in the Province are so adamantly opposed to any unification with the Catholic Republic in the South. Indeed, they are prepared to wage full-scale civil war to prevent it. The self-styled champion of the "loyalists" who are fiercely determined to remain British is the "big man" the Reverend Ian Paisley. Both Mr. Paisley's party, the Democratic Unionist Party (DUP) and the more moderate Ulster Unionist Party led by James Molyneaux, see themselves as defending the survival of their Protestant Unionist identity. They know that in any unified all-Ireland state they would become a one million strong minority in a state dominated by 3.25 million Catholics. They point to the powerful Catholic influence in shaping key elements in the present Republic's political system, for example in relation to laws on divorce and abortion. They fear the elimination of the Protestant education system. Above all they fear the loss of their right to be subjects of the British Crown in an alien Republic.

It is important to understand that this divide between Catholic Irish Nationalists and Protestant Unionists is not merely a matter of inter-communal suspicion and friction. It is a truly ethnic divide. The northern Catholic nationalists feel themselves to be "Irish", an identity totally rejected by the Protestant Unionists. They have a traditional deep hatred not only for the Protestant Unionists for taking over their lands when they settled there four centuries ago in the Ulster plantations, and for monopolising economic and political control in the north thereafter, but also for the British whom they blame for creating and perpetuating their subordination. The resentment of the militant northern Catholic republicans was intensified during the 50 years of Unionist hegemony in Ulster, following the partition of Ireland and the establishment of the independent Irish Free State in the South in 1921. The Northern Ireland Civil Rights Association (NICRA) flared into life in the late 1960s when it brought the Catholic minority on the streets to campaign against anti-Catholic discrimination in housing, local goverment and employment.

Tragically the situation polarised in 1969–1970. Before legislative reforms and closer attention from the Westminster government could bring about peaceful change and reconciliation, militant paramilitary groups on both sides of the sectarian divide began to use violence and terrorism.

The central reason for the intractability of the Northern Ireland conflict is that it is a dual minority problem. Both the Northern Protestants and Catholic minority in Northern Ireland see themselves as beleaguered groups waging a zero-sum conflict for the right to maintain their way of life on their own terms.

*Northern Ireland: Reappraising Republican Violence* 3

The Catholic minority fear a repressive Unionist hegemony in which they would continue to suffer discrimination and the second-class status in jobs, housing, and political decision-making. Northern Ireland Protestants, on the other hand, fear above all the idea of a united Ireland, in which they believe they would lose their right to maintain their own way of life in a state that would inevitably be dominated by the Catholic majority and the pervasive influence of the Catholic Church. Indeed the Protestant Unionists have bitterly opposed the Anglo-Irish Agreement (1985) and all schemes to introduce a power-sharing system of devolved government combining Unionist and Nationalist parties in key decision-making, because they see these as steps down the slippery slope towards ultimate unification.

A major reason for the intractable nature of the conflict is that extremists both in the Loyalist and Republican camps have been fully committed to the use of terror and intimidation from the beginning of the present phase of the Troubles. On the Republican side the Provisional Irish Republican Army (PIRA) emerged from a split in the IRA in 1969. The old IRA members who had opposed the Anglo-Irish Treaty of 1921 because they bitterly opposed the Partition fought an unsuccessful civil war against the Irish Free State, 1922–1923, and continued, throughout the inter-war and post-war years, to deny the right of Britain to sovereignty over the six counties. After the failure of their bombing campaigns against British rule in Northern Ireland in the 1930s and again in the late '50s and early '60s, the IRA turned towards an explicit Marxist view in the mid '60s. Under the leadership of Cathal Goulding, a group on the IRA Army Council planned to create a non-sectarian left wing revolutionary movement to unite the working class throughout Ireland. They down-graded the role of violence and placed great emphasis on political and economic action.

This shift towards a Marxist strategy caused a profound split within the movement. It was Brendan Behan, the Irish writer, who said the first item on the agenda of any Irish meeting is "The Split". Many leading members of the IRA Old Guard were totally opposed to the policy of downgrading the movement's "military role". They were particularly angered by what they regarded as a betrayal by the 1969 IRA Special Convention in ending the policy of abstentionism and thus allowing Sinn Fein, their political wing, to send elected candidates to the parliaments of Dublin, Belfast and London. The lurch towards Marxism also greatly upset many hard-core IRA members: Catholicism and conservatism still dominated their social and political ideas. But the really big split in 1969 occurred when militant Republicans in the North rebelled against the IRA leadership over the latter's failure to militarily defend the northern Catholic population when sectarian rioting broke out in 1969. Graffiti appeared in Belfast streets saying "IRA – I Ran Away!" Hasty moves were made to establish an armed organisation, initially at parish level, for the protection of the Catholic enclaves. Under the leadership of Sean MacStiofain, Rory O'Brady, Bill McKee, and Seamus Twomey, the militant physical force Republicans established their own "Provisional" IRA organisation with its own PIRA Army Council, Brigades and Battalions. A month later they set up their own political wing, Provisional Sinn Fein (PSF).

4                           *Research Institute for the Study of Conflict and Terrorism*

There is no doubt that the PIRA has become the most dangerous of all the terrorist organisations in Northern Ireland, and one of the most dangerous in Europe. It is this movement that we shall be examining in some detail in this study. Its ruthless campaign of terrorism is directed primarily against the British state, its security forces, government, and its citizens, with the aim of sickening them into withdrawing the British presence from Northern Ireland. But despite their frequent denials, they have also become mired in the savage violence of tit-for-tat sectarian murders directed at the Loyalist organisations and often at random members of the Protestant population. There is no doubt that PIRA members also see themselves as the self-appointed "defenders" of the Catholic community, avenging assassinations of Catholics by the Loyalist terror groups.

Like the IRA, the Loyalist paramilitaries also use the titles and symbols of their own tradition of armed organisations. For example, the Ulster Volunteer Force (formed in 1966), takes its titles from the armed force set up by the Unionist leader Lord Carson to resist Irish Rule before the First World War. The UVF declared war on the IRA in 1966. At the peak of its strength in the early '70s it probably numbered over 1000 men. It has been responsible for numerous assassinations. The Ulster Freedom Fighters (UFF) is another notorious Loyalist terror gang. It is widely believed to have been set up under the aegis of the Ulster Defence Association, the largest Protestant paramilitary organisation, though since the mid '70s the UDA has disclaimed any connection with it, and the UDA has remained a legal organisation. Yet another notorious Loyalist terror group is the Red Hand Commandos, formed in 1972 and responsible for a number of sectarian murders.

In the light of the recent spate of tit-for-tat sectarian murders it should hardly be necessary to remind the reader that there are *two* terrorist traditions in Northern Ireland: Loyalist and Republican. Loyalist terrorists have been responsible for over 30 per cent of the killings since 1969, while the PIRA has caused roughly 60 per cent of the total fatalities through terrorism. While it is true that the Loyalist terrorists' attacks are not directed at the security forces and the British state they have helped to fuel an orgy of sectarian violence, which has sometimes come close to triggering a full-scale civil war. One of the largely unsung achievements of the British Army and the Royal Ulster Constabulary has been to prevent an escalation to civil war with all its attendant death and destruction. The corollary is that the security forces have succeeded in "buying time" for the politicians to find a stable political framework acceptable to the overwhelming majority of both the Protestant and Catholic communities.

However, it is all too evident that the security forces, for all their courage and patience and their success in preventing civil war, have not been able to eradicate the cancer of terrorism in Northern Ireland or its spill-over into the mainland and the Continent. This is partly because terrorism is all too easy to wage in an open democratic society. It takes only small numbers of fanatics to conduct hit-and-run bombings and assassination campaigns. The terrorists have the great advantage of surprise. It is only when the security forces have the rare asset of high-calibre intelligence giving detailed advance warning of an attack that they can know where and when the next blow will fall and can plan to catch the terrorists in the act. The democratic authorities are forced to respond at mid-levels of coerciveness because they are committed to preserving the framework of democratic liberties and the rule of law.

It is true that successive British governments have sought to strengthen the hand of the security forces by the use of emergency measures. For example, they have allowed non-jury courts in Northern Ireland in order to avoid the problem of terrorist intimidation of juries. (The Republic of Ireland also employs a non-jury court to try terrorist cases, but they have three judges rather than the single judge employed in the Diplock courts in Northern Ireland.) Nevertheless, despite numerous emergency measures, the British authorities have remained determined to avoid the imposition of martial law and other extremely draconian measures. The cost of operating at mid-levels of coerciveness is, however, very high. The conviction rate for terrorist offences is appallingly low, and the terrorists' supply of manpower and weaponry does not appear to have been significantly reduced by *any* recent security measures. This is not to deny that the security forces have had many outstanding successes in preventing major loss of life, especially through their courage and skill in locating and defusing terrorist bombs.

Another major factor contributing to the intractability of the conflict is the ease with which the PIRA can exploit the long and tortuous border with the Republic, with its vast number of unmarked crossing-points. The Provisionals gain considerably from their ability to move terrorists and weapons and explosives across the border. They have the huge benefit of being able to use the territory of the Republic for planning, for logistic support from PIRA's Southern command, and for recruiting, training, safe-haven and R and R (rest and recreation), knowing that they cannot be reached by the British security forces. Last but not least, what makes it so hard for the British security forces to eradicate or even substantially reduce the terrorist threat to below its present level is the sheer all-round capability, experience and skill of the PIRA as a terrorist organisation. Indeed when one takes into account their successes in gathering intelligence and to a large extent preventing penetration by the security forces of their own organisation, and the sophistication of their terrorist techniques, tactics, fund-raising and arms-procurement, it would be accurate to describe the PIRA as one of the most dangerous terrorist movements in the world.

For those concerned with the defence of democracy against terrorism there is no axiom more important, than "know thine enemy". The present study is designed to assist in this task. It will examine PIRA's ideology and aims, strategy and tactics, organisational structure, weaponry, finances, links with the Republic and other foreign states, and their propaganda and political warfare.

## 2. PIRA IDEOLOGY, STRATEGY AND TACTICS

It is probably an exaggeration to describe the political slogans and obsessions of the PIRA as an ideology. The movement's broad aims and beliefs hark

6                    *Research Institute for the Study of Conflict and Terrorism*

back to the old IRA of the 1920s and '30s. "The Green Book", the PIRA's official manual, states that a key aim is to establish "an Irish Socialist Republic based on the 1916 Proclamation". The reference to 1916 identifies the organisation with the Easter Rising in Dublin in which the rebels claimed to be establishing a Provisional Government for an independent Ireland. PIRA see themselves as the true successors to this tradition, as the true vanguard of the nationalist struggle for the liberation of the whole of Ireland, dedicated to the use of physical force to achieve their goals. The term Provisional in the PIRA's title is of course a deliberate attempt to claim this legitimacy of the true succession for themselves. In the eyes of PIRA, those who supported the Irish Free State and opposed the "Irregulars" in the Irish Civil War of 1922–1923, betrayed their trust by selling out to the British, accepting Partition in the Anglo-Irish Treaty, and setting up what PIRA regard as a traitorous "imperialist" parliament in Dublin. The PIRA also perceive the old "Official" IRA as having betrayed the Irish people by abandoning the policy of abstentionism in 1969 and by failing to provide military protection for the people of the Catholic enclaves in the North.

The PIRA's attempt to hijack the whole mainstream tradition of Irish nationalism of course makes a mockery of their claim to be a "democratic" movement. They simply assert that the PIRA Army Council is the legitimate government of the whole of Ireland, on the grounds that: (i) the legitimate authority for the government of an independent Ireland originally passed to those members of the *Dail Eireann* who voted against the Anglo-Irish Treaty; (ii) as these members transferred their authority to the IRA Army Council in 1938, and the old IRA Army Council betrayed its trust to the Irish people, the authority passed to the PIRA Army Council. In truth the PIRA do not care a jot for the legitimacy of genuine support from an elected majority of the people. The PIRA's political Wing, Provisional Sinn Fein, obtained less than 2 per cent of the vote in the last Irish General Election. In the PIRA's eyes the majority of Irish people are simply wrong and invalid. The PIRA know best and have the moral right to force the Irish people to follow the destiny laid down for them by PIRA's self-appointed vanguard. Small wonder that the PIRA ignore democratic methods in their own internal structures and procedures. While on the one hand they use their political wing, PSF, to exploit the political opportunities of the ballot box in electoral contests, they rule their "military" organisation with draconian authoritarianism, all key policy decisions being handed down to the grass roots from the Army Council and the General Staff. The price for disobedience is severe, and may be death or maiming after "trial" before a kangaroo court.

The core belief of the PIRA can be briefly summarised: the ending of Partition and the establishment of a socialist republic in the whole of Ireland on lines approved by the PIRA: a passionate hatred of the British and the aim of expelling every vestige of the British presence from Northern Ireland; and an unshakable belief that violence followed by more violence is the only way to pursue their goals. This blind faith in the efficacy of political violence also explains the crude banality of the PIRA's military strategy. The PIRA's "Green Book" describes the strategy thus:

*Northern Ireland: Reappraising Republican Violence* 7

1. A war of attrition against enemy personnel which is aimed at causing as many casualties and deaths as possible so as to create a demand from their people at home for their withdrawal.
2. A bombing campaign aimed at making the enemy's financial interest in our country unprofitable while at the same time curbing long term financial investment in our country.
3. To make the Six Counties as at present and for the past several years ungovernable except by colonial military rule.
4. To sustain the war and gain support for its ends by national and international propaganda and publicity campaigns.
5. By defending the war of liberation by punishing criminals, collaborators and informers.

In the early years of their terrorist campaign the PIRA believed that they could rapidly escalate it to render Northern Ireland ungovernable. Their achievement in bringing about the end of the Northern Irish government at Stormont almost certainly led the PIRA's leaders to underestimate the difficulties of following this up by securing British withdrawal. Up until the mid-'70s the PIRA kept promising its members that "one more push" would bring total victory. This optimism had been modified by 1977, and since then great stress has been placed on the need to fight a protracted war, long-drawn out but nevertheless destined to bring an inevitable final victory.

The most significant strategic development has occurred since 1981, when Bobby Sands, the H-Block hunger striker was elected to a seat in the House of Commons. The political wing of the PIRA, PSF, realised the great possibilities of building a mass political base of support in West Belfast and other Nationalist areas. Thus evolved the strategy of "the ballot box in one hand and the Armalite in the other". PSF threw themselves into community-style politics in areas such as West Belfast, taking up complaints about housing, pavements and social services and trying to prove that they could be far more effective in meeting the needs of the general public than the other parties. The strategy appeared to pay off. PSF surprised its opponents by winning over 11 per cent of the vote in Northern Ireland in the general elections of 1983 and 1987. Yet more recently the PSF's support has slipped badly, especially in the Republic, where it dipped below 2 per cent of the total vote. It is inadequate to explain this as a failure of energy in political work by PSF. One major reason is undoubtedly growing public revulsion over PIRA terrorist attacks in which civilians have been killed. Repeated statements by Gerry Adams, president of PSF, apologise for these "accidents" but this does not convince anybody. The more politically realistic of PSF's organisers must know that the more Adams reiterates the total solidarity of PSF with the "armed struggle" of the PIRA the more they destroy their chances of winning major gains in electoral support. The fact is that between Remembrance Day, 1987, when 11 civilians died in the PIRA bombing at Enniskillen, and Autumn 1990 a further 22 civilians died as a result of what Adams calls "mistakes" by the PIRA.

8                    *Research Institute for the Study of Conflict and Terrorism*

In 1989 PIRA gunmen "accidentally" killed the six-months-old daughter of a British RAF Corporal stationed in Germany and the German-born wife of a British soldier. In May 1990 PIRA gunmen in the Netherlands murdered two Australian tourists whom they mistook for British off-duty soldiers. In July 1990 a PIRA bomb aimed at a police patrol also killed a young nun. In November 1991 the PIRA bombed a hospital in Belfast: two soldiers were killed and children in the children's ward were among the injured. The savage brutality of the PIRA's terrorist tactics outrages the vast majority of Irishmen and all decent men and women everywhere. Only the hard men of the PIRA, their tunnel vision fixed on violence and maximum carnage, fail to understand that, even in terms of their own political objectives, the heavy cost of the PIRA's massacres outweighs any political benefit.

Yet there are faint glimmerings of a real debate going on behind closed doors. The more astute members of PIRA's political wing are at last beginning to ask how PSF can possibly hope to make any political gains, or even to hold the ground it occupied in previous elections, if the PIRA continue to launch attacks which kill or injure innocent civilians. These criticisms were openly expressed at the 85th Sinn Fein *ard fheis* (annual conference) in February 1990, and there have been signs of internal policy debates on the issue during and since the round of interparty talks promoted by the Brooke initiative in Summer, 1991. Predictably, the Provisionals' propaganda has bitterly attacked the talks. PIRA leaders hold stubbornly to the belief that the British government will be forced to sue for peace and to talk to the PIRA on the terrorists' own terms. The reality is that no credible democratic government could ever agree to do deals with those who use the bomb to achieve what they cannot win through the ballot box. They would be signing the death warrant of democracy.

## 3. THE PATTERN OF PIRA TACTICS AND TARGETING

The PIRA have been using Northern Ireland as a veritable laboratory for the development of tactics and techniques of terrorism since the start of the "the Troubles". They are among the most experienced and expert terrorist organisations in the world in such matters as the design and manufacture of radio-controlled and time-delay bombs, booby-trap bombs, car bombs, and improvised grenades and mortars. They have a huge knowledge within the organisation of the *modus operandi* and resources of the security forces, and have perfected techniques of penetrating government and security organisations and gathering intelligence of major value in their campaign. But the terrorists have by no means had it all their own way. The security forces in Northern Ireland have also gained formidable knowledge and understanding of the tactics and methods of the PIRA, and have become expert in the means of combating them. In this constant battle of terrorism and counter-terrorism the security forces have managed significantly to reduce the total number of PIRA bombings. From the peak of over 1500 bombings and defusings per year in the period 1971–1973 they have been cut to between 215 a year (1985)

*Northern Ireland: Reappraising Republican Violence*          9

and 458 a year (1988) since the mid-'70s. There has been a dramatic reduction in the number of shooting attacks annually from a peak of 10,628 in 1972 to a low of 237 in 1985. The figure for the nine months period to the end of September 1991 shows a welcome fall from the 1990 total of 559 attacks.

However, the reduction in the number of PIRA attacks does not indicate any lessening of brutality on the part of the PIRA. This was clearly demonstrated on 24 October 1990, when they forced three Catholic civilians whom they described as "collaborators" to serve as human bombs by driving explosive devices to military installations while their families were held hostage. This tactic, which Mr. Peter Brooke described as marking "new depths of depravity" by the PIRA, was clearly aimed at killing the maximum number of soldiers with the minimum risk to the PIRA. It was also designed to further their ongoing campaign of terrorist intimidation against all those serving or supplying the security forces in any way. PIRA clearly intended the "human bomb" drivers to be killed in the explosions, and claimed to have selected them because they "collaborated" with or served the security forces in some capacity. Thus they hoped that the deaths of the civilian drivers of the proxy bombs would act as a means of dissuading other members of the population from providing goods or services to the security forces.

In this cowardly campaign against suppliers and services the PIRA have killed 15 people since 1985, including a number of directors and executives in the building industry and two workmen, aged 63 and 59, who died when the PIRA fired 99 bullets into their car. Some companies have surrendered to the terrorists' pressure and placed advertisements in the press declaring that they did not supply the security forces. Other firms have bravely stood their ground and continued to work for the Army and Police. However, there is no doubt that this particular campaign by PIRA placed an additional burden on the Northern Ireland authorities, who are now forced to take expensive security measures in order to proceed with the vital £150 million building programme needed as a result of the expansion of the RUC.

However, it would be grossly inadequate to seek to analyse the patterns of PIRA terrorism purely by reference to Northern Ireland. The PIRA leadership have always regarded attacks on the British mainland, particularly in London, as of enormous potential value in their overall struggle. In the words of one PIRA leader: "One bomb in London is worth 10 in Belfast". The PIRA leaders believe that attacks on the mainland will help to sicken the British public and politicians into adopting a policy of withdrawal from Northern Ireland. They know that attacks in England will yield huge publicity. They also know that this publicity helps to compensate for their failures and setbacks in Northern Ireland. Last but by no means least, they have since the late '80s built up considerable expertise and success in deploying hypermobile PIRA Active Service Units (ASUs) on the mainland which can escape detection from the police and intelligence services for very long periods: their expertise and their much-improved intelligence have enabled them to attack numerous soft targets in Britain with apparent impunity.

The PIRA's reasons for venturing into the terrorist attacks against British military bases and personnel on the Continent are very similar, though they only began the latter form of activity in the late 1970s. Moreover their campaign in 1989–1990, in which PIRA "mistakes" led to the deaths of civilians became a major embarrassment to the PIRA leadership, causing outrage among the public and politicians on the Continent. Since the arrests of a number of suspects in France, the Netherlands and Belgium in 1989 and 1990, the PIRA terrorist campaign on the Continent appears to have been at least temporarily suspended. However, it would be unwise to assume that this will continue indefinitely. There are indications that they have already been restoring their Active Service Unit on the Continent ready for action.

In their campaign on the British mainland the PIRA have also tended to go increasingly for the softer targets. With the exception of their daring mortar attack on a Cabinet meeting in Downing Street in January 1991, the majority of mainland attacks have been against soft military targets such as the young Marine bandsmen at Deal, the boy soldiers at Lichfield station, and recruiting offices in various cities.

The PIRA's mainland civilian targets have ranged from "establishment" targets such as the Stock Exchange and the Carlton Club to public facilities such as Victoria Station. The PIRA's cowardly murder of Mr Ian Gow MP, and their attempts to murder Sir Peter Terry, the former Governor of Gibraltar, and other leading figures, demonstrate that the terrorists have the organisation and resources to conduct major terrorist operations on the mainland, and that this capability is by no means confined to the London area. It is also clear that the PIRA had been exporting some of its more successful terrorist methods from Northern Ireland. For example, the PIRA have frequently used small but effective incendiary devices against shops and businesses in Northern Ireland. It is now clear that the PIRA have used these devices in Manchester and London. They have also frequently attacked railway stations, track, and trains in Northern Ireland, causing considerable disruption. The PIRA's Victoria Station bombing suggests that they have been attracted to the possibilities of causing much greater mayhem by attacking the major transport systems of the mainland. It is inherently extremely difficult to protect the public against this type of indiscriminate attack.

It is quite clear that there *are* discernible patterns in the PIRA's terrorist tactics and targeting. This is particularly true of the PIRA's campaign in Northern Ireland It is obvious that the terrorists are committed to sustaining their attacks against the police and the Army throughout the Province. This campaign includes more audacious attacks on hardened targets, such as police stations and Army posts, for example using powerful vehicle bombs and mortar attacks. But it also includes a wide range of attacks on soft targets, such as policemen and reservists shot down in their homes, in front of their wives and children, ambushed in the streets, or killed or injured by car bombs. There have also been other clearly established patterns of targeting, such as the campaign against civilian personnel and firms involved in supplying goods or services to the security forces, a campaign which has particularly focused on building firms employed for repair and building work for the security forces. There has also been a long-term campaign of sectarian murders which the PIRA have seen themselves as entitled to retaliate in kind against the

Northern Ireland: Reappraising Republican Violence        11

murder of Catholics by Loyalist terrorist gangs. These tit-for-tat murders reached a crescendo in the mid-1970s. They have again intensified so much in recent months that the RUC has established a much-needed specialist squad to concentrate exclusively on combating sectarian murders. On the night of 13 November 1991 the PIRA murdered four Protestants and seriously wounded a five-weeks-old baby girl. The following night Loyalist terrorists gunned down three men at a factory near Portadown. In the wake of this bloodshed the government deployed extra troops and decided to increase the strength of the RUC by an additional 441 officers.

There have been predictable and understandable calls from Unionists and senior army officers for the reintroduction of internment. However, the government is unlikely to adopt this draconian measure. The level of sectarian murders has escalated dramatically, but the level of violence has not yet reached potential civil war proportions as it did in the early '70s. The last time internment was tried in 1971 it was a disaster. Many unconnected with terrorism were detained. The government knows that it would give a huge propaganda and recruiting weapon to the PIRA. It would put at risk the whole framework of security and political co-operation with the Republic and would alienate Britain's allies.

In their terrorist campaigns on the British mainland, as was noted above, the PIRA have attacked a very wide variety of targets, both military and civilian. Sadly, it is the case that the PIRA find it easier to kill members of the British armed forces on the mainland and the Continent, where security and awareness of the threat are much laxer than in Northern Ireland. Indeed in the period from December 1988 to June 1990 the PIRA killed more soldiers in England and on the Continent than they did in Ulster. The campaign has been marked by sharp switches in targets and the introduction of tactics already tried and tested in Northern Ireland. While it is true that the overwhelming majority of their attacks have hit soft military targets or soft civilian targets, it would be a great mistake to assume that the PIRA have abandoned attacking hard targets. For example in the trial of Liam O'Dhuibir and Damien McComb at the Old Bailey in November 1990 on charges of "conspiring to cause explosions with persons unknown", it was revealed that detailed hit-lists were found in a flat used by the PIRA, including the names of all members of the Cabinet. Also found in the flat were 12 forged Home Office security passes and Ordnance Survey maps of key military base areas such as Aldershot and Salisbury Plain. These should surely be regarded as hard targets. It is also worth remembering that the PIRA came very close to blowing up Prime Minister Margaret Thatcher and senior members of her Government at Brighton in 1984, and in January 1991 they launched a daring mortar attack in Whitehall in broad daylight, narrowly missing the room in Downing Street where the Cabinet meeting was taking place. It should not need emphasising that the PIRA will continue to seek out any opportunity to hit a high-value hard target, because of the enormous publicity and psychological potential of such attacks. Key targets are not immune simply because they are the subject of high-grade security, and those responsible for protecting major targets must therefore maintain the highest vigilance and standards of security in every aspect, constantly on the lookout to correct weaknesses.

At the other end of the targeting spectrum, we have abundant evidence that the terrorists are quite prepared to bomb indiscriminately, knowing full well that by attacking public places, such as the concourses of major railway stations, they are almost bound to cause deaths and serious injuries among the general public. As was noted earlier, we know that at least some members of the PIRA's political wing, PSF, realise the enormous damage these random bombings can do to their support and their much-vaunted political campaign. This does not appear to have deterred the hard-men of the PIRA leadership. It should also be recognised that the leaders of PIRA Active Service Units (ASUs) on the mainland are given considerable discretion as to the way they carry out their attacks. The PIRA leadership give them only broad policy direction as to the nature of the targets to be attacked and aims to be achieved. Hence, even if they find it politically inconvenient to be faced with criticism from within their own movement, they are more than ready to defend the activities of their ASUs and, when necessary, to give them retrospective authorisation for any attack. However, there is no doubt that this readiness of the PIRA to launch indiscriminate bombing and incendiary attacks in public places creates huge problems for the security forces, the emergency services, and the private sector management and personnel responsible for the security of shops, hotels and other places open to the public. In an open society it is practically impossible to provide adequate security to prevent such attacks.

On 15 November 1991 a PIRA bomb exploded in St. Albans' city centre. It was apparently aimed at the military band of the Blues and Royals which had been performing in a charity concert. The two people killed in the explosion had been priming or planting the bomb. If it had gone off six minutes later, when the audience was due to leave the concert, many civilians would have been killed. Once again the PIRA appears ready to cause indiscriminate attacks in public places. Commander Churchill-Coleman, head of the Anti-Terrorist Squad, was right to ask for maximum vigilance and co-operation from the public against the terrorists. The authorities suspected that the PIRA were planning one of their Christmas bombing campaigns.

In the long term, as will be argued later, the only really effective means of preventing attacks of this kind in public places is by developing such effective counter-terrorist intelligence and police work that the cells conspiring to commit such attacks are identified and brought to justice. This is not intended to be a counsel of despair. There are, of course, numerous ways in which the general public and alert employees can help prevent an explosion, for example by sharp observation in identifying suspicious persons or packages, and by swift action in clearing buildings and alerting the police and emergency services. Experience has shown that public vigilance and co-operation of this kind can save hundreds of lives.

## 4. ORGANISATIONAL STRUCTURE

The PIRA have quite a complex organisational structure. Not surprisingly they have derived much of their format and terminology from the old pre-1960s IRA. There is a General Army Convention which meets every two years and which chooses the Army Executive, the supreme authority in the PIRA in between conventions. This consists of a small number of senior members with a record of hard-core activism within the organisation. They in turn elect the Army Council, which is far and away the most powerful body in the movement and which provides the day to day direction of the organisation. This body normally meets monthly, though it can meet more frequently when required. It consists of the key leadership of the PIRA, including the President of PSF, the political wing, and the PIRA Chief of Staff. Its tasks are to appoint the Chief of Staff and to direct the overall campaign, providing the guidelines for the Chief of Staff and his Headquarters staff to carry out. The Chief of Staff and the top directorate of the PIRA he appoints, including the heads of operations in Northern Ireland, the British mainland and the Continent, are responsible for conducting the "military" (ie terrorist) campaign. To assist in this task the Chief of Staff has specialist cells concerned with weapons and weapon-procurement, intelligence gathering, other logistic support and propaganda and publicity.

In the early days of the PIRA campaign the grass-roots structure was modelled on an army or militia, with a "brigade", "battalion" and "company" structure. However, this structure had grave disadvantages; it was difficult to prevent infiltration by the security forces; inevitably the members tended to be widely known in the locality from which they were drawn; and the structure proved particularly vulnerable during the Army crackdown in the mid-'70s. In an effort to remove these weaknesses the PIRA leadership switched to a cell structure, more on the Continental model, which they introduced in the late '70s. The Active Service Units (ASUs) constitute the clandestine cells which carry out the terrorist operations of PIRA, and these have proved much more difficult for the security forces to penetrate. The backbone of the ASUs, varying between five and 12 members according to requirements, are the 80 or so hard-core PIRA members. These are experienced in the tactics and techniques of terrorism and expert in the art of avoiding been caught with evidence in their possession. The hard core are assisted by PIRA volunteers, estimated to total between 200 and 250. These volunteers are the foot-soldiers of the terrorist organisation, selected both for their reliability and commitment to the cause and for their suitability for ASU operations. Once "blooded", trained and experienced, these volunteers become the pool from which the hard-core is derived. The hard-core themselves generally move to senior positions as commanders, godfathers or political organisers when they become too old for ASU operations. Finally, there are the "auxiliaries", the active supporters of the PIRA who are ready to carry out useful back-up tasks for the ASUs, such as acting as look-outs, carrying weapons, or driving vehicles. Last but not least we should not overlook the much larger body of PIRA sympathisers among the general population. It is a mistake to assume that all those who have voted for the PSF fully support the methods and actions of the PIRA: at the peak of their electoral impact (over 100,000 votes) the PSF undoubtedly collected a large number of protest votes. However, even if only a quarter of PSF supporters are fully committed to the PIRA this still constitutes a formidable reservoir for potential recruits, fund-raising and other assistance which can be tapped by the terrorists. There is certainly no evidence of any serious lack of supply of recruits to the organisation: indeed the Catholic Church has recently warned of the success of the PIRA in intensive recruiting efforts in Dublin and elsewhere.

It would be a grave mistake, however, to overlook the brutally coercive aspect of the PIRA's relations with their own members and Nationalist communities in areas such as West Belfast and parts of South Armagh and Tyrone, where they have used coercion and intimidation to control their own population. Recently there has been a record number of kneecappings and other "punishments" meted out by the PIRA. Moreover, testimony such as that produced at the recent trial of Danny Morrison, former PSF publicity director, reveals the PIRA's savage treatment of alleged informers. In an organisation demanding blind obedience, and paranoid about penetration by the security forces, torture and death are the stock-in-trade of methods of internal discipline.

Finally, one should not underestimate the intensity of the PIRA's efforts constantly to improve the training and expertise of their operations. One has only to study "The Green Book" and the track record of the organisation to recognise the emphasis given to the acquisition of basic terrorist skills, such as intelligence gathering, weaponry, internal security, use of safehouses, false documents, acquisition of vehicles for terrorist operations and so on. Recently it has also become clear that the PIRA are striving to obtain more sophisticated technological expertise by giving their members advanced training in such fields as electronics and telecommunications.

## 5. WEAPONRY

The PIRA, thanks to the Libyan dictator Colonel Qadhafi, are one of the best-armed terrorist organisations in the world. For example, the PIRA obtained the Soviet RPG7 hand-held surface-to-surface missile, so widely used among terrorists in the '70s and early '80s. This weapon first appeared 30 years ago but it can still be effective, and fired under proper conditions it can penetrate 320 mm of armour. On the other hand it can easily be deflected by cross-winds and by wire mesh protection around buildings. It has to detonate at right angles and at the correct range to be effective, and it is therefore a highly unreliable weapon for terrorists.

The PIRA have also developed their own improvised multi-barrelled mortars mounted on trucks. Early versions of these weapons were highly unreliable but recent attacks have shown the PIRA using them with greater skill and accuracy, as in the case of the attack on Downing Street. Another weapon developed by the PIRA is their own improvised drogue grenade, which has proved to be a dangerous device, especially against the armoured troop carriers and Land-Rovers of the security forces. It is basically a hollow charge weapon, shaped like a stick grenade. It consists of a charge of Semtex in a standard food can and a plastic tube which contains the firing mechanism. The release of the grenade pin and lever releases a drogue which is intended to make the grenade strike with the base of the can to direct the charge with maximum destructive effect against the target. It is not a reliable weapon, but when aimed accurately it is a lethal addition to the terrorist armoury. The PIRA also have ample supplies of Armalites and AK47 assault rifles. It is estimated that the PIRA acquired around 1000 AK47s from Libya in the mid-'80s, a number of heavy machine guns capable of use against aircraft, 12 SAM-7 shoulder-launched ground-to-air missiles, and over a tonne of Semtex explosive. Only a small proportion of this armoury, smuggled into the Republic in the mid-'80s, has been recovered by the security forces, despite intensive searches in the Border area. The PIRA's acquisition of Semtex has presented a particularly serious threat to the security forces and the population because it is more destructive than conventional high explosives, is easy for terrorists to use, and difficult to detect, owing to its extremely low vapour content.

The PIRA's supply of Semtex is an even greater threat owing to the very considerable expertise the PIRA have developed in the design and manufacture of bombs. Their sophistication in making use of precise time delay mechanisms for bombs (of the kind used in the 1984 Brighton bombing) has been matched by their growing skill in developing radio-controlled bombs. However, they have not been so successful at utilising other parts of their armoury, such as SAM-7s. It is clear that the terrorists have used their heavy machine guns against Army helicopters in Northern Ireland, but so far they have not proved very effective. In July 1991 there was a press report that the PIRA had tried to use a SAM-7 missile to shoot down an Army helicopter, while two helicopters were preparing to land at Kinawley, Co. Fermanagh. It is reported that the attack missed. If this is the case it can be assumed that the PIRA will try to improve its performance with this weapon, and the security forces will need to review their counter-measures against ground-to-air attack. Far more worrying to the security forces are well-authenticated reports, for example from the FBI, that the PIRA have been trying to obtain the Stinger missile, used with such devastating effect against Soviet aircraft in the Afghan conflict. This missile is far more accurate and effective than the SAM-7. There have been a number of press reports of terrorist movements attempting to purchase these weapons and other man-portable, ground-to-air missiles on the international arms black market.

It is already clear from the above that the PIRA are one of the most heavily armed terrorist groups in the world today. They have been remarkably successful in hiding their weapons from the security forces. Many of the finds of arms caches have occurred through the sharp observation of the public rather than from successful intelligence work by the authorities. The Libyan regime has recently claimed that it has ceased to provide weapons for the PIRA. Qadhafi's word cannot be trusted. In any case even if this is the case, the PIRA already have sufficient weaponry hidden away to keep them going for another decade, and enough cash to continue to acquire weapons from other sources.

## 6. FINANCES

The PIRA, like other major terrorist organisations, require substantial funds in order to pay for weapons, to support the activities of their ASUs in Northern Ireland, the mainland and the Continent, and to pay the considerable costs of general administration, the propaganda and publicity campaigns of their political wing and the costs of contesting elections, to provide assistance for the families of jailed IRA members, and to invest in their own legitimate and illegitimate "business" enterprises with the aim of making more money for the organisation.

The Northern Ireland Office has recently estimated that the PIRA have an annual income of £5.3 million. According to their figures the largest sums are derived from tax fraud (£1 million) and legitimate businesses (£1 million) and from drinking clubs and gaming machines (£1 million). Pirate videos and smuggling are thought to bring in £600,000 and protection and extortion £500,000. Donations from NORAID and other foreign-based support groups are thought to total no more than £100,000, a far less significant sum than the amount provided a decade ago. In 1981 alone NORAID admitted remitting 550,000 US dollars.

Racketeering is clearly an extremely important source of PIRA funding. Pirate videos provide a major example. In February 1984 the RUC reported that they had discovered that illegal tapes worth millions of pounds on the black market were pouring into Northern Ireland and the PIRA were behind the operation. It has been claimed that in a 12-month period the Northern Ireland anti-fraud team recovered over 50,000 illegal tapes and hard-porn films. Recently there have been persistent reports that the PIRA have been taking a cut from the lucrative drugs trade to help finance terrorist activities. If these claims are proved correct it will make a mockery of the PIRA's repeated claims that they are deeply opposed to drugs and that they are trying to enforce their anti-drugs stance by stern warnings to owners of clubs and pubs. The PIRA know that if they were discovered to be taking any share of profit from the activities of drug-dealers it would rebound against them politically.

The PIRA have claimed that it is the tiny Republican splinter group, the Irish People's Liberation Organization (IPLO), which has been involved in drug trafficking, along with the Loyalist paramilitaries. Some are claiming that the PIRA have also secretly planned to take a cut from the trade of London drugs dealers supplying the Province. If this is the case it would certainly be an extremely high risk strategy for the Provisionals. Until there is clear cut evidence to back up these allegations it would be wise to suspend judgement.

The authorities in Northern Ireland have long been aware of the need to staunch the flow of funds to the PIRA and other terrorist groups. In 1988 Mr Tom King, at that time Secretary of State for Northern Ireland, announced the establishment of a special anti-racketeering co-ordinating task force to combat the problem, consisting of members of the police, tax authorities and Customs and Excise, and the intelligence services. This was seen as an attempt

*Northern Ireland: Reappraising Republican Violence*          17

to overcome the weaknesses which were perceived to have limited the old C13 anti-rackets squad of the RUC, which had less than two dozen policemen and too little clout.

Secretary of State Peter Brooke has given major emphasis to the need to combat PIRA racketeering and extortion. In October 1990 he denounced the PIRA's extortion activities in the strongest terms:

> "The IRA is a parasitic organisation . . . it has lived off the backs of the people. Its members have stolen and extorted money to sustain themselves and their activities. People in small businesses have been forced to pay protection money . . . Local enterprises have become subject to the Mafia–like empire of the IRA boss in the area."

And in a speech to the House of Commons in March 1991 Mr Brooke warned that businessmen and accountants were becoming increasingly involved in raising and laundering funds to finance terrorism. He won general support for the new powers inserted in the Northern Ireland (Emergency Provisions) Bill to enable the courts to confiscate the assets of anyone who has benefited from terrorist-related activities. Mr Brooke has repeatedly called upon businessmen in Northern Ireland to stop paying protection money to terrorist organisations. However, this is easier said than done. Businessmen under threat are advised to contact the RUC, but they fear that the police will be unable to guarantee protection for their families and their businesses. Yet in order to provide such protection the RUC, already overstretched with its wide range of tasks in countering terrorism, clearly needs more resources.

Government action against terrorist racketeering has not been confined to the North of the Border. In February 1985 the Dail passed an emergency law enabling the Government to seize up to £10 million in funds that it alleged had been obtained by the PIRA under threat of kidnap and murder. The amendment to the Offences against the State Act is potentially extremely useful because the Irish Government can now seize additional terrorist funds that may be held under Irish jurisdiction.

The need for firm governmental action to staunch the flow of terrorists' funds and to seize their assets has been reinforced by recent reports of the activities of the Bank of Credit and Commerce International (BCCI). In particular much stronger co-ordination of the national and international intelligence and police effort against the financing of terror is required. Terrorists are already taking advantage of the weaknesses of controls on international financial activities. When the internal barriers in the European Community come down at the end of 1992 the PIRA, like other organised criminal groups, will seize their opportunities in the larger market. Community governments are in principle committed to strengthening their co-operation against terrorist racketeering, drug-trafficking, and money-laundering, community-wide. Sadly they still lack the means, if not the will, to implement these commitments.

## 7. THE PIRA: A THREAT TO THE REPUBLIC

It is important for the general public in Northern Ireland, the British mainland, and in the Republic of Ireland to understand that the terrorism of the PIRA is a threat to them all. The reality of the threat to the Republic is far less well understood than it should be.

From their inception the PIRA have made no secret of the fact that they hate the present parliamentary system and government in the Republic. They invariably refer to it with contempt as an "imperialist" entity which they accuse of betraying the cause of true Irish nationalism through collaboration with the British government. It is clear that if, heaven forbid, the PIRA got their way in forcing the British to abandon their responsibilities in Ulster, the inevitable ensuing civil war with the Unionist population for control of the Province would spill over into the Republic, developing into a bloody all-Ireland civil war. It is also clear that if the PIRA ever got the opportunity they would seek to remove the present form of government in the Republic and replace it with an all-Ireland "Socialist Republic" in a form laid down by the PIRA's dictatorship.

The paranoid obsession of many Ulster Unionists who insist on viewing the Republic as an "enemy" state blinds them to the glaring reality that it is in the mutual long-term self-interest of the Republic as well as the North to co-operate effectively and wholeheartedly in eradicating the scourge of terrorism from the whole island. They conveniently ignore the evidence of the relatively heavy burden of security costs borne by the Republic to deploy substantial numbers of the Irish Army and the Garda in the border areas. Ireland is one of the poorer countries in the EC, and there is surely a strong case for a Community fund to assist Ireland and other economically disadvantaged member states with severe cross-border terrorist problems.

On the other hand it is certainly true that Irish governments and judicial authorities have sometimes shown a prejudice against close co-operation with the British authorities and a blindspot towards their responsibilities in respect of taking firm action against the PIRA, often showing a surprising vulnerability to PIRA propaganda tactics, such as the clever anti-extradition protests orchestrated by PSF.

In the long term, however, the prospects for enhancing British-Irish co-operation look promising, for four major reasons:

  (i) the mutual recognition by Westminster and Dublin of the value of the Anglo-Irish Agreement and consultative council as a framework for close bilateral co-operation;

  (ii) the strong and consistent support given by Dublin to the continuing efforts at revitalising political dialogue between the mainstream political parties in the North, to achieve constitutional reform acceptable to the majority of both the majority and minority communities;

  (iii) the impetus given to greater co-operation against terrorism and other serious forms of crime by both countries' membership of the EC, and the prospect of the Single European Act (SEA);

*Northern Ireland: Reappraising Republican Violence* 19

(iv) the strong revulsion felt in the Republic against the savage brutality of the PIRA's terrorism, and particularly the killing of civilians.

In the light of the geography, history and politics of the whole island of Ireland it would clearly be absurd to attempt to resolve the conflict and violence in the North without full co-operation of the authorities on both sides of the Border. The militant Unionists' inability to understand this is part of the problem, not part of the answer.

## 8. IRSP, INLA AND IPLO

When the Provisionals broke away from the old IRA in 1969, its rump, known as the Officials or the "Stickies", continued to be committed to conducting a violent campaign against the British security forces, although it lacked the resources and organisation to make much impact and it was rapidly eclipsed by the violent struggle of the Provisionals. In 1972 the Officials declared a truce followed by an indefinite cease-fire, and many of the old leadership channelled their energies into the Workers' Party dedicated to pursuing Irish unification by political means.

However, in 1974, another splinter group broke away from the official IRA: a more militant Marxist-minded group formed the Irish Republican Socialist Party (IRSP) favouring a violent revolutionary struggle against the British. In late 1974 the IRSP spawned a paramilitary wing, the Irish National Liberation Army (INLA). This organisation is much smaller than the PIRA, amounting to probably no more than 50 activists, but it has a reputation for ruthless terrorist violence. Dominic McGlinchey, a former PIRA man, who became leader of INLA in the early '80s, boasted of having killed 30 people. It has been estimated that in Belfast as many as a third of the members of the old Official IRA went over to the IRSP. The "Stickies" were afraid that IRSP would undermine their organisation completely. They set up four hit squads to eradicate the rebels. In the bloody feud that ensued three Official IRA and two IRSP men were killed. Although many of the Belfast PIRA shared INLA's detestation of the Official IRA and their desire for military action, INLA remained a small splinter group.

In 1987 another savage internal feud broke out in which over a dozen people were killed, following the emergence of a further splinter group, the Irish People's Liberation Organization (IPLO). More have been killed in internal feuding among these fringe groups in the period since 1988. Yet although these small organisations have nothing like the firepower, organisation and support apparatus of the PIRA, it would be foolish to overlook their capacity to launch occasional bloody attacks on members of the security forces and on civilian targets.

INLA and IPLO have been far more influenced by neo-Marxist and Trotskyist ideas than PIRA. It is perhaps not surprising, therefore, that these groups have been very active in cultivating links with extreme left revolutionary groups on the Continent. Evidence emerged in the late '80s and early '90s of INLA and IPLO arms-smuggling activities in France and the Low Countries.

They have also developed links with a number of European extreme left Irish Solidarity groups. For example the IRSP/INLA is linked to the West German Ireland Solidarity Committee.

## 9. PIRA'S INTERNATIONAL LINKS

There has been a widespread tendency to exaggerate the extent and significance of the Provisionals' international links. It should always be remembered that the PIRA originated in Northern Ireland and have their roots in the bitter and protracted Ulster conflict which can be traced back over centuries. The latest phase of "the Troubles" did not need any foreign *deus ex machina* to set it alight. PIRA's leadership, hard-core and volunteers are all drawn from the Republican community on both sides of the Border. They have many sympathisers abroad, especially in countries like the USA and Australia where there are large numbers of people of Irish descent. But the crucial focus, political support, and fund-raising for the movement comes from within Northern Ireland or the Republic.

It is true that PIRA directs a great deal of propaganda activity towards mobilising support among the 45 million or so Americans of Irish descent. But the amount of cash raised by pro-PIRA organisations such as the Irish Northern Aid Committee (NORAID) and similar groups in America has dropped sharply in recent years. As was noted earlier, it is now estimated that the annual donations from NORAID and other foreign-based support groups total no more than £100,000, a tiny fraction of PIRA's income. However, it would be wrong to underestimate the value of the USA as a convenient platform for anti-British propaganda and as a potential source of arms.

The PIRA has been quite assiduous in building up political contacts with Irish Solidarity groups in Europe, such as Comité Solidarité-Irlande, Ireland Komitee Nederland and many others. The numbers of foreign sympathisers involved are relatively small, and they are of little importance as fund-raising organisations. The more significant role of these Solidarity groups is to assist in promoting pro-PIRA and anti-British propaganda, and mobilising pressure against the extradition, trial and conviction of PIRA members wanted for crimes committed on the Continent or elsewhere.

But even taking all these foreign based support activities in combination, they cannot compare to the significance of the Libyan link. It is Colonel Qadhafi's huge supply of weapons to the PIRA in the mid '80s that converted the organisation into one of the best-armed terrorist movements in the world.

## 10. CAUGHT ON THE TREADMILL OF TERRORISM: THE PROSPECTS FOR THE PIRA

A major conclusion of this report is that the PIRA are likely to continue to pose a serious threat to the life and limb and well-being of civilians and the security forces for some time ahead. They have the recruits, the weaponry and the funds to sustain their campaign for at least another decade if they so

*Northern Ireland: Reappraising Republican Violence* 21

desire. Open, democratic societies are by their very nature vulnerable to those who are determined to exploit their freedom to wage an underground terrorist campaign against their fellow citizens. The PIRA have also been quite astute at making propaganda capital out of the dilemmas and occasional grave errors of the authorities such as the tragic miscarriages of justice in England which recently came to light.

The conclusion of this study is that while the PIRA's terrorist organisation may survive for quite a long time ahead, it cannot win. The fundamental reason why it cannot win is that the PIRA are apparently totally locked on to the treadmill of terrorism, and terrorism cannot succeed in overthrowing a state which, whatever its shortcomings, is seen by the vast majority of its citizens as being legitimate.

The plain fact is that the PIRA are a terrorist movement representing the view of only a minority of a minority. They pretend to be a national liberation movement and yet they are rejected by the overwhelming majority of the inhabitants of the island of Ireland, by over 98 per cent of the voting population in the Republic and by at least 89 per cent of the voting population in the North of Ireland.

Secondly, the PIRA are doomed to fail because they have no viable democratic solution to the conflict between the Unionists and the Nationalists in the North. The PIRA claim to recognise the rights of Unionists, but in reality their only response to the adamant desire of the Unionists to maintain their British identity is the threat of unification at the point of a gun. The government of the Republic has formally declared its acceptance of the principle that the unification of Ireland could only take place with the consent of the one million Unionists of the North. The PIRA do not care a jot for the principle of consent or for the politics of bargaining and compromise which is the stuff of the real world of politics. In reality by their terrorism the PIRA have only increased polarisation and made the attainment of unification far more difficult, if not impossible.

The PIRA are so habituated to the savagery of the bomb and the bullet, so brutalised and criminalised by their bloody career of murder, maiming and destruction, that it seems somewhat unlikely that the movement will lay down their weapons of their own accord.

A far more likely long-term scenario is that they will ultimately be driven into "suspending operations" by the mounting hostility and outright rejection from the Catholic community. It is highly significant that Dr Cahal Daly, the new Primate of All Ireland, warned the PIRA at his installation ceremony:

"The longer you continue with your campaign of violence, the more ignominious in the end will be the memory you will leave behind you, and the further away from attainment will be any of your aims and objectives".

There is absolutely no doubt that if the leaders and members of the community on both sides of the Irish Sea continue to show clarity, courage and determination in combating the evil of terrorism the PIRA will become increasingly irrelevant and will ultimately be defeated.

### TABLE 1    DEATHS AS A RESULT OF SECURITY SITUATION
### *1969–1991*

|  | RUC | RUC 'R' | ARMY | UDR | CIVILIAN | TOTAL |
|---|---|---|---|---|---|---|
| 1969 | 1 | — | — | — | 12 | 13 |
| 1970 | 2 | — | — | — | 23 | 25 |
| 1971 | 11 | — | 43 | 5 | 115 | 174 |
| 1972 | 14 | 3 | 103 | 26 | 321 | 467 |
| 1973 | 10 | 3 | 58 | 8 | 171 | 250 |
| 1974 | 12 | 3 | 28 | 7 | 166 | 216 |
| 1975 | 7 | 4 | 14 | 6 | 216 | 247 |
| 1976 | 13 | 10 | 14 | 15 | 245 | 297 |
| 1977 | 8 | 6 | 15 | 14 | 69 | 112 |
| 1978 | 4 | 6 | 14 | 7 | 50 | 81 |
| 1979 | 9 | 5 | 38 | 10 | 51 | 113 |
| 1980 | 3 | 6 | 8 | 9 | 50 | 76 |
| 1981 | 13 | 8 | 10 | 13 | 57 | 101 |
| 1982 | 8 | 4 | 21 | 7 | 57 | 97 |
| 1983 | 9 | 9 | 5 | 10 | 44 | 77 |
| 1984 | 7 | 2 | 9 | 10 | 36 | 64 |
| 1985 | 14 | 9 | 2 | 4 | 25 | 54 |
| 1986 | 10 | 2 | 4 | 8 | 37 | 61 |
| 1987 | 9 | 7 | 3 | 8 | 66 | 93 |
| 1988 | 4 | 2 | 21 | 12 | 54 | 93 |
| 1989 | 7 | 2 | 12 | 2 | 39 | 62 |
| 1990 | 7 | 5 | 7 | 8 | 49 | 76 |
| 1991 to 13 Oct | 5 | 1 | 3 | 6 | 52 | 67 |
| TOTAL | 187 | 97 | 432 | 195 | 2005 | 2196 |

*Northern Ireland: Reappraising Republican Violence* 23

**TABLE 2    INJURIES AS A RESULT OF SECURITY SITUATION**

*1968–1991*

|  | *RUC* | *ARMY* | *UDR* | *CIVILIAN* |
|---|---|---|---|---|
| 1968 | 379 | — | — | — |
| 1969 | 711 | 54 | — | — |
| 1970 | 191 | 620 | — | — |
| 1971 | 315 | 381 | 9 | 1887 |
| 1972 | 485 | 542 | 36 | 3813 |
| 1973 | 291 | 525 | 23 | 1812 |
| 1974 | 235 | 453 | 30 | 1680 |
| 1975 | 263 | 151 | 16 | 2044 |
| 1976 | 303 | 242 | 22 | 2162 |
| 1977 | 183 | 172 | 15 | 1017 |
| 1978 | 302 | 127 | 8 | 548 |
| 1979 | 165 | 132 | 21 | 557 |
| 1980 | 194 | 53 | 24 | 530 |
| 1981 | 332 | 112 | 28 | 878 |
| 1982 | 99 | 80 | 18 | 328 |
| 1983 | 142 | 66 | 22 | 280 |
| 1984 | 267 | 64 | 22 | 513 |
| 1985 | 415 | 20 | 13 | 468 |
| 1986 | 622 | 45 | 10 | 773 |
| 1987 | 246 | 92 | 12 | 780 |
| 1988 | 218 | 211 | 18 | 600 |
| 1989 | 163 | 175 | 15 | 606 |
| 1990 | 214 | 190 | 24 | 478 |
| 1991 to 30 Sept | 112 | 123 | 44 | 367 |
| TOTAL | 6847 | 4630 | 434 | 24,121 |

24                    *Research Institute for the Study of Conflict and Terrorism*

*TABLE 3*            ***SECURITY SITUATION STATISTICS***

***1969–1991***

| | *SHOOTINGS* | *DEVICES USED (Explosions & Defusings)* | *ARMED ROBBERIES* |
|---|---|---|---|
| **1969** | 73 | 10 | — |
| **1970** | 213 | 170 | — |
| **1971** | 1756 | 1515 | 489 |
| **1972** | 10,628 | 1853 | 1931 |
| **1973** | 5018 | 1520 | 1317 |
| **1974** | 3206 | 1113 | 1353 |
| **1975** | 1803 | 635 | 1325 |
| **1976** | 1908 | 1192 | 889 |
| **1977** | 1081 | 535 | 676 |
| **1978** | 755 | 633 | 493 |
| **1979** | 728 | 564 | 504 |
| **1980** | 642 | 400 | 467 |
| **1981** | 1142 | 529 | 689 |
| **1982** | 547 | 332 | 693 |
| **1983** | 424 | 367 | 718 |
| **1984** | 334 | 248 | 710 |
| **1985** | 237 | 215 | 542 |
| **1986** | 392 | 254 | 839 |
| **1987** | 674 | 384 | 955 |
| **1988** | 537 | 458 | 742 |
| **1989** | 566 | 420 | 604 |
| **1990** | 559 | 287 | 492 |
| **1991** to 30 Sept | 369 | 276 | 432 |
| **TOTAL** | 33,592 | 13,910 | 16,680 |

## TABLE 4   PERSONS CHARGED WITH TERRORIST OFFENCES

### *1972–1991*

| | |
|---|---|
| From 31.7.1972 | 531 |
| 1973 | 1418 |
| 1974 | 1374 |
| 1975 | 1197 |
| 1976 | 1276 |
| 1977 | 1308 |
| 1978 | 843 |
| 1979 | 670 |
| 1980 | 550 |
| 1981 | 918 |
| 1982 | 686 |
| 1983 | 613 |
| 1984 | 528 |
| 1985 | 522 |
| 1986 | 655 |
| 1987 | 468 |
| 1988 | 439 |
| 1989 | 433 |
| 1990 | 380 |
| 1991 to 30 Sept | 280 |
| **TOTAL** | **15,089** |

*TABLE 5*        *FIREARMS AND EXPLOSIVES FINDS*

*1969–1991*

| | FIREARMS | EXPLOSIVES (TONS) |
|---|---|---|
| 1969 | 14 | 0.1 |
| 1970 | 324 | 0.3 |
| 1971 | 716 | 1.2 |
| 1972 | 1259 | 18.5 |
| 1973 | 1313 | 17.2 |
| 1974 | 1236 | 11.7 |
| 1975 | 820 | 4.9 |
| 1976 | 736 | 9.7 |
| 1977 | 563 | 1.7 |
| 1978 | 393 | 0.9 |
| 1979 | 300 | 0.9 |
| 1980 | 203 | 0.8 |
| 1981 | 357 | 3.4 |
| 1982 | 288 | 2.3 |
| 1983 | 166 | 1.7 |
| 1984 | 187 | 3.8 |
| 1985 | 173 | 3.3 |
| 1986 | 174 | 2.4 |
| 1987 | 206 | 5.8 |
| 1988 | 489 | 4.7 |
| 1989 | 246 | 1.4 |
| 1990 | 179 | 1.9 |
| 1991 to 30 Sept | 116 | 3.8 |
| **TOTAL** | **10,458** | **102.4** |

*TABLE 6    NOTIFIABLE OFFENCES KNOWN AND CLEARED*

*1969–1990*

|      | *KNOWN* | *CLEARED* | *DETECTION RATE* |
|------|---------|-----------|------------------|
| 1969 | 20,303  | 8732      | 43               |
| 1970 | 24,810  | 10,069    | 40.6             |
| 1971 | 30,828  | 9822      | 31.9             |
| 1972 | 35,884  | 7525      | 21               |
| 1973 | 32,057  | 8850      | 27.6             |
| 1974 | 33,314  | 9676      | 29               |
| 1975 | 37,239  | 7771      | 20.9             |
| 1976 | 39,779  | 9367      | 23.5             |
| 1977 | 45,335  | 9940      | 21.9             |
| 1978 | 45,335  | 10,535    | 23.2             |
| 1979 | 54,262  | 11,308    | 20.8             |
| 1980 | 56,316  | 14,391    | 25.6             |
| 1981 | 62,496  | 16,802    | 26.9             |
| 1982 | 62,020  | 11,768    | 19               |
| 1983 | 63,984  | 17,775    | 27.8             |
| 1984 | 66,779  | 20,491    | 30.7             |
| 1985 | 64,584  | 22,581    | 35               |
| 1986 | 68,255  | 25,336    | 37.1             |
| 1987 | 63,860  | 27,743    | 43.4             |
| 1988 | 55,890  | 25,226    | 45.1             |
| 1989 | 55,147  | 23,808    | 43.2             |
| 1990 | 57,198  | 21,475    | 37.5             |

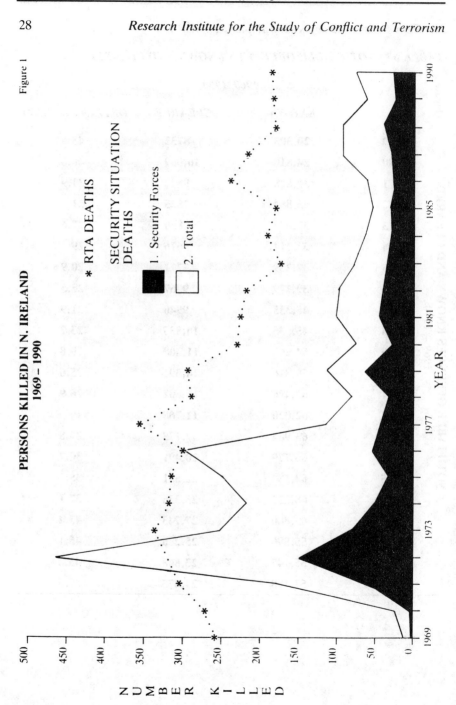

Figure 1

PERSONS KILLED IN N. IRELAND
1969 – 1990

* RTA DEATHS

SECURITY SITUATION
DEATHS

1. Security Forces

2. Total

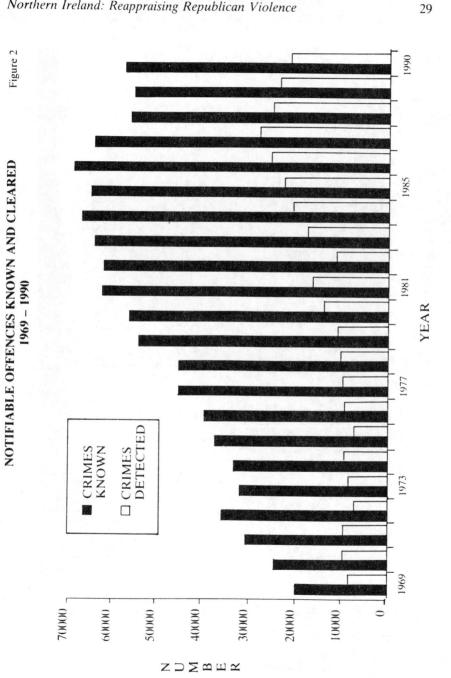

Figure 2

NOTIFIABLE OFFENCES KNOWN AND CLEARED
1969 – 1990

CRIMES KNOWN
CRIMES DETECTED

# [8]

# Northern Ireland: Reappraising Loyalist Violence

## Steve Bruce

1991 was the 25th anniversary of loyalist paramilitary activity in the present Ulster Troubles. It was also the year of a significant resurgence of loyalist violence.[1] In the early years of the present Northern Ireland conflict, between 1972 and the end of 1976, loyalist paramilitaries killed just over 500 people but in 1977 the campaign of retaliatory murder was all but abandoned; in the next 12 years, loyalists averaged between 12 and 13 victims per year. However, in 1991 loyalists claimed 39 victims by the end of November and a brief description of some of those murders is a good place to start a study of the Ulster Volunteer Force (UVF) and the Ulster Defence Association (UDA).

The 1991 murders are typical of loyalist attacks in coming in three types. First there are the retaliatory killings of easy targets, people selected simply because of their ethnic identity and the ease of attacking them: a Falls Road shopkeeper, six taxi drivers. Often the targets are especially easy because they are "out of place", Catholics in Protestant areas. A Catholic woman and her son were killed when loyalists petrol-bombed their home in the predominantly Protestant suburb of Glengormley. A Catholic workman on a site in a Protestant area was shot dead. Then there are those that more narrowly represent retaliation, where the murder has obvious parallels with an IRA action. So after the IRA murdered a Protestant businessman, the Mid-Ulster UVF murdered two young girls serving in a Catholic mobile shop on a Catholic housing estate in Craigavon. Thirdly, there were a number of attacks on active republicans. The Mid-Ulster UVF murdered a man who had served a sentence for an arms offence and the Belfast UVF killed a leader of the Irish People's Liberation Organization (IPLO) in the Divis area. The UFF murdered two Sinn Fein councillors (one across the border in Buncrana) and two Sinn Fein members.

But in addition to stepping up their murder campaign, the UVF and UFF also produced a surprising political initiative when they announced a cease-fire for the duration of the Secretary of State's summer talks with the major political parties. Although very few commentators paid any attention to the joint statement, it was interesting in offering support for some sort of accommodation with the Catholic minority in Northern Ireland, provided devolution was accompanied by an end to any role for the Dublin government. The paramilitaries thus took up a position more accommodating than that of many Unionist politicians. However, and this is another important theme, nobody took much notice. Although by their increase in murder and then by their truce, the UVF and UDA had forced themselves back into the attention of local politicians, journalists and the general public, they could not force anyone to take their political innovations seriously.

1

2                    *Research Institute for the Study of Conflict and Terrorism*

## 1. A BRIEF HISTORY OF LOYALIST PARAMILITARISM

The first "Ulster Volunteer Force" was formed in 1912. When it became clear that a British government would give independence or "home rule" to Ireland, the Protestants of Ulster and elsewhere began to mobilise against the home rule movement and as part of that mobilisation a popular and probably illegal army – the Ulster Volunteer Force (UVF) – was raised.[2] The UVF was a well-organised mass movement (well over 200,000 people joined it), commanded by the Ulster aristocracy, and trained by retired British army officers in the gardens of stately homes. For a year it drilled and planned and organised without any significant number of weapons but on 24 April 1914, a consignment of 20,000 rifles and matching ammunition was brought into Larne harbour and distributed; the UVF was now a real army. Rebellion was averted by the arrival of the First World War. The British army badly wanted to enlist the UVF and unionist politicians were able to extract as concessions the principles that the Force should be kept together and that constitutional change should be postponed until the end of the war. As the 36th (Ulster) Division, the men of the UVF fought gallantly and died in their droves at the battle of the Somme. After the war the British government accepted the unionist case and partitioned the island, giving independence to three-quarters but allowing Ulster to remain in the United Kingdom.

In 1920 and 1921 there was considerable violence in the north as republicans fought against partition.[3] Protestants began to reorganise the old UVF units as a peace-keeping vigilante movement. Once again there was elite support (the Fermanagh Volunteer Force was raised by Sir Basil Brooke, later Lord Brookeborough) and once again these units were incorporated in the crown forces, this time as a part-time or "B" element in the Ulster Special Constabulary.[4]

It is a common but mistaken view that Northern Ireland was then at peace until the present wave of violence. There were sectarian riots in the 1930s. In 1942, the IRA killed three RUC officers and two B Specials. In its 1957–61 campaign the IRA killed six RUC officers. If one is to understand loyalist reactions to reform in the late 1960s, it is important to realise that, while insignificant in the context of what was to come, these campaigns did enough to remind Protestants of the future that Irish nationalism offered them. At the start of the Troubles loyalists may have exaggerated the threat of the IRA but they did not invent it out of thin air. In 1912 and 1920, Protestant militias were formed and then incorporated in the state's security forces. The disturbances of the 1930s, '40s and '50s did not see a recreation of the UVF because the security forces were widely perceived as able to contain the threat and there were not corresponding changes within the Unionist government of Northern Ireland that could be seen as imminent capitulation to republicanism.

The present revival of paramilitarism has its origins in militant loyalist reaction to the tentative reforms of the premiership of Terence O'Neill. Ian Paisley, at that time little known outside the world of evangelical missions and gospel halls, stimulated concern that O'Neill was "selling out" Ulster and organised his Ulster Protestant Volunteers (UPV), a name clearly chosen to

*Northern Ireland: Reappraising Loyalist Violence*     3

show continuity with the original UVF.[5] Although officially the UPV confined itself to marching and obstructing marches, some of its members, impressed more by the possibility of the IRA becoming active again than by the then lack of IRA activity, collected weapons and blew up a number of public utilities in the hope that the explosions would be blamed on the IRA and hence would dramatise Dr Paisley's claims about the consequences of O'Neillism. The scheme worked.

UPV members were also involved in re-forming the UVF. Of a number of groups who assembled under the UVF banner in 1966, the most active was that made up mostly of ex-servicemen Shankill Road loyalists, led by Augustus 'Gusty' Spence. That group drilled, collected weapons, and practised taking up positions to defend loyalist areas of the city. It also robbed a few shops and an armoury, murdered a drunk Catholic man who was overheard singing republican songs, and then shot at and killed a young Catholic barman leaving a pub off the Shankill Road. The UVF was banned and Spence and his colleagues were sentenced to very long jail terms.

Although popular with a small core of the Belfast working class, Spence's "team" drew little support from the wider Protestant community and was firmly denounced by the middle classes and by religious leaders. He lingered in prison, unheeded, from 1966 until 1970 when the increase in violence and the instability which followed the civil rights movement gradually led many loyalists to suppose that Gusty had been right all along; the Catholics had been plotting once again to overthrow the government and drag Ulster into a united Ireland. The UVF began to grow and its members started killing.

Apart from a brief period in 1974–75 when the government was encouraging loyalist paramilitaries to abandon violence for politics, the UVF has always been illegal, small and secretive. The more public face of paramilitarism was provided by the Ulster Defence Association (UDA), which grew out of a variety of vigilante groups. In 1970 and subsequently, there was a massive eruption of violence. There was rioting every night. For six months the IRA planted large bombs inside or outside pubs used by Protestants or in cars in busy city streets (there were 153 explosions in 1970, almost all of them in Belfast). There was constant sniper fire from Catholic ghettos into Protestant streets and vice-versa (the police recorded 213 shooting incidents in 1970; the following year it was 1,756).

In almost all working class areas of Belfast, men formed vigilante groups to blockade their streets and keep out the enemy. Each protected a small area of five or six streets; so there was the Woodvale Defence Association, the Shankill Defence Association, the Hammer Defence Association, the East Belfast Defence Association, the Roden Street Defenders and so on. These were genuinely popular movements, often involving all the able-bodied men in the area. Here it is worth noting the difference in the distribution of the sense of threat. In 1912 and 1920, all classes of Ulster Protestants supported vigilante action because there was a widespread sense that something valued by all Ulster Protestants was being threatened. Although the political implications of the civil rights movement and the republican challenge to the state reached all sections of Ulster unionism, the middle classes in 1970 were largely

4                    *Research Institute for the Study of Conflict and Terrorism*

absent from the vigilante response, which came only from the residents of those areas in the "front line" of sectarian conflict.

Many of the activists were already acquainted through the UVF, the UPV, the Orange Order or the Unionist party. Meetings held to recruit members also served to bring the leaders together and in the summer of 1971 the various groups merged to form the Ulster Defence Association. Not long after formation, it was re-structured on military lines, with each area being a brigade, sub-divided into companies: for example, the Shankill Defence Association became A company of the West Belfast brigade, the Woodvale Defence Association became B company and the outlying Protestant estates of Highfield and Glencairn became C company.

Although the original purpose was "defence", from the start there were many people who advocated taking the fight to the enemy. At one vigilante group meeting, an ex-soldier gave an impassioned address, arguing that, unarmed, the vigilantes were just sitting ducks. He should have known: he had tried to murder vigilantes in Catholic areas from a fast moving car. UDA men, often operating under the cover name of the Ulster Freedom Fighters, took to bombing Catholic pubs and murdering randomly chosen Catholics. Often such attacks would be justified with the claim that the victim was in the IRA but the reality was that loyalists had no more idea who was in the IRA than the IRA had of who was in the UVF or UDA. People were killed simply because they were Catholics and were, by virtue of walking home late at night or driving a taxi for a Catholic firm, available. The reasoning was that, if they were not IRA men, then they supported the IRA or wanted the same thing as the IRA, which was to kill Protestants, so Protestants should kill them first.[6]

TABLE 1.   *Victims of republican and loyalist paramilitaries, 1969–89*

| Status of victim | Republican No. | % | Loyalist No. | % |
|---|---|---|---|---|
| Security forces | 847 | 52.7 | 10 | 1.4 |
| Republican paramilitaries | 146 | 9.1 | 21 | 3.0 |
| Loyalist paramilitaries | 18 | 1.1 | 40 | 5.7 |
| Civilians | | | | |
|    Catholic | 173 | 10.8 | 506 | 71.8 |
|    Protestant | 379 | 23.6 | 14 | 16.2 |
|    Other | 22 | 1.4 | 12 | 1.7 |
| Prison officers | 23 | 1.4 | 2 | 0.3 |
| TOTAL | 1,608 | 100.1 | 705 | 100.1 |

*Source*: Adapted from Irish Information Partnership. *Agenda: Information Service on Northern Ireland and Anglo–Irish Relations* (6th edn., London, 1990), 295.

There is always a problem in knowing who to believe in the arguments over the status of victims. Criminal damages compensation is not given to the families of those who have "brought their own fate" on themselves by being active in a paramilitary organisation, which gives all groups a good reason to

*Northern Ireland: Reappraising Loyalist Violence* 5

deny that the victim was one of their own people if they can get away with the denial. There is also the purpose of denying the murderers the propaganda value of a "good hit". It may be a year or more before a paramilitary organisation claims a victim as one of its own (by for example listing him on a memorial plaque). To give an example, when the UVF killed Liam Ryan in a bar in Ardboe, the IRA denied that he was a member but over a year later, *Republican News* printed a photograph of a colour party firing a salute over the grave of Volunteer Ryan.[7] But even if we contest 20 or 30 identifications, the broad sweep of the figures compiled by the Irish Information Partnership seems reliable, and, as we can see from Table 1, republican paramilitaries form only a very small proportion of the victims of loyalist violence. 71.8 per cent were "Civilian Catholics" and even allowing for a number of cases of covert involvement, at least half the victims of the UDA and UVF were ordinary Catholics. If they were to be cold bloodied about this, the paramilitaries could describe the sectarian murder campaign as "successful" in that it frightened a lot of Catholics and "makes the fuckers appreciate the cost of not getting rid of the IRA", as one man put it. If the purpose is simply to terrorise or to exact communal revenge, then it succeeded. However, very few loyalist paramilitaries' leaders defined their goals in those terms and for good reasons: it would be quite at odds with their self-image as being, in contrast to republicans, decent law-abiding and reluctant soldiers.

The IRA also fails to live up to its self-image. A large proportion of its victims do not fall into its own categories of "legitimate targets". Nonetheless, the IRA proportionately kills more members of the security forces and representatives of the British state than the UDA and UVF do leading republicans. But one needs to be careful of the contrast. If we say that the IRA are better at killing the targets they have selected, this could mean (a) that they are more skilled or (b) that they can choose from a wider range of targets which are easier to hit. Both of these seem to be the case.

Taking the second point first, an anti-state terrorist organisation has a relatively easy job in identifying and finding its targets. The agents of the state – the police and the army – must be identified by their uniforms. Indeed, far from being able to merge into the background, they have to stand out and be visible; a large part of their purpose is not so much to do anything as to be seen. They represent, in their visible persons, the continuity and security of the state. Although small units can, for particular purposes, disguise themselves (the E4A RUC units or the SAS), the bulk of the security forces have to be seen in order to be doing their jobs.

Furthermore, the range of people who can be defined by an anti-state organisation as "legitimate targets" is extremely wide. Not only the security forces but anyone who assists them can, with varying degrees of acceptance by the supporting population, be a target. Where, as in the Ulster case, one has a majority population who are not just acquiescent but active supporters of the status quo, there is a huge population of legitimate targets. First it is policemen who are killed when their station is mortared. Then it is the builders who accept the contracts to rebuild those stations. Then it is public utility engineers who repair services to the stations. Finally, the IRA adds the men who deliver the bread and the milk. When one includes those who do not refuse to serve members of the security forces (the owners of the Dropping Well pub in Ballykelly, for example) then one has defined almost all Protestants (with the possible general exception of women and children) as "legitimate targets". Even old age does not exclude someone if they have been earlier in their lives in any sense active in support of the status quo.

The UDA and UVF have a much narrower target to aim at. In their own theory they must confine themselves to attacking anti-state terrorists and those who actively support them. Such people are hard to find. Unlike the targets of the IRA, who have to put themselves on show, the majority of the "legitimate" targets of the UDA and UVF – IRA gunmen – keep themselves hidden. Even the public fronts – Sinn Fein politicians, for example – are better hidden than people playing a similar role in the majority community. Even without their taking active steps to avoid loyalist assassination, such people are harder to find because they generally stay in the bosom of the minority (and hence small, introverted, and secretive) population. It is noticeable that the rise of popular IRA fronts (such as the National H Block Committee) and Sinn Fein has been accompanied by an increase in accuracy of loyalist murders.

The response of the loyalist gunmen in such a situation was to maintain the martial rhetoric and engage in random sectarian killings. To an extent, this reduced the popularity of the UDA and UVF within their own communities and exacerbated problems of morale, fund-raising, and recruitment. That this is seen as a problem by the paramilitaries is clear from the frequent apologies for the past and promises to do better that are made in the UDA's *Ulster* or the UVF's *Combat*. What makes random anti-Catholic violence damaging to the public standing of loyalist paramilitaries is the contrast between those actions and the martial rhetoric which is so important a part of their claims to legitimate descent from the 1912 UVF. Carson's UVF did not have "romper rooms"[8], Lenny Murphy[9] (whose Shankill Road gang committed a very large number of gruesome murders with knifes and hatchets), or the east Belfast gang which left bodies by the Connswater river. However, one should not exaggerate the problem. One cannot quantify it but some working class loyalists do appear quite happy with sectarian murder. The 1991 Christmas edition of *Red Hand* (a magazine which encourages Scottish support for the UVF's Loyalist Prisoner's Welfare Association) happily listed Lenny Murphy in a list of UVF heroes. Just as the IRA's core support seems indifferent to its "mistakes", so there is a loyalist core which thinks "the only good Taig's a dead Taig" but it is very small.

People do not respond to the objective reality of a situation; they respond to their perceptions of that reality and perceptions can be shaped. Whether a particular murder is legitimate or not is in the end a matter of competing rhetorics. Each side tries to persuade its public to accept its definition of the situation. Large parts of the Catholic population are not receptive to government definitions of the situation. Although not uncritical of their "defenders", their general disposition is to be more favourable towards the IRA's own interpretations of its actions than to the government's interpretations. The UDA and UVF compete with the agencies of the state they claim to defend. Their natural support base is receptive to the views of the government. The IRA finds it easier than do the UDA and UVF to persuade its people that sectarian assassination campaigns are necessary evils of a just war.

Let us turn from the nature of the victims of loyalist violence to a consideration of its frequency. The murder rate is an extremely complicated outcome of many decisions and actions. When the total amount of activity is small, the competence of the assassins can make all the difference between 20 and 40 victims. Teams may be more and less active as their leaders are arrested and released. It is clearly possible for the leadership of the UVF and UDA to dampen down their members' ardour for killing and they may do so for personal and for political reasons. In trying to explain the general pattern of loyalist activity, I want to suggest three phases. The defence of provocation is so commonly used that we should always be suspicious of people who claim their action is a response to the evil doing of others. Nonetheless, in this case it does seem that republican and loyalist aggression were closely related and that, as one can see in Figure 1, the surge of republican activity comes *before* the increase in loyalist killing.[10] The rise of large-scale loyalist paramilitarism (as distinct from Spence's vanguard operations) was a response to republicanism. There was then a lengthy lull before the increase of 1991, which will be discussed below.

**The 1974 Strike and After**

The highpoint for the paramilitaries was the 1974 Ulster Workers Council (UWC) constitutional stoppage or general strike. The British government had devised a form of power-sharing in which the Social Democratic and Labour Party, as representatives of the Catholic people, would be guaranteed a number of cabinet positions and thus a share of power. The scheme was accepted by Brian Faulkner, the leader of the Unionist party and the last Prime Minister of Northern Ireland but opposed by many within his own party (who either joined Bill Craig in his Vanguard Party or identified themselves as "Official" Unionists) and by Ian Paisley's Democratic Unionists. In addition to such constitutional actions as fighting and winning elections on an anti-powersharing slate, unionists accepted the offer of the UDA and their allies in the trade union movement to use the industrial muscle of the Protestant working class to bring the province to its knees with a general strike.[11]

The strike was more effective than anyone imagined. UDA and UVF men blocked all the main roads of the province and made movement very difficult. Those people who could get to work round the barriers found they were wasting their time because the electricity workers reduced power to a level where only emergency supplies to hospitals could be guaranteed and all industrial production was stopped. The dockers closed the ports and prevented the import of food, coal, and agricultural feed. After 10 days the power-sharing executive had no choice but to resign. From that high point of being

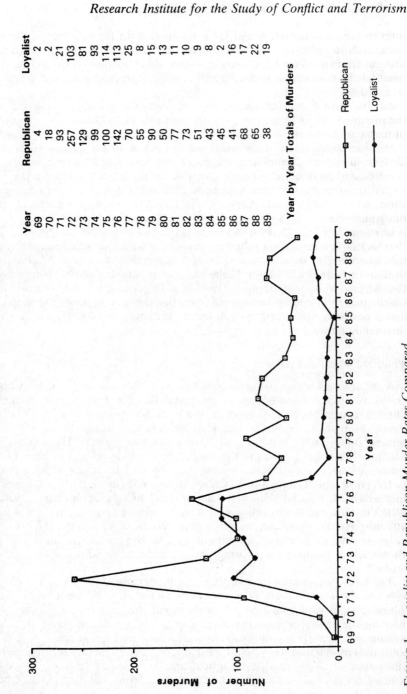

**Republican and Loyalist Murder Rates Compared**

| Year | Republican | Loyalist |
|------|------------|----------|
| 69 | 4 | 2 |
| 70 | 18 | 2 |
| 71 | 93 | 21 |
| 72 | 257 | 103 |
| 73 | 129 | 81 |
| 74 | 99 | 93 |
| 75 | 100 | 114 |
| 76 | 142 | 113 |
| 77 | 70 | 25 |
| 78 | 55 | 8 |
| 79 | 90 | 15 |
| 80 | 50 | 13 |
| 81 | 77 | 11 |
| 82 | 73 | 10 |
| 83 | 51 | 9 |
| 84 | 43 | 8 |
| 85 | 45 | 2 |
| 86 | 41 | 16 |
| 87 | 68 | 17 |
| 88 | 65 | 22 |
| 89 | 38 | 19 |

Year by Year Totals of Murders

Republican

Loyalist

Number of Murders

Year

FIGURE 1. *Loyalist and Republican Murder Rates Compared*

able to veto a government initiative the paramilitaries went into something of a decline. Although unionist politicians willingly benefited from their muscle, the paramilitaries were given no reward. Once the dust settled they were less rather than more influential because the politicians closed ranks to freeze them out. Indeed, this was partly an ironic consequence of the strike itself. By putting an end to a scheme for devolution, it removed politics from the province and sent them back to Westminster, where the unionist members of parliament had a (very small) voice but the loyalists had none.

Second, the security forces began to get on top of the violence. The RUC underwent a massive reorganisation and expansion after 1976 and gradually became a highly effective and well-trained force. Intelligence gathering improved so that large numbers of terrorists, loyalist as well as nationalist, could be put in court and convicted. This disrupted the loyalist organisations but more importantly the general improvement in the security situation reduced Protestant support for paramilitary initiatives. As one UDA brigadier put it:

"Once the police started to get on top of it our support just dropped. When they saw that the RUC and the UDR [Ulster Defence Regiment] was willing to take on the IRA and the bombings pretty well stopped, well, what's an east Belfast Prod going to think? That he needs us?"[12]

An attempt in 1977 to repeat the 1974 strike failed miserably. In trying to find a new role for the UDA, Glen Barr, who had led the UWC strike but then fallen out with Supreme Commander Andy Tyrie, was invited back and given the remit of developing his ideas for negotiated independence into a distinctive political platform, which he did but none of the major parties took it up and internal suspicion of Barr's proposals led to him again resigning.

Although the Ulster Loyalist Democratic Party was formed, the UDA gradually lost its ambitions to develop a significant political and social presence. The UDA and UVF both reduced their activities to a low-level but fairly steady campaign of retaliatory murder. As the number of killings fell, so they became slightly more selective, although tit-for-tat sectarian killing remained a feature of the work of both organisations.

In recent years there has been a wholesale clear-out at the top of the UDA. In December 1987, John McMichael, who was both commander of the UFF and political spokesman for the UDA, was killed by the Provisional IRA (PIRA). Two weeks later, Davey Payne, brigadier of North Belfast UDA, was arrested while leading a procession of Ford Granadas stuffed with weapons. The mid-Ulster brigadier was charged with extortion after falling for television reporter Roger Cook pretending to be a building contractor. Andy Tyrie, Supreme Commander for 16 years, resigned after failing to win a vote of confidence in his leadership. Shortly after, those who took over were themselves removed, either arrested during police investigations into collusion between paramilitaries and the security forces[13] or pushed out by their own members. Only half of those now running the brigades held any position in 1974. The new leadership has all but abandoned any social or political agenda and in recent newspaper interviews has shown a new willingness to accept the designation "terrorist".[14] The UDA, which is now little more than the UFF, is almost indistinguishable from the UVF.

In contrast to that of the UDA, the central command of the UVF has seen few changes since the late 1970s. Although the chief of staff was in prison for a number of years in the early 1980s during the "supergrass" trials, he was restored to office on his release. Not surprising given its different origins, the UVF has been less involved than the UDA in developing an alternative loyalist political agenda but it too reduced its level of violence considerably after 1977 so that, until the upsurge of 1991, it seemed almost to be maintaining itself on a "care and maintenance" basis.

## 2. POLITICS AND SOCIAL WORK

Unlike the IRA, which was able to translate the nationalist response to the hunger strikes into electoral success for Sinn Fein, the UDA and UVF have not been successful in building a political party or a network of community groups to solidify the base of support for the paramilitary action.

This is not for want of trying. During his time in command of UVF prisoners in Long Kesh, Gusty Spence tried hard to encourage them to learn about the history and politics of their country and developed his own rather radical approach to the Ulster crisis (which might be briefly described as allowing Northern Catholics a fair share of power and responsibility but maintaining the bar on any Dublin involvement) but most of his words fell on deaf ears. For a period in the early 1970s brigade staff did not even bother replying to Spence's letters from prison. When policy positions were taken, it was often without consulting the membership. Rather than starting with a policy and then attracting members, the UVF's short-lived 1975 Volunteer Party enrolled its members and then asked them if they had any policies.

The UDA had a better chance of developing a political agenda. Many of its early leaders had been trade union activists or community leaders. They were influential (but not as influential as they would have liked to have been) in Craig's Vanguard Party and under Glen Barr and Harry Chicken the New Ulster Political Research Group produced well thought out proposals for negotiated independence for Ulster in *Beyond the Religious Divide* (1978). Barr was always aware that the reputation of the UDA was such that his initiative could only succeed if taken up by mainstream politicians and negotiated independence failed to attract such support. Worse, it was criticised by senior figures within the UDA as being too radical a departure from traditional unionism.[15] John McMichael, who played a major part in pushing Barr out of the UDA, re-presented some of the ideas in more acceptably unionist clothes in *Common Sense* (full independence became commonwealth status) but by then the trade union and community activist element had mostly defected to conventional unionist parties and McMichael's electoral performance (in a Westminster by-election in February 1982 he won just 2 per cent of the unionist vote) was miserable. In the response to the Anglo–Irish inter-governmental accord of 1985, McMichael mistakenly saw an opportunity for the UDA to combine with working class Unionists and Democratic Unionists in a new grass-roots political organisation but any such opportunity for broadening the paramilitary organisation was ruined by the actions of UDA men in confronting the police during demonstrations against the Accord and in burning RUC officers out of their homes in what had previously been safe Protestant areas. By the late 1980s, most people in the UDA had come to the UVF's conclusion that the paramilitary organisations could not provide an alternative to mainstream unionist parties.

One can see another important aspect of the competition between paramilitaries and mainstream unionism in the contrast between loyalist and republican literature. While the republican movement is supported by a literature of ideological writing, biography and poetry, there is almost nothing comparable on the loyalist side. A potential IRA recruit could read the works of Gerry Adams or Bobby Sands. What would a potential UVF man read? However slim the chances of the IRA succeeding in its mission, it has a goal which is clear and which is minimally consistent with republicanism's past. It has to compete with constitutional nationalism and although it loses in that competition its cause remains clear enough. It can call on the whole history of nationalism to serve as a focus for political action. The history and literature that the UVF and UDA want to use to justify their struggle has already been taken over by the state and by the mainstream. Although the UDA and UVF can argue that the Orange Order and the unionist parties are betraying the symbols of unionist history by not supporting the men whose "only crime was loyalty" (and there have been regular disputes between the paramilitaries and the mainstream over those symbols) they cannot as successfully claim such symbols for themselves as the IRA can with the Easter Rising and other touchstones of Irish nationalism.

A similar principle of competition with the state allows us to see why the loyalist paramilitaries have been less successful than the IRA in using various forms of community action to build popular support. The only times the UDA and UVF have been obviously good at community action were when civil unrest prevented Protestant people using the state's agencies: for example, when the "no go" areas or the UWC strike temporarily disrupted social services. The Catholic ghettoes that support the IRA are peopled by men and women who are almost permanently disaffected from the state and willing to participate in a variety of "community" activities (such as Irish language schools) which are at root minor forms of rejection of the state. Many residents of Ballymurphy and the Divis flats are unwilling to call on the RUC to police hooliganism and anti-social behaviour; there is therefore a space for the IRA to take on that role. The anti-state group can set itself up as an alternative "state" in those communities which are its support and in so far as it provides for their needs, it acquires additional support and legitimacy. The pro-state group is competing with the state itself: the UDA cannot set up "loyalist" schools.

When loyalist paramilitaries do offer themselves to the electorate on fairly conventional platforms, they are not generally well supported. As one UDA man who unsuccessfully stood for the Belfast city council a number of times put it:

"When the Taigs was running up the streets with guns, then I was the boy. Just the ticket. Come and save us. But when it settles down, it's thank you and goodbye. It comes to voting and the Protestant people would rather vote for some respectable wanker."

To summarise, modern societies have clear divisions of labour: policing is done by professional policemen, politics is done by political parties, the administration of justice is done by a legal system, and so on. Only in the extreme circumstances of, say, Lebanon, when civil society and its institutions collapse is that division of labour replaced by paramilitary organisations offering a variety of roles. That the worse expectations of the early 1970s were not fulfilled and the network of institutions that make up civil society did not collapse meant that there was still a full range of unionist political parties to pick from and hence plenty of "respectable wankers" for unionists to elect in preference to their self-appointed protectors. That the government continued to function in loyalist areas meant that there was little call for paramilitary organisations to supplant the operations of the state.

## 3. PARAMILITARIES AND THE SECURITY FORCES

We can distinguish between "anti-state" and "pro-state" terrorism. The IRA uses terror to attempt to destroy the state; the UVF and UDA use it to retaliate and thus seek to preserve the state. It is also possible for a state to use illegal violence and hence we need the category of "state terror". It is common for critics of British policy in Northern Ireland to claim that there is no meaningful distinction between the "pro-state" terror of the loyalist paramilitary organisations and the "state" terror of the crown forces. Relations between the paramilitaries and the security forces will now be considered.

The first point – and the one made by the critics – is that both recruit from the same population. Approximately 90 per cent of the RUC officers are Protestant[16] and despite it initially attracting Catholics, the Ulster Defence Regiment is now around 98 per cent Protestant.[17] Although the fact of crown forces and paramilitaries recruiting from the same population is often seen as being to the latter's advantage, one can make a better case for saying that it deprives the UDA and UVF of good recruits. If a working class Protestant wishes to do something positive to combat IRA terrorism, to safeguard his family, or to defend Ulster, he can join the police or the UDR. If he wishes to combine such a commitment with a full-time job, he can join the RUC Reserve or become a part-time UDR soldier. The police and the army are selective. Many of the people who might in only slightly altered circumstances have become competent operatives in loyalist paramilitary organisations have been siphoned off and thus, in comparison with the IRA, the UDA and UVF have a narrower base from which to recruit. There is no doubt that many UVF and UDA volunteers were motivated by a spirit of patriotism. Most of the early activists were ex-servicemen. Many early UDA commanders were trade union activists or community leaders who were pressed into paramilitary leadership by already occupying a leadership role within their communities. But there were also many who joined because of the opportunities for vicious thrills, excitement, easy money and prestige. The two types competed to define the ethos of the organisations and as popular support for paramilitarism declined, so the second sort came to the fore.

It is frequently claimed that the security forces regularly assist the UDA and UVF. Or, to be more precise, the same claims are frequently repeated. To evaluate such claims we can separate those cases (a) where the crown forces use the paramilitaries from those (b) in which the paramilitaries use the state forces. The most dramatic stories of security force assistance in loyalist murders come from just two ex-service sources – Fred Holroyd[18] and Colin Wallace[19] – whose evidence has been assessed by a number of competent and impartial analysts and found seriously wanting.[20] It seems that the claim for security force collusion with loyalists in this or that murder is made, not because there is any evidence, but because (a) critics of the security forces *expect* them to be colluding and (b) critics of loyalist paramilitaries suppose them incapable of organising anything more complicated than the simplest sectarian killing without professional help. The UDA and UVF wish to be seen as allies of the security forces, serving the same goal by different means. In order to claim legitimacy for their actions, they want wherever possible to show security force support (and their magazines *Ulster* and *Combat* have often made what they can of the very small number of convicted terrorists with a security force background). That so few claims for army or police assistance have been made by the UDA and UVF (either in the existing journalistic record or in my own interviews) strongly suggests a dearth of such assistance.

The one area in which there is clear evidence of collusion is in the passing to loyalists of security force intelligence on republicans and nationalists. Even here there are few cases (almost all involving low ranking British soldiers and part-time members of the UDR) and good reason to suppose they made little difference to the overall operational capacity of the loyalist terrorists. It is instructive to consider the recent case of Brian Nelson, who in January 1992 pleaded guilty to a number of serious crimes. Nelson was a Belfast UDA man who in 1973 was caught red-handed while kidnapping an educationally sub-normal and registered blind Catholic man who, had the UDA team not been stopped on their way from a loyalist club on the Shankill to the outskirts of Belfast, would have been yet another sectarian murder statistic. On release from prison Nelson became involved again in the UDA and volunteered his services to the army as a spy. In the late 1980s he served as the UDA's chief collector and compiler of information on potential murder targets and routinely passed on his information to army handlers. In at least two cases, planned UDA attacks were foiled by the security forces. According to Nelson, on only two occasions did his handlers provide him with information and one of those was in the context of dissuading him from trying to target a particular IRA activist.[21] When Nelson was arrested during the enquiry into security force collusion led by John Stevens, he was able to provide information that led to the arrest and conviction of a large number of UDA men. Although the Nelson case raises important issues of the morality of undercover operations, it is very difficult to construe it as a case of the army helping the UDA when Nelson provided regular briefings on the UDA and finally shopped his colleagues.

The rank and status of those crown force personnel who have helped the UDA and UVF is interesting. Almost all were of very low rank and/or short service and their unsuccessful careers suggest personality or behavioural problems. That is, these are people who left or were forced to resign because, for a variety of reasons, they were not very good soldiers or policemen. This should not be a surprise. Those people who are successful in any organisation or occupation and find it personally rewarding tend to become strongly committed to the ethos of the organisation and highly loyal to their colleagues. No matter what residual personal sympathies they may have for the cause of the people they grew up amongst, these are over-ridden by their commitment to their role as "soldier" or "policeman".

Links in the other direction – the UDA and UVF using the security forces – have been more important in that many loyalist paramilitaries have deliberately joined the UDR in order to gain access to training, weapons and intelligence and have then used those resources for their own purposes. One Belfast UFF commander was also a serving UDR man and in the mid-1970s the Mid-Ulster UVF had a number of members who were also in the UDR. However, it is important to move from weighing anecdotes to considering the statistical evidence of overall criminality and this does not support the general claim that the security forces have been of great assistance to the loyalist paramilitaries.

TABLE 2A.    *Conviction rates for scheduled offences, 1985–9*

| Offenders | Total | Rate per thousand |
|---|---|---|
| Civilian population | 2,662 | 5.9 |
| RUC | 6 | 0.9 |
| UDR | 29 | 9.1 |
| British army | 8 | 1.7 |

*Source*: Adapted from Irish Information Partnership, *Agenda: Information Service on Northern Ireland and Anglo–Irish Relations* (6th edn., London, 1990). table A7iv.

TABLE 2B.    *Adjusted conviction rates for scheduled offences, 1985–9*

| Offenders | Total | Rate per thousand |
|---|---|---|
| Male 18–35 civilian population | 2,600[a] | 23.0 |
| RUC | 6 | 0.9 |
| UDR | 29 | 9.1 |
| British army | 8 | 1.7 |

[a] Total estimated by removing known female and juvenile offenders.

The figures in Table 2 allow us to get some perspective on the issue. To generate a "rate" that can be used to compare the criminality of each group, the total number of convictions was divided by the average population of each group during the period. At first sight this seems sound but consider what we know about the sort of person who commits terrorist offences: they are almost

*Northern Ireland: Reappraising Loyalist Violence*     15

all young men. The British Army, RUC and UDR populations are almost all young men also, but the total civilian population which has been used to produce the "rate" includes all adults, male and female. One can hardly fault the RUC or UDR for not turning their young male members into retired women. A much more sensible comparison is of the terrorist crimes of young civilian men, RUC officers, UDR soldiers and British army soldiers and the figures in column B present such a comparison. We can now see that, far from being involved in more terrorism than the average civilian, UDR members are considerably *less likely* to be engaged in terrorist offences than are young male members of the public.

Curiously the major contribution of the state to the UDA and UVF has rarely been mentioned or discussed and that is in providing places in the armed forces *before* the "Troubles". Many of the older paramilitaries were ex-servicemen and brought to the first generation skills that were important in the commission of violence (the most effective country UDA unit was led by an ex-paratrooper) and a discipline that allowed the men imprisoned in Long Kesh to maintain a high degree of morale through their internment and imprisonment.

What is often missed from the many partisan discussions of this issue is any consideration of problems that recruiting from the same population as the security forces might cause for the UDA and UVF. The RUC and the British army have managed to insert their own personnel into the IRA and to 'turn' IRA activists. They have also used various "trawl" methods to build up very detailed profiles of republican areas. With far less effort, the security forces have been able to know what is going on in loyalist circles and been able to bring a group of perpetrators into the net.

Of course, the extent to which close ties to members of state security forces will be detrimental to pro-state terror groups depends on the attitude of the state to those groups. Through either an unwillingness to believe that Protestants did that sort of thing or an unwillingness to fight a war on two fronts, the security forces have at times been reluctant to act against loyalist paramilitaries. The first year of sectarian murders and the lack of a response to them anything like as vigorous as the army's Falls Road curfew would be an example, as was the inertia of the security forces during the 1974 strike. However, when the state does turn its attention to its pro-state terror groups, it can pursue them with far more success than anti-state groups, as we can see from the data in Table 3.

Under the headings "Loyalist" and "Republican", the number of murders committed by each side, and the number of people charged with murder (athough these generally related to the murders of previous years) are listed. There are weaknesses with this presentation. It would be more informative to know for what percentage of murders people were made amenable and to have data on convictions rather than charges because that would remove the possibility that there is a significant difference between loyalist and republican successes in turning a charge into a conviction. But the differences between the two sets of figures are so large that such considerations do not change the big picture. In all but two of the eight years, the number of loyalists charged

TABLE 3. *Policing efficacy, 1981–7*

| | Republican | | Loyalist | |
|---|---|---|---|---|
| Year | Political murders | Persons charged with murder | Political murders | Persons charged with murder |
| 1981 | 69 | 27 | 12 | 21 |
| 1982 | 71 | 32 | 13 | 18 |
| 1983 | 54 | 23 | 7 | 52 |
| 1984 | 40 | 36 | 7 | 5 |
| 1985 | 42 | 17 | 5 | 7 |
| 1986 | 41 | 5 | 14 | 7 |
| 1987 | 69 | 8 | 11 | 20 |
| TOTAL | 386 | 112 | 69 | 130 |

*Source*: RUC Information Office.

with murder was greater than the number of victims of loyalist murder and in those two, the totals were close. In the same period, the number of IRA personnel charged with murder was considerably less (often less than half) the total of victims. Or to describe the same data in another way: very similar numbers of loyalists and republicans were charged with murder but the republicans killed 386 people while loyalists killed only 69. To put it simply, the RUC is far more successful at making someone "amenable" for loyalist murders than it is for republican killings. The purges of the UDA leadership between 1988 and 1991 have reduced security force intelligence and permitted a greater level of loyalist paramilitary activity but we may suppose that the differences between loyalist and republican communities in terms of the ease with which they can be policed will continue.

Finally, it is worth noting that the various control strategies that have been so widely criticised for the infringement of basic civil liberties have been used as enthusiastically on loyalists as on nationalists. Although internment was initially conceived as a way of stopping republican terrorism, it was also used against loyalists when it proved difficult to build a convincing case for a normal prosecution. The "trial without jury" system of the Diplock courts was introduced after a number of cases in which juries returned implausible verdicts to free loyalist paramilitaries. Given that the police and the Crown Prosecution service can always offer a good reason for very lengthy periods of remand, we cannot go beyond a suspicion that there is often no great hurry to bring leading paramilitaries to court but "internment by remand", as its critics call it, seems as much a characteristic of loyalist paramilitary trials as republican ones. The first "supergrass" trial (in which large numbers of defendants were charged on the uncorroborated evidence of one person) was the 1974 trial of alleged east Belfast UFF men which depended on the word of Albert "Ginger" Baker. The second was the 1976 conviction of more than 20 east Antrim UVF men on the word of a UVF man turned informer.

*Northern Ireland: Reappraising Loyalist Violence* 17

Between 1981 and 1984, four UVF "supergrasses" allowed over 90 alleged UVF men to be charged with serious crimes. In one case, the informer retracted his evidence, in two the convictions were overturned on appeal, and in the fourth, the informer's evidence was dismissed in the first trial. The only convictions secured in the four trials were those of the informers and a handful of others who pleaded guilty at the start of their cases. Despite the legal failure of the "supergrass" system, it resulted in a large number of alleged UVF men being in custody for an average of two years (and some for longer as their release as one case collapsed was followed immediately by their arrest to be tried with the evidence of a subsequent informer). Whether the use of uncorroborated testimony was legally good or bad is not my concern. My point is that one cannot insist that the state has offered succour to loyalist paramilitaries and overlook the very many evidences of the state being perfectly happy to use the same methods to control loyalist violence as to try to stem republican violence.

## RACKETS

Paramilitary organisations are expensive. There are weapons to be bought, salaries of full-time officers to be paid, and prisoners and their families to be supported. Even when they were at their largest the UVF and UDA were not able to be survive on the voluntary donations of members and "rackets" of one sort or another have always played a part. From the start loyalist paramilitaries robbed banks and shops. They ran illegal drinking clubs and used the poor accounting systems of such clubs as a way of laundering bank robbery money.

Unlike the IRA, the UDA and UVF have almost no support outside the province for the very simple reason that any external population or government that wants to prevent republican violence will support the government and not the UDA or UVF. The reliance on rackets has brought two sorts of problem for the loyalist paramilitaries. First, it has fuelled internal conflict by creating many opportunities for self-enrichment or for the suspicion of self-enrichment. When money is raised by bank-robbing, extortion, prostitution, and the sale of drugs and pornography, the flow of money cannot be controlled by good accounts and skilled accountants. One has a cash economy and large sums of cash create the temptation for some of it to stick to the fingers of those who raise it. Some leaders tried to reduce the scope for fiddling: "I never handled big sums of money. When we need money to buy 'toys' and 'sweets' like, I instructed the company commanders to raise so much by such a date", which protected him but still relied on the integrity of the company commanders. A climate of perpetual suspicion was created. As a senior figure said: "If I get killed they'll say I took the money and that's yer own people". There is no doubt that many senior paramilitary figures did take the money. Throughout the 1980s, Jimmy Craig, who had been the UDA boss in Long Kesh, ran a building site protection racket that netted hundreds of thousands a year and was only ended when his own people decided that he was too much of a liability and killed him. As well as causing constant friction within the organisations, the rackets made it very easy for the police and the media to portray the UDA and UVF as unprincipled gangsters, often in cahoots with their supposed republican enemies.

That both the UDA and UVF have periodically promised to end gangsterism shows that they see such deviations from their preferred self-images as armies of principled soldiers as damaging. In a reflective mood, a very senior UVF man told me that he sometimes felt that the paramilitaries of both communities had done more damage to their own people than they had to the other side. However, one should place such reflections in context and note that how much working class Protestants condemn the gangsterism of the paramilitaries will depend on the equation of the extent of IRA threat and the value of the UDA and UVF. A UDA man said "I don't mind some wee bastard getting a new car if he's doing the job, you know". It is when the "wee bastards" are seen to be putting holidays in Spain and new cars before defending Protestants against the IRA that resentment begins to undermine the standing of the organisations and it does so in a downward spiral. As the Jimmy Craigs came more to the fore, the more respectable elements (who had not joined the UDA to rob banks and frighten builders) withdrew and the gangsters came more and more to define the organisation. Whether the present UDA leadership's attempts to purge some of its gangsters or the UVF brigade staff's attacks on members suspected of drug dealing can do anything to change public perceptions is doubtful. So long as the organisations are dependent on illegal fund-raising and so long as the Protestant working class remain more responsive than the Catholic working class to government persuasion, the UDA and UVF will be unable to regain the widespread support they enjoyed in the early 1970s when the perilousness of the situation and considerable ignorance about their methods made them more attractive than they now appear.

## THE FUTURE OF LOYALIST PARAMILITARISM

Although this discussion has been extremely compressed, I have implied that many of the features of loyalist paramilitarism can be explained by the awkwardness of "pro-state terrorism" in a situation where the state remains reasonably solid and does not co-opt its self-appointed guardians. So long as the state itself is not in terminal disarray, then its security forces will be better legitimated to do policing and more competent. The pro-state terrorist organisation is the corner shop against the hypermarket: a struggling firm in a competition which it is bound to lose. In terms of ideology, there is a fundamental ambiguity in the pro-state terrorist project which can be seen in its attitude towards the government. Travel up the loyalist Shankill Road and one sees a large mural which declares "Shankill Road Loyalists Welcome the British Army". Yet at times in the last 20 years the loyalists have shot at and killed soldiers. In September 1975, the UVF was claiming to be receiving intelligence from the security forces; a month later it was threatening to bomb pubs used by soldiers! The loyalists see themselves as law-abiding yet at times, most recently in the aftermath of the signing of the Anglo–Irish accord, loyalists have attacked policemen and prison guards.

However, the present difficulties of the UDA and UVF should not be taken to mean that loyalist paramilitarism has been exhausted as an option. The response to the Anglo-Irish has been muted in comparison with the hostility to the 1974 power-sharing innovation and on every front the UDA and UVF, even after the surge in 1991, are less active now than they were 17 years ago. But many of the gunmen from the early 1970s were never arrested. Though retired, they can still return to their former ways and there are thousands of young men who will follow them if the circumstances demand it. This is a point often missed by those who argue for the return of "selective internment". That would only end paramilitary activity if it was the case that the present activists are irreplaceable. Circumstances produce the activists, not vice-versa. A removal of 100 leading loyalist paramilitaries, without a complete halt to IRA violence, would only create 100 job opportunities for would-be paramilitaries and if the recent changes in the UDA are anything to go by, the new wave will be more committed to violence than those they replace. There are some killers who give so little thought to their killing that their actions are immune to self-examination but many paramilitaries are reasonably thoughtful people who are able to reflect on their actions. Many of them began enthusiastically, driven by the sense of a correct cause and by the thrill of danger but for many something akin to disillusionment set in. As one convicted murderer said to me: "After a while you have to wonder why you bother. We kill 10, 20, 30 of them and what for? We can't kill all of them". And it has gone on so long. When he was first convicted, he expected to be out in a matter of months: "Sometimes I thought we would win, you know or there would be some solution and an amnesty and we'd be out by Christmas. Its always Christmas, isn't it? It was all amnesty, amnesty. None of us reckoned on serving a year, let alone 15."

Some of the early leaders thought that having proved they could stand up to the IRA and having established their credentials as hard men, they would be able to negotiate a settlement with their enemies but for any number of reasons, that did not happen. A long career has brought war-weariness to many older paramilitaries. Some retired when they could no longer see any obvious benefit. Others stayed in their positions but did their best to mute the sectarian murder campaign and to find more positive directions. As the changes in the UDA post-Stevens showed, a wholesale removal of an older generation that has become tired merely opens the way for younger men who have not yet had the experience to make them doubt the value of an extensive murder campaign.

History can never simply repeat itself. Even at the height of their influence in 1974, the UDA and UVF were sufficiently unacceptable that they had to work behind such fronts as the Ulster Workers Council. The poor reputations the UDA and UVF have acquired since 1974 will be an even greater obstacle to popular mobilisation. The considerable improvements in the efficiency of the RUC will ensure that any return to murder on the scale of the early 1970s will attract a much more effective response. Having said that, what brought the UVF and UDA into being and allowed them to grow was the belief that the government was not doing enough to counter challenges to the state, the disruptions of the civil rights movement and then the threat of armed republicanism. Far from simply being another version of "state terror", the UDA and UVF came into being because many loyalists felt the state had left a gap which they should fill. Any change in political or security circumstances that again gives wide credence to the belief that the state is unwilling to, or incapable of, defending itself will cause a resurgence in support for these organisations or the rise of new forces.

*Northern Ireland: Reappraising Loyalist Violence*        21

## NOTES

[1] My research on loyalist paramilitary groups was supported by a grant from the Economic and Social Research Council and is reported more fully in *The Red Hand: Loyalist Paramilitaries in Northern Ireland*, Oxford, 1992. I would like to acknowledge the help of the many people I interviewed who, for obvious reasons, cannot be identified.

[2] On the first UVF, see Phillip Orr: *The Road to the Somme*, Belfast, 1987.

[3] Arthur Hezlet: *The B Specials: a History of the Ulster Special Constabulary*, London, 1972.

[4] Michael Farrell: *Arming the Protestants: the Formation of the Ulster Special Constabulary and the Royal Ulster Constabulary*, London, 1983.

[5] On the career of Ian Paisley, see Steve Bruce: *God Save Ulster: The Religion and Politics of Paisleyism*, Oxford, 1986.

[6] For a more detailed account of early attitudes to Catholic victims of loyalist violence, see the discussion of responses to the bombing of McGurk's Bar in Steve Bruce, "Protestantism and Terrorism in Northern Ireland", in A. O'Day and Y. Alexander: *Ireland's Terrorist Trauma*, Brighton, 1989.

[7] *Republican News* 14 February 1991, p. 2.

[8] The term "romper room" was borrowed from a popular children's TV programme of the early 1970s and used to describe places of torture.

[9] Even by the standards set in the present Troubles, Murphy was a vicious killer who killed more Protestants than Catholics (some by mistake; others as a deliberate response to some usually petty insult) and who was eventually set up for the IRA by loyalists. Many loyalists regard it as a major failing of UVF leaders of the period that either they did not know what Murphy was up to or they knew but did nothing to stop him. For an account that has all the faults of popular journalism but suitably conveys the sense of Murphy's life, see Martin Dillon: *The Shankill Butchers*, London, 1989.

[10] The statistical relationship between republican and loyalist murder rates is extremely close, even when one takes the month by month figures instead of annual totals. For the 240 months from 1969–89, the Pearson's 'r' measure of correlation between republican and loyalist rates was 0.58 at $p < 0.001$. The 'r' for the year-by-year totals is 0.74 at $p < 0.001$.

[11] Robert Fisk: *The Point of No Return: The Strike Which Broke the British in Ulster*, London, 1976, is a reasonably reliable and very well-written journalistic account which only errs in underestimating the UDA's control of the strike and exaggerating the autonomous role of the UWC and the importance of some of the smaller loyalist paramilitary groups.

[12] This quotation, and all others without cited sources, is from an interview conducted between 1989 and 1991.

[13] Since the start of the Troubles there have been reports of security force intelligence finding its way to terrorists. In August 1989, the UDA leadership, stung by having yet another of what they regarded as "legitimate" murders being described as sectarian, none too brightly decided to show a BBC reporter various documents that identified the victim as IRA suspect and a video, apparently shot inside a briefing room of a UDR base. The subsequent outcry led to an enquiry into collusion, led by John Stevens, then the deputy chief constable of Cambridgeshire.

[14] During his time as Supreme Commander, Tyrie steadfastly denied knowledge of the UFF and denied that UDA men committed murder. In a number of interviews in December 1991, the brigadier who uses the pseudonym "John Montgomery" happily owned the UFF and proudly announced that the old racketeers of the UDA had been replaced by terrorists.

[15] Barr tried to build cross-community support for his plans with a body called the Northern Ireland Negotiated Independence Association. Some UDA men wanted it named the "Ulster . . ." and innocently wondered why Catholics might find that off-putting.

[16] John Brewer: *Inside the RUC*, Oxford, 1991, p. 138.

[17] Chris Ryder: *The Ulster Defence Regiment: An Instrument of Peace*, London, 1991, p. 196.

[18] Fred Holroyd and N. Burbridge: *War Without Honour*, Hull, 1989.

[19] See Paul Foot: *Who Framed Colin Wallace?*, London, 1990. Raymond Murray: *The SAS in Ireland*, Cork, 1991, has very little about the SAS but contains every claim ever made for security force collusion. Most are extremely flimsy.

[20] Martin Dillon: *The Dirty War*, London, 1990 and Steve Bruce: *The Red Hand*, Oxford, 1992 discuss the allegations at length.

[21] *Independent* 9 January 1992.

# [9]

# Collaboration

*New legal and judicial procedures for countering terrorism*

### Alison Jamieson

**"Law is nothing else than an ordinance of reason for the common good, promulgated by him who has the care of the community."**
Thomas Aquinas, *Treatise on Law*

This report is a study of attempted pacification rather than of conflict. It looks at a specific phenomenon – the collaboration of self-confessed criminals in court trials – in the context of political violence in Italy and in Northern Ireland. Examples will be given of Northern Irish supergrasses, of left wing *pentiti* from the Italian Red Brigades and Front Line organisations, and of collaborators from the Sicilian Mafia, *Cosa Nostra*.

It should be stated immediately that no attempt will be made to compare "like with like" in terms of the organisations themselves. To weave tortuous psychological webs linking together the ideologies, aims and characteristics of Northern Irish militants with Italian *brigatisti* and Sicilian *mafiosi* would be a time-consuming and probably fruitless task. Nor is it the intention to set Italy beside the United Kingdom and try to establish which has "done better" against organised crime and terrorism.

The truth – and the heart of this study – is that the legal systems of two Western European countries have been stretched to the limit (some would say have exceeded it) in reacting to political violence with democratic means. Under two very different jurisdictions – the British common law system with its accusatorial form of criminal trial, and the Italian European law system, which until 1989 used the inquisitorial form of trial – the administration of justice has been bent towards utilitarian objectives, permitting unrepentent criminals to go free or serve token prison sentences in exchange for providing incriminating evidence against former accomplices.

The use of accomplice evidence raises many issues. What factors determine the choice of collaboration? Does it matter that punishment no longer fits the crime, but is redefined according to the amount of information a collaborator can give and how many associates he names? What ethical and legal arguments need to be overcome to justify such a pragmatic approach to justice? Is it possible for a judicial system to deal with problems of political violence without becoming or seeming to become a tool of political anti-terrorist strategy?

In seeking answers to these and other questions it is hoped that the differences between the militant organisations under consideration as well as those between juridical and political systems, rather than being an obstacle to study, will enrich and extend it.

1

2                    *Research Institute for the Study of Conflict and Terrorism*

## BACKGROUND

### The Italian "years of lead"

The most striking characteristic of Italian left wing militancy during the decade 1968–1978 was its broad mass following. Italy's liberation from dictatorship was widely experienced as a precarious and temporary interlude, constantly under threat from the continuing fascist presence in the police and in public administration, and from right wing protectors and supporters in Spain, Portugal and Greece. The student revolution of 1968, industrial unrest throughout 1969 and an indiscriminate bomb attack in Milan in December 1969 (17 dead) whose attribution to the far left was sanctioned by senior political figures, all contributed to a sense that the left needed to unite and arm itself against covert forces of the right.

In contrast with the spate of right wing bomb attacks which continued until 1974 without significant arrests or attribution of responsibility, the Red Brigades (BR) and the multitude of extremist groups that mushroomed on the area of the extra-parliamentary left were unequivocal in proclaiming their corporate identity and objectives. "Militant antifascism" was the common denominator from which a wide spectrum of attitudes to violence and to social and political change emerged.

The Red Brigades were the first group to use violence as an offensive strategy rather than a defensive tactic, and saw industrial action, sabotage and attacks on industrial targets essentially as a means to manoeuvre themselves into a position from which the real struggle – the overthrow of the "sham democracy" – could be launched.

After a wave of arrests and relative calm in 1975–76, 1977 saw a further explosion of spontaneous and not-so-spontaneous protest which ranged from violent clashes between police and demonstrators in cities all over Italy with deaths and injuries on both sides, to the kidnapping, leg-shooting and murder of prominent public figures, mostly at the hands of the Red Brigades. The line between the indiscriminate, almost nihilistic protest of the "77 Movement" and the carefully planned escalation of Red Brigades' terrorism blurred perceptions, not just for the authorities but for the brigadists themselves, who deduced from the confusion that a "pre-revolutionary moment" had arrived. This misplaced confidence was a crucial factor in the decision to kidnap Christian Democrat President Aldo Moro in the spring of 1978. The murder of Moro and of his five bodyguards signalled the beginning of the Red Brigades' isolation and of their ultimate decline. It also forced the government to react with a series of repressive measures specifically directed against terrorism. Police powers to stop, search and detain were extended, prison sentences were increased and maximum pre-trial detention periods lengthened.

### Northern Ireland

The long history of conflict in Northern Ireland takes as its contemporary flash point the British government's decision to deploy army troops in the Bogside area of Londonderry in August 1969. The riots of the following weeks

*Collaboration* 3

and months caused a steady deterioration in the security situation and, in August 1971, the British government authorised the Northern Ireland Security Council and the Northern Ireland Minister of Home Affairs to revive a clause of the Civil Authorities (Special Powers) Act (NI) of 1922, permitting the arrest without charge and internment of over 300 suspected Republican extremists.

An uneasy balance between Stormont government and rule from London collapsed after the breakup of a civil rights march on "Bloody Sunday" in January 1972 when 13 civilians were shot dead by army troops; direct rule was formally imposed in March 1972. The IRA, bolstered by the sympathy that internment had aroused, reached an unprecedented level of violence in that year, killing 467 persons, or an average of 39 per month, including 103 army personnel and 321 civilians.[1]

A Royal Commission chaired by Lord Diplock was appointed in the autumn of 1972 to examine the administration of justice in Northern Ireland and make recommendations. Most of these were incorporated into the Northern Ireland (Emergency Provisions) Act 1973. They included extending the powers of police to stop, search, detain and question; rules of evidence were altered in such a way that confessions made under police interrogation were admissible and in themselves sufficient to convict in court, and trial without jury was suspended for a "schedule" of potentially terrorist-related offences to eliminate the risk of jury intimidation. Contrary to Lord Diplock's recommendation, the use of internment was phased out and abolished altogether in 1975.

Between 1976 and 1979 some 3,000 persons were charged with terrorist offences, many on the basis of confessions obtained under interrogation.[2] According to Greer,[3] the police came under increased pressure to show a satisfactory conviction rate after internment ceased:

"Until the advent of the supergrass strategy the critical point in the Diplock process was whether a suspect confessed or not. Only 32 confessions out of nearly 4,000 were declared inadmissible by the courts between 1976 and 1980, and 75 to 80 per cent of the 93 per cent conviction rate in scheduled offence cases in the first six months of 1978, a not untypical period, rested on confessions alone."

Concern about the treatment of political prisoners in Northern Ireland prompted a visit at the end of 1977 from an Amnesty International delegation, which in its 1978 report denounced maltreatment of detainees and brutal interrogation procedures. This provoked a new official enquiry, headed by the English judge Lord Bennett, which substantially confirmed the Amnesty findings. Amongst the Bennett recommendations were: that interviews were to be more closely supervised; prisoners were to be seen by a medical officer every 24 hours and offered an examination; detectives were to be rotated and their duties varied; close circuit television was to be installed in interview rooms; late night interrogation was to be discontinued.[4] Most of these were introduced in 1979.

By the early 1980s, after more than 10 years of renewed hostilities, some disillusion was evident amongst Republican militants. RUC and Army intelligence had improved and the British government under Margaret

4                    *Research Institute for the Study of Conflict and Terrorism*

Thatcher had shown an impressive determination to resist all forms of blackmail, including the hunger strike of 1981 and the 10 deaths that ensued.

## Cosa Nostra

*Cosa Nostra* does not have a political ideology as such,[5] but it is included in this study because it uses violence in the context of objectives and strategies which are political, such as the erosion of democratic rule and the election or subordination of malleable politicians. The Mafia resorts to terror to intimidate or eliminate its enemies, including political or institutional figures who stand between it and the realisation of its goals. Between 1979 and 1983 the Mafia murdered the Sicilian leaders of the two largest national political parties; the President of the Sicilian Region; the head of the Police Flying Squad; a *carabinieri* commander; three senior judges and the Prefect of Palermo. The peak of "mafia terrorism" was reached in 1992 with the murders in May and July of judges Giovanni Falcone and Paolo Borsellino, and in March and September of two presumed political ex-allies, Christian Democrat Euro-MP Salvo Lima and Mafia businessman Ignazio Salvo, discarded either because they knew too much or because they no longer served any useful function, or both.

*Cosa Nostra* is a secret society *par excellence*; the initiation ceremony involves pricking a finger of the novitiate who lets blood fall on the picture of a sacred image which is then ignited and burnt in his hand. He is then informed that he is "a man of honour" for life and that, just as he entered the society through blood, he can only leave it through blood – in death.

The Mafia has survived for over 100 years in Sicily, continually regenerating itself and consolidating its powers through a unique ability to adapt archaic values and codes of conduct to the management of the most sophisticated national and international criminal activities. Its greatest strength comes from below, consisting of absolute territorial control of many areas of Sicily and consequently of the activities that go on there: of who can live, work, build housing, offices or schools, commit crimes – or represent the area politically. Observance of rigid rules of behaviour is maintained by a combination of trust and fear, – with violence as the main sanction when the rules are broken.

*Cosa Nostra*'s development from rural to urban Mafia and its massive expansion into the international drugs trade has been charted elsewhere.[6] It was a process whereby *mafiosi* gradually ceased to exercise their original role of mediators between rural landlord and peasant crofter and became entrepreneurs in their own right. Fortunes were made in the 1960s and 1970s through land speculation and inner city construction projects, by the acquisition of permits and licences to deal in the wholesale food markets, in raw material supplies to the building industry and for the maintenance of public services – in many cases facilitated by the compliance of local politicians and public administrators, whose approval was bought with the promise of electoral support.

The need to rely on non *mafiosi* for crucial areas of business competence came with the expanding drugs trade. All the Palermo families were involved

*Collaboration* 5

in drug trafficiking to some degree,[7] though specialities developed – some saw to importing morphine base from the production zones, others to transportation or to refining in Sicilian laboratories and others (those with well-established North American links) to trans-Atlantic distribution and sales. In drugs, as with tobacco smuggling, traditional alliances and divisions between Mafia families ceased to operate and each boss could decide how and with whom to do business. *Cosa Nostra*'s "hermetic seal" was broken when it began to involve in its drug operations not only non-Mafia Italians but also Chinese, Lebanese, Turks, French, Belgians and Swiss as couriers, financiers or suppliers. No oaths of silence or allegiance bound the outsiders to *Cosa Nostra*, merely the common goal of making money.

## STAGES TO COLLABORATION

### Crisis and identity on the Italian left

The Moro kidnap split the far left in Italy between those who judged it a politically foolhardy and over-ambitious action destined to fail, or who distanced themselves from the excess of bloodshed, and those who admired and envied the military prowess of the Red Brigades. Many withdrew from militancy at the end of the 1970s, but those intent on continuing were forced into clandestinity and increasing social isolation.

The "squeezing in of (our) environment"[8] which the far left terrorist groups in Italy experienced in the late 1970s and early 1980s was not simply the effect of increased police pressure, but had as much to do with their own perceptions of themselves and the perception of them by those who, if not direct supporters, had at least provided a degree of non-rejection or passive consensus. Shortly before Moro was killed, a meeting had been held in Rome university attended by hundreds of far left militants who had urged the BR to release Moro alive; when their advice was ignored, statements of outright condemnation were issued.

Two murders in 1979 – one of a factory labourer and Communist party member in Genoa, the other of a Milanese judge who had diligently investigated the 1969 right wing bomb attack – turned such sympathy as remained for the Red Brigades and Front Line groups into outright rejection. The murder of the factory worker – "justified" by the BR because he had reported a colleague distributing BR propaganda – changed the image of the organisation in the eyes of hitherto acquiescent observers. Enrico Fenzi, member of the Genoa BR, remembers, "It was no longer me against them but them against me; I was ashamed, I was afraid . . . I was the enemy."[9]

Towards the end of 1978 the new anti-terrorist laws which galvanised police and intelligence services and a specialised anti-terrorist unit under the authority of General Carlo Alberto Dalla Chiesa began to show results – within two months of his appointment in September, 10 leading brigadists had been arrested and an important base discovered in Milan. The risks and isolation of clandestine living – especially for those on the run with arrest warrants issued in their names – initially served to intensify group identity and solidarity through mutual dependence and the shared commitment to the aims and values of the group. Moreover there was a strong sense of obligation to those who had been killed in gun battles and to those in prison: "a moral responsibility towards those who had fallen and to the blood that had been shed – death is a tremendous bond".[10] Yet at the same time an anguish crept in, "a sacrificial sense of going forward simply because we were incapable of finding a way out".[11]

Under pressure, cracks began to appear: the political handling of the Moro kidnap was widely criticised inside the BR and by rival groups; opposition to his killing expressed during the kidnap by a minority of the Rome column but suppressed out of respect for the majority view at the time, led to a split and the exit of the dissenters. Other factions formed, fragmented and argued incessantly over the direction and strategies of armed struggle.

Neither the Red Brigades nor Front Line, the other principal far left group, could afford to forget that their long term aim was a proletarian revolution for which, logically, the support of the working classes was indispensable. Yet it was becoming apparent at the turn of the decade that things simply were not working:

"The struggle took on more and more the characteristics of terrorism, it was an instrument that was contrary to proletarian interests. The proletariat was against armed struggle and against terrorism. It recognised the limits, the dangers and the mistakes of armed struggle and fought it."[12]

In the autumn of 1980, the announcement of large-scale redundancies in the Fiat works in Turin had led to the occupation of the premises, but when Fiat offered to lay off workers on 90 per cent of pay for up to three years instead, opposition crumbled. BR founder member Alberto Franceschini, who was imprisoned at the time but still committed to armed struggle, recalls:

"The Fiat working class, the continuing point of reference for our analyses and our struggles, had finally knuckled under. A new period was beginning in which the certainties of the past, about the working class, revolution, armed struggle and communism were gradually becoming museum pieces."[13]

In February 1980 Patrizio Peci, member of the BR executive Committee and Turin column leader, was arrested after several weeks of police surveillance. Within a month he had begun to collaborate with General Dalla Chiesa and with examining magistrate Giancarlo Caselli. According to Peci's own account[14] disillusionment with armed struggle had already set in. But it was his first impact with prison – left for several days in solitary confinement and warned that the least serious of his charges, illegal possession of a gun, would earn him over three years of imprisonment – which was decisive. With direct and indirect responsibilities for eight murders and numerous shootings Peci could only have received a sentence of prison for life.

He admits that initially he felt no remorse for his crimes, but decided to collaborate for the simple reason that – "All in all we were beaten, militarily and politically".[15]

Before beginning his collaboration, Peci claims he sought guarantees for a lighter sentence, security precautions for himself and the chance of starting a new life abroad. Neither General Dalla Chiesa nor judge Caselli was in a position to make such promises, yet Peci's evidence was deemed of such value that his interlocutors, as well as most of the swelling "pool" of judges specialising in terrorist cases, became strenuous advocates of premium legislation over the following months. Peci's information led to the arrest of 100 other brigadists; the capture in the same year of Front Line leaders Michele Viscardi and Roberto Sandalo and their collaboration set in motion a domino effect. Arrests of far left militants leapt from 63 in 1979 to 345 in 1980.[16]

**Northern Ireland – informers and collaborators**

Former members of the Provisional IRA are less inclined to offer up critical assessments of their militancy for public scrutiny. However there is evidence at the end of the 1970s of a weariness with violence inside and outside the Republican movement, and of a perceived gap between the mythology of battle and mundane reality. Christopher Black had joined the Provos,

"to be accepted and established in the area. I think I thought it would be a game really, and that there would be excitement."[17]

His first job in an Active Service Unit was to take over a house in the Ardoyne from which to shoot soldiers.

"Before leaving they donned hats and spectacles in a half-hearted attempt at disguise. It was an early job and Black recalled feeling pleased because he would be home in time to see England playing at Wembley on the television."[18]

In 1981 the recruits that had come to swell the Provos' ranks after the introduction of internment were coming up for 10 years of militancy: the "excitement" was beginning to wear off. As Boyd points out:

"Most of the informers were mere schoolboys when the present phase of communal violence began in Northern Ireland. The only politics they have ever known is the politics of violence. And when the politics of violence fails they fail."

He continues: "Much the same explanation has been given by Fr Denis Faul. He says that until 1978 or thereabouts the Provisional IRA and the INLA were convinced they would soon win the struggle to force the British out of Northern Ireland. After the British withdrew those who had been sent to jail assumed they would be set free under an amnesty and be acclaimed heroes, like the Republicans freed in 1917 after the Easter Rising."[19]

Intelligence had improved since the opening of the Castlereagh interrogation centre in 1977 and the RUC's successful infiltration of the H-Block Committees. Prisons were no longer compact paramilitary training and indoctrination camps offering an impervious face to the enemy; special status given to political detainees had ended in 1976 and prison conditions were hard. Of those newly arrested, many faced second sentences not only for recently-committed crimes but for uncompleted terms of previous sentences.[20]

Black was 27 years old and had already spent five years inside Long Kesh when he was re-arrested in November 1981. His decision to collaborate, in common with nearly all the supergrasses who followed him whether Republican or Loyalist, stemmed from dread of another extended prison sentence and the prospect of a long separation from his wife and young children.

## Collaboration and *Cosa Nostra*

The prospect of members of *Cosa Nostra* becoming "repentant" or dissociating themselves from their organisation in the way that former terrorists had done was not considered a credible option in Italy. The Mafia's ethos was based on the principle of *omertà*, literally "the ability to be a man" – to remain silent. An invitation to join the organisation could only have followed a rigorous selection procedure based on proven courage and resilience of character. Any signs of cowardice, weakness or a disposition to inform were punished with death well before they reached the stage at which they could threaten the organisation; *mafiosi* were murdered in prison if they could not maintain a dignity and aloofness in difficult conditions.

The sociologist Nando Dalla Chiesa (son of the General murdered by the Mafia in 1982) suggests there are four factors which created the conditions for collaboration within the Mafia:
"**1** its capacity to represent local culture is diminished;
**2** there occurs a weakening of internal cohesion;
**3** there are changes in the contacts between the Mafia and other criminal worlds.
**4** there is a reduced sense of 'otherness' from the state;"[21]
(According to Dalla Chiesa such was the collusion between Mafia and state institutions in the 1970s and 1980s that the Mafia could not feel itself sufficiently "separate" from a system of power with which it was deeply compromised.)

Tommaso Buscetta was an important boss of the Porta Nuova clan in Palermo. Officially owner/manager of the family glazing business, his alleged crimes in Italy included involvement in several murders and in tobacco smuggling. Strong suspicions that he subsequently ran extensive drug trafficking networks between South and North America were never proven and always denied by him. Having served a prison sentence in Italy in the 1970s, he escaped house arrest and fled abroad, firstly to North America and then to Brazil whence he was extradited to Italy in 1984. By that time he had done eight years in prisons in the US, Brazil and Italy. In Brazil he had been given electric shock treatment and had his toenails pulled out, but had refused to talk.

Buscetta's alienation from *Cosa Nostra*, which he claims began with his refusal to go into drug trafficking, was objectively sealed by his continued friendship with the "losers" in the internecine Mafia war of 1981–83, which left 400 dead on the ground and another 600 victims whose bodies were never found. This was a vicious struggle of double cross and betrayal between and within Mafia "families"; it had broken the traditional bonds and rewritten the rules of the honoured society. Buscetta, in relative safety in Brazil, was punished by the murders of seven of his close relatives at the end of 1982. This violation of the conventional family unit, once considered "the cardinal point of consensus in the organisation of consensus around Mafia power"[22] severed his allegiance definitively.


## Revenge and survival

In September 1984, with his extradition from Brazil imminent, Tommaso Buscetta tried to save his wife and children from further reprisals by committing suicide with strychnine. When the attempt failed, according to the Palermo judiciary,

"Buscetta decided to entrust his fate and the secrets of *Cosa Nostra* to the Courts at a time when the State . . . was beginning to show a real determination to pursue Mafia crimes. A *mafioso* of the old school, he had realised that the inspiring principles of *Cosa Nostra* had irredeemably been overturned by the blind ferocity of his enemies, who had transformed it into a criminal organisation of the worst kind in which he no longer recognised himself. Thus there was no sense in paying homage to the rules of an organisation in which he no longer believed, no sense in remaining true to the law of *omertà*. He had to contribute to the destruction of the "new Mafia", had to take his revenge for all his mourning, but the overwhelming superiority of his enemies left him few hopes; he had no alternative but to turn to Italian justice to consume his vendetta and save his life."[23]

The urge for revenge is a strong and frequent motive for collaboration in the Mafia, as is advance notice of a death sentence decreed by rival factions. Salvatore Contorno, footsoldier of an important Palermo clan also on the losing side of the Mafia war, had witnessed the systematic extermination of his "family" bosses and was therefore prepared for the attempt on his own life which he narrowly escaped. He was arrested in Rome whilst preparing a revenge attack but refused to begin his collaboration until he received formal blessing to do so from Buscetta himself. Like Buscetta, he entrusted his hatred for the "band of cowards and assassins"[24] to the process of state justice.

Mafia "chemist" Francesco Marino Mannoia, who admitted to having refined "quintals of heroin" on behalf of *Cosa Nostra*, realised his danger after his brother's murder in 1988 for which he received, ominously, neither an explanation nor an apology. After his arrest, desire to make a new life with his companion and their child were the prime factors in his decision to collaborate.

Internal conflicts were bitter and frequent in the history of the Red Brigades but never in themselves drove a militant to collaborate; however this was a factor for a collaborator from the Loyalist Ulster Volunteer Force, Joseph Bennett, sentenced to death by a UVF Court Martial for stealing money from his employer.[25] Given his involvement in one murder and seven other serious crimes, Bennett's choice on his arrest in May 1982 appeared to him to be one of a life sentence in prison or a death sentence outside it.

"The future was bleak. The police offered a third alternative . . . My life depended on impressing the police and on my first day in custody I mentioned immunity . . . There was a strong incentive to co-operate. . . . At the end of the day my usefulness to the police would be measured in the number of men I put away.[26]

There is only one known case in Northern Ireland and one in Italy where genuine remorse was the stimulus for collaboration. Leonardo Vitale, the first ever Mafia *pentito*, was apparently overcome by a crisis of conscience in 1973 and poured out details of *Cosa Nostra's* criminal activities to the Palermo police, including his own responsibility, with accomplices, for several murders. He was considered partially unsound of mind and locked up in a mental asylum. Shortly after his release in 1984 he was assassinated.

Kevin McGrady had joined the IRA in 1975. He was arrested in December of that year and had served three months of a prison sentence when a murder charge against him was dropped. After joining a religious sect in Amsterdam he reportedly became obsessed with the need to expiate his crimes and returned to Belfast in early 1982 where he gave himself up to the police. He neither asked for nor initially obtained any material benefits from giving evidence and was sentenced to life imprisonment later that year; he was released in 1988.

## Conclusions

Although the circumstances that led to Tommaso Buscetta's collaboration differ radically from those of the Red Brigades and of PIRA militants, there is a common denominator: they all coincide in a state of personal crisis, in which the values and identity of the individual are seen by him, perhaps for the first time, as separate from and directly conflicting with those of the group. The individual who cuts free from the group acknowledges the superiority of the state over his former organisation and henceforth looks to it for revenge, for protection or occasionally, as a means to spiritual redemption.

Other factors which are present to varying degrees of relevance include rejection of the values of the group by a significant sector of society – a loss of consensus; altered perceptions of victory and defeat so that the organisation loses credibility and/or legitimacy in the eyes of its own members; internal conflict, such that group identity and solidarity are weakened; a perceived breaking of the rules, or betrayal of the values for which an individual joined the group, by some of its members; the dread of facing a long prison sentence, and an individual's fear for the physical safety, either outside or inside prison, of himself and/or his family.

## THE INTERLOCUTOR

Little research has been done on the relationship between the collaborator and his police or judicial interlocutor. Clearly, the person or persons to whom the potential collaborator speaks during an initial period of resistance to or uncertainty over collaboration are of crucial importance. An ordinary police informer builds up a relationship of trust with his handler which is vital to both sides but it remains essentially a private relationship. The collaborator is under immeasurably greater pressure. Once his statements have been taken he will either be kept isolated in prison or else relocated with his family to a safe place where the demands of security make ordinary human existence impossible. If he reaches trial, the combination of stress from the social upheaval, from public exposure and from threats of reprisals can prevent it from going ahead – indeed this was the case with 14, or over half of the 26 supergrasses that originally offered collaboration in Northern Ireland.

The dependence of a collaborator on his police or judicial interlocutor is often likened to the Stockholm syndrome, the sense of shared destiny and mutual dependence experienced by a hostage towards his captors. The interlocutor is not only a confessor figure but also a physical protector and a morale raiser. As Lord Gifford points out in his detailed examination of the supergrass system, "Once the supergrass has chosen the escape route from prison by agreeing to give information, his relationship with the investigating police officers becomes one of total dependence. He has cut himself off from his friends in the movement of which he was part. He needs the goodwill of the police officers in order to secure his immunity, or his light sentence, or his recommendation for an early release. He is in no position to resist any suggestions which they may make to him."[27]

This seems to be true up to a point. But attempts at emotional blackmail can destroy the possibility of trust and may result in the retraction of evidence, as with IRA supergrass Robert Lean who claimed the police threatened to arrest his wife and put his children into a home if he did not collaborate. Lean escaped from protective custody and signed an affidavit retracting all his previous statements.

In Italy the judiciary, plus a handful of senior police or *carabinieri* officers have had a leading role in encouraging collaboration. Psychological difficulties may not be unique to the collaborator, since the interlocutor may well have colleagues or friends murdered by the very person whose confessions he is called upon to evaluate.

The importance of the rapport between Mafia collaborators and their interlocutors has frequently been stressed. For proud and taciturn Sicilians, the arrival of prestigious judges of the calibre of Paolo Borsellino or Giovanni Falcone to hear their statements was an important endorsement of their own importance and thus a boost to self esteem. "Function, grade and notoriety are all important" according to an official from the witness protection service.[28]

After these initial requirements a considerable effort is demanded of the interlocutor, as the official explains:

"We need judges not just willing to take down the collaborators' statements but also willing to live their moments of sadness with them. It means giving up on an afternoon's questioning if the *pentito* starts to cry from doubts and torments. . . . They live through an incredible interior drama. Whatever the reason, when these people decide to dissociate, they end up by tearing their own skin off in order to uproot themselves from their culture, from their world. And it's not easy. They can't do it alone. They need an expert, someone who understands the parabolas, the moments of falling tension, the recurring states of apprehension; someone who respects silence, understands moments of discomfort, who knows how to be close without insisting, and who is able to use that moment when the person is ready to open up to make his statements."

The fact that Borsellino and Falcone were Sicilian and could understand the dialect ensured that a particular turn of phrase, gesture or even a silence was instantly comprehended. Falcone described his discussions with Tommaso Buscetta as being "entirely coded", in which "everything was communicated in the form of a message, every detail had significance".[29] Above all, Falcone understood the importance of respect:

"I tried to immerse myself in their human drama and before passing on to proper interrogations I always forced myself to understand each one's human problems and put them in a precise context. I never called them "*tu*", as many others did, I never insulted them, as some people think they have the right to do, nor did I take them Sicilian sweets as others have insinuated. Between me and them there is always a table – in the literal and metaphoric sense of the word."[30]

The respect was reciprocal: the Mafia collaborators witnessed the dedication and integrity of Borsellino and Falcone at first hand and learned to trust them. After their murders, collaborators such as Buscetta, Contorno and Antonino Calderone all returned to Italy as free men and at considerable personal risk to offer their contribution after years of silence – no longer for vendetta, but from an acknowledged debt to two old adversaries who had believed in them.

Calderone commented, after hearing of Falcone's death on television:

"It was a shock. It was enough for me just to know that he was there doing his job. He gave me such confidence. He never misled or disappointed me."[31]

Paolo Borsellino had listened to the account of a young Sicilian woman whose father and brother had been killed in Mafia feuds. Safe but lonely in an apartment provided for her in Rome, she killed herself exactly one week after Borsellino's murder. Her suicide note said "I'm so overcome by the death of judge Paolo Borsellino, now there's no one left to protect me, I'm sickened, I can't go on."[32]

## LEGAL INCENTIVES TO COLLABORATE

### The supergrass phenomenon

The term "supergrass" – probably derived from the Cockney rhyming slang, grasshopper-copper[33] – was first coined in the early 1970s when a number of London bank robbers gave Queen's evidence against former accomplices. Some 26 supergrasses came forward in Northern Ireland in the years 1981–1983, seven Loyalist and 19 Republican, of whom 10 (three Loyalist, seven Republican) gave evidence against accomplices before the Diplock courts.

No new laws were introduced to encourage collaboration in Northern Ireland, although changes to the rules of evidence contained in the Northern Ireland (Emergency Provisions) Act of 1973, discussed earlier, undoubtedly facilitated the use of accomplice evidence. In reality, the supergrass phenomenon appears to have been a direct outgrowth of the extensive informer system, stimulated by the RUC and the security forces and adopted by the judiciary for a significant but limited period of time.

*Collaboration* 13

In marked contrast to Italy, where there is a constitutional obligation to prosecute every crime, under the British common law system the Crown Prosecution Service has a number of options at its discretion. These include the granting of immunity; the procedure known as "offering no evidence", which is tantamount to immunity, since by offering no evidence the prosecution renounces any future right to try the individual for the crimes to which he has admitted; and *nolle prosequi* – not to proceed. Unlike the previous two options, this can be revoked at a later date.

In general, such initiatives come from the police, who make a recommendation to the Director of Public Prosecutions who in turn is answerable to the Attorney General – a member of government and therefore part of the executive. (Since 1985 Crown Prosecutors have the same powers as the DPP.) The decision to grant immunity can only be taken on the personal authority of the DPP on the recommendation of the Chief Constable.[34] It can either be granted before trial takes place or afterwards, although practice with Northern Ireland supergrass cases seems to have been to grant it before trial.

In 1983 the Attorney General, Sir Michael Havers, explained before Parliament the circumstances that would justify immunity:
"Where the evidence which the accomplice can give is credible and cogent and involves perhaps a large number of alleged terrorists who cannot otherwise be charged or brought before the court, the prospect of saving lives, whether the lives of the ordinary members of the public or members of the security forces, and the prevention of further violent crime must weigh heavily with the Director in making that decision."[35]

Unofficially, there seem to have been three criteria for granting immunity in Northern Ireland: the witness had to convince police his knowledge was first hand and not hearsay, he had to provide a long list of accomplices, and he always had to deny having pulled the trigger in a murder, although attempted murder or being present at a murder was acceptable.[36]

According to the Attorney General's Department, 15 immunities were granted in November 1981–November 1983 to members of Northern Ireland paramilitary groups of which 13 have been identified.[37] Seven were given to individuals who later retracted their evidence but who were not re-arrested thanks to their immunity.

The 10 supergrass trials that took place in the Belfast Diplock courts ended with very diverse results for the key Crown witnesses: six received immunity, three were sent to prison for life (though one was released after six years) and one (UVF) collaborator sentenced to fourteen years in 1984 was released in 1986 after exercise of the Royal prerogative.[38]

There was no official "contract" specifying terms of immunity, nor were precise offers of money, protection or general assistance made public, although such details were supposed to be disclosed to defence lawyers. It has been alleged that some collaborators were paid up to £300,000; one has said he was offered £25,000–£30,000 plus a house, a job and a new identity abroad if he testified against all the people he had named; others claim that no cash sum was offered but a pension for life and resettlement in another country. Both Northern Ireland Secretary James Prior and Sir Michael Havers denied

14                    *Research Institute for the Study of Conflict and Terrorism*

in November 1983 that large cash sums had been paid to informers: Sir Michael told the House of Commons that cash allowances ranged from £35 per week for someone with no dependents to a maximum of £120 for those with families, in addition to free accommodation. Mr. Prior stated that up to 17 November 1983 the protection of police informers – including crown witnesses, presumably – had cost over £500,000.[39] In 1985 Northern Ireland Secretary of State Douglas Hurd revealed that the cost of providing protection for those who had given evidence against former accomplices in terrorist organisations had cost £1.3m over the previous seven years.[40]

### The Italian "premium laws"

Unlike its British counterpart, the Italian judiciary is genuinely independent of the executive. As a counterbalance, its margins for discretion are narrower, hence the constitutional obligation to prosecute all crimes committed. The granting of immunity is not an option.

The Italian government responded to the kidnap of Aldo Moro on 16 March 1978 with a Law Decree passed on 21 March, converted into Law 191 of 18 May 1978. It introduced the crime of "kidnap with the aim of terrorism or subversion", for which the law reduced prison sentences for those who broke with the criminal group and contributed to the safe release of a kidnap victim.

Law Decree of 15 December 1979, converted into Law 15 of 6 February 1980, was known as the "Cossiga Law" after the then Minister of the Interior: it increased penalties severely for all crimes bearing the aggravating factor "with the aim of terrorism and subversion of the democratic order" and increased maximum terms of pre-trial detention. For terrorists who dissociated themselves from their companions, intervened to prevent the further consequences of their acts or gave concrete assistance to the police to identify or capture their associates, the aggravating factor of terrorism was dropped; sentences were reduced by a third to a half, and life sentences cut to between 12 and 20 years.

Law 304 of 29 May 1982, referred to as "the penitence law", was applicable to all crimes bearing the aggravating factor of terrorism, with the exception of *strage* or massacre (thus excluding attacks like the 1980 bomb at Bologna station). Despite the name, it was only marginally concerned with genuine repentence. It applied to those who made a full confession of all crimes committed, furnished decisive evidence for the identification or the capture of one or more associates, or gave evidence that led to the exact reconstruction of crimes or the discovery of those responsible for them. In such cases associative crimes were not punishable and arrest was not necessary for those who voluntarily gave themselves up. Life sentences were reduced to between 10 and 12 years, other sentences were reduced by half and not to exceed 10 years. If the contribution of the *pentito* was considered "of exceptional relevance" then prison sentences could be reduced by a further third and provisional liberty (liberty with specified restrictions) could be granted after sentence had been passed. In all cases, conditional release (equivalent to parole) could be granted once half the sentence had been served if behaviour indicated *ravvedimento* or genuine repentence. The category of *pentito* was differentiated from that of the *dissociato* or dissociated terrorist. If the latter confessed personal responsibilities and acted to "annul or attenuate the dangerous or harmful consequences of their crimes", "life" was reduced to 15 to 21 years and all other crimes by a third, not to exceed 15 years.

This law was applicable only to crimes committed prior to 31 January 1982 and ran for 120 days. It was extended by a further 120 days (until 31 January 1983) by special decree.

Law 34 of 18 February 1987, known as the "dissociation law", modified the terms of dissociation contained in Law 304/82. Dissociation now comprised: definitive abandonment of the terrorist group; confession of the activities undertaken; formal renunciation of the use of violence as a means of political struggle, behaviour compatible with all the above. In return, prison sentences were reduced from "life" to 30 years for the most serious crimes, for other crimes of bloodshed sentences were cut by a quarter; for less serious crimes by a third to a half, and those serving sentences of less than 10 years were granted conditional release. Dissociation had to be declared within a month of the law's enactment, was only applicable to crimes committed up until 31 December 1983 and excluded "massacre".

## Mafia collaborators and the law

Repeated calls from a variety of political groups and by the Palermo judiciary for special legislation to encourage and protect Mafia collaborators went unheeded throughout the 1980s. The lack of formal procedures resulted in a haphazard and unsystematic treatment of collaborators, who were passed along a chain of four separate and sometimes conflicting authorities – the judiciary, the police, the security services and the office of the High Commissioner for the Mafia Fight. It could happen that instead of benefiting from his collaboration, the witness received a longer sentence and worse prison conditions; and such benefits as he might receive came primarily from the personal efforts of individual judges.

The most common argument used against the passing of appropriate legislation was that unlike the terrorist *pentito*, eminently capable of shedding a subversive ideology that was intellectually constructed, abstract and symbolic, the *mafioso* could not "convert" or abandon the group; moreover his allegations would be largely unverifiable and instrinsically unreliable because they were based on reasons of personal vendetta or self preservation. An alternative theory holds that adequate legislation was continually blocked by a dominant political class fearful of having *pentiti* step forward to reveal the extent of its own connivance with the Mafia.

In a report of January 1990, the authoritative all-party Parliamentary Antimafia Commission insisted on "the necessity to enact legislation in this delicate area as rapidly as possible".[41] Fourteen months later, Law 82 of 15 March 1991 was passed, although even this remained on paper for a further seven months and was not fully activated until the summer of 1992.

Modelled on the highly successful US Witness Security Program which had been studied in depth, it was a radical departure from the terrorism premium legislation in that it specified no sentence reductions but concentrated on the physical and economic security of the witness and involved a clear assumption of certain obligations on his part. A Central Protection Commission was established within the Ministry of the Interior, presided over by an under-secretary and comprising a judge and five other members with expertise in the area. The Commission was given responsibility for setting up and running individual protection programmes in consultation with the police and judicial authorities and where appropriate, with the Director of the Prison Service.

The law specifies various types of programme together with appropriate costings, ranging from the simple protection of the collaborator's dwelling 40m lire, (£18,700) to general assistance and economic support. This could involve a one-off payment of 30m lire (£14,000) for a six month period or, at the top limit of protection, a change of identity and relocation abroad with economic and housing assistance – estimated at 210m lire (£98,000). The total estimated cost of the various types of protection was estimated at £4.5m.

Modifications were introduced by a Law Decree of 8 June 1992 (passed in the wake of the Falcone murder), subsequently converted into Law 356 of 7 August 1992. Henceforth, in the presence of "grave and urgent reasons of security" the collaborator serving a prison sentence could be relocated with his family to a "place other than prison, for the time strictly necessary to define the special protection programme." Whether this in practice will prove to be an indirect method of granting immunity for Mafia collaborators is not clear at the time of writing.

### Protection of terrorist collaborators

No special laws were passed to guarantee the physical protection of terrorist collaborators in Italy or in the UK. Supergrasses came under the responsibility of the Home Office but measures were, it seems, taken on an ad hoc basis. In both countries the main dangers came from prison reprisals, (especially in Italy where immunity was not granted) and special annexes were provided accordingly. Reprisals against Italian terrorist *pentiti* were most severe in 1980 when the phenomenon was beginning – nine prison murders took place in that year. The only example of Mafia-style revenge on a family was the two-month kidnap and then murder of Patrizio Peci's brother Roberto – the Red Brigades' unsuccessful attempt to prevent Patrizio from continuing his collaboration. Relatives of the supergrasses were also kidnapped for similar reasons but were released unharmed, usually when they voiced disapproval of the collaboration being given.

The major Italian *pentiti* served prison sentences of two or three years, were given limited economic assistance in order to start a new life under a false name and were provided initially with police protection and "sheltered" housing.

Northern Ireland collaborators to whom immunity was granted were kept until trial with their immediate family in Army barracks or accommodated in or beside police premises in Northern Ireland or on the mainland. Frequent changes of address were common. In one case an entire family was flown to Cyprus for a four week "winter holiday"[42] Little information is available on the supergrass's life after trial.

## THE CONTRIBUTION OF THE COLLABORATOR

The use of accomplice evidence can be said to have made a notable contribution if, without compromising the rule of law, guilty persons are identified, arrested and tried for the crimes they have committed; if lives are saved that otherwise might have been lost, and if criminal organisations are weakened. To what extent is this true of the cases examined here?

### The supergrass

If we look at the proceedings of the 10 supergrass trials that took place in Northern Ireland it would be hard to argue that these objectives were met.

Of an estimated 593 persons arrested or charged on the basis of supergrass evidence, 217 were sent for trial. Greer notes:

"In the 10 supergrass trials to date, 55 per cent of defendants, or 120 out of 217, tried at first instance were convicted or pleaded guilty. Of these, 57 per cent of convictions were based on uncorroborated single witness accomplice evidence. However in the five cases in which appeals were lodged, 67 out of the 74 convictions appealed against were quashed, bringing the overall conviction rate down to 42 per cent."[43]

Convictions were annulled thanks to the weakness of uncorroborated evidence and to the lack of "intrinsic credibility" of the collaborator. On two separate occasions during the trial involving supergrass Joseph Bennett (UVF), Bennett's evidence "was shown to be wrong, if not deliberately false".[44] IRA supergrass Christopher Black gave evidence against 38 persons of whom 18 were convicted on Black's evidence alone, including one man who had provided 40 alibis against Black's allegations. All 18 had their convictions overturned on appeal.[45]

Lord Chief Justice Lowry's summing up in the case of McGrady, the former IRA man who had voluntarily given himself up, described some of McGrady's evidence as "contradictory, bizarre and in some respects incredible" and his manner of giving it "devious and deliberately evasive".[46] One accomplice named by McGrady turned out to have been in prison at the time of the alleged offence, and McGrady substituted his brother's name instead. Yet Lord Lowry went on to convict three men, two of them on McGrady's uncorroborated evidence on the grounds that it "had the ring of authenticity." The Appeal Court judges overturned the two convictions, finding McGrady's evidence to be "quite unpersuasive and incredible".[47]

Former INLA member John Grimley was granted immunity before trial despite an involvement in crime stretching back to his schooldays and a long history of mental illness. He may also have been a police agent. When he told the court that police had given him the names of 22 persons whom they wanted convicted, the trial collapsed.

On the question of saving lives, the 1983 report of RUC Chief Constable Sir John Hermon praised the use of what he called "converted terrorists" whose "evidence so provided has contributed significantly to the removal from society of a considerable number of persons convicted by the courts of the most appalling crimes . . . many people who would otherwise be dead are alive today because of the converted terrorist process".[48]

Sir John's viewpoint must be respected, since it may conceal knowledge about thwarted attacks of which the general public is unaware. However on the legal evidence available – the record of supergrass retractions, of immunities granted for evidence which was either retracted or collapsed in court as unreliable or sheer invention, not to mention the conspicuous absence, bar one case, of "conversion" in the moral sense, the Chief Constable's thesis does not stand up to scrutiny. Even if a number of people were correctly arrested and tried, many others were held in custody for long periods without trial, particularly if named by more than one supergrass – a practice that led to accusations of "internment by remand".

There is no evidence that the bumpy but generally downward trend of murders that commenced in 1977 was directly attributable to the supergrass phenomenon. PIRA (the Provisional IRA) was undoubtedly damaged by informers and feared the consequences of collaboration, but in fact supergrass evidence did not lead to the capture of any leading figures, nor did the supergrasses themselves tend to have key positions in the organisation (in contrast to many BR *pentiti* and Mafia collaborators). One directly counterproductive effect was that the organisation was remodelled from the old company system into a smaller, tighter cell structure which was more difficult to penetrate. PIRA militants may be less numerous in the early 1990s than 10 years previously, but it has become a more professional and more deadly army, to the extent that a senior British security official described it as "Without doubt . . . the most professional terrorist organisation in the world today."[49]

## The left wing *pentito*

Almost all left wing terrorist trials in Italy from 1980 onwards involved collaboration and/or dissociation. The contributions made by the first *pentiti* such as Patrizio Peci and Michele Viscardi were crucial because they had laid bare the organisational structure and method of operation of the Red Brigades and Front Line groups respectively, and, by sowing doubt and distrust, precipitated the wavering commitment of a generation of militants into irreversible crisis and decline. The timing of the two-pronged approach of repression and reward was crucial, as it surely was for saving lives, judging by the hit lists and in-depth surveys of potential targets discovered in bases raided on the word of the *pentiti*. On the whole, the state's – and in particular the judiciary's – credibility rose in the process, since court verdicts passed virtually unaltered through the stages of Court of Assizes, Appeal and Supreme Court.

The collaboration of Red Brigades *pentiti* was crucial in the trial of 59 defendants for the kidnap and murder of Aldo Moro and his five bodyguards which concluded in the Rome Court of Assizes in January 1983 with 32 life sentences and 256 years of prison. The Appeal Court verdict in March 1985 substantially confirmed the pattern of convictions and acquittals but, with collaboration and dissociation, 10 of the life sentences were commuted into sentences totalling 260 years and the 256 were reduced to 157 years of prison.[50] These were reduced again after the implementation of the dissociation law in 1987.

When the penitence law expired in December 1983, a total of 449 militants had taken advantage of the premium provisions: of these, 330 had dissociated and 119 had actively collaborated.[51] A parliamentary report of December 1988 showed that a total of 561 militants had benefited from the 1987 dissociation law.[52] Recidivism in left wing collaborators has not been reported.

Left wing violence peaked in Italy during the years 1978 to 1980, with a death toll of 29, 23 and 29 in the three year period. This fell to 14, 17 and one in the following triennial. Persons injured in left wing attacks also dropped from 42, 45 and 19 in 1978 to 1980 to 15, 18 and one.[53]

But as in Northern Ireland, innocent people were wrongly arrested and held for long periods without trial; it was argued that the package of "emergency laws" was a means of social control, of taking suspects off the streets and then looking for the evidence against them – the Italian version of internment by remand. Nonetheless, these laws certainly contributed to the eventual decline of left wing terrorism.

## Mafia collaborators – their contribution

The overall contribution of Mafia collaborators to the completion of court trials has been considerable. Well aware of the potential weaknesses of such evidence, Sicilian judges were forced to scrutinize every statement with particular rigour and to reject any allegations that did not stand the test of corroboration. Particular problems arose from the sheer numbers involved in the "maxi-trials" – 475 defendants in the first Palermo maxi-trial – and from the difficulties of proving beyond all reasonable doubt many crimes of association. There were instances where accomplice evidence was rejected at the final hurdle by the Supreme Court, causing the annulment of verdicts and the re-running of trials, sometimes several times over.

Giovanni Falcone assessed the contribution of the various Mafia *pentiti* in his interview-autobiography, remembering that until the late 1970s it was still common to hear discussions of whether the Mafia actually existed or not. Even the Sicilian judiciary had only a sketchy understanding until Tommaso Buscetta opened the door.

"He gave us innumerable confirmations of the structure, the recruitment techniques, the functions of *Cosa Nostra*. But most of all he gave us a broad, global vision, the whole spectrum of the phenomenon. He gave us an essential key to reading and understanding, a language and a code to decipher it. For us it was like having a language teacher who helps you to speak to the Turks without using sign language . . . Buscetta gave me the co-ordinates that permitted me to devise a working method."[54]

Falcone had dealings with some 35 collaborators from *Cosa Nostra*: Buscetta was the most useful because he was the first, and for his personal knowledge of the command structure; Salvatore Contorno had a limited vision but represented "the perfect footsoldier" of *Cosa Nostra*. Their statements, given in the autumn of 1984, led to the issue of 366 and 127 arrest warrants respectively and led directly to the first Palermo "maxi-trial" which ran from February 1986 to December 1987.

The developments of the late 1980s were revealed by Catania boss Antonino Calderone and the *Cosa Nostra* "chemist" Francesco Marino Mannoia, who updated the judges' knowledge of *Cosa Nostra's* operations, its internal alliances and divisions, and gave important insights into its political and electoral preferences and how these were used.

The Mafia was seriously depleted by the revelations of the collaborators and reacted savagely. Between rival clan attacks and acts of vengeance for his betrayal, Buscetta lost 10 relatives, Salvatore Contorno no fewer than 35. Francesco Marino Mannoia's mother, sister and aunt were killed in a single attack when news of his collaboration leaked out. It is also no coincidence that the Mafia murdered the two judges who had the closest rapport with the collaborators and who had most strenuously campaigned for measures to protect them.

Like the IRA, the *Cosa Nostra* leadership reorganised its traditional structures to limit future damage. Falcone described the process as "implosion": "The structure is more compact, more vertical and there is a greater control from the top. At local level there is still considerable autonomy but I believe there are 'regents', men totally trusted by the leaders who answer directly to them."[55]

Scepticism and reluctance in some quarters to recognise the value of Mafia collaborators was finally put to rest in January 1992 with the confirmation in the Supreme Court of the veracity of Buscetta and Contorno's declarations. Although some of the 19 life sentences and 342 other convictions had been modified on Appeal, the core of the "Buscetta theorem" – the principle of the single, hierarchical structure of *Cosa Nostra*, its control by a central decision-making body known as the Commission and its joint responsibility for most, if not all the politico-institutional murders – was accepted.

The experience of collaboration is in full flow as far as *Cosa Nostra* is concerned. The repercussions on the organisation of all the approximately 200 collaborators under protection in the autumn of 1992 are not yet clear, but in the short term, violence can be expected to intensify rather than abate. This could be directed at collaborators and their families but also the most dedicated and diligent politicians, policemen and judges.

## ACCOMPLICE EVIDENCE – THEORY AND PRACTICE

### England and Northern Ireland

The rules governing the use of accomplice evidence in England and Northern Ireland are identical in theory although legal practice in the two countries has diverged. From 1972 onwards, no immunity was granted in England for collaboration; however two rulings of the Court of Appeal in 1970 and in 1978 established that any defendant found guilty should not be sentenced to more than five years imprisonment if he or she had collaborated, whatever crimes had been committed.[56]

Accomplice evidence may be admitted or excluded in courts in England and Northern Ireland at a judge's discretion, but if admitted, the law states that the jury must be warned to pay special attention to its evaluation, given the risks involved of a witness with a criminal past and vested interests in his evidence being accepted. The judge is obliged to inform the jury that they may convict on such evidence but that it is dangerous to do so unless it is corroborated by one or more alternative sources. If this warning is not given then any convictions must be annulled.

With the abolition of jury trial for scheduled offences in Northern Ireland from 1973, the single judge sitting in a Diplock court was placed in the position of warning himself. As Gifford points out,

" . . . This is a somewhat unreal mental operation. The efficacy of the warning consists in the separation of identity and function between the judge as arbiter of the law and the jury as finders of fact."[57]

The restricted possibilities for supergrass evidence to be examined in a wider context were tightened further in Northern Ireland by a ruling that, subject to the approval of the Attorney General or of the court, the prosecution could commit the accused for trial without the holding of a preliminary enquiry in a magistrates' court. This is known as the Voluntary Bill of Indictment procedure, and was used in two supergrass cases.[58] It helped the collaborator in that defence lawyers for the accused did not know the content of his allegations prior to full trial, and potential weaknesses in his evidence were not revealed.

### Corroboration

The standard definition of corroboration in British judicial practice is that given in 1916 by the then Lord Chief Justice, Lord Reading:

"We hold that evidence in corroboration must be independent testimony which affects the accused by connecting or tending to connect him with the crime. In other words it must be evidence which implicates him, that is, which confirms in some material particular not only the evidence that the crime has been committed, but also that the prisoner committed it . . ."[59]

This definition draws the line between corroborative evidence as above and other independent or circumstantial evidence which gives weight to the veracity of the evidence without implicating the accused. This latter constitutes supportive evidence.

The Northern Ireland judiciary indicated that, where supergrasses were involved, there might be an even greater need for "clear and compelling corroboration".[60] They appear not to have followed their own advice, however. In the Bennett, Black and McGrady cases, Mr. Justice Murray, Mr. Justice Kelly and Lord Lowry based 31 convictions (61 per cent of the total) on uncorroborated single witness testimonies.[61] In six of the seven trials that followed, the percentage dropped to 22 per cent, but if the seventh case involving INLA collaborator Kirkpatrick is taken into account, where 25 convictions were the result of single witness uncorroborated testimony, it rises overall to 53 per cent. All these convictions were annulled by the Northern Ireland Court of Appeal.

**Italian theory and practice**

To its credit, Italy has never renounced the practice of trial by jury, despite threats and intimidation by terrorists and *mafiosi*. The jury is composed of six "popular" jurors, or ordinary members of the community, plus the President of the Court and one other judge. In theory the opinion of each member has equal weight, although the ultimate verdict is inevitably determined by the *guidici togati*, the "robed judges".

One important difference between accomplice witness trials in Italy and in Britain is that according to the Italian criminal code a defendant (*imputato*) cannot at the same time be a witness (*testimone*). The Italian accomplice witness remains a defendant throughout, with all his defendant's rights: he is not under oath to tell the truth and therefore cannot commit perjury; he may also remain silent.

Some jurists maintained that the role of defendant/collaborator sat uneasily in the Italian inquisitorial system, since the role of the examining magistrate was formally *super partes*. It was argued that the practice "overturns the function of the interrogation of the defendant, transforming it from an instrument of defence into an instrument of investigation".[62] In this sense the Italian move towards an accusatorial system, where defence and prosecution confront each other as equal "sparring partners" in open court, was seen as giving the use of accomplice evidence a greater degree of ethical propriety.

Many of the British preoccupations regarding the dangers of accomplice evidence have also emerged in Italian legal debates. A Supreme Court ruling of 1964 states that accomplice evidence (*chiamata di correo*),

"in order to assume the dignity of a legitimate source of evidence, not only must be spontaneous, detailed, constant, unequivocal and disinterested but must find confirmation in other elements of an objective nature which confer upon it a character of certainty concerning the facts to be proven."[63]

Another ruling in 1972 mentions the "intrinsically suspect nature of the confession of someone who accuses others as accomplices to his own crime, given the variable and multiple reasons for falsification connected to such a confession."[64] And in 1978 the Supreme Court insisted that accomplice evidence "be subjected to meticulous rigour consonant with the reasons for suspicion connected to this form of evidence".[65]

*Collaboration* 23

A 1967 interpretation of the law permitted the use of accomplice evidence alone when, according to the *libero convincimento* or "freely reached conviction of the jury", it had decisive value. The principle of *libero convincimento* is fundamental in Italian criminal law; it constitutes a synthesis of the evidence of the specific case with the "maximum of judicial experience" (roughly corresponding to precedent in common law). The new code of criminal procedure introduced in October 1989 has maintained the principle of "freely-reached conviction" but gives greater weight to the motivation of this conviction according to strict criteria of corroboration. As with all criminal verdicts in Italian courts, written motivation is obligatory.

In practice, the courts seem to have been sufficiently aware of the dangers of evidence given for reasons of vengeance, self protection or personal antagonism and with the exception of a notorious maxi-trial in Naples, have weathered the collaboration trials with dignity.

The motivation for the verdicts given by the Palermo Court of Assizes in the first maxi-trial states, with regard to the accomplice evidence, that

"the declarations were subjected to a rigorous critical examination in open court, were recognised as truthful and genuine for their logic, constancy, spontaneity and reiteration, as well as having been given in full autonomy and therefore with the capacity to constitute reciprocal corroboration."[66]

The judges were careful to distinguish between the *chiamata in correità* – accomplice evidence, and the *chiamata in reità* – where the accusation is made for a crime from which the accuser excludes his own participation, this obviously having weaker evidential weight. The criteria used to evaluate the accomplice evidence in the maxi-trial were, first the immediacy and spontaneity of response; second, the veracity of the affirmations; third, the plurality of sources and finally the absence of all reasonable doubt as to whether the evidence was contaminated or not.[67]

The Palermo court believed it had "ascertained beyond all reasonable doubt the autonomy of the evidence given by Buscetta and Contorno which was not affected by *contaminatio* precisely because they were at variance with each other on several quite crucial aspects of the structure and composition of *Cosa Nostra*. This divergence guaranteed the non-coincidence of means of knowledge of the two".[68]

Answering the defence's charges that the accomplice evidence was contaminated by the wish to settle private scores, the court recalled the personal travail that both men had gone through before deciding to collaborate – Buscetta's attempted suicide and a long reluctance on Contorno's part to give evidence. It was said that both had collaborated in order to gain reductions in prison sentences and to obtain economic rehabilitation in the United States. This was demonstrably false on both counts – there were generic attenuating factors connected to the collaboration which could be evaluated at the discretion of an individual judge, but no premium legislation as such; secondly, the Italians were indeed "lent" to the US authorities in order to testify in the "Pizza Connection" trial in 1985 and were given a maintenance allowance in recognition for this assistance, but this was quite separate from and uninfluential on legal proceedings in Italy.[69]

With regard to the accomplice evidence, the Palermo Court of Assizes was explicit: "The more generic is the accusation, the more the possibilities increase of making an error which would fatally compromise the judge, making him the blind instrument of every response of the accomplice. . . . And therefore on the single indication of an accomplice, this Court, in the absence of corroboration of a subjective nature (confirmation by another source whose autonomy is obvious) or else by verification of an objective nature (unequivocal findings of police investigations, curriculum vitae, previous convictions for crimes consonant with the present charges), has opted for acquittal for insufficiency of proof."[70]

## REFLECTIONS AND CONCLUSIONS

### Italy

Although it may seem from a distance that the anti-terrorist fight in Italy was conducted with political parties and public opinion united in joint cause, this was not the case: some 30 per cent of Italians disapproved of the premium laws, including a number of influential public figures like Sandro Pertini, Italy's President from 1978 to 1985, and symbol of unquestionable moral probity.

The main objections concerned the penitence law of 1982 and the fact that it rewarded "political realism and not moral internal change".[71] There were criticisms of excessively favourable treatment of the *grandi pentiti* – those who after making a contribution of "exceptional relevance" were given provisional liberty once sentence had been passed, whilst those guilty of lesser crimes but who chose silence remained in prison. In some cases it transpires that genuine moral repentence did follow, and privately, a number of *pentiti* and *dissociati* made peace with the families of their victims. This cannot of course be attributed purely to legislation, but for this group of collaborators at least, tends to support the function of law not simply as repressive but also as a rehabilitative tool.

In purely functional terms, the Italian terrorist *pentiti* had no interest in falsifying their statements or in withholding evidence. Their statements invariably implicated their own circle of associates and rarely compromised public figures. *Cosa Nostra*, on the other hand, has traditionally flourished thanks to subordination of and connivance with public administration and political power. Between 1984 and 1992 Tommaso Buscetta refused to discuss Mafia/political links with the Palermo judges because, in his view, the state was not ready to accept or react seriously to such information. Some of the later collaborators named a few names but usually without convincing evidence of criminal responsibility and therefore their evidence never came before a court.

In 1992 three factors changed the status of Mafia collaborators: the confirmation by the Supreme Court of the verdicts of the Palermo maxi-trial, the murders of judges Falcone and Borsellino, and the implementation of sound legislation to protect those who wished to dissociate from the organisation. Since the state has begun to demonstrate greater determination and credibility in fighting the Mafia, the willingness of its members to contribute to its downfall has grown. Hundreds of arrest warrants have been issued and a number of important fugitives captured. The former reluctance to speak of politico-mafia links has been overcome: allegations have been made of political deals done at the highest level, of murders carried out at political request and of trial verdicts suitably "adjusted" by compliant judges. The credibility of these statements awaited corroboration at the time of writing.

### Northern Ireland

Perhaps the greatest proof that the supergrass system was not of overall value in the form it was utilised is the fact that it gradually dropped out of use. Laws were neither passed nor abrogated, indicating either a policy change prompted by political considerations, or else a critical reassessment of a judicial experiment that had not survived the test of a democratic criminal law system and had begun to drag the Northern Ireland Crown prosecutors into professional disrepute. Lord Gifford's carefully argued report of 1984, amply quoted here, may also have been influential in the issue of a statement by Sir Michael Havers in 1986 that uncorroborated single witness evidence would no longer be grounds for conviction in Northern Ireland.[72]

It is interesting to note that although only a minority of seven out of 26 supergrasses in Northern Ireland were Loyalist, the system was widely opposed by public opinion and by most of the religious and political groupings in Northern Ireland, in the Republic and elsewhere. The leading Belfast Unionist and Grand Master of the Orange Order Thomas Passmore described the system as "an affront to British justice" and that the "inbuilt immunity by which informers were rewarded" was "utterly immoral".[73] The Democratic Unionist Party pronounced itself officially in favour of using informers but against granting immunity, although the Rev. Ian Paisley personally criticised the supergrass system as dangerous and potentially manipulative. Both the British Liberal and Labour parties officially denounced it, as did the Irish Congress of Trade Unions. The Catholic and the Protestant Bishop of Derry issued a joint condemnation of the practice on the grounds that the end did not justify the means. Families of those accused by supergrasses formed solidarity associations in order to give themselves a political voice. In sum, few apart from the RUC appear to have attempted a serious defence of the system.

### Conclusions

Why did the collaborator system by and large overcome the judicial and ethical hurdles in Italy and not in Northern Ireland? The clearest judicial explanation appears to be an excessive reliance in Northern Ireland on uncorroborated accomplice evidence and the lack of an adequate distinction between corroborative and supportive evidence. The disregard for standard judicial practice in the face of demonstrably unreliable witnesses led to allegations that the supergrass system was little more than the implementation of a political counter-terrorist strategy by means of a willing or pressurised judiciary.

A similar charge might originally have been levelled in Italy, where the most articulate and influential sectors of society – the politicians, judges and businessmen, who were also those most at risk – constituted a powerful pressure group for the introduction of means that would hasten the end of violence. But political conditions in the two countries were very different. In contrast to Britain's confidence in the robustness of its democracy, Italy lived, and still does to some extent, close to the memory of a dictatorship. There was a lurking and not-implausible fear that were serious action not taken, continuing violence against the state might provoke an authoritarian intervention.

In this context the requirement that the legislation be democratically approved, temporarily and uniquely to deal with an emergency situation, was never forgotten. The penitence law was passed by an almost unanimous vote of Parliament and ran for 120 days; after further debate and a special law decree, again submitted for parliamentary approval, it was extended for another 120 days and then expired definitively. The dissociation law was valid for one month from its official publication; thereafter those wishing to collaborate or dissociate from a criminal organisation were left with the Cossiga law, which is still in force, but is much less generous to accomplice witnesses. The legislation on behalf of Mafia collaborators does not include legal inducements such as sentence reduction, and perhaps for this reason does not have an expiry date.

An important aspect to consider is the difference in the characteristics of the collaborators concerned. Some of the supergrasses had combined a long history of common crime with politically-motivated activities and may have had fewer inhibitions about tailoring evidence to their own ends. Italian left wing militants and *mafiosi* had lived by spurious but, in their own way, rigid moral codes which were less contaminated by the artful dodging of the common criminal.

Of the three groups, the left wing *pentiti* appear to be the most "straightforward" category of collaborators: on the whole, Italian revolutionaries had come to realise by the early 1980s that they had missed their moment, if ever it had come, that Italy's industrial democracy was too well established to be overthrown, and that they might as well make the best of defeat.

The collaboration of members of *Cosa Nostra* and of Northern Ireland paramilitary organisations is more complex and demanded – or should have – special study and preparation. Tardily, the Italian Parliament set up an independent central commission to evaluate each Mafia collaborator's situation with a collegiality of decision-making and an impartiality that would not be possible within investigating authorities. This lesson, learned from the US experience, in itself merits further study.

The Mafia imposes its rules and protects itself by violence but has no concrete set of goals which in themselves constitute "victory". *Cosa Nostra* is certainly in crisis: it has lost much though not all of the consensus that guarantees *omertà* and it is torn by internal conflict, but because its goals are centred on power and money, collaborators are unlikely to deal it a death blow; depending on the efforts put in over the next few years, *Cosa Nostra* is more likely either to fade away slowly, or else to undergo a generational change involving a reduction of anti-institutional violence and a return to a less aggressive co-existence with political power.

The Provisional IRA has a very precise idea of victory and it is not unrealisable. Victory may be unlikely or it may be a long way off, but from PIRA's point of view it is not totally utopian to think that the British may one day withdraw from the six provinces. This must be an important element that has helped to keep the ideology from collapsing and has encouraged the fighting spirit.

## Future research

This study has only scratched the surface of a largely unresearched topic. In psychological terms the experience of collaboration is complex, but almost certainly is linked in some coherent pattern to the reasons for entry into the organisation as well as to the elements that bind an individual to it for many years. If one understood such processes better it might be possible to devise means of exit that were also coherent and acceptable within a given set of conditions.

Themes touched on here such as credibility, legitimacy and identity are crucial, and concern the state just as much as the potential collaborator. Consensus is a vital condition for survival for all three of the subject groups studied, hence the importance of the link between external perceptions of the group and its view of itself. The making and breaking of rules in organisations with a self-created system of justice is also relevant.

Collaboration and dissociation may be poles apart or they may come very close in certain cases; "active" and "silent" dissociation are important variants. Silence can be interpreted as "honourable" in some instances, "criminally reticent" in others.

An important but overlooked area is "post-collaboration" -- what happens to collaborators once they have regained freedom. At least one Mafia *pentito* has bitterly regretted his decision, whilst others such as Tommaso Buscetta and Antonino Calderone have publicly exhorted former associates to abandon the now dishonoured society. What sort of lives do collaborators live under their new identities, far from home? Is it a case of blissful obscurity or frustrated inaction?

The legal path is better explored but not exhaustively so, particularly in comparative terms, or when linked more closely to psychological aspects. Why, for example, when the same laws were open to all Italian terrorists did the far left take more advantage than the far right? A partial answer is that the crime of *strage* or massacre is excluded from the premium benefits, but there are undoubtedly other reasons.

Further research into the subject of collaboration will be incomplete unless

28 *Research Institute for the Study of Conflict and Terrorism*

a joint-track approach is pursued, one that combines psychological study with legal analysis. On this basis, it could yield fruitful and fascinating results.

---

## NOTES

[1] Clutterbuck, R: *Terrorism, Drugs & Crime in Europe After 1992*, Routledge, London, 1990, p. 73.
[2] Bishop, P. and Mallie E.: *The Provisional IRA*, Heinemann, London, 1987, p. 255.
[3] Greer, S.: The Supergrass System, in *Justice Under Fire*, Jennings, A. (ed): Pluto Press, London 1990, p. 84.
[4] Bishop & Mallie *op. cit.* p. 257.
[5] Interview of Giovanni Falcone with author, 28 February 1989.
[6] Jamieson A.: *The Modern Mafia: Its Role and Record*, Conflict Studies 224, RISCT, London, 1989; *Global Drug Trafficking*; Conflict Studies 234; RISCT, London 1990.
[7] Stajano, C. (ed): *Mafia, L'Atto di Accusa dei giudici di Palermo*, Editori Riuniti, Rome 1986, p. 96.
[8] Interview of BR member Adriana Faranda with author in Paliano prison, 26 February 1987 in Jamieson, A.: *The Heart Attacked: Terrorism and Conflict in the Italian State*, Marion Boyars Publishers, London 1989, p. 270.
[9] Fenzi, E.: *Armi e Bagagli; Un diario dalle Brigate Rosse*, edizioni Costa & Nolan, Genova, 1987, p. 104.
[10] "Una premessa d'obbligo" – a document dated 18 February 1986 produced by left wing detainees in Bergamo prison and presented at a conference held in Bergamo prison on 13 March 1986, p. 20.
[11] ibidem.
[12] Buonavita, A. (former BR leader): open letter to weekly magazine "L'Espresso", 14 June 1981.
[13] Franceschini, A.: *Mara, Renato ed Io*, Arnaldo Mondadori Editore, Milano, 1988, p. 199.
[14] Peci, Patrizio: *Io, L'Infame*, a cura di Giordano Bruno Guerri, Arnaldo Mondadori Editore, Milano 1983.
[15] ibidem, p. 194.
[16] Della Porta, D.: *Il Terrorismo di Sinistra*, il Mulino, Bologna, 1990, p. 265.
[17] Bishop & Mallie, *op. cit.* p. 313.
[18] ibidem p. 314.
[19] Boyd, S.: *The Informers*, Mercier Press, Dublin 1984, p. 82.
[20] ibidem.
[21] Dalla Chiesa, N.: Gli Effetti Sociali del "pentitismo" in *Stato e Mafia Oggi*, a cura di Smuraglia C., Editori riuniti reviste, supplemento al n. 6, novembre–dicembre 1985 di Democrazia e Diritto.
[22] Santino, U.: Mafia e Maxiprocessi Dalle "Supplenze" alla "Crisi della Giustizia" in Chinici, G.: Santino U.; La Fiura, G.; Dragna U.; *Gabbie Vuote*, Franco Angeli, Milano, 1992, p. 142–3.
[23] Stajano, *op. cit.* p. 39.
[24] Falcone G., in collaboration with Padovani, M.; *Cose di Cosa Nostra*, Rizzoli, Milano 1991, p. 65.
[25] Greer, *op. cit.*, p. 86.
[26] R. v. Graham (1983) 7 NIJB pp. 25–6, quoted in Greer, *op. cit.* p. 86 note 64.
[27] Gifford T., QC: *Supergrasses: The Use of Accomplice Evidence in Northern Ireland*, The Cobden Trust, London, 1984, p. 27.
[28] Corriere de la Sera, 29 July 1992.
[29] Falcone, *op. cit.* p. 51.
[30] ibidem, pp. 70–71.
[31] La Repubblica, 30 May 1992.
[32] Corriere de la Sera, 29 July 1992.
[33] Greer, *op. cit.* p. 74.
[34] Gifford, *op. cit.* p. 11.
[35] ibidem.
[36] Boyd, *op. cit.* p. 87.
[37] Gifford, *op. cit.* p. 10.
[38] Greer, *op. cit.* p. 75.
[39] Boyd, *op. cit.* p. 80.
[40] Greer, *op. cit.* p. 101 note 61.
[41] Commissione Parlamentare d'Inchiesta sul Fenomeno della Mafia e sulle altre associazioni criminali similari, Relazione annuale, 24 January 1990, p. 43.
[42] Gifford, *op. cit.* p. 31.

*Collaboration*     29

[43] Greer, *op. cit.* p. 74.

[44] Gifford, *op. cit.* p. 16.

[45] Greer, *op. cit.* p. 75.

[46] Gifford, *op. cit.* p. 22.

[47] ibidem p. 57.

[48] Boyd, *op. cit.* p. 97.

[49] Sunday Times, 17 June 1990, "War Without End", by Adams, J. and Clarke, L.

[50] La Nazione, 15 March 1985.

[51] Musco, E.: "La premialità nel delitto penale" in *La Legislazione Premiale*, convegno in ricordo di Nuvolone, P., Giuffre Editore, Milano, 1987, p. 120.

[52] Ministero di Grazia e Giustizia, in report presented to Parliament on 17 December 1988 by On. Trabacchi.

[53] Della Porta, *op. cit.* p. 237.

[54] Falcone, *op. cit.* p. 41.

[55] Interview of Giovanni Falcone with author, 28 February 1989.

[56] Mazzoleno, I. and Pintus, L.: "L'esperienza del processo inglese e nordirlandese" in Maxiprocessi e pentiti nell'esperienze continentale e del sistema del common law, *Documenti Giustizia*, Roma n. 12, Dec. 1988.

[57] Gifford, *op. cit.* p. 5.

[58] ibidem p. 9.

[59] Greer, *op. cit.* p. 81.

[60] 1982 3 NIJB p. 8 quoted in Greer, *op. cit.* p. 82.

[61] ibidem p. 83.

[62] Onorato, P.: "Processi di terrorismo e inquinamenti della giurisdizione" in *La Magistratura di fronte al Terrorismo e all'Eversione di Sinistra*, Franco Angeli editore, Milano, 1982 p. 135.

[63] Neppi Modona, G.: "Dichiarazione dei 'pentiti' e problemi della prova" in Nuvolone, *op. cit.* p. 250, with reference to decision of Cassazione Penale Sezione II of 17 November 1967.

[64] ibidem, reference to decision of 16 February 1972 p. 249.

[65] ibidem, reference to decision of 4 May 1978.

[66] Santino, U.: *op. cit.* p. 128; quoting from Sentenza, Tribunale di Palermo, sentenza contro Abbate Giovanni + 459, Palermo, 1987.

[67] ibidem.

[68] La Fiura, G.: "Gli 'imputati Dichiaranti' nelle motivazioni della sentenza di primo grado del maxiprocesso di Palermo", in Santino et al, *op. cit.* p. 181.

[69] ibidem p. 182.

[70] ibidem p. 185.

[71] Ferracuti, F.: *Ideology and Repentence, Terrorism in Italy.* (Paper presented at conference on the psychology of terrorism, Washington DC, 16–18 March, 1987).

[72] Greer, *op. cit.* p. 94 quote 90 (from H. C. Debs, vol. 94, col. 186.)

# Name Index